ARTHURIAN AND COURTLY CULTURES

The dynamic field of Arthurian Studies is the subject for this book series, *Arthurian and Courtly Cultures*, which explores the great variety of literary and cultural expression inspired by the lore of King Arthur, the Round Table, and the Grail. In forms that range from medieval chronicles to popular films, from chivalric romances to contemporary comics, from magic realism to feminist fantasy—and from the sixth through the twenty-first centuries—few literary subjects provide such fertile ground for cultural elaboration. Including works in literary criticism, cultural studies, and history, *Arthurian and Courtly Cultures* highlights the most significant new Arthurian Studies.

Bonnie Wheeler, *Southern Methodist University*
Series Editor

Editorial Board:

James Carley, *York University*
Jeffrey Jerome Cohen, *George Washington University*
Virginie Greene, *Harvard University*
Siân Echard, *University of British Columbia*
Sharon Kinoshita, *University of California, Santa Cruz*
Alan Lupack, *University of Rochester*
Andrew Lynch, *University of Western Australia*

MEDIEVAL LITERACY AND TEXTUALITY
IN MIDDLE HIGH GERMAN

MEDIEVAL LITERACY AND TEXTUALITY IN MIDDLE HIGH GERMAN

READING AND WRITING IN ALBRECHT'S *JÜNGERER TITUREL*

Annette Volfing

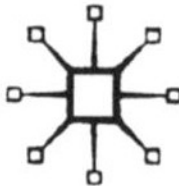

MEDIEVAL LITERACY AND TEXTUALITY IN MIDDLE HIGH GERMAN
Copyright © Annette Volfing, 2007.

First published in 2007 by
PALGRAVE MACMILLAN™
175 Fifth Avenue, New York, N.Y. 10010 and
Houndmills, Basingstoke, Hampshire, England RG21 6XS
Companies and representatives throughout the world.

PALGRAVE MACMILLAN is the global academic imprint of the Palgrave Macmillan division of St. Martin's Press, LLC and of Palgrave Macmillan Ltd. Macmillan® is a registered trademark in the United States, United Kingdom and other countries. Palgrave is a registered trademark in the European Union and other countries.

ISBN-13: 978–1–4039–7017–6
ISBN-10: 1–4039–7017–3

Library of Congress Cataloging-in-Publication Data

Volfing, Annette.
    Medieval literacy and textuality in Middle High German : reading and writing in Albrecht's Jüngerer Titurel / Annette Volfing.
        p. cm.—(Arthurian and courtly cultures)
    Includes bibliographical references and index.
    ISBN: 1–4039–7017–3 (alk. paper)
        1. Albrecht, von Scharfenberg, 13th cent. Jüngere Titurel—Criticism, Textual.
    2. Romances, German. I. Title.

PT1501.A4T4347 2007
831′.22—dc22   2007061458

A catalogue record for this book is available from the British Library.

Design by Newgen Imaging Systems (P) Ltd., Chennai, India.

First edition: September 2007

10 9 8 7 6 5 4 3 2 1

Printed in the United States of America.

For Katinka and Anja

CONTENTS

ACKNOWLEDGMENTS

I would like to thank the Arts and Humanities Research Council for awarding me a term of special research leave to enable me to complete this book.

I have received valuable input from a large number of friends and colleagues. I am particularly grateful for the continuous stream of advice and help which I have received from Undine Brückner, Alastair Matthews, Stephen Mossman, Nigel Palmer, and the other members of the Medieval German Seminar at Oxford. I would also like to thank Henrike Lähnemann, Timothy McFarland, and Kerstin Rüther for their comments on draft chapters.

INTRODUCTION

In the late twelfth century and throughout the thirteenth century, Middle High German literature manifests a new readiness to reflect on its own nature, status, and function.[1] This collective theoretical reflection—most pronounced in narrative works—consists of a variety of strands. Some texts engage directly with the nature of fictionality, either by highlighting the experiential opposition between life and literature, or by expressing outright unease with the supposed mendacity of fiction,[2] whilst others concern themselves with related issues of authorship and narration, including the appropriate adaptation of foreign language sources and the formation of a literary canon in German.[3] Although one finds relatively little theoretical reflection on genre, there is an abundance of intertextual reference, particularly within Arthurian romance, as well as outright criticism of other texts, indicating an on-going concern amongst later writers as to how to position their output favorably in relation to earlier, established works.[4] These various considerations have their specific and understandable parts to play within the development of Middle High German as a literary language, but they also testify to an ambivalent fascination with the written medium itself.

On the one hand, the works of the period constitute an implicit celebration of the power of writing: notwithstanding the fact that many, particularly earlier, texts are likely to have been intended for recital rather than for private reading,[5] and accordingly operate with a narrator-figure who supposedly "speaks" to his audience, it is accepted that without the materiality of the book, there would be no guarantee of the survival of the work and no succession of further performances extending into an indefinite future. For example, at the start of Wirnt von Gravenberg's *Wigalois* (written before 1230) it is the book itself which speaks, asking *Wer hât mich guoter ûf getân?* [What good person has opened me?], thereby underscoring the point that—reciter or no reciter—one cannot access the story other than through the book.[6] In addition, the construction of authorial and narratorial authority often hinges on the relevance and reliability of the written sources consulted. Literacy, and particularly the ability to read another language, thus becomes a marker of prestige. Whilst this is most obviously the case for author/narrator figures who need to engage with the right sources, it also applies to the fictional protagonists: although the foregrounding of the theme of literacy becomes more widespread in the thirteenth century, even a very early text such as Heinrich von Veldeke's *Eneasroman* (ca. 1170) presents its royal protagonists as being able to read and write.[7]

On the other hand, the written word was not universally associated with power and prestige. As early as 1200, the authorial narrator of Wolfram von Eschenbach's *Parzival* expresses outrage that his work might be regarded as a book and claims not to know a single letter of the alphabet.[8] In the same author's slightly later *Willehalm*, the narrator appears once again to distance himself from all that is associated with book-learning.[9] The interpretation of these claims to illiteracy and ignorance is problematic and critics disagree as to what exactly Wolfram meant. Those who read the statements autobiographically have wondered whether the historical author was illiterate in the modern sense or merely without access to Latin, whilst others have sought to explain the literary function of the statements by reference to a notion of divine literary inspiration, according to which it is better to derive one's authority from the living word of God than from the inherently lifeless writing of other human beings.[10] Whilst the opposition between the *logos* and the material fallibility of human writing had formed a long-standing topos amongst ascetically-minded Latin philosophers and theologians, Wolfram's vernacular recognition of the disjuncture of divine inspiration and human writing preempts a more fundamental unease experienced in the thirteenth century with regard to the increasingly mundane uses of writing. Although the Bible itself had to some extent been exempted from the ascetic critique of the written word on the grounds that the authors of its various books were in receipt of direct divine inspiration, Hagenlocher has argued that with the expansion of literacy and the shift from oral to written culture in the thirteenth century, the written word, which had previously been endowed with authority and even sanctity as a result of its almost exclusive association with the Church, came to be seen as a mere medium of communication, used by virtually anybody for any purpose.[11] With this irrevocable dissociation of script and Scripture, writing seemed increasingly untrustworthy and unreliable, capable of taking on as many meanings as a harlot takes on partners (to use a striking analogy formulated by the Wolfram-aficionado Brun von Schönebeck in the second half of the thirteenth century).[12] The unease with which certain writers approached the question of the truth-value of fiction is thus matched by an unease with the reliability of the medium in which fiction is codified.

The aim of this study is to use Albrecht's *Jüngerer Titurel* (J.T.) as a case-study for exploring this cluster of issues relating to the presentation of literacy and textuality in the Middle High German Arthurian romance.[13] The J.T. is particularly well suited to this, given the varied and imaginative ways in which it addresses the problems of its own written medium. Whilst the story line, which focuses on the ability of a highly literate group of protagonists to possess and to interpret certain elusive textual objects, highlights both the materiality and the unreliability of script, the J.T. also engages polemically and playfully with the narratorial conventions of Arthurian romance and with the literary authority of Wolfram von Eschenbach.

This large-scale and widely disseminated narrative, consisting of more than 6,000 four-line strophes,[14] represents an attempt to supplement, harmonize, and didacticize the interlinking story lines of Wolfram von Eschenbach's *Parzival* and *Titurel*.[15] The new version of events set out in the J.T. is also mediated by a narrator named 'Wolfram von Eschenbach'—at least until J.T. 5961 when the text suddenly presents itself as being the work of a hitherto unnamed 'Albrecht'. This unusual complexity in the construction of the narrator-figure(s) means that the J.T.'s engagement with the two earlier works goes well beyond merely appropriating and adapting their story lines. Written around 1270,[16] Albrecht's text therefore not only reflects a general thirteenth-century fashion for producing prequels and sequels to "the classics,"[17] but also a specific fascination with the literary persona of Wolfram von Eschenbach.[18] Indeed, the J.T.'s deployment of a 'Wolfram'-narrator appears to have provided an appealing model for near-contemporary authors.[19]

As is the case with its French counterpart, the Middle High German Grail romance develops out of the genre of the Arthurian romance.[20] Drawing on the *Perceval* of Chrétien de Troyes, Wolfram's *Parzival* is not only the earliest and most significant of the German Grail romance, but also stands as one of the most popular and influential of all Middle High German texts. Although later authors' preoccupation with the persona of Wolfram von Eschenbach may in some measure derive from a general admiration extended to the literary skill and reputation of the historical author, a large part of it is due specifically to the personal charisma of the *Parzival*-narrator, a high-profile and idiosyncratic figure who, being explicitly named 'Wolfram von Eschenbach,'[21] is readily conflated with the historical author.

Parzival, the only one of Wolfram's three narrative works that is undoubtedly complete, charts the eponymous hero's eventual attainment of Grail kingship. Whilst *Willehalm* deals with religious conflict in the tradition of the French *chanson de geste*, *Titurel*—of which only two short and apparently fragmentary sections are extant—revisits the narrative universe of *Parzival*. Protagonists who played a relatively minor part in the earlier work are now moved to the centre of attention: although *Titurel* initially appears to be about Parzival's great-grandfather, the Grail King Titurel, the work soon shifts its focus from the Grail community to Parzival's cousin Sigune and her love-relationship with Schionatulander. In *Parzival*, Schionatulander is a very minor figure, featuring only as a corpse held in the arms of the distraught Sigune.[22] In choosing to make this knight the central protagonist of *Titurel*, Wolfram takes the unusual step of producing a work that, although still nominally "Arthurian," actually thematizes the failure and death of its hero. This break with tradition is also marked formally: whilst Arthurian romances are normally written in rhymed couplets, the strophic *Titurel* is metrically similar to the *Nibelungenlied*, a Germanic epic characterized by a bleak world-view and featuring death and destruction on a large scale.[23]

In terms of story line, the J.T. combines *Parzival*'s focus on the Grail with *Titurel*'s interest in the way in which Schionatulander's quest for the 'Brackenseil' (a valuable inscribed dog's leash) brings about his doom.[24] As *Parzival* already contains a brief and enigmatic reference to the Brackenseil,[25] even *Titurel* itself may, on the face of it, be regarded as an attempt by Wolfram to tie up a particular narrative loose end. In fact, the effect of *Titurel* is quite the opposite: the two fragments cover only a short time span, with no hint as to what exactly happens between Schionatulander's departure in pursuit of the Brackenseil at the end of *Titurel* and Parzival's initial encounter with Sigune and the dead hero.

The J.T. plugs the "factual" gap with a thoroughness entirely at odds with the allusive, elliptical style of *Titurel*. As well as giving an exhaustive account of the

military career of Tschinotulander,[26] it also provides numerous other points of
information deemed to be missing from *Parzival*: on the nature and origins of the
Grail, on the historical role of Artus (Arthur), and on geography and natural
science more generally. Wolfram's *Titurel* also provides no clear guidance as to
how the Brackenseil catastrophe relates conceptually to the Grail (celebrated at the
start of the first fragment). In addressing this matter, J.T. takes further issue with the
ethos and outlook associated with Wolfram: by essentially presenting itself as a
moral corrective to *Parzival*, it suggests that the code of behavior sanctioned by the
Grail is stricter, more ascetic, and less tolerant of secular, courtly values than is
suggested in the earlier work.[27] This difference may be illustrated by reference to
the moral codes imposed on the Grail communities in the two works. Wolfram's
Grail is by no means easygoing: it expects chastity from all ordinary members of its
community and will permit the Grail King to marry only the woman of its choice.
Indeed, the terrible groin wound suffered by Anfortas is presented as a punishment
for his disobedient courtship of a woman not singled out for him by the Grail.[28]
However, Albrecht's Grail manifests an additional level of hostility to secular love:
if anybody thinks even chaste and faithful thoughts about his beloved while in the
presence of the Grail, he will be physically debilitated for a week (J.T. 646); and if
his thoughts are impure and lustful, he will die immediately (J.T. 647).[29]

Whilst the J.T. thus places itself in polemical opposition to *Parzival*, it does not
even acknowledge the separate existence of Wolfram's *Titurel*. Instead, it presents
itself as the "intact," original version of the *Titurel*, the two fragments of Wolfram's
text being integrated more or less seamlessly into this much longer work.[30] It is consistent with this approach that 'Wolfram', the primary narrator of the J.T., should
refer to *Parzival*, but not *Titurel*, as "his" earlier work (e.g., J.T. 18, 86–87).

Although a project such as Albrecht's naturally entails an evaluative engagement
with the processes of reading and writing literature, this aspect of the work has so
far received little critical attention. The body of secondary literature on the J.T. is
in any case somewhat smaller than one might expect for so monumental a text.
Although this is partly attributable to the fact that the last volume of the critical
edition was only published in 1992, the J.T.'s ornate style, overt didacticism, and
supposed "inferiority" to the works of Wolfram have made it deeply unfashionable
for much of the twentieth century.

The text had enjoyed popularity and prestige, not only in the Middle Ages,[31]
but also amongst early nineteenth-century scholars, who took the identity of the
'Wolfram'-narrator at face value (notwithstanding the fact that the literary technique and moral outlook of this work are radically different from those that one
encounters in the actual works of this author).[32] However, when Lachmann finally
discredited the notion of Wolfram as the author of the J.T., his correction of the
factual error was accompanied by a knee-jerk repudiation of any literary merit in
the work that he terms "den ganz langweiligen und albernen Titurel" [the utterly
tedious and silly *Titurel*].[33] Having been praised by Rosenkranz as a masterpiece
rivaling the *Divine Comedy*,[34] the J.T. sunk to being regarded as an incompetent
attempt on the part of Albrecht to pass himself off as Wolfram.[35] Only in the
second half of the twentieth century did critics start to approach the J.T. as a self-
standing text and to address the question of the extent to which it provided an

alternative world view to that of Wolfram's works.[36] At the same time, more sophisticated narratological approaches to *Parzival* also started to have an impact on J.T. scholarship. For example, Curschmann's groundbreaking presentation of the *Parzival*-narrator as a figure assuming a series of differing masks paved the way for acceptance of the premise that the figure of 'Wolfram' in the J.T. is also a fictional construct intended to be recognized as such.[37] Nonetheless, the notion of the J.T. as a piece of plagiarism still persisted into the 1980s.[38] Equally detrimental to a wider engagement with the text has been a tradition of subjective claims to the effect that the J.T. is simply unappealing or not worth the effort.[39] Lachmann's 1833 designation of the text as tedious and silly finds its modern counterpart exactly one hundred and fifty years later in Wyss' 1983 assertion that "Wer sich mit dem 'Jüngeren Titurel' einläßt, den packt zuerst eine tiefe, unwiderstehliche Unlust am Text." [Whoever takes on the *Jüngerer Titurel* is initially overcome with a deep and irresistible aversion for the text.][40] Whilst Wyss admittedly goes on to suggest tentative ways in which this presumed aesthetic aversion might be overcome, his study is still predicated on the premise that the J.T. is uniquely unpalatable. Fortunately, this premise has been abandoned in more recent interpretations by Guggenberger, by Lorenz and, most recently, by Mertens, whose analysis fully acknowledges the complex narratorial role-play carried out in the J.T.[41] It is now no longer deemed necessary, or even appropriate, for critics to adopt an apologist stance with respect to the overall literary quality—or the "enjoyment factor"—of the J.T. This monograph presents the J.T. as an intellectually ambitious work that reflects extensively on its own textual status and which deploys the themes of reading and writing with considerable narratological and poetological sophistication as part of this process.

In the J.T., reading and writing are not only of paramount importance for the protagonists, whose lives revolve around texts and textual objects, but also for the narrator(s) engaging discursively with the status of the literary enterprise and its ambiguous relationship to *Parzival*. Accordingly, whilst the first half of this monograph (chapters 1–3) covers various aspects of intradiegetic textuality,[42] the second half will address the construction of the narrator-figures (chapter 4) and the case made by the text itself for its ultimate validation (chapter 5). This division of the monograph into two halves reflects its central contention that there is a fundamental difference in the attitudes expressed, on the one hand, toward the textual pursuits of the protagonists, and, on the other hand, toward the J.T. itself. Nonetheless, the narratorial and authorial perspectives are important to the analysis from the very outset, given that the numerous cases of reading and writing on the part of the protagonists cannot be adequately assessed solely by reference to the specific intradiegetic situation: when protagonists are criticized for reading literature (e.g., Ovid) or for trying to write it (e.g., the Brackenseil inscription), this inevitably draws attention to the fact that the J.T. is also a piece of literature with subject matter not too far removed from that of Ovid or from that of the Brackenseil. This begs the question of why this text should succeed in aesthetic and moral terms, when everything that is read or written intradiegetically appears to fail.

On the narrative level, Albrecht inherits from Wolfram a narrative world dominated by two very different, yet equally enigmatic, textual objects: the Grail and the Brackenseil. The Grail, "ein Stück Schrift, das wie ein Stein vom Himmel gefallen ist" [a piece of text, which has fallen from the heavens like a stone],[43] is of divine provenance. Although its textual function is to reveal the will of God in a series of written messages,[44] it often comes across as an autonomous, anthropomorphic being, addressing a core audience that it has selected for itself.[45] This impression of animation on the part of the Grail is brought about in a number of ways. For example, the fact that the written messages, which are not fixed, but change as the Grail apparently reacts to what is going on in the world, are sometimes formulated in the first person singular creates the impression that the Grail has a personal identity.[46] This impression is reinforced when the narrator uses metaphors of speech when discussing these written messages.[47]

Despite the undisputed miraculous (or "unnatural") properties of Wolfram's Grail, the fact that this object is no human artifact, but owes its existence directly to God, gives it a certain affinity with "readable" natural phenomena in the world (such as the stars) and reinforces the impression that all of God's creation is ultimately decipherable.[48] Admittedly, Albrecht's Grail differs from Wolfram's principally in that it is identified (at least toward the end of the work) as the chalice from the Last Supper.[49] For this reason, it might be taken to constitute a human artifact as much as an extension of the natural world.[50] Nonetheless, Albrecht embraces Wolfram's interest in the interpretability of natural phenomena (stones, plants, stars, and animals) and explores this area not least in connection with the Grail and its surrounding temple.[51]

By contrast with the Grail, the Brackenseil is a purely human construction.[52] It is a compelling hybrid of love-story, love-letter, and moral treatise, composed by Clauditte for her lover Ekunat, with the script constructed out of precious stones and fixed onto the leash. The central crisis involving this object is set out in *Titurel*: when Sigune unravels the knot in the leash in order to read the text in full, the dog makes a bid for freedom and the leash slips through her fingers. The Brackenseil therefore constitutes the ultimate elusive text, literally running away from the reader. The processes of reading and of writing are thus embedded into the story line from the very start, while the opposition between the sacred Grail and the secular Brackenseil encourages a broader evaluation of human writing in all its manifestations. While the Brackenseil might be exceptionally exotic, it is by no means the only textual composition to feature within the narrative. On the contrary, an almost obsessive preoccupation with the written word is one of the most striking features of the courtly cultures represented in the J.T.

As will be shown in chapter 1, this over-reliance on the efficacy and social prestige of human writing is presented as fundamentally misguided. On a practical level, messages may be lost or misunderstood, whilst on a moral level, most forms of textual activity will fall foul of the ascetic values implicit in the J.T. The problem is not only the licentiousness of certain literary texts favored by the protagonists (e.g., the works of Ovid): disapproval of human eroticism and sexuality is just one, albeit a very obvious, part of Albrecht's asceticism, which entails a hostile engagement with the body in all its manifestations. This includes a negative evaluation of the corporeality of the written word, which the ascetic tradition tends to present in opposition to the immediacy of the spoken word, by analogy with equivalent oppositions between flesh and spirit, or between humanity and God. Chapter 1 presents a case for seeing Albrecht's pessimism regarding intradiegetic writing as standing in a broad and well-documented ascetic tradition. Building on this, chapter 2 examines Albrecht's equally pessimistic approach to human language, which is presented as an arbitrary system of signs lacking any compelling connection to the relevant objects and individuals in the world. In particular, the spurious (and multilingual) etymologies associated with the names of protagonists serve not only to highlight the severance of *verbum* and *res*, but also to draw attention to the illusory nature of the personal identity of the protagonists: the protagonists themselves, as well as their attempts at spoken and written communication are to be seen as verbal constructs and therefore as inferior in nature to natural phenomena in the world that constitute the true "language" of God. Finally, after these more theoretical considerations, chapter 3 focuses on the contrast between the Brackenseil and the Grail: whilst the former serves as a specific case-study in the nullity of even the most morally well-intentioned human writing, Albrecht's inscripted Grail, identified with the chalice used at the Last Supper, is uniquely able to link sacrament with writing and hence to bridge the gap between divine orality and human textuality. This tentative equivalence that is posited between a eucharistically themed text and the eucharist itself also entails the metaphor of a communion of readers who all "receive" the Grail in textual form.

Turning to textual activity on the narratorial and authorial level, chapter 4 examines the identities of the two narrators, named 'Wolfram' and 'Albrecht'. Whilst 'Albrecht' only introduces himself toward the very end of the work, the former makes his presence felt from start to finish, much like the narrator of *Parzival* and *Willehalm*. Whereas 'Albrecht' represents the authorial narrator who retains overall artistic control (as well as interacting with patrons), 'Wolfram' is essentially an unwilling mouthpiece for vrou Aventiure, the allegorical authority who determines how this narrative material ought to be presented. We are therefore confronted with a 'Wolfram' whose views and attitudes have changed dramatically since the writing of *Parzival*, and who is now supposedly ready to tell the story "correctly," by reference to clerical rather than secular values. The narrative is interspersed with a series of conflicts between 'Wolfram' and vrou Aventiure, in which the unreconstructed courtly voice of the former attempts to rebel both against the facts and the morality of the tale that he is forced to narrate. At other times, however, the narrator, while still calling himself 'Wolfram,' apparently articulates the new morality and related didactic contents on his own authority and it therefore becomes more difficult to focus on the distinction between 'Wolfram' and 'Albrecht.'[53]

With the separation of the authorial persona from the primary narrative voice, the work introduces considerable extradiegetic reflection on the textual processes implicit in the act of narration. This involves highlighting, and playfully undercutting, the opposition between oral performance and written text. Like his historical counterpart Albrecht, 'Albrecht' must be deemed to have received and internalized the earlier work(s), although it is unclear whether this is the result of reading or of listening. When these works are then recast in their new, morally appropriate form, 'Wolfram'—the interlocutor of vrou Aventiure—is associated with an immediate oral articulation of the contents, whereas 'Albrecht' is associated primarily with the authorship of a written text. A further twist to the opposition between speaking and writing arises from the historical Albrecht's didactic agenda, which impels the narrator(s) to draw on the literary traditions of the biblical commentary and of the allegorical exposition of scientific data. Both of these traditions are associated with a purely written circulation, as opposed to the coexistence of oral performance and written text that is typical of classical courtly romance. However, by contrast both with the works of Wolfram von Eschenbach and with its own extensive thematization of oral narration (through the figures of 'Wolfram' and vrou Aventiure), the J.T. ends with a strong affirmation of its textual status: *Nu pruͤfet, alle werden, die wirde dises buͦches!* (J.T. 6327) [Now acknowledge, all you worthy ones, the worth of this book!][54] Of course, oral reception of this *buͦch* remains a distinct possibility,[55] but there is no sustained pretence that the role(s) of the narrator(s) should be seen as coinciding entirely with that of a performer addressing an audience directly.

Finally, chapter 5 seeks to determine the basis on which 'Albrecht' believes himself justified in celebrating the worth of his book, notwithstanding the otherwise pessimistic stance adopted toward the adequacy of written texts. After considering the ways in which the J.T. distinguishes itself from other Middle High German works, the chapter addresses the text's evaluation of its own didacticism. It will be arguing that although a devoutly didactic intent is clearly deemed preferable to a more frivolous stance, the J.T. does not try to present its didacticism as the primary basis of its worth. Although the J.T. contains numerous individual points of information and observations about appropriate Christian lifestyle, the presentation of the narrative material as a whole appears not to have been undertaken with a view to didactic transparency or effectiveness. On the contrary, the fact that the text remains deliberately ambivalent both in its treatment of courtly values and in its deployment of exemplary figures from the past suggests that the J.T. ultimately remains doubtful about the viability of effecting moral improvement through the medium of human writing. The point that even clear-cut and well-formulated moral advice is unlikely to be followed has, of course, been illustrated only too clearly within the narrative by the failings of the well-intentioned Brackenseil.

Instead, the J.T. justifies its supposedly unique exemption from the fallibility of human writing by reference to a model of literary cooperation between God and human author. This is articulated most clearly in the prologue, in connection with a discussion of the sacraments, where it is suggested that only the direct involvement of God will enable writing to transcend its natural limitations, just as divine grace is required for the transformation of the hosts in the eucharist, or for the supernatural efficacy of water in baptism. Albrecht's (metaphorical) association of his text with the sacraments also provides a solution of sorts to the unease expressed in the text at the status of words as an infinitely regressive system of signs (cf. chapter 2). Sacramental language differs from ordinary language precisely because of its efficacy: as Aquinas puts it, the words *non pronuntiantur solum causa significandi, sed etiam causa efficiendi* [are not pronounced solely in order to signify, but rather in order to effect change].[56] The metaphorical recourse to an ideal of sacramental writing is therefore based not only on an attempt to use the vitality of sacred pronouncements to offset the perceived "deadness" of script, but also on a desire to transfer to the text (in all its vernacular and generic inadequacy) the salvatory efficacy of the sacraments and to the audience the collective identity of a religious community.

The model whereby authorship is shared between God and human being is far from unusual for the Middle Ages. In the case of the J.T., however, it is endowed with unusual depth and complexity. This is brought about partly through the association of the Grail with the eucharist (and hence through the ascription of "sacramental" status to the text by virtue of its subject matter, as suggested in chapter 3), and partly through the way in which the model is adapted to fit the particular narrative situation. The last section of chapter 5 examines the way in which the prologue to the J.T. accommodates the difficult relationship between 'Wolfram' and 'Albrecht' within its poetological program. As part of a wider exposition of the nature of the element water (in scientific and sacramental contexts), the prologue presents the miraculous properties of the porous stone *enidorium* in such a way as to suggest an analogy for the pivotal position of 'Wolfram' within the work. Just as the *enidorium* allows water to flow through itself, whilst remaining solid (literally), so the fallible outlook of 'Wolfram' flows through the J.T., which still remains (morally) solid. The J.T. has thus found a careful formula that allows it to concede to sharing some of the general fallibility of the written word (and particularly of courtly literature), whilst at the same time invoking the special grace of God in order to separate itself from 'Wolfram' and all that he stands for.

PART I

THE NARRATIVE UNIVERSE

CHAPTER 1

LITERACY AND TEXTUAL CULTURE: LETTERS, LETTERING, AND LITERATURE

The J.T. presents a series of courtly environments characterized by a common reliance on, and regard for, the written word. To the extent that one accepts Stock's definition of literacy as the ability to "read and write a language for which in theory at least there was a set of articulated rules, applicable to a written, and, by implication, a spoken language," virtually every protagonist—heathen as well as Christian—is literate.[1] Furthermore, this literacy is accompanied by what at first sight looks like a strong textual orientation. Whilst it may seem unsurprising that a group of literate people should also be conscious of the numerous benefits of reading and writing, the coexistence of literacy and textuality (at least as defined by Stock) should not be taken for granted. As Stock points out, "Literacy is not textuality. One can be literate without the overt use of texts, and one can use texts extensively without evidencing genuine literacy."[2] In other words, it is possible for literate people to choose not to engage with texts on a regular basis, just as it is possible to see texts less as bearers of meaning and more as material objects, which may be visually attractive, commercially or political valuable, or even endowed with quasi-magical powers. In fact, as chapter 3 will show, the Brackenseil is one text that elicits a remarkably "nonliterate" response from most of the protagonists, who are much more anxious to possess it than to assimilate its written contents.

Of course, it is also possible to operate with a looser, more metaphorical definition of literacy, whereby the term is not confined to the ability to negotiate the letters of the alphabet, but is used to describe a wider spectrum of interpretative skills: fathoming the true meaning behind the words of a text, reading a situation correctly, and even appreciating the whole world as a decipherable text written by God. Once the definition of literacy is broadened in this way, the term starts to overlap with categories such as intelligence or moral judgment. As this study will aim to show, interpretational challenges (in the widest sense) lie at the heart of the J.T., with the failure to respond correctly to written texts being associated with moral failure. For that reason, an extended, metaphorical notion of literacy will be appropriate for most of this book, and it will be shown that when the term is understood in this way, most of the protagonists are fundamentally illiterate. The fact that they are, at least on the surface, both able and willing to engage with the written word, makes this deeper deficiency all the more poignant. It also raises the question of whether there is a more fundamental link between the two: in other words, does the J.T. suggest that is there something morally suspect about a culture in which reading and writing are integral to the pursuit of an elite, secular lifestyle? Accordingly, this chapter will take Stock's conceptions of literacy and textuality as its starting point in order to highlight the unusual attention that Albrecht accords to the presentation of habitual reading and writing. The chapter aims to provide a general characterization of the textual culture within which the narrative unfurls, by examining both the protagonists' engagement with, and the narrator's evaluation of three different forms of written output: pragmatic documents, ornamental lettering and inscriptions, and literature.

The protagonists of the J.T. manage to deal competently, and sometimes multilingually,[3] with personal letters and other forms of practical written communication (e.g., contracts and battle plans). Although the events of the narrative are set in the last years of the Roman Empire, the pronounced literacy of the protagonists reflects the cultural environment of Albrecht and his audience, illustrating the extent to which the thirteenth century may be seen as a "mediale Umbruchszeit" [period of transition in the use of media],[4] characterized by a shift from oral to written culture. Of course, the opposition between oral and written culture is by no means an absolute one: recent studies have focused strongly on the interplay between the two modes of communication.[5] Nonetheless, the J.T. accords particular importance to individual literacy, as may be demonstrated in the case of letters: although scribes are sometimes employed, and documents sometimes read out loud to a larger group, the default position is that protagonists are able and accustomed to reading letters in private.[6] Such a predilection for integrating letters into the flow of a narrative is typical of the so-called postclassical narratives of the thirteenth century.[7] Albrecht may not be as "briefwütig" [letter-fixated] as the authors of the *Virginal, Wilhelm von Österreich*, and all versions of the Alexander-material.[8] However, the reliance on written communication in the J.T. is still striking in comparison with those of the twelfth century, where news tends to be announced orally by messengers. The works of Hartmann von Aue, for example, do not include any letters at all. Wolfram's *Parzival* occupies an intermediate position, in that it features five letters: Gahmuret to Belacane (55,21–56,26); Ampflise to Gahmuret (76,23–77,18); Gawan to Artus and Ginover (625,16–626,8); Gramoflanz to Itonje (715,1–30); Feirefiz to his followers (785,27–30).[9] However, although all these characters are presented as fully literate, the agency of the messenger and the public reading of letters remain culturally important in *Parzival*, as Kiening notes with respect to the elaborate ritual surrounding the reception and public reading of Gawan's letter (645,19–651,30); Kiening's formulation that "Die Schrift muß zum Leben gebracht werden" [The writing has to be brought to life] is consistent with the reflections later in this chapter on the perceived "deadness" script.[10]

However, the real difference between the presentation of letters in *Parzival* and in the J.T. concerns not so much the quantity of letters or even the question of how they are received, but rather the inherent importance of the contents. In *Parzival*, the letters are all written by key figures and tend to be associated with turning points in the narrative. In short, these letters matter. Whilst the J.T. contains some important letters, as will be discussed below, others are routine and ephemeral, written by minor characters and relate to subject matter that cannot interest the audience for very long. The J.T. creates the impression that because everybody is writing all the time, the bulk of written documents—including letters—simply become part of the detritus of everyday life.

The importance attached by the protagonists of the J.T. to the processes of reading and writing indicates that the culture in question is not merely literate, but has a strong, and misguidedly optimistic, textual orientation. The enthusiastic production of letters—and of other forms of written records—is seen by the protagonists as a way of ensuring appropriate outcomes, and of guaranteeing both the truth-value and the survival of the information in question. Their respect for the written word extends into frequent use of metaphor, so that any authoritative oral statement or strongly held opinion might be said to have been "written."[11]

In fact, such indiscriminate reliance on human writing is subjected to implicit criticism. As far as the letters are concerned, these commonly held assumptions are thoroughly undermined by the story line itself, which features extensive failures of communication: written missives are lost, misunderstood, or otherwise fail to achieve their objective. As the "historical" records created in the course of the narrative do not have such clear, short-term objectives, there is perhaps not the same scope for demonstrating their failure, but there are narratorial comments questioning the relevance and the durability of these texts.

However, while references even to such pragmatic forms of writing contribute to the construction of a textual culture within the narrative world of the J.T., the full extent of the protagonists' textual orientation only becomes clear when one considers their engagement with two further categories of text: the decorative inscriptions on buildings, objects and even persons; and certain classics of world literature.

These two categories of text, which will be examined in separate detail in sections II and III below, play an important role in enhancing cultural bonding, given that they are accessible to the entire literate community. To this extent, these kinds of text differ from letters that, although capable of being "shared" through public reading, tend to have one exclusive personal addressee.[12] Furthermore, given the predominantly aesthetic, ceremonial, or sacral function of these kinds of writing, it seems reasonable to credit them with a more self-consciously "textual" status than would be characteristic of the typical letter, contract, or battle plan. In the case of an inscription, for example, the intimate connection between meaning and physical context (i.e., the artifact on which the lettering appears) serves to differentiate its mode of reception from that of a letter simply conveying a point of information. In the case of such information, it arguably makes relatively little practical difference whether the addressee receives it orally (from a messenger), or textually (through private reading), or through a combination of the two (e.g., another person reading out a letter). By contrast, the effect of an inscription is diminished unless the viewer/reader is capable of receiving and internalizing the wording without mediation, in its full visual context.

One crucial difference between an inscription and a canonical literary text is that the latter is not uniquely tied to a particular material object but might be available in copies in many different locations. For this reason, the mode of reception and the literacy of the receiver actually become less important than in the case of an inscription. For example, when the young Titurel reads Ovid, the crucial point is that he is engaging intellectually with a text that belongs to the Latin literary tradition, and that also exercises the minds of other members of the same aristocratic textual community.[13] The appearance of the manuscript and the fact that the well-educated Titurel reads the work for himself, rather than having another person read it out to him, are subordinate to the more fundamental point that this reception of Ovid leads him to define his own ethical position in opposition to a core text—and in opposition to other members of the courtly world. This in turn means that while all examples of reading and writing within the work underscore the fact that the literate protagonists share an educational framework and common set of assumptions, references to the reception of literary texts can be particularly important for emphasizing the textual orientation as well as the literacy of the protagonists.

The enthusiasm for making inscriptions and quoting the classics cuts across the Christian/heathen divide, members of both faiths being equally keen to reinforce their aristocratic identities through regular affirmation of literacy and of textual orientation (including the use of metaphors of reading and writing). Nonetheless, the very fact that secular writing is also accessible to the heathen world is enough to render it suspect within the moral system of the J.T.: according to the narrator, the heathens combine *kunst* [knowledge of the arts] with a profound folly (J.T. 2603–2605) and are, in their approach to language, like talking animals,[14] capable of producing form without meaning. It therefore becomes necessary to use the reception of certain texts as a device for cultural differentiation rather than for cultural bonding. The texts in question include not only the Bible,[15] but also the Grail messages and the inscriptions on the temple, all of which may be deemed to be of divine rather than human provenance and which are therefore set apart from the arguably frivolous and futile written output featured elsewhere in the narrative. When, for example, Sigune addresses God with the words: *Din rein gebot ich schribe besunder zu dem herzen* (J.T. 5196,1) [I inscribe your pure commandments onto my heart], her chosen image certainly hints at her ability to write, but, by echoing a biblical formulation,[16] she also underscores her position as a member of a broadly Christian textual community united, in opposition to the heathens, through its reception of the Bible.[17]

Within the broad Christian community, the written word clearly has a particular significance for the Grail family, given the way in which God uses the Grail as a surface for written communications.[18] These messages on the Grail constitute a unique phenomenon that straddles the categories of pragmatic letter and of aesthetic-sacral inscription and that might be thought to promote the view that writing (in the ordinary sense, with letters, syllables, and words) is a divine as well as a human activity: on this account, the mysterious writing on the Grail might be more authoritative, effective, and beneficial than most human communications,[19] but not fundamentally different in kind. As such it is comparable to 'Himmelsbriefe,'[20] or to the Tablets of the Law, which were literally written with the finger of God.[21] This perspective on God as a writer is supplemented by the narrator's extensive use of the commonplace of God's cosmic authorship.[22] According to this, all things in world might be read *quasi liber* [like a book] by those who possess the correct kind of intellectual and spiritual literacy.[23] All these examples of God's authorship run counter to Ong's assertion that ". . . God is thought always as 'speaking to human beings,' not as writing to them."[24] Furthermore, the topos of the divine authorship of the cosmos establishes a fundamental link between the act of reading in the narrow sense of assimilating the significance behind letters and words, and reading in the broader sense of making sense of the world within an overall devotional context.[25] Furthermore, this line of thought implies that human language, although deployed imperfectly by fallen man, is fundamentally tied to divine creation, with *vox* mapping onto *res* in such a way that the world created by God may be adequately re-created in discourse or in text. Writing, at least as carried out by the devout and the theologically enlightened (such as the members of the Grail community), might therefore readily be understood as an appropriate form of *imitatio Dei.*

In fact, as far as the protagonists are concerned, the narrative ultimately argues against such an optimistic approach to human writing. Although, as will be shown in chapters 4 and 5, the narrator has no qualms about harnessing to his own extradiegetic opus the traditional poetological strategy of glorifying the creative "word" in all its manifestations,[26] this does not mean that he is prepared to accept an equivalent transfer of *auctoritas* from divine "writing" to intradiegetic human writing. Instead, the narrator chooses to stress the disjuncture between the two: the texts read, produced, and celebrated by the protagonists are shown to be largely pointless and ineffective, if not downright sinful (as in the case of Ovid), and the very pronounced textual orientation of every segment of society (even of the Grail family) is presented as at least partly vain and misguided: although their attitude to the written word is not intrinsically sinful, it is most often evoked as a marker of their limitations and fallen state.

The J.T. is not only profoundly ascetic with regard to sexuality and to the body, but also manifests an approach to writing that is consistent with that adopted within the ascetic tradition, according to which "the corporeal form of script anchors it to the world of death" and writing therefore constitutes "a deformation . . . secondary, belated, contaminatory, parodic, dead."[27] Even in the case of divinely authored texts, the ascetic tradition ranks the spoken word more highly than its written equivalent, since Christ (being God's spoken word) was seen as the fulfillment of the written Law.[28] Nonetheless, on the human level, all language (i.e., the spoken as well as the written word) is intrinsically flawed. For Augustine, the limitations in human textual activity are ultimately tied up precisely with the structure of human language. As Irvine puts it:

> Language, Augustine finds, has a structure consisting of the continual temporal deferring of meaning and of presences and absences that require a form of memory to unite at any cognitive moment linguistic sign functions and the suspension or duration of syntax over time . . . Mankind is circumscribed by the temporality of conceiving and interpreting through signs; language is discursive, sequential, and determined by temporal relations and differences.[29]

Albrecht's narrator adopts a view very similar to that of Augustine, who distinguishes the human act of reading from the way in which the angels read the will of God directly, *sine syllabis temporum* [without the syllables of time], and without recourse to the web of signs that underlies human language.[30]

The dependence on linguistic signs and impossibility of unmediated cognition are seen as consequences of the Fall. These premises that underlie Augustine's realization that words are not just the signs of things, but may refer to other words in infinite regression, potentially lead the way to a theory of linguistic indeterminacy that calls into question the very possibility of meaningful discourse. It is this pessimism regarding the scope of intradiegetic written communication that forms the overall subject of the first part of this book. In this chapter it will be examined in relation to each of the three categories of written output that have been identified (pragmatic texts, decorative inscriptions, literature); in chapter 2 it is related to the meaningfulness of names and etymologies, and to the interpretability of the natural world; and in chapter 3 it is applied to the special cases of the Brackenseil and of the Grail. The narrator's difficulties in reconciling this approach with a celebration of his own complex and ambitious literary enterprise then form the subject matter of chapters 4 and 5.

Section I: Pragmatic Literacy

At the most pragmatic end of the spectrum, the narrative features a number of personal letters, which constitute the preferred device for summoning people, or for communicating points of information to correspondents in remote locations.[31] While scribes are sometimes involved both in the production and in the public recitation of these letters,[32] the narrative makes it clear that, as in *Parzival*, basic skills of reading and writing are by no means confined to a specialist professional group. For example, while Artus has scribes at his disposal to write letters for him, he is able to read incoming mail privately.[33] Heathen royals are equally literate, allowing for the same alternation of aural and visual reception on the part of the addressee. For example, most of the love-letters received by the heathen queen Secundille from her twenty-five suitors appear to have been read out in public (with *man* [one] as the ambiguous grammatical subject undertaking the reading).[34] However, she is specifically said to have read one of the letters herself, possibly out loud.[35]

The narrator tends not to dwell extensively on the contents of letters, but generally contents himself with stating that a letter was sent or received, and possibly providing some brief assurances as to its stylistic adequacy. For example, when three hundred ladies go missing from the Arthurian court, apparently stolen by the King of Morocco, Artus' attempt at a diplomatic solution to a hostage crisis involves sending this king a letter written *mit worten wol gesu^ezet* (J.T. 2474,4) [with well-sweetened word] in which he describes the sorrow of the court and politely requests the return of the ladies. On the whole, however, the narrator appears to attach relatively little importance to the aesthetic or rhetorical aspects of personal letters. While the fact that Secundille receives love-letters from her twenty-five suitors indicates that letters in the J.T. may have a persuasive function, as well as just serving to transmit orders or to communicate facts, it is significant that

Secundille is ultimately unable to make her selection on the basis of these written documents. Instead, all the letters are returned to the suitors (J.T. 5345,3) and a tournament is proclaimed, the winner of which will be entitled to her hand. In matters of love, rhetorical flair is therefore shown to be less effective and less relevant than chivalric prowess. Similarly, in the case of the Brackenseil (which constitutes a letter of sorts), it will be argued in chapter 3 that this document is strikingly ineffective at persuading either the primary addressee or the other recipients to adopt the outlook that it advocates.

Only occasionally is a letter so important that its contents are cited verbatim. The Brackenseil stands out in that it is quoted more or less in full.[36] Furthermore, extracts are quoted from certain other letters, which, like the Brackenseil, may to some extent be regarded as communicative failures, serving neither to benefit the recipient(s) nor to achieve the objectives of the sender.

One straightforwardly abortive letter is written by Secureiz to some of the Christian leaders in an attempt to bribe them to desert Tschinotulander in favor of Ypomidon (extract quoted in J.T. 3352–3354): this offer is simply turned down (J.T. 3374). A more subtle style of communicative failure is exemplified by the reply sent by the King of Morocco to Artus regarding the fate of the three hundred ladies. Although Artus, poignantly styled *der witze riche* (J.T. 2480,1) [well-endowed with intelligence], is able to read this letter, neither he nor the rest of the court is able to make constructive use of the information imparted, namely that it is in fact Klinschor who has taken the ladies:

wa Klinschor mit den vrowen   wer, des waren si di kunste vrien.
(J.T. 2480,4)

[They had no idea at all as to where Klinschor might be with the ladies.]

Furthermore, even though Artus is clearly literate (in Stock's sense), he lacks the more fundamental insight necessary to "read" the overall situation. Presumably acting on the assumption that the best thing to do in a crisis is to write a letter, he is about to send yet more messengers out into the world (J.T. 2482,4), when his wise aunt Accedille steps in to explain that the loss of the ladies is to be understood as a punishment for the immoderate hedonism of the Arthurian court and that everybody will simply have to wait patiently until a single knight (i.e., Gawan) takes on this challenge in the future (J.T. 2484–2496).

As far as the overall story line is concerned, the most important letter, other than the Brackenseil, is that written by the *baruc* [heathen potentate] Ackerin to Tschinotulander promising to send a further portion of the magical *golt der selden* [gold of good fortune]. This letter, quoted verbatim in J.T. 4721–4726, is a success in the sense that it is received and understood, but a failure in that it achieves precisely the opposite of what was intended by the writer. The background is that Ackerin had previously sent Tschinotulander a set of lavish gifts in order to persuade him to return to the east on a second campaign. These gifts, including a shield with a live salamander set within it, a set of armor and various items of clothing, were fashioned out of the so-called *tiger-golt*, a magical substance formed in the vicinity of paradise whenever a tiger defecates on yellow flowers.[37] When *tiger-golt* is combined with diamonds and other precious substances, it turns into the *golt der selden*, a substance that brings good fortune to its owner, but also disaster to anybody who loses it. However, on his departure from Ackerïn, Tschinotulander makes the mistake of taking these gifts on a sea journey, not appreciating either the need to take particular care of the *golt der selden* or the fact that the conflict between the elements of water and of fire (represented by the live salamander fixed within his shield) will cause a tempest that can only be calmed once the gold has been jettisoned.[38] From this point on, Tschinotulander's good fortune is at an end. Although Ackerin attempts to undo the damage by sending more gold (in the form of a ring and a brooch), his initiative only makes things worse: although Tschinotulander receives the letter, the precious objects fall into the wrong hands owing to a verbal ambiguity. The original messenger carrying these dies on the way and with his dying breath, passes them on to a huntsman, with the instruction to give them to *dem fursten in dem lande* (J.T. 4969,2) [the prince ruling the land]. However, the denotation of this phrase is unclear, given that the land in question is Waleis, which belongs to Parzifal, has been entrusted to Tschinotulander, and is now illegally occupied by Orilus. The huntsman, who is disinclined to reflect on the finer points of territorial entitlement, decides that Orilus is as suitable a recipient as any and hands the gifts over to him.[39] Once this fresh *golt der selden* is in the hands of his arch-enemy, Tschinotulander is doubly disadvantaged, and his death can therefore be attributed at least in part to the combination of Ackerin's two well-intentioned dispatches. This fatal aspect of Ackerin's (second) letter is given particular prominence, since its discovery after Tschinotulander's death also serves to make the various causal connections even clearer in the minds of the audience:

> Bi dem talfine   het Sigun ein prievel funden,
> do er nach todes pine   entwapent wart. si behielt iz an den stunden.
> franzois si las, wie im der paruk wolde
> senden hort der selden.   zwei stucke rich von steine in selden golde.
>
> (J.T. 5509)

[Sigune found a small letter on the Dauphin, when he was disarmed after the agony of death. She took it straight away. In French she read how the *baruc* intended to send the treasure of good fortune: two precious pieces, with stones set in the *golt der selden*.]

This letter also provides a further link with episodes in the life of Parzifal/Parzival that will be familiar from Wolfram's work. When Sigune later entrusts the letter to him, he realizes that the replacement gift mistakenly handed to Orilus is in fact none other than the set of ornaments that he himself stole from Jescute during his period of youthful folly and which he used to pay the churlish fisherman for his night's lodging (J.T. 5510–5511; cf. *Parzival* 129,27–143,14).

As well as availing themselves of letters as a medium of communication, the protagonists rely on written texts for planning, for setting out contractual obligations, accounts and inventories, and for founding institutions.[40] Above all, texts matter for historical record keeping,[41] the protagonists subscribing to an almost naive assumption that if something is written down it is more likely to be true, and that the act of writing makes something more believable. To some extent, a written document can simply have a representative function, substituting for the presence of an absent authority-figure. For example, when Ypomidon is briefing Secureiz orally as to general military strategy, he also provides him with an accompanying written document (*brief*) setting out points of detail, including the names of the thirty kings who are to serve under Secureiz' leadership (J.T. 3363,1–2)—and he urges Secureiz to show this document to anyone who does not accept the overall plan (J.T. 3363 B). However, the use of writing is also seen as psychologically comforting in other situations. For examples, those warriors who witnessed the combat between Hernant and Fridebant later insist on having written records drawn up on the basis of their memories,[42] because oral reports of the event would not have been regarded as convincing:

> Si liezen niht beliben durch sagebære wunder,
> si hiezen alle schriben den strit ieclicher in sin lant besunder
> an sin gehugde bu°ch, wan si des jahen,
> daz iz unglouplich wære von allen, di iz horten oder sahen.
> (J.T. 2730)

[They did not content themselves with having the marvels talked about. Instead, each one of them ordered an account of the battle to be written into the book of his recollections and sent to his own land, for they claimed that it would be unbelievable for anybody who heard it or saw it.]

When questioned about the prowess of the Christians in the Orient, Lehelin's claim that *geschriben und gepruˆfet ist unser striten* (J.T. 4606,2) [our fighting has been documented and accounted for] also testifies to the widespread view that written records are, if not indisputable, then at least more authoritative than oral reports. However, as there is no such written document specifically mentioned within the text, it is possible that Lehelin is speaking metaphorically on this occasion. On this account, his statement would mean that the achievements of the Christians are as widely acknowledged as if they had been recorded in writing—or "carved in stone." While apparently blurring the distinction between speech and writing, such a metaphorical designation of the accumulation of oral reports as a "quasi-text" nonetheless implicitly affirms the default position, namely that there is greater credibility inherent in the written word.

The enthusiasm for written documentation also becomes apparent in the scene in which the heathen queen Ekuba reports to the Arthurian court the attempts of the twenty-five suitors to woo Secundille. Here, rather than just being content with an oral reception of the story, Ginover commands that all the details of the narrative be taken down even as Ekuba is speaking:

> Ekuba si vragete, diu sagt ir sus (do hiez diu wol versunnen
> die rede von ir munde schriben alle)
> wer durch Secundillen pris gewan und ouch verlos mit valle.
> (J.T. 5300,2–4)

[She asked Ekuba to tell her (and commanded, wisely, that the whole of her spoken account be written down) who had won renown through Secundille and who had lost out in disgrace.]

The insistence on immediate written documentation of a story distinguishes this episode from otherwise similar episodes in other works, when the Arthurian court is being regaled with an entertaining narrative (e.g., Kalogrenant's story in *Iwein*).[43] There is no clear reason why the story of Secundille's suitors is so compelling that it should merit this treatment. A possible parallel may be found in *Die Klage*, in which Bishop Pilgerin has a Latin text composed on the basis of the eyewitness accounts of Swemmel and others.[44] However, even allowing for the differences in genre, the complications in Secundille's love life hardly have an historic impact comparable to that of the destruction of the Burgundians. Even within the framework of the J.T., the Secundille material is peripheral, as vrou Aventiure is the first to point out in her conversation with the narrator:

> Min friunt von Blienvelden,   waz wiltu an mir rechen?
> wes sol Sigun engelden,   durch was sold ich von Secundillen sprechen?
>
> (J.T. 5295,1–2)

[My friend from Pleinfeld,[45] why are you making things difficult for me? Why should Sigune lose out [in terms of our attention]? Why should I talk about Secundille?]

The narrator's justification for insisting on discussing Secundille at this particular point is essentially that he wants a cheerful report of courtship and marriage to redress the balance after the mournful account of Sigune's anguish.[46] However, this extradiegetic piece of motivation has no bearing on Ginover's decision to call for immediate written documentation. In intradiegetic terms, it could be argued that the Arthurian court is wasting resources by misdirecting its historiographical zeal toward an area that does not merit being singled out in this way.

On the other hand, it could be maintained that it is precisely the apparent unimportance of Ekuba's discourse that makes its immortalization in script revealing and even poignant. The crucial link between writing and (collective) memory is widely appreciated in the Middle Ages. Isidore argues that writing was invented in order that things might be remembered; speech vanishes but writing lends permanence to things which would otherwise be forgotten.[47] Once the advantages of "script memory" over "brain memory" have been understood,[48] it follows, at least in theory, that if something is worth hearing in the first place, it will be worth remembering, and consequently worth writing down. In practice, there are resource implications that make it necessary for any society to be rather more selective about what is recorded. However, the decision to record Ekuba's storytelling may be seen as a symbolic acknowledgment both of the transience of speech and of the comforting solidity of the written word; the fact that her discourse is being recorded does not mean that it is uniquely important, but simply that this is how all oral contributions ought to be approached.

While the Ekuba episode is thus predicated on a conscious concern about the passage of time and the inadequacy of individual memories, the importance accorded to the process of documentation also illustrates an unwillingness on the part of the protagonists to accept the inevitable limitations of the written word. After all, despite its usefulness as a bulwark against the ravages of time, the permanence of writing is only relative: a text will only last as long as the letters are discernible, and the surface still intact. This ultimate transience and vulnerability of the written word is widely acknowledged in Latin texts reflecting on the role of grammar. Irvine draws attention to the fact that one popular etymology for the term *littera* links it to *litura* [erasure], on the grounds that writing on wax tablets was frequently rubbed out to make space for new lettering. As Irvine puts it, this trope "exposes the temporality and impermanence of even recorded utterances" and underscores "the text as what is iterable, writing as a system of deferral and memory."[49] Commonplaces such as that of "writing one's name in water" also highlight the fact that script is not immortal per se, but depends entirely on having an appropriate physical framework.[50]

Although the protagonists in the J.T. do not dwell explicitly on the fact that textual documents are physically fragile and liable to become smudged, blurred, or otherwise illegible, Ekunat's celebration of the power of the beryl to magnify script implicitly draws attention to the risk that a text might be inaccessible to the naked eye due to the size or quality of its lettering.[51] Similarly, when a group of learned masters explain to Tschinotulander the nature of the four elements and of the beasts that inhabit these, they point out that in the domain of the bird Gamaniol,[52] fourteen miles above the earth, the air is so pure that letters written even in dust will last for a thousand years:

> Wan in dem selben lufte   ist regn und wint gestillet,
> noch blikz mit doners gufte   kumt niht zu tusent jaren dar gezillet.
> und wer ein schrift geschriben in stoup al wesende,
> di wer von wind und regene   uber tusent jar da gu°t zulesene.
>
> (J.T. 2808)

[For in that same air rain and wind have been appeased, nor does lightning come with the roar of thunder even in a thousand years. And if a text were written in dust, the impact of wind and rain would be so minimal that it could be read for over a thousand years.]

This comment underscores the fact that in the normal course of events on earth, even a text constructed from far nobler materials is unlikely to last for a thousand years.[53] Finally, the narrative itself provides a crucial illustration of textual fragility, clearly demonstrating the inappropriateness of placing too much confidence in the endurance of the written word. When the Brackenseil is shredded in a joust between Ekunat and Orilus, the jewels used in the inscription are scattered all over the ground, losing their former status as bearers of literary contents.[54] The narrator poignantly expresses the disintegration of meaning by punning on the two meanings of *lesen* [to read / to gather up], the point being that people might become materially rich by gathering up the jewels, but there is no longer any possibility of reading the text:

> Swer si do was lesende   nach in uf dem plane,
> ob Artus were wesende   so rich, als ich wen, des was er ane.
>
> (J.T. 5896,1–2)

[If anybody were later to gather them up from the battle-field, I do not think that even Artus, had he been present, would be so rich.]

Section II: Inscriptions and Ornamental Letting

Although the deployment of decorative inscriptions and other forms of lettering is popular throughout the courtly world represented in the J.T, the inscriptions produced by the Grail community in order to adorn the temple can usefully be distinguished from other purely secular forms of lettering. The difference arises from the fact that in the case of the temple, the Grail artisans are building directly onto a divinely sanctioned model: as the plan for the temple is God-given, they only have to expand this into a program of text and image, rather than producing autonomous work from their own initiative.[55]

As the building is completed, it is adorned with many images that are cast, engraved, or sculpted (J.T. 345,1). Inside the temple, these images represent the saints (J.T. 384,4) or the apostles, confessors, virgins, patriarchs, martyrs, and prophets (J.T. 417,3–4). Each of these is supported by a *brief*, which in this case means a written statement identifying the figure, telling his *historje* [life-story] (J.T. 384,4), and otherwise elucidating the subject matter in question. The complementary relationship between text and image underscores the medieval conceit that visual representations constitute a secondary form of script that is accessible to the illiterate members of the laity.[56]

On the outside, the temple supports a program of secular virtues (J.T. 575,1), whereby visual representations of knights and ladies are accompanied by inscriptions that are inlaid with gold (J.T. 580,1) and that set out guidelines for speech and behavior in all social contexts, be it at table (J.T. 580,4) or during tournaments (J.T. 585). The fact that the knights are said to act in accordance with these inscriptions (J.T. 581,4) implicitly credits the external temple inscriptions with the same authority as the Grail communications. However, the meaning of the inscriptions is complicated by the inclusion of jewels amongst the building materials underpinning this didactic program. The fact that each gemstone has its own specific allegorical meanings, irrespective of the wider textual or visual context into which it is embedded, introduces a certain ambiguity into the act of reading. Thus, when the narrator notes that nobody might enter the temple without reading the stones that are on the outside (J.T. 576,1–2), it is unclear what kind of cognitive or spiritual process is being stipulated. In particular, when the narrator raises the possibility that a visitor might be unable to read the stones without assistance (J.T. 576,3–4), the question arises as to whether he is talking about illiteracy in the conventional sense, or about a lack of information about the meaning of gemstones, or about a kind of spiritual blindness that prevents the visitor from appreciating the true significance of natural phenomena.

Superficially, at least, the programmatic combination of text and image is duplicated within the secular domain, although with very different effect. This occurs most notably in the context of promoting Tschinotulander's status as an exemplary knight. Just as the saints represented within the temple carry a textual banner setting out their *vitae*, so Ackerin, not content with adorning Gamuret's coffin with rich inscriptions (J.T. 1002,4), also produces a banner bearing both the image of Gamuret/Tschinotulander (whose identities have to some extent merged) and a piece of text proclaiming the valor of Gamuret, who was treacherously slain (J.T. 3695–3697).[57] Such inscriptions are not confined to the image of Tschinotulander, but are also applied to his actual body. His identity, defined in terms of dynastic relationships, is inscribed in French and Arabic on the armor given to him by Ackerin, the text being made up of green characters (signifying the greenness suggested by the place-name *Graswalt* [grass-wood]) engraved onto red gold (J.T. 1684).[58] This armor, made of *golt der selden*, later turns out to be the undoing of Tschinotulander: as has already been explained, Ackerin fails to inform Tschinotulander of the particular importance of not losing the armor, and then compounds the damage by sending Tschinotulander a further portion of *golt der selden*. When Ackerin first realizes that Tschinotulander has departed without proper explanation of the nature of this armor, he is consumed with worry; and at this point, the text presents the problem, not just in terms of Tschinotulander's general ownership of the item, but specifically in relation to the inscription. The crucial fact is that the armor has Tschinotulander's name on it:

> Swie manz geschriben funde   an der vil richen sarwe,
> gehelfen daz niht kunde   Ackerin. der het vergezzen garwe,
> daz er im al di kraft niht undersagte
> durch vliz der werden hu^ete,   und im daz golt durch selde wol behagte.
>
> (J.T. 4409)

[Ackerin could do nothing about that which one found written on the very precious armor. He had completely forgotten to explain to him all the power [associated with] caring worthily and diligently [for this object] and to make him appreciate the gold for the sake of *selde*.]

Tschinotulander's identity, as expressed through the decorative writing of his name, thus becomes inextricably bound up with the theme of his demise.

Another key aspect of Tschinotulander's identity is his love for Sigune. Before he sets out to assist Ackerin, this too is inscripted onto his person, or rather, onto his helmet and lance, which constitute extensions of his knightly body.[59] First, his helmet is adorned with a textual garland affirming the purity of his lady, as well as his devotion to her:

> Zwei zirkel stab der bu°che   alumb daz schapel drungen.
> di schrift mit eren ru°che   seit, iz gebz ein herzogin dem jungen,
> und ditz schapel wer ein werdiu krone
> ir ku^eschen magetu°mes.   der ritter wurbe nach ir minne lone.
>
> (J.T. 1247)[60]

[Two rounds of letters encircled the garland. The text made the honorable proclamation that it was given by a Duchess to the young man, and that this garland was a worthy crown of her chaste virginity. The knight was serving her to win her love.]

This text also stresses its materiality in a self-referential way by informing onlookers of the fact that the garland was given to Tschinotulander by Sigune. Similarly, an inscribed veil taken from Sigune's headdress offers hope of reward:[61]

> Ein sidin risel clare,   darin erwebn von golde
> bu°chstaben rich furware.   di seiten, daz er sich des tro°sten solde,
> ob sin reise nem mit eren ende.

(J.T. 1248,1–3)

[A bright silken veil, interwoven with rich letters of gold, proclaimed that he would obtain the desired reward if his journey came to an honorable conclusion.]

This veil is tied to Tschinotulander's lance, in accordance with Sigune's wishes (J.T. 1249,1–2).

As texts, the garland and the veil are clearly more complex and elaborate than the inscription on the armor, which merely names Tschinotulander. It is therefore appropriate to see Sigune fulfilling the role both of author (formulating the texts) and of scribe (creating the textual artifacts). In commenting on this elaborate inscripting of Tschinotulander, Ekunat transfers the role of scribe from Sigune to Love personified:

> der minne schrift din sper, din helme fu°ret.

(J.T. 1428,3)

[Your lance and helmet bear the inscription of Love.]

It could be maintained that at this point in the narrative, Sigune is so focused on the secular side of the love relationship that her actions (in producing the writing) do indeed coincide so fully with those associated with the traditional vrou Minne [Lady Love] that she is virtually a tool of the latter.[62] Nonetheless, by thus inscripting Tschinotulander, Sigune is also (vainly) modeling her authorial activity directly on that of God drawing on the perceived continuum between divine and human writing. Her output is shown at least to some extent as a reaction to the fact that her beloved was not summoned to the Grail. As she laments this circumstance, Sigune refers to Tschinotulander as being *ungeschriben*, meaning that his name was "unwritten" on the Grail:

> Daz du der ungeschribene   bestu°nde vor dem grale,
> von vreuden diu vertribene   bin ich der selben schulde sunder twale.

(J.T. 5456,1–2)

[On account of the fact you should remain unwritten with respect to the Grail, I am constantly banished from joy.]

In the metonymic construction chosen by Sigune, Tschinotulander himself replaces his name. This means that, while the primary sense is simply that the name was never written on the Grail, the passage actually evokes a different image, namely of Tschinotulander, not as the text that might or might not appear on the "page" represented by the Grail, but rather as the blank "page" itself that is waiting to be inscripted. Sigune's decision to provide him with a set of courtly inscriptions before he sets out into battle may therefore be understood as an attempt to compensate him for the painful absence of divine lettering. In fact, no such compensation is possible, least of all through the means chosen by Sigune: notwithstanding her membership of the Grail family, the flimsy physical fabric (especially the veil) and the secular content (focusing on the erotic fulfillment following love service) of her output are both clearly illustrative of the transience and vanity which, according to Albrecht, characterize intradiegetic human writing.

Finally, it could also be argued that the extravagant inscripting of Tschinotulander in these passages constitutes a foreboding of his death. As Harpham puts it (with reference to hagiography and to the ascetic conception of the "deadness" of script): "Textuality constitutes an ascesis, a deadening, a purging of materiality and mutability that anticipates the release of the soul from the body at death."[63] Inscription often serves specifically as a metaphor for martyrdom, the wounds inflicted on the believer being presented as letters on a page.[64] While Tschinotulander falls short of martyrdom, the *minne*-oriented inscription of his person possibly points toward his death in courtly combat. Sigune's reduction of Tschinotulander to a textual construct may be regarded as a mise-en-abyme of an equivalent process of textualization of the hero on the part of the narrator(s): as will be shown in chapter 2, section I, the text plays an elaborate textual game with Tschinotulander's name, involving its deconstruction (through etymology) and partial obliteration (through the use of the Gamuret-mask as an identifier for the hero).

Section III: Reading Literature

In the J.T., the Christian and heathen courts are presented as sharing an established literary canon, which may broadly be described as being that of classical antiquity. There is no evidence of the characters having access to Middle High German literature—by contrast with the narrator, who makes intertextual references to the works of Hartmann von Aue, Heinrich von Veldeke, and Neidhart, and to figures from the heroic epic such as Witege and Siegfried.[65] The reason for this distinction between the intradiegetic and extradiegetic frames of literary reference undoubtedly stems from an attempt at achieving historical verisimilitude: the protagonists are deemed to have lived during the late years of the Roman Empire, many centuries before the Middle High German authors just mentioned. In view of this, and in view of the fact that Ovid constitutes the most prominent and controversial literary figure known to the protagonists,[66] it is particularly ironic that the one Ovidian work to be mentioned by name should prove strikingly anachronistic: when the young Titurel expresses his distaste for Ovid's *puellere* (J.T. 190,1), he is in fact referring to a medieval, rather than to a classical work: *Ovidius puellarum* or *De nuncio sagaci* is an (incompletely transmitted) erotic comedy thought to have been composed in France in the first half of the twelfth century.[67] However, it seems reasonable to understand Titurel's response in terms of Ovid's general status as a master of secular love, rather than to focus specifically on the contents of this text.[68]

Despite the fact that in the J.T. the Christians and the heathens both draw on the literature of classical antiquity, considerably more attention is devoted to examining the complexities of literary reception and interpretation within the Christian community. The heathen world is certainly presented as learned: for example, the entourage of the King of Morocco includes men of *meisterschefte* [learning] versed in jurisprudence, medicine, and the seven liberal arts (J.T. 2355).[69] However, although the *trivium* portion of the liberal arts is broadly language oriented, and although both grammar and rhetoric have clear literary dimensions, there is little indication that this proliferation of scholarship within the heathen world has affected the protagonists in such a way as to turn them into sophisticated readers of literary texts. Instead, on the two occasions when a heathen protagonist refers to books that he has read, his main objective is to draw out historical *exempla* that have a potential bearing on military strategy. In an inspirational speech to his ally, Gloramatis of Persia, Ackerin relies on the authority of *den alten bu°chen* (J.T. 3125,1) [the old books] to back up his claim that small but excellent teams of fighters are capable of defeating much larger forces that have grown complacent.[70] Similarly, Secureiz formulates his own principles of military conduct on his reading of the Trojan war *in dem bu°ch Omere* (J.T. 3549,1) [in the book of Homer]—by which he most probably means the pro-Trojan narrative by Dares and Dictys.[71] Admittedly, given that these speakers are rulers and warriors, and not the kinds of professional scholars mentioned in J.T. 2355, this pragmatic approach is perhaps unsurprising—indeed, the very fact that they should present themselves as readers in the first place testifies to the respect accorded to the written word in every culture depicted in this work. Nonetheless, it is noteworthy that when the Christians are presented as readers of classical texts, there is less emphasis on the military lessons to be drawn from the past, and considerably more on a subjective engagement with literature as part of the broadening of man's aesthetic and ethical sensibilities. This in turn raises the possibility of divergent readings of particular authors and of the moral ambiguity of certain literary texts. These issues are exemplified most clearly with reference to the chasm developing between the young Titurel, who is shocked by what he finds in Ovid, and many of the adult protagonists, who appear to have the highest admiration for the *praeceptor amoris* [expert on love] and wish to draw on his linguistic flair (if not his practical advice) as they pursue their courtly love relationships.[72]

In the figure of Titurel, the narrator attempts to combine the topoi of the learned *puer senex* and of the courtly youth impatient to embark on chivalry.[73] Accordingly, Titurel progresses onto the first rung of the liberal arts (J.T. 183,3: *an der grammatik wart er schier vol varnde* [he was soon accomplished in *grammatica*]) and yet these studies are burdensome to him (J.T. 184,3: *sin wille stu°nt gen ritterschaft, kunst der bu°che wold er sin nu sparnde.* [his will inclined toward chivalry, and he now wanted to leave book-learning behind.]).[74] However, he enjoys reading about chivalry and *manheit* (J.T. 185,1) [manly / military activities]. It is unclear what the material referred to in this line might have been: although Ovid is the great authority on love, he is by no means an obvious source of information about knighthood and military prowess.[75] It is similarly unclear whether the line refers to extracurricular reading or to material selected by the tutor. Be this as it may, Titurel's reading leads him to his first contact with the notion of *minne* (J.T. 185,2). At this point, his situation is complicated by the fact that his mother Elizabel, prefiguring the famous overprotectiveness of Herzeloyde in *Parzival*, has decreed that Titurel is not to be told about the nature of love. Titurel becomes convinced that *minne* is a ghost or hellish spirit (J.T. 190,3: *ein schrat, ein geist von helle*), and develops the habit of uttering prayers and crossing himself whenever the term is mentioned, much to the amusement of the court (J.T. 187,4). His tutor is initially unwilling to enlighten him because of Elizabel's edict but finally asks Titurel why is it that he is worried by *minne* At this point, Titurel claims to have been troubled specifically by *Ovidium puellere*, this text having supposedly caused him to form a very negative impression of *minne*, although he realizes that many people in the world regard this personified force as their friend and companion (J.T. 190). Again, it is unclear whether this work (or indeed, any work by Ovid with erotic content) has actually been prescribed for Titurel as part of his study of the *trivium*.[76] Although nothing is said to suggest that Titurel should not have read the book, the tutor nonetheless distances himself from carnal love, which is claimed to imperil the soul and ought therefore to be called *unminne* (J.T. 196,1) [the opposite of love]. At the same time, he reassures Titurel on the value of chaste, spiritual love, and urges the boy to extend this kind of love to God and to all created things. In operating with such a distinction between different forms of love, the tutor's approach is superficially similar to the common justification for using Ovid for educational purposes: namely that Ovid's erotic works include models of "good" as well as of "bad" love.[77] However, the implication here is that everything Ovidian falls into the category *unminne*, and that *minne* is something entirely different (and specifically Christian).[78]

On the one hand, therefore, Titurel's rejection of Ovid serves to underscore his exceptional purity and hence his unique suitability for the role as guardian of the ethically stringent Grail. Although he comes across as somewhat naive in his assessment, the fundamental rightness of his reaction is endorsed shortly afterward in the narrator's general admonition:

> Und daz sich nieman kere   an Ovidium den lecker!
> (J.T. 263,1)

[And let nobody follow the lecherous Ovid!][79]

According to the narrator, Ovid's principal crime is to have dishonored women, any worthy praise that he might have formulated being outweighed by his slander and wickedness (J.T. 263–264).

On the other hand, Ovid is clearly a literary force to be contended with and the incident under discussion illustrates the fact that even within the Grail community, divergent reactions are possible: Titurel and Elizabel constitute one extreme of radical hostility to secular love, while others (e.g., the laughing courtiers) are able to retain a certain intellectual distance without, in their own view, jeopardizing their virtue. Furthermore, within the Arthurian world, admiration for the skill of the *amorigraphus* is commonplace.[80] Whereas Titurel does not appear to have responded to the aesthetic qualities of Ovid (unsurprisingly, perhaps, if all he has read is *Ovidius puellarum*!), others habitually invoke the master in topoi of ineffability, as when Ekunat says to Clauditte:

> Ovidius, ob der lebte,   din tugent im wer zu prisen unbenennet!
> (J.T. 2539,4)

[Even if Ovid lived, he would not be able to do full justice to your virtue].

This particular formulation draws attention not only to Ovid's eloquence, but also to his surprising status (promoted in many academic commentaries) as an arbiter of morals.[81] Furthermore, whereas one might perhaps expect worldly figures such as Ekunat, Clauditte, and Ekuba to express enthusiasm for Ovid,[82] it is striking that even Sigune should refer to Ovid in very similar manner, as she laments her own inability to record the well-formulated terms of endearment that Tschinotulander addressed to her in the past:[83]

> wie moht ich, herr, erzeln unde schriben
> allen den zart, den ich von dir ie horte?
> und wer Ovidius lebende,   er moht sich niht gevlizen solcher worte!
> (J.T. 5227,2–4)

[How might I, my Lord, speak and write down all the tender words which I ever heard from you? Even if Ovid were alive, he would not be able to avail himself of such words!]

'Wolfram,' the primary narrator, is certainly not prepared to follow Titurel in his absolute rejection of the master. In a much later exchange with vrou Aventiure, he takes a rather different view of Ovid's alleged misogyny: when vrou Aventiure protests at his claim that women can shed tears at will, he argues that he is merely repeating that which has already been said by *Ovidius der wise* (J.T. 5152,1). Furthermore, other Middle High German authors supposedly view women just as negatively; Hartmann's presentation of Laudine being cited as a case in point (J.T. 5153).[84] Admittedly, in all the dialogues with vrou Aventiure, the narratorial voice is explicitly identified as being that of 'Wolfram,' and so it cannot be assumed that the views expressed on these occasions reflect the values otherwise promoted in the text.[85] It could therefore be argued that this interchange does not constitute even a limited endorsement of Ovid, but should rather be seen as a dig at 'Wolfram': a man with his misguidedly liberal approach to courtly love might indeed find Ovid wise.

However, even when the narratorial voice is not coupled unambiguously with the 'Wolfram'-role, it is still capable of invoking Ovid as part of an ineffability topos, thereby implicitly endorsing the protagonists' view that Ovid constitutes the cynosure of style and literary competence:

> Ovidius und Ercules,   ich wen, in gar zerunne an disem prise.
> (J.T. 108,4)

[Ovid and Heraclius—I believe that they would not be able to do justice to all this merit.][86]

There is, nonetheless, a fundamental difference in function between the references to Ovid made by the protagonists and the seemingly similar ones made by the narrator(s). When Ekunat and Sigune speak of Ovid, it is in the context of their secular love relationships, and so, even when they are only talking about literary categories (e.g., style and eloquence), they are still basically paying inappropriate homage to a corpus of texts that ostensibly provides incitement to, and advice on how to achieve sexual consummation. By contrast, when Ovid features within the narratorial discourse, the context is that of one littérateur speaking about another. The emphasis is thus on the common process of producing literature, rather than on the personal pursuit of love.

Admittedly, even the production of literature—and especially of 'Ovidian' literature—is not unproblematic from as ascetic perspective. In illustrating the nexus between sin, body, and text, Kiening adduces the case of Guibert of Nogent, an eleventh-century Benedictine monk who produced a three-part biography known as the *libri monodiae*.[87] As a young monk, Guibert was plagued by bodily desires and the desire for power and literary renown. Stimulated by the works of Ovid, he would hide under the bed-clothes at night, reading the erotic verses of the master and attempting to write versions of his own, with his sinful hand functioning, in the words of Kiening, as "ein schillerndes *membrum*" [a quivering member], which later features in Guibert's own dreams.[88]

However, an anecdote such as this not only illustrates the nature of the carnal temptation from which Albrecht wishes to exempt the young Titurel, but also suggests a model of writing very different to that of the J.T. itself. Whilst the night-time scribblings of Guibert appear to copy Ovid in the most obvious way (in terms of erotic subject matter and titillating turns of phrase), they do not appear to take account either of the complexity of the medieval construction of Ovid's persona, or of the subtlety with which Ovid's texts undercut their own eroticism. As Ginsberg has argued (with particular reference to the *Ars amatoria*), Ovid's work "enacts and cancels it own program . . . [and] . . . subverts the pretense that it is educative, or that it mimetically represents the social world."[89] Furthermore, "its writing displaces men and women both," presenting itself as a surrogate for the body and its desires.[90] The J.T., in turn, constitutes a similarly extreme case of "textualization" of the body, highlighted not only by the subordination of human destinies to the analytical exegesis of the narrator(s), but also by the literal inscription of bodies (as discussed in the previous section) and by means of the deconstruction of personal identities through etymologies (to be discussed in chapter 2). Ginsberg's conclusion, that "the connection . . . between Ovidian sexuality and the ascetic impulses of the commentaries is less strange that one might think, since Christian self-denial was also an exercise based on textuality,"[91] could therefore equally well be reformulated to apply to the connection between Ovid and the J.T. On this account, it becomes possible even for the authorial narrator ('Albrecht') to designate Ovid as wise, without any trace of irony. However, the intellectual luxury of embracing the paradox whereby Ovid is both *der lecker* and *der wise*, is one that he reserves for himself. As far as the protagonists are concerned, there is ultimately only one appropriate response to the Ovidian corpus. Within the narrative world of the J.T., this set of texts not only constitutes yet another example of the futility of human writing, but, given its particular raciness, it serves as a kind of litmus paper revealing the precise degree of moral purity of all who come into contact with it—and only Titurel passes with flying colors.[92]

CHAPTER 2

FIRST AND SECOND LANGUAGE: NAMES, ETYMOLOGIES, AND NATURAL PHENOMENA

Whereas the discussion of textual culture in the previous chapter focused on the fallibility inherent to the processes of reading and writing, this chapter will concern itself with the way in which the J.T. reflects more broadly on the reliability and interpretability of language. Language is here understood in the widest possible sense covering the interplay between the "first" language of ordinary verbal communication between human beings and the "second" language used by God to communicate with humans by means of created objects.[1]

This terminological opposition between first and second language is coined by Brinkmann on the basis of the Augustinian theory of signs.[2] The ordinary words that make up the first language are understood as signs (*signa*) substituting for objects or phenomena (*res*) in the world. Additionally, many objects created by God are in themselves deemed to be bearers of meaning and thus to stand in an hermeneutic relationship with further elements of reality (objects, persons, or facts):[3] to take one very common example, the pelican, which has the property of piercing its own breast in order to feed its young, is deemed to signify Christ's self-sacrifice in undertaking the redemption of the human race.[4] The essential difference between first and second language has been summarized by Hegener as follows:[5]

1. Sprache besteht aus Worten als Zeichen für Dinge (Ersatzcharakter der Sprache).
2. Sprache besteht aus Dingen als Zeichen für andere Dinge (Verweisungscharakter der Sprache).

   [1. Language consists of words that are the signs of things (The substitution-function of language).
2. Language consists of things that are the signs of other things (The reference-function of language).]

The notion of second language hinges on the assumption that objects in the natural world were created to benefit human beings, not only physically (e.g., by providing them with foodstuffs), but also morally and intellectually, by encouraging them to interpret their properties in such a way as to arrive at spiritual truths.[6] The learning of the second language thus coincides with the assimilation of the Christian tradition of the allegorical interpretation of natural phenomena such as animals, plants, and gemstones. It is also an approach that encourages the widespread conceit of the physical universe as a readable text authored by God.[7]

The relationship between first and second language is complex. On the one hand, the former is generally presented as inferior to the latter. Words have no "real" existence but only substitute for objects.[8] Furthermore, as Augustine notes, and as later thinkers tend to agree, there is no inherent or God-given connection between words and the objects to which they relate—these being linked not by nature but by human convention.[9] While it is sometimes accepted that an inherent or "natural" connection might have existed at the point when Adam, in his pre-lapsarian state, named all objects in Paradise in accordance with a true understanding of their natures,[10] this connection was later severed, not only by the Fall, but also by the proliferation of languages arising after the destruction of the Tower of Babel. In theory, therefore, the process of scrutinizing the names of objects in order to fathom the true nature of them or of their creator ought to be deemed entirely otiose. Certain writers, such as Abelard, do take this approach.[11]

The viability of medieval etymology, founded as it is on the Isidorean maxim that *Nisi enim nomen scieris, cognitio rerum perit* [without knowledge of the name, there is no understanding of the object],[12] is only "saved" by the tradition that singles out the three languages that featured on the Cross (Hebrew, Latin, and Greek), and accords these with an element of that sanctity which characterized Adam's original utterances.[13] Vernacular etymologies are more problematic.[14] They find a defender in Petrus Helias, who side-steps the whole issue of Adam and Babel, taking the line that all languages have been developed by human beings along rational principles and that a similarity between words should therefore reflect as similarity between the things that they are intended to designate.[15] While this is a pleasing argument that underscores the rationalism of the human mind, it can easily be attacked with reference to homonyms with entirely different meanings. As will be shown in section I below, the J.T. deploys a number of such counter-examples to good effect. In any case, the general popularity of etymological statements in vernacular works does not hinge on this academic defence, but is more likely to be a function either of the lower philosophical stringency of these texts (which would make them more ready to affirm a pleasing but slightly simplistic notion of all language as being God-given) or else of the fact that etymologies, however spurious, serve a useful expository and mnemonic purpose.[16]

As against all these limitations in the scope of first language, second language offers a comforting solidity and reliability. Ohly even uses the term "pfingstlich" [pentecostal] to characterize this allegorical language, thereby placing the second language on a par with the miracle described in Acts 2, when the Holy Spirit descended on the Apostles to bridge the linguistic chasms resulting from Babel.[17]

On the other hand, the second language is not without its own difficulties and cannot be mastered without recourse to the first language. The web of connections between objects has to be learned, a process that is complicated by the fact that a given object does not have a single *significatio*, but as many *significationes* as it has properties. Augustine notes by way of example that people must study and memorize the properties of the serpent, the garnet, the beryl, the diamond, and the olive—and, recognizing the challenges involved in this, he encourages the compilation of allegorical encyclopedias.[18] This emphasis on education clearly restores some prestige to the first language in which information about the physical world is transmitted. The written words used in the study of the quadrivium and of other scientific texts may only be signs of signs, but without them, the objects forming the units of discourse in the second language would remain uninterpretable.[19] Nonetheless, just as with first language, there are areas of ambiguity and open-endedness. In addition to the well-established problem of objects being interpretable either *in bonum* or *in malum partem* (positively or negatively, in the sense that the lion, for example, can signify either God or the devil), the hermeneutic poly-valency of created objects means that it can be difficult to distinguish between God-given *significatio* and man-made metaphor.[20]

There is considerable evidence to suggest that Albrecht shares not only Augustine's enthusiasm for second language, but also his pessimism about the scope and reliability of first language. The final destruction of the Brackenseil (whereby Clauditte's first-language text disappears, while the jewels continue to exist as independent bearers of meaning) neatly illustrates the enduring superiority of second language over first language. As Finckh puts it:

> Die aufgestickte Botschaft wurde mißverstanden und vernichtet, aber die Edelsteine als natürliche Vermittler der christlichen Lehre sind nicht so leicht zu zerstören; sie bleiben erhalten als Gottes Inschrift im "Buch der Welt", verständlich für den Gelehrten, der sie zu "lesen" versteht, ungefährlich für den Maßvollen, der mit ihrem Wert vernünftig umzugehen weiß.[21]

> [The stitched-on message was misunderstood and annihilated, but the jewels, as natural transmitters of Christian doctrine, are not destroyed so easily; they are preserved as God's inscription in the "Book of the World," comprehensible to the learned, who know how to "read" them, and harmless to those of moderate temperament, who know how to handle them sensibly.]

Admittedly, there are passages in which Albrecht appears to celebrate *wort* [words] as something God-given, forming part of creation on a par with other natural phenomena. Examples of this stance include:

> Got sterne, steine, krute,   wort, wurze git sus orden
> dem senften alein zu trute.   sus kan sin hort ob allen horden horden.
> (J.T. 284,1–2)

> [God allows only the gentle-spirited man to become familiar with the *ordo* of stars, stones, herbs, words, and roots. Thus his treasure-trove outdoes all other treasure.]

and

> Mit sternen gotes girde   und vil mit steinen wundert.
> chraft mit grozer wirde   git er worten, wurzen ouch besundert.
> (J.T. 1662,1–2)

[God's will, as manifested in stars and stones, causes great amazement. In particular,
he grants power and great worthiness to words and roots.]

Nonetheless, Albrecht is also fully aware of the limitations and ambivalence of ordinary language. One striking case of linguistic ambiguity is central to the story line of the J.T.: Ackerin's second gift of the *golt der selden* falls into the wrong hands because the phrase *dem fursten in dem lande* (J.T. 4969,2) [the prince ruling the land] may reasonably be taken to refer to either Tschinotulander, who has been entrusted with the country, or to Orilus, who wields power *de facto*. Place-names can also be a source of ambiguity, particularly when, as in the case of Paradise, a particular place becomes so strongly associated with particular qualities that its name starts to be used as a common noun and thereby loses its function as a unique identifier.[22] When the two aggressive heathens, Philip and Alexander, confront Tschinotulander with the battle-cry *Paradis* (J.T. 4754,1), it takes the hero a moment to realise that he is not dealing with divine emissaries from the terrestrial paradise (J.T. 4757), and he remains puzzled until it is explained that *Paradis* also happens to be the name of heathen land. The slight connection between this land and its more famous namesake, distinguished in J.T. 4814,4 as the proper (*daz rechte*) Paradise, is based on the fact that the heathen land is particularly rich in natural resources and therefore provides its inhabitants with a supposedly paradisical quality of life (J.T. 4823).

It is in the potentially Adam-like act of naming his characters that Albrecht reveals his nominalist tendencies most clearly and section I will focus on this aspect of the J.T. As will be shown, the narrator invokes the traditions of etymology, including those of vernacular etymology, only in order to subvert them.[23] Despite extensive discussion about the principles involved in naming, there is no real attempt to use names to express fundamental aspects of characters' natures. On the contrary, the unusual importance ascribed by the protagonists to the exact spelling of certain names ties in with the comments made in chapter 1 about the futility of intradiegetic writing generally, while the practice (on the part of the narrator as well as of the protagonists) of transferring names from one figure to another undercuts the solidity of the personal identity of the protagonists and thereby serves to highlight the fictionality of the narrative.

Section II will examine Albrecht's engagement with the second language (i.e., with the allegorical interpretation of natural phenomena). In many respects, the narrator of the J.T. takes a fairly conventional line, arguing that God created the world, here exemplified by animals, for the practical and spiritual benefit of man:

Got hat menschen bilde　　geschaffen gar zeheile
daz zam und ouch daz wilde,　　ze gu°t, ze nutze lib und sele ze teile.
einhalp den lip mit manger vrucht iz spiset,
anderhalp geistlichen　　mit tugende ler di sel iz paradiset.

(J.T. 2805)[24]

[God has created both tame and wild animals for the benefit of man, for the good and
the use of both body and soul. On the one hand, they feed the body in many different
ways, and on the other hand, they provide the soul with a spiritual paradise through
teaching about the virtues.]

Consequently, man has a duty to study and interpret the *proprietates* of created objects in the world. This doctrine is embedded into the story line: for example, after Tschinotulander has found to his detriment that taking a salamander out to sea will trigger a tremendous storm, three learned masters give him a tutorial explaining just why it is that fire and water are naturally hostile to each other.[25] Their teaching culminates with a general injunction to study the elements and the humors—not so much for the practical benefit of knowing how to avoid future perils at sea, but rather in order to obtain a scientific basis for a moral lesson: how to achieve *maze* [balance; moderation] within the soul (J.T. 2819–2820).

However, Albrecht's position on the second language immediately becomes more interesting in situations where there is some blurring of the boundaries between "natural" objects (with their divinely ordained *significations* [meanings]) and man-made objects with a representative function. A natural object (such as a gemstone) will have its particular, and sometimes quasi-magical properties and will have various meanings based on these properties. However, if such an object is then used within a human work of art to depict a different natural object (e.g., gemstones being used to represent the heavenly bodies), there is suddenly a new layer of meanings to be taken into account. Furthermore, there are cases in which man-made copies of a natural object appears to possess not only the *significationes* but also the actual properties of the original. Finally, in a rather special case of the "man-made" replacing the natural, reality and allegorical meaning are ascribed to an animal (the *bestia de funde*) which is clearly Albrecht's own creation: a fictional compilation of properties taken from a variety of "real" animals.

Section I: Names and Etymologies

The J.T. contains approximately 1,280 names of persons and places, of which approximately six hundred are taken over from the works of Wolfram, approximately seventy derived from other sources, and the remainder invented by Albrecht.[26] The varied techniques employed by Albrecht in coining this impressive array of names have been analyzed by Zatloukal, who argues that Albrecht had a clear sense of the semantic value attaching to particular components such as suffixes and that he used these smaller linguistic units to distinguish consistently between, for example, male and female names, or heathen and Christian names.[27] From these facts alone it can be deduced that Albrecht took a particular interest in names as linguistic and literary entities. Furthermore, although the vast majority of the names in the J.T. are understandably introduced into the text without any kind of commentary or glossing, there are some instances in which explicit attention is drawn to the status of names as textual constructs. While the importance of this textual dimension is underscored even by the narrator's practice of breaking down certain names into constituent parts and subjecting these parts to etymological analysis (usually translations of stem elements), more striking evidence for a textual understanding of names comes from two separate episodes within the narrative, when the infants Titurel and Secundille are given newly invented names designed to signal their parentage.[28] In both cases, careful attention is paid by all involved to the building blocks (i.e., syllables and letters) of these onomastic neologisms. It will be argued that this focus on names as accumulations of inherently meaningless individual letters or of semantically neutral individual syllables points toward a dissociation (already latent in the narrator's handling of etymologies) of names from identities, and of the written word from the "reality" of the narrative situation.

Although proper names differ from common (appellative) nouns precisely in that it is possible for them to carry out their denotative function without any descriptive content or wider meaning, Western rhetorical tradition often accords the personal proper name the additional, connotative function of serving as a prophetic indicator (*veriloquium* or *praesagium*) of the bearer's nature, qualities, or destiny.[29] On the face of it, there is evidence in the J.T. that Albrecht too draws on this tradition and intends his audience to engage with the possibility that at least some of the names constitute meaningful descriptors of their bearers.

In some cases, the meaning of a name is entirely transparent and requires no elucidation. The name of Senabor's son Parille is in fact a common noun (beryl):

> Ein sin sun Parille   hiez er nach dem steine
> (J.T. 99,1)

[He called one of his sons Parille/Beryl after the stone]

This does not require any elaborate etymological analysis, although the narrator chooses to remind the audience of those particular properties of the stone that provides that *tertium comparationis* which explains the choice of name.[30] Similarly, Richaude's punning prediction that Herzeloude will die of *herzeleide* [heartache] hinges on an implicit assumption that a name "means" what it sounds like.[31] Finally, when the narrator comments that the green color of this hero's armor is commensurate with his place of provenance, he implicitly highlights the fact that *Graswalt*, which serves both as a place-name and as part of the personal name of Tschinotulander, is readable as a German compound (grass-forest):

> Von Graswalt geheizen,   nach Graswalt geverwet
> (J.T. 1428,1)

[named after Graswalt, colored like Graswalt]

Graswalt evokes greenness to such an extent that Tschinotulander's green armor may be understood as a visual reference to his own name.[32]

In other cases, the meaning of a name is veiled and can only be accessed through the techniques of etymological analysis. For the most part, the narrator's chosen etymological technique is that of (more or less spurious) translation.[33] Heathen or French names are thus rendered into German so as to provide a description of the bearer on the model provided in Wolfram's *Parzival*, where the hero's name is glossed by Sigune as meaning *Rehte enmitten durch* (140,17) [straight through the middle].[34] In this context, the dog Gardivias, whose names is not only translated (J. T. 1190,4: *hu᷎te wol der verte* [stay well on the track]), but subjected to an extensive allegorical interpretation, constitutes a special case that will be treated in chapter 3.[35] The same applies to Ekunat de Silvat, who plays a central part in the quest for the Brackenseil and whose name is translated both in the J.T. and in Wolfram's *Titurel*.[36]

Whereas one might normally expect the topos of the name as *veriloquium / praesagium* to be applied primarily to those figures whose natures and careers are of central interest to the audience, Albrecht's narrator is in fact very uneven in his distribution of etymological translations, ignoring the names of most major protagonists, and sometimes devoting considerable attention to the names of characters who only engage the audience's attention for the briefest moment. For example, the interest shown in the meanings of the names of Feirefiz's three rather ephemeral mistresses is hardly justified by any interest that the audience might be assumed to have in their individual destinies:

> Iedoch so pflak er minne   der kunigin Alberosen.
> lip, lant, ir sinne   het im verselt diu sueze "liljen rosen".
> (alsus genant so was ir nam zeduᵉte
> ze Proventz in der sprache,   ob Kyot niht entriegen kan die luᵉte.
> (J.T. 5354)

[And yet he loved the Queen Alberose. The sweet "lilies and roses" had devoted to him her self, her land and her thoughts. (This is how her name was interpreted in the language of Provence, if Kyot is to be trusted)];[37]

> Diu ander Bardidele,   der name sich glosieret
> "noch lieber dann diu sele"
> (J.T. 5355,1–2)

[The second one was Bardidele. This name may be glossed as "more precious even than the soul"];[38]

> "In herzen gar beslozzen",   daz spricht enduᵉt Clauditte,
> in herzen unverdrozzen   minnet er die. seht, daz ist diu dritte!
> (J.T. 5358,1–2)

["Entirely enclosed in the heart" is the meaning of "Clauditte." He loves her utterly in his heart. Behold, she is the third one!][39]

Examples such as these suggest that in the J.T., the etymologies offered do not necessarily serve to support the narrative.[40] We are not provided with the etymologies because they reveal something about the characters or because the characters matter for the story line, but because the names themselves (as distinct from their bearers) are of aesthetic or moral interest, simply as individual words on the page. For example, as Nyholm has shown, Albrecht has a predilection for floral images and compounds, using the term *blume* to encapsulate his conception of an absolute, even Christ-like, form of moral excellence.[41] Accordingly, he is particularly willing to construct and translate names involving this quasi-totemic stem, regardless of who the bearers actually are; and so we learn not only the meaning of *Alberose*, but also of *Flordiprintze* (J.T. 5785,1: *Der hohen fursten bluᵒme* [the flower of noble princes]) and of *Floramie* (J.T. 5782,3: *der bluᵒmen friundin* [the lover of flowers]).[42]

Additionally, on the two occasions when the narrative focuses on the efforts involved in inventing suitable new names for children, the principle adopted is one of genealogy rather than etymology: the children's names are constructed from elements taken from those of the parents (*Titurel* from *Titur*ison and Elizab*el*; *Secundille* from *Secu*reiz and Araba*dille*), with no regard to what these elements might actually "mean."

Names were regularly used in the Middle Ages to give expression to a genealogical relationship: in this context, Haubrichs draws attention to the techniques of "Alliteration," "Namensvariation," and "Namensrepetition (Nachbenennung)" [alliteration, variation on a name, repetition of a name (being named after somebody)].[43] However, while it is relatively common in Middle High German fiction for boys to share a first letter, a prominent stem, or even a full name with their fathers,[44] or other male relatives;[45] for girls to be named after their mothers;[46] or even for entire nuclear families to share a common stem,[47] Albrecht's strategy of fusing two parental components into a single name is very unusual.[48] An early historical parallel is provided by the case of the eleventh-century Bishop Wulfstan, who was named after his parents *Wulf*geua and Aethel*stan*, supposedly on the basis that the sanctity of each parent would be passed on to the child through the partial bequest of the name.[49] It seems reasonable to assume that a similar line of thought underlies the decisions taken with respect to the naming of Titurel and Secundille; and given Wolfram's preoccupation with issues of maternal and paternal inheritance on all levels, such a naming strategy may be seen as particularly appropriate within a literary universe that purports to overlap with that of Wolfram's works.

Furthermore, it might be argued that in the cases of Titurel and Secundille, the names, as textual entities, have a life of their own, which parallels that of the characters that they designate: just as the children have their human parents, so the names have their textual parents. This is turn ties in with the grammatical conceit of presenting a particular linguistic form as the product or offspring of other linguistic forms: so, for example, the union of *nomen* [noun] and *verbum* [verb] is said to give rise, not only to the *oratio* [sentence],[50] but also to the past participle: a single word, which, like the names under discussion, contains traces of both of its grammatical parents.[51]

The naming of Titurel is more controversial than that of Secundille because it unleashes a quarrel concerning the exact number and selection of letters to feature in the child's name. The apparently harmless suggestion in J.T. 171,3 *daz sin nam ir beider name ru^erte* [that his name should touch on both of their names][52] triggers the question as to the exact proportion of the paternal and maternal contribution:

und wurden des zu kriege,   von wederm iz den gro^ezern teil da fu^erte.
(J.T. 171,4)

[and a quarrel broke out as to which of them should be the parent from whom the name derived its greatest part.]

This leads the learned masters to rule that the child's name should contain at least two *teil* [parts] from that of the father in order to reflect (or even to bring about) a predominance of the paternal heritage within the child:

> di seiten bi ir eiden   des vater nam im zwei teil oder mere.
> so vil mer wer iz dem vater nahen
> vereigent an geburte.

(J.T. 172,2–4)

> [On their oaths they recommended two parts or more from the father's name. The child would be so much more closely linked to the father at birth.]

Nothing is said about the number of *teil* to come from the mother, or indeed about how a *teil* is to be quantified. However, the implication of the rulings appears to be that the mother should be deemed to contribute one *teil* and the input from the father's name should be at least twice as great as that from the mother's, regardless of whether this is calculated on the basis of syllables or of letters.

In the subsequent strophe, describing Elizabel's dissatisfaction both with this general principle and with the three-syllable name actually proposed, the focus turns to the number of letters, when she notes that the name contains five letters *von des vater teile* (J.T. 173,3) [from the father's part] and only two from her name.[53] The strife is only resolved when the learned masters point out that the name proposed contains not merely two, but four letters from the name Elizabel (since E and L feature both at the beginning and at the end). This new ratio 4:5 apparently satisfies Elizabel as being an improvement on 2:5 (J.T. 174,4). Furthermore, even though the masters do not say this, she may also have spotted that the letter I is common to both parents, thus giving her a full half-share in the baby's name.

While Zatloukal argues that the last point made by the masters should be understood as a mere sop to appease the wounded feelings of Elizabel,[54] it seems that this curious solution reached may be interpreted more seriously as an indictment of the ambivalence of the written word, the analysis of which can differ so markedly according to individual perspective (e.g., according to whether one focuses on syllables or on letters). On the one hand, all the parties concerned apparently subscribe to the view that there is a direct correlation between linguistic forms and the real world (i.e., the physical and moral contributions of both parents are quite literally tied up with their share of the child's name). On the other hand, the duplication of certain letters within one name, or between the names of two people, underscores the fact that letters, being infinitely recyclable, ultimately elude both meaning and ownership, and make a mockery of the dispute between the two parents.

This is, after all, not a text in which characters are associated uniquely and metonymically with certain letters of the alphabet, in the way that Margarethe, for example, is associated with the letter M in *Der Ackermann aus Böhmen* 3.3 and 4.9.[55] Nor does the text draw on the tradition of etymological *expositio* according to the "meaning" of individual letters.[56] On the contrary, the narrator goes out of his way elsewhere to demonstrate that exactly the same arrangement of letters can mean quite different things, according to context. In the case of certain names, puns (*aequivoca*) are designed to show that apparent and actual meaning, rather than coinciding as they did in the cases of *Parille* and *Graswalt*, are at odds with each other. Conversely, in the case of the *Herzeloude* / *herzeleide* pun, the fact that homonyms can be spelled differently highlights the irrelevance of *litterae* [letters], at least as far as the spoken language is concerned. The intrinsic meaninglessness of *litterae* is also illustrated in the following passage in which exactly the same letters are used to convey two entirely different things, namely the place-name *Anschowe(n)* [Anjou] and the verb *anschowen* [to look at]:

> si [Herzeloude] enachte weder tanzes noch der blu^emen,
> wan den von Anschowen anzeschowen.
>
> (J.T. 4443,2–3)

[She cared neither for dancing nor for the flowers, but only for looking at the one belonging to the house of Anjou.]

This joke hinges on the coincidental homonymity between a German verb and a foreign place-name, but the text is equally ready to juxtapose purely German homonyms, as when vrou Aventiure deconstructs the narratorial name *Wolfram* by separating the constituent elements and highlighting the different possible meanings of *ram* and its derivatives in German:

> Min fru^ent, ein ram der Wolfe,   ir sult min so nicht ramen!
>
> (J.T. 3598,1)

[My friend, you branch/kinsman of the wolves, you should not attack/besmirch me in this way.]⁵⁷

Here, although the name *Wolfram* is on one level shown to be interpretable, the plurality of possible meanings for the different segments contributes to the sense that any interpretation is ultimately open-ended and unreliable. Between them, these passages exemplify the two categories on multilingual (*aequivoca ex diversitate linguarum*) and monolingual puns (*aequivoca in una lingua*),⁵⁸ both of which clearly undermine some of the fundamental premises of etymology, such as the claim formulated by Peter Helias that it is *litterarum similitudo* [similarity in spelling or letters] which provides the key to the properties of things.⁵⁹ This in turn raises at least the possibility that the coincidence of certain letters (i.e., *litterarum similitudo*) which apparently links the name of Titurel to those of his parents is as unreliable and irrelevant as that which links *Anschowe(n)* and *anschowen*.

By contrast with the domestic tensions just outlined, the naming of Secundille involves no conflict of any sort for the heathen couple, Secureiz and Arabadille. For that reason, perhaps, no recourse is made to the level of *littera*. Instead, a distinctive element or cluster of syllables is lifted from the name of each parent, with no concern for the number of letters involved, or for the fact that a new letter N is introduced to link the two parental elements:

> Nu wart daz kint geheizen   nach vater und nach mu^oter.
> ir liebe daz wol reizen   kunde. iedoch wart iz ein name gu^eter,
> swie er doch von in zweien wart gespalten:
> also kan diu liebe   und die minne manger wunder walten.
>
> (J.T. 2990)

[Now the child was named after its father and its mother. It was well able to evoke their affection. It was a good name, although it was cut out of their two names. Thus affection and love can work many marvels.]

Although the name chosen for the little girl is deemed good and appropriate, this strophe nonetheless presents the linguistic quarrying of each parent's name as an act of violence and invasion: the original names are cut or split open (*gespalten*), in a process that is comparable to the infliction of wounds by affection and love. This choice of imagery points forward to the death of Secureiz in battle and to the narrator's rhetorical question as to whether Arabadille's subsequent fatal decline should be attributed to *herzenliebe* or *herzenleide* (J.T. 4888–4889) [heartfelt love or heartache]. In this case, therefore, although the elements making up the new name are not shown to have meaning as such (i.e., no attempt is made to translate them into German), they are nonetheless intimately connected with the identities of the original bearers. The same might have held true for the elements *Titur* and *el* in the previous case, had it not been for the crucial shift away from syllables toward letters.[60] On the other hand, lest too much weight be attached to the genealogical meaningfulness of the constituent elements in either of these cases, it should be noted that other characters in the work share some of these same elements, without any genealogical connection. So, for example, that *dille*-segment that apparently links Secundille uniquely to her mother Arabadille is also shared by completely unrelated figures, namely Accedille (Artus' aunt) and Dillibande (a heathen knight). Furthermore, the narrator is quite happy to jettison this apparently significant segment in the interests of rhyme: at one point, he changes the form *Secundille* to *Secundare* (J.T. 3813,3) so that it will rhyme with *clare*.[61]

Given that letters figure so prominently in the case of Titurel, it might be argued that the textual status of the name is accorded more importance there than in the case of Secundille. Whereas a purely oral mode of reception would be conceivable for many parts of the work, including the episode about the naming of Secundille, this is not really possible for the episode about the naming of Titurel: in order to understand the nature and resolution of the conflict involved, an audience listening to it (rather than reading it) would be forced mentally to visualize the written forms of the three names involved.

This contrast between the two naming episodes is in some ways comparable to that between the two revelations of the name *Eneas* in Veldeke's *Eneasroman*, in which Dido pronounces the name syllable by syllable (1530–1534), whereas Lavine writes it down letter by letter (10624–10627). With respect to Veldeke's text, Wuth argues that this doubling is conceived by analogy with the paradigm according to which the written word matches but also surpasses the spoken word; whilst speech is broken down into syllables, the linearity of writing is characterized by individual letters.[62] However, as there is no structural opposition between Titurel and Secundille as individuals in the way that there is between Dido and Lavine, any attempt to see one naming episode as surpassing another would have to focus on the differences between Christian and heathen culture more broadly, and the heathen culture of Secundille is not presented as being any less competent at the manipulation of letters than is the Christian culture of Titurel. As has been shown in chapter 1, the heathens are not only fully reliant on pragmatic literacy (sending letters, writing down battle plans), but also adept at citing literature; it is only in fathoming Scripture (as opposed to script more generally) that they lag behind the Christians.[63] Furthermore, the pun on *lesen* [to choose / to read] in connection with Secundille's name also adds an element of textuality to this episode:

> durch dz si aller kinde lang entwesende
> waren durch sin liebe,   was man im einen erwelten namen lesende.
> (J.T. 2989,3–4)

> [Because they had been without a child for so long, out of affection one chose/read a special name for it.]

Rather than pursuing any opposition between Titurel and Secundille as representatives respectively of 'Schriftlichkeit' and 'Mündlichkeit,'[64] it is more useful to focus on the fact that both names are presented as being hermeneutically opaque (i.e., as untranslatable rearrangements of letters and syllables) and to consider the implications of this, not only for the narrator's reflections on the reliability of written forms, but also for the extent to which an individual's identity in the J.T. may be dissociated from his actual name. For example, the understanding of names as arbitrary and consequently disposable forms is communicated to the audience, not only by these two cases and by the examples of *aequivoca*, but also by the narrator's curious attitude toward name/identity of the two heroes, Gamuret and Tschinotulander.

In his treatment of Tschinotulander, the narrator not only avails himself extensively of the device of antonomasia (i.e., using sometimes elaborate epithets, rather than the actual name, to refer to the hero),[65] but also presents Tschinotulander in the guise of the dead Gamuret for a large portion of the narrative. What starts out as a genuine misunderstanding on the part of the heathens, who believe that Tschinotulander really is Gamuret risen from the dead, gradually turns into a "fact" that even the audience is apparently expected to accept: there really are two 'Gamurets,' one living and one dead.[66] Furthermore, this pattern of twinning the living and the dead is extended to include Tschinotulander and Parzifal. When Parzifal, bearing the heraldic emblem of the anchor, approaches Sigune's cell toward the end of the work, the sight of the anchor (which had formed part of the visual identities of both Gamuret and Tschinotulander), confuses her to such an extent that she believes that her beloved has come back to life. She actually has to look into the coffin in order to convince herself that this is not the case (J.T. 5849–5850).

Finally, as will be discussed further in chapters 4 and 5, this blurring of identities is discernible even on the narratorial level, with 'Albrecht' hiding behind the 'Wolfram'-identity for a large proportion of the work, in the same way as Tschinotulander hides behind the Gamuret identity. Just as the audience has to cope with the fact that there are two Gamurets, they have to cope with the fact that there are two narrators whose assertions can only be distinguished contextually (for example, the narratorial voice arguing with vrou Aventiure is specifically that of 'Wolfram'). However, such contextual markers are often absent, with the result that a large number of narratorial *ich*-statements are fundamentally ambiguous in their reference. Whilst this problem is to some extent a function of the specifically deictic nature of pronouns, it also points to a fluidity in the conception of the names or nouns represented by the pronoun *ich*: although 'Albrecht' and 'Wolfram' occupy different positions in the ascetic spectrum, their personal identities fade away as soon as the contrast between these positions is no longer functionalized.

Section II: Natural Phenomena

The scope of Albrecht's scientific knowledge has been the subject of individual studies by Leckie, Rausch, and Wegner.[67] Although 'Wolfram' claims to be *kunstlos, an meisterschefte . . . der schrifte* (J.T. 68,2) [unskilled and without mastery of the written word],[68] there is little reason to challenge Wegner's view that Albrecht qualifies as a *poeta doctus rerum naturae* [poet learned in natural science] who prides himself precisely on this "Buchgelehrsamkeit" [academic learning].[69] Such pride may be justified by reference to the accepted view outlined in section I above that a detailed knowledge of *realia*[objects in the natural world] constitutes an essential basis for obtaining the spiritual insights conducive to salvation.

At the most basic level, *realia* are presented as being of devotional interest because of the so-called "argument from creation": the existence of created objects allows one rationally to deduce the existence of the creator. This principle of using sensory perception as the basis for spiritual extrapolation is clearly formulated by Titurel in his dying speech:

Ich su°che den gehiuren   schaffer aller dinge,
aller creatu°ren,   und vind in an in allen sunderlinge:
ich vind in an dem su°zen vogel sange,
an aller blu°men varwe,   wurtze smak und an der seiten clange.
(J.T. 6302)[70]

[I seek the benevolent creator of all things, of all creatures, and I find him in every individual object: I find him in the sweet song of the birds, in the color of all the flowers, in the taste of herbs and in the sound of strings.]

Additionally, Albrecht focuses on the status of *realia* as units of second-language discourse that point not just to the fundamental truth of God's existence, but also to other entities, either concrete or abstract. Given this interest in the Christian *significatio* of natural objects and phenomena, Albrecht's treatment of these is therefore inevitably oriented toward the exposition of their powers and properties. The catalogue of the planets in J.T. 2801–2804 constitutes a particularly telling case in point, given its superficial similarity to the nonexegetical discussion of the planets by Kundrie in *Parzival* 782. In both cases, the astronomical information is imparted to the hero by a learned figure (or group) standing on the cusp of the heathen and the Christian worlds, and therefore able to combine the technical knowledge of the former with the religious perspective of the latter.[71] However, while the movement of the planets is central to the events of *Parzival*, this is not the case in the J.T.: although the discourse on the planets is addressed to Tschinotulander, the contents are no more relevant to his particular situation than they would be to that of any other Christian. Furthermore, whereas Kundrie achieves a sense of mystery by naming the planets only in Arabic, with the briefest of hints as to their impact on Parzival himself and no general explanations, the masters in the J.T. proceed in a much more systematically didactic fashion. As a first step, they give the familiar Latin names of the planets. Next, they gloss some of these names in secular terms:

> Merkurjus mittelere,   Jovis der helfeliche
> Venus der minnebære,   so ist Saturnus ganzer stæte riche.
> (J.T. 2803,1–2)

[Mercury is the mediator, Jove the helper, Venus the loving one, and Saturn entirely steadfast.]

Finally they set out the way in which each planet impacts the spiritual life of a Christian: the sun teaches faith, the moon induces humility,[72] Mars helps in the battle against sin, Jupiter teaches generosity, Venus teaches love, Mercury furthers peace and reconciliation, and Saturn assists in all good causes. Strictly speaking, this is an exposition of the actual powers of the planets, rather than of their *significatio* or reference function. However, it is characteristic of Albrecht's handling of *realia* that it is difficult to distinguish power from *significatio*. For example, if Jupiter teaches generosity, this is not just because the planet has the power to influence the disposition in a particular way (almost, as it were, against the wishes of the human subject), but also because the human subject is supposed to understand the connection between Jupiter and generosity and to "read" the planet as a reminder of God's endorsement of that particular virtue. *Realia* cannot make people virtuous without such intellectual cooperation on their part. This is borne out in the case of gemstones, which are only of real benefit when their *significatio* is understood and valued. As will be discussed in chapter 3, the "magical" impact of the stones in the Brackenseil is only short-lived because most of the listeners lack the ability and desire to understand the way in which the stones form a part of second language.[73] The narrator also notes that in the case of really entrenched human sinfulness, gemstones will lose their powers completely (J.T. 4896–4897).

A further example of how Albrecht's use of allegorical interpretation distinguishes his literary approach from that of Wolfram may be found in the allegorization of *meie* [May], which triggers an astronomical excursus in J.T. 1651–1663. *Parzival* and the J.T. both engage polemically with the traditional understanding of Artus being *meienbaere* (i.e., existing in a state of unblemished excellence characterized by permanent summery weather).[74] While Wolfram explicitly takes issue with this notion by inflicting a sudden snowfall on the Arthurian in court,[75] Albrecht uses the technique of allegorization in order to undermine the intrinsic value of the Arthurian *meie* and to underpin his programme of opposing secular courtliness with Christian spirituality. Having evoked the May-like quality of Artus, the narrator proceeds to set out the nature of seasonal change and to relate this to the movement of the planets, especially of the sun. After reminding the audience not to value the created object (the sun) more than its creator (God), he switches to the allegorical mode, presenting God as the true sun (J.T. 1656,1), which bring welcome relief from the winter of sin (J.T. 1656,3). The joys of the literal, earthly May are contrasted with those of the heavenly one, and the crowds of well-dressed ladies with the hosts of angels in heaven (J.T. 1659). Furthermore, in a programmatic endorsement of second language, it is pointed out that the approach that is here taken to the month of May could just as well be taken to any other thing:

> Swer alle dinc bedehte   alsus nach gotes eren,
> vil selicheit im brehte   ein ieclich dinc, wolt erz zu gu°te keren,
> dar nach iz got dem menschen hat geordent.
>
> (J.T. 1660,1–3)

[If anybody were to consider all things in this way so as to honor God, every single thing would bring him great blessedness, as long as he turned it to good use, just as God has arranged it for man.]

Finally the narrator argues that this technique should be applied to the text of the J.T. itself, or rather, to the joy that the audience might derive from experiencing the text and taking vicarious pleasure in its depictions of courtly celebrations.

> Swer hie nu vreude si lessened   oder ho°re an disem bu°che,
> der denk mit vreude genesende   ewiclich mit aller vreuden ru°che.
> di ist da baz mit wunsch gemangerleiet.
> vrowen unde ritterschaft   und meien tusentvalt sie uber meiet.
>
> (J.T. 1663)

[Whoever is now deriving enjoyment from reading or listening to this book, let him think joyfully about obtaining eternal salvation, with joys of every kind. These are multiplied as much as one may desire. They "out-may" ladies and chivalry and May-time a thousand times over.]

In other words, courtly pleasures are to be read as pointing toward, or "signifying" heavenly pleasures, and therefore as implicitly negating their own value.

In taking this final step, the narrator goes well beyond the ordinary parameters of the second language, within which objects in the natural world have a series of established properties, and these properties have meanings. To interpret the month of May is in itself a little unusual, but falls within these parameters once it is understood that it is really the sun that is being discussed. However, concepts such as courtly culture or courtly pleasure are not the kinds of *realia* that are normally associated with God-given *significationes*. The easy transition that the narrator makes from interpreting *ein ieclich dinc* (J.T. 1660,2) as a manifestation of second language, to interpreting whole aspects of his own narrative world as pointing toward the importance of salvation, illustrates how readily second-language explications given in a fictional context lose their apparent objectivity, dissolving into metaphor and literary conceit—or pointing toward the poetological hermeneutics of *integumentum*.

In the J.T., the model of the world as a two-tier system of signs (verbal/human versus nonverbal/divine) is complicated by the profusion of manmade objects which, like the God-given *realia*, are also are nonverbal bearers of meaning and open to verbal interpretation. The ceiling of the Grail temple, featuring an *orolei* [horologium] with moving replicas (*exempel*) of the sun, the moon, and the heavens (J.T. 375–376),[76] constitutes one particularly striking example. This composite object made up of *karfunkel* [carbuncles or garnets] set in *saphire* [sapphire] has a triple function. First, it is decorative.[77] Secondly, it serves as a scientific instrument with the practical purpose of marking the seven liturgical hours (J.T. 376,4). Thirdly, it provides a springboard for an allegorical interpretation of the heavens (articulated by Titurel):

> Im tempel daz gestirne   lert iuch gen himel kriegen,
> so daz diu sele ein dirne   si bi got, da si kein uppik triegen
> an hohen selden nimmer mer entsitzet.
> der sus di stern ist sehende,   der wirt an richer kunst vil wol gewitzt.
> (J.T. 574)

[In the temple the stars will teach you to strive toward heaven so that the soul will be a hand-maiden close to God, with no presumptuous trickery ever unseating it from [its place] in high bliss. Whoever beholds the stars like this will be imbued with rich knowledge.]

Although the *orolei* is manmade, its constituent gemstones are part of God's natural creation and therefore obvious elements of second-language discourse. However, their independent meanings are here subordinated to the manmade context, within which they substitute for the heavenly bodies that constitute a separate element of second-language discourse.[78] When Titurel refers to there being stars in the temple (J.T. 574,1), there is a deliberate blurring of the distinction between the manmade *signa* (the stones in their horologium context) and that which they signify (the stars).

A corresponding ambiguity between *signa* and *realia* characterizes the discussion of heraldic beasts. There is not only the predictable conflation of the natures of the beasts and the natures of those who bear them,[79] but, as with the stars in the temple, there is also a blurring of the distinction between, on the one hand, heraldic representations of beasts made out of gemstones and other precious raw materials, and on the other hand, actual living beasts that have been embedded into a heraldic tableau, on par with gemstones.[80] Sometimes the heraldic beasts fall unambiguously into one of these two categories. For example, it is made clear that Tschinotulander's shield contains a living salamander whose "proper" fiery heat enhances the powers of the surrounding gemstones.[81] Conversely, there is also no doubt that the hound adorning Ekunat's helmet is a representation of Gardivias, rather than the real animal.[82] Other heraldic beasts are more puzzling: although they are not explicitly said to be real, they appear to take active part in battle.[83] Sometimes this impression is simply a result of metonymic constructions:

> gen dem anker wiz in grase gru^ene
> sol des tracken ro^ete   streben, des pflac Daries, der ku^ene.
> (J.T. 3884,3–4)

[The red of the dragon (wielded by the brave Daries) will fight against the white anchor set in green grass.]

However, Ledobodantz von Gredimonte is not only covered in ornamental basilisk (J.T. 3985,1), but also seems to carry the "real" beast, with all that that entails in the way of danger to onlookers,[84] and the dragon adorning Orilus' helmet constitutes a further case in point. The association of Orilus with the dragon derives from *Parzival*, in which the beast is clearly a representation on a shield, albeit a very vivid one:

> ûf des schilde vander
> einen trachen als er lebte (262,4–5)

> [on the shield he saw a dragon that seemed to be alive]

In the J.T., however, Orilus' dragon-helmet apparently gives off fire to such an extent that it ignites the hound on the helmet of his opponent Ekunat:

> Der bracke mu°st ouch brinnen,   der was von harm velle.
> von swamben was er innen,   da von daz fiur vienc er hie so snelle.
> der tracke was von rechte fiur gebende.
> owe, daz nu der bracke   was vor im also kranklichen lebende!
> (J.T. 5889)

> [The hound also had to burn. It was made of ermine with sponge inside. That is why it caught fire so quickly. The dragon gave off fire in accordance with its nature. Alas, that the hound had to die before it!]

The ambiguity in the presentation of Orilus' dragon suggests that the audience is being discouraged from expecting a simple answer as to the reality or otherwise of this dragon, and indeed from distinguishing too closely between the categories of image and original. Instead, it would seem that Albrecht is implicitly using the *signum*-status of natural objects in order to argue for a certain equivalence between original and image. After all, if the *significatio* of creatures is related to their powers and properties, and if an image of a creature signifies the same as the beast itself, then the powers and properties of the original beast must be deemed to inhere in the image. This in turn may be understood as an implicit argument for equivalence between the creative output of God and man: while there is no doubt that human constructions are fundamentally derivative, they can still function as meaningfully, and in every sense as powerfully, as the originals on which they are based. Such an argument constitutes a celebration, not only of the human craftsmanship that goes into the construction of the kind of decorative armor under discussion, but also of the craftsmanship involved in constructing a text featuring extensive representation of objects from the real world.

While salamanders, basilisks, and dragons are clearly exotic creatures, they are not, in the medieval context, regarded as unreal or not forming part of God's creation, and there is thus no difficulty with regarding them as an interpretable unit of second-language discourse. The situation is rather different in the case of a creature that is distinctively unique to one particular text, as the *bestia de funde* is to the J.T. Amongst the various properties of this unique sea creature, particular attention is paid to its habit of emitting a foam which after three days turns into amber. The foam is important for the narrative in that it serves to cure Tschinotulander of the wounds that he has incurred in his battle with the Gaylotten; but it also has a spiritual *significatio* (set out in J.T. 2791–2792) which link it to repentance and salvation. As Rausch's detailed study of the *bestia de funde* demonstrates,[85] this creature, the function of which is not only to heal Tschinotulander's wounds, but also to provide him with a compelling image of the temptations and dangers of the world, constitutes a *res composita*, a selective fusion of the bundles of properties associated with the whale and the chimera, and, to a lesser extent, with the dragon and the leviathan. On one level, such a composite creature may be well-suited for this particular didactic purpose, but there are obvious difficulties with an attempt to read nonexistent objects as units of second-language discourse, even if the *significatio* suggested is a good and worthy one. Although God may be speaking through the whale and the chimera (the existence of which is assured by Latin authorities), he does not speak through novel combinations of properties, which are fictitious as well as fictional. Here, Albrecht's deconstruction of "established" creatures matches his deconstruction of established names (Titurel and Secundille) in section I above, with properties, like letters, being liable to capricious rearrangement. In both cases, this deconstruction serves to remind the audience that they are dealing with a fictional universe that bears the hallmarks of more than one creator: notwithstanding Albrecht's enthusiastic promotion of Christian teaching and his predilection for allegorical interpretation as a didactic tool, his narrative strategy ultimately challenges God's monopoly on language. By presenting manmade *signa* (be it on the level of physical objects crafted by the protagonists, or on the level of literary constructions such as the *bestia de funde*) as capable of yielding messages that are just as true as those attaching to purely natural objects, Albrecht severs that exclusive connection presumed by supporters of second language to exist between divinely created sign and Christian *significatio*. At the same time, Albrecht's attitude to his own creative medium is complex. As has been shown in section I above, he repeatedly chooses to highlight the various respects in which first language—particularly in its written form—may be regarded as a web of arbitrary and impenetrable signs that are dissociated from reality. However, this does not constitute a disadvantage. On the contrary, his nominalist approach to language gives him the freedom necessary to subordinate the narrative material to his didactic purposes. It is precisely because the audience has a strong sense of the protagonists as being made "of words" rather than of "flesh and blood," and of them being rooted on the page rather than in reality, that it seems entirely appropriate for the story line to become fragmented through its continuous use as a springboard for moralization and allegorical interpretation: the literary creator is merely asserting his right to take apart that world which he had assembled in the first place.

CHAPTER 3

THE BRACKENSEIL AND THE GRAIL:
CHASING THE TEXTS

Despite their many differences, the two most important inscripted objects in the J.T.—the Brackenseil and the Grail—share the quality of elusiveness. Both are highly desirable, and yet also surprisingly mobile and resistant to human ownership. While the enduring image of the Brackenseil is perhaps that of an uncontrolled hound crashing through the undergrowth on the run from its various owners and dragging the text with it, the Grail is also presented as strikingly, and almost wilfully, evasive. During a large portion of the years that it spends in the care of Titurel's family, it does not allow anybody to hold it, and only eventually consents to rest on the cushion held by Titurel's granddaughter Tschoysiane (J.T. 605). Furthermore, by the end of the J.T., both textual objects are effectively lost to the Western world: the Brackenseil is shattered after the final confrontation between Ekunat and Orilus, while the Grail, although intact, has disappeared into the remote ideality of India, the kingdom of Prester John. However, despite this shared elusiveness, the factors that prevented the protagonists from grasping these objects (either physically or intellectually) differ in each case. Whereas the Grail itself is faultless, the responsibility for its departure from the secular world lying firmly with the sinful *mores* of the protagonists, the reasons for the communicative failure of the Brackenseil are more complex. While the inadequacy of the potential recipients certainly plays a part, the Brackenseil itself is also conceptually flawed: not only is it tainted with the ethically suspect eroticism of a courtly love relationship, but the mismatch between textual message and material form is so fundamental as to render the former effectively unreadable as far as most recipients are concerned.

On a literal level, the motif of the quest for the Grail is largely peripheral to the J.T.: while Albrecht's work serves to bridge the information gap between Wolfram's *Parzival* and Wolfram's *Titurel*, his aim is clearly not to narrate the tribulations of Parzifal *in extenso*. Nonetheless, it is partly against an audience awareness of this major Grail quest that Albrecht's very detailed account of the Brackenseil quest is to be understood. Some critics, such as Haug, go as far as to see the Brackenseil as a kind of secular precursor to the Grail, that is as something which promotes broadly the same values, whilst also being slightly more accessible to the courtly world.[1] As Haug sees it, Parzifal's attainment of the Grail marks the the start of a new phase, in which the Brackenseil has become redundant. Accordingly, its destruction in the joust is not to be seen as unduly problematic.[2]

This chapter, however, takes a different approach to that of Haug. Rather than seeing the Brackenseil and the Grail as forming an almost seamless continuum, it will focus on the ethical disjuncture between the two, whilst still acknowledging the virtues of the Brackenseil inscription itself. This approach highlights the irony in the fact that most of the protagonists of the J.T. pursue the lesser of the two textual objects with such vehemence, yet show little awareness of, or interest in, the Grail.[3] This irony is exacerbated by the fact that the knights (Tschinotulander, Ekunat, Orilus, and Teanglis) who are at the forefront of the quest for the Brackenseil and the related conflict over its ownership also show very little appreciation for the moral contents inscribed on the object that they are chasing. While the men focus firmly on the materiality of the object, or even on the hound to which it is attached, it is the women—notably Clauditte (the author) and Sigune (the principal reader)—who, although by no means entirely exemplary, at least perceive the Brackenseil as a text rather than as a trophy. To some extent, this striking association of female gender with the production and the appreciation of literature is already present in Wolfram, whose second *Titurel* fragment features both Clauditte's authorship and Sigune's intensive reading of the inscription.[4] However, as the discussion in section I below will show, Albrecht strengthens this gender alignment by letting the subsequent narrative dwell extensively on the inadequacy of male receptiveness to the message of the Brackenseil. Furthermore, section II will argue that this backdrop of intradiegetic inadequacy forms part of the didactic challenge that Albrecht sets his audience. Whereas in textual terms, the lesser of the two objects is effectively handed to the readers on a plate, Albrecht's recourse to the allegorical level of interpretation allows him to encourage the members of his audience to embark on an ethical—and literary—quest for the personal attainment of the "Grail."

Section I: The Brackenseil

Given the complexity of the conflict over the Brackenseil, a brief summary of the developments may be useful at this point. The narrative divides into three principal sections, focusing on Tschinotulander's deeds respectively in the West, in the Orient, and back in the West. While the Brackenseil features most dominantly in the first section, it provides an element of structural unity linking all three sections.

1. The Brackenseil, consisting of the inscripted leash attached to the dog Gardivias, is sent by Queen Clauditte to Ekunat, the man whom she wishes to marry. Gardivias escapes from Ekunat, is caught by Tschinotulander, but escapes again as Sigune unties the leash in order to read the full text. Sigune insists that the leash must be recovered before she will grant Tschinotulander her love; however, before he sets off in pursuit of the hound, she agrees to let him have a glimpse of her naked body. Gardivias is caught up in a thorn bush and is found by Teanglis,

who surrenders the dog to Orilus upon being defeated by the latter. Having set off on his quest, Tschinotulander happens to arrive at the Arthurian court, where he accidentally kills Arbidol, the nephew of Orilus and Lehelin, and thereby incurs the enmity of these two knights. Tschinotulander and Orilus fight (without knowing each other's identity or connection with the leash), but the battle is interrupted by Ekunat, who recognizes Tschinotulander. Tschinotulander tells Ekunat of the condition imposed by Sigune and then leaves the court suddenly, in pursuit of a dog that resembles Gardivias. Orilus and Jescute also leave angrily, after an exchange with Ekunat about the ownership of Gardivias. Ekunat initiates public discussion of Tschinotulander's plight; the common view is that the Brackenseil belongs to Orilus because he has won it in battle and that anybody else who wants it must win it from him. Orilus is invited back to court, Ekunat challenges him, and a date is set for eighteen weeks later. Although Artus wishes to take charge of the Brackenseil for this intermediate period, Jescute refuses to relinquish it. Ekunat tells the court about Sigune's interest in the writing on the leash and Jescute agrees to the first public reading of the text. This reading has a quasi-miraculous effect on the court, elevating spirits and inducing a (short-lived) phase of universal harmony, when even Orilus forgets his grudge against Tschinotulander. Tschinotulander returns to the court and is later joined by Sigune. At this point, the *baruc* Ackerin contacts Tschinotulander to request military assistance in the Orient. Ackerin also sends him the magnificent but problematic gifts made out of the *golt der selden*, including the shield with a living salamander enclosed (cf. chapter 1, section I). Artus organizes a great feast and tournament, in which Tschinotulander excels and as a result of which he obtains pledges from all his defeated opponents, including Orilus, that they should join him in his expedition to assist Ackerin. Sigune is invited to enter the select ranks of the Ehrenjungfrauen [maids of honor], but declines on various grounds, including the fact that she has not yet read the Brackenseil. She is then permitted (presumably by Jescute) to read it three times in private. She also listens to a second public reading. As a result, her relentless desire is satiated and Tschinotulander's quest should theoretically lapse. Furthermore, a definitive solution appears to be achievable, given that Orilus and Lehelin are reluctant to honor their pledge to join Tschinotulander on his military expedition, and offer to hand over the leash to Sigune in return for being released from their obligation. Clauditte, however, opposes this development, since it would remove Ekunat's chance of winning it from Orilus in combat. At the point of Tschinotulander's departure for the East, Sigune suggests that they marry, since she requires no further service from him, but Tschinotulander refuses, declaring himself still unworthy. However, he requests a further viewing of her naked body. She agrees to this request, in the hope that this inspirational experience will imbue him with strength and fighting prowess.

2. Tschinotulander's military triumphs in the East are largely unaffected by the Brackenseil quest, which is only briefly foregrounded when Ackerin offers Lehelin a large amount of gold if Lehelin will persuade Orilus to become reconciled to Tschinotulander and to pass on the leash to Sigune. However, nothing comes of this proposal.[5] On the way back from the East, Tschinotulander loses the magical *golt der selden*. This is of crucial importance to his future conflict with Orilus,

because this gold protects its wearer, but brings misfortune upon anybody who loses it. When Ackerin sends replacement gold to try to alleviate this misfortune, the disaster is in fact exacerbated, because the replacement gold is mistakenly delivered to Orilus.

3. Upon Tschinotulander's return to the West, Artus attempts to resolve the Brackenseil issue by offering the magical tented city of Tasme to be shared between Clauditte and Jescute, in return for their surrendering the leash to Sigune.[6] This offer is turned down by the two women as well as by Tschinotulander, who wishes to gain the leash in battle. Tschinotulander starts to focus on the task of regaining Parzifal's lands, unjustly occupied by Orilus. He fights Orilus for the third time and is on the point of winning when the battle is interrupted by Jescute who fears for her husband's life and therefore offers to give the leash to Sigune. Tschinotulander refuses to accept it, reaffirming the position that he can only gain it in battle. A further duel is scheduled, but in the meantime Jescute secretly sends the leash to Sigune. Shortly before the final duel, Sigune reads the text to Tschinotulander, but it appears to have lost its capacity to cause its listeners to experience joy. Ekunat requests the return of the leash to himself and Clauditte, and Sigune agrees; she and Tschinotulander set out for Munt Salvasch. They encounter Orilus, who is now in possession of the *golt der selden* and in the ensuing battle, Tschinotulander inevitably dies. Finally, Ekunat avenges Tschinotulander in a battle in which Orilus is killed, and the Brackenseil itself destroyed.

When the Brackenseil is first introduced into the narrative, the attention of the audience is immediately directed to its material form, with no mention of the fact that this is a written text rather than just a decorative object. The exotic styling of the leash is emphasized:

> Do er den bracken horte,   do spranc er gen der verte.
> arabisch ein borte   sin halse was, geslagen mit drihen herte.
> dar uf kos man tiur und lieht gesteine.
> di glesten sam di sunne.
>
> (J.T. 1181,1–4)

[When he heard the hound, he leapt in its direction. Its collar was of Arabian braid,[7] very tightly pounded by the needle. On it one could see precious and bright stones. They shone like the sun.][8]

The attention of the audience is also directed toward its colors and its intriguing texture, which combines metallic hardness with textile pliancy:

> zwelf klafter was mit lenge   daz seil, des varwe vier von siden waren:
> gel, brun, gru^ene, rot so was diu vierde,
> immer swa diu spanne erwant,   geworht in ein ander mit gezierde.
>
> Da obe lagen ringe   mit berlin verblenket.
> da zwischen richer dinge   ie spanne lanc, mit steinen nicht verkrenket,
> vier blat, vier varwe vingers breit di maze.
>
> (J.T. 1185,2–1186,3)

[The leash was twelve fathoms long, consisting of braid-silk in four colors—yellow, purple, green, with red as the fourth—elegantly interwoven at the joins. Over these were laid rings of metal, whitened with pearls. There, between these rich things, were four ribbons in four colors, each one span in length, and as wide as a finger, without any jewels.]

The designation of the collar as *arabisch* serves to associate the Brackenseil with other treasures of oriental provenance, such as Tschinotulander's salamander shield.[9] It has also been suggested that the leash is eroticized through its resemblance to a woman's girdle and therefore has a strong association with Clauditte's body.[10]

Even when the existence of the *schrift* is first mentioned in J.T. 1187,2, the emphasis is primarily on the beauty and costliness of the jewels out of which the script is constructed (J.T. 1187–1189) with no clues given as to the contents relayed. The reader of the J.T. is thus initially placed in a position similar to that of the illiterate Teanglis, who is able to see the stones and to speculate about the kind of *aventiure* that is linked to it, but who has no access to the text. The strategy of teasing the audience so as to arouse their curiosity is already present in *Titurel*;[11] however, whereas in *Titurel*, neither Sigune nor the audience ever have their curiosity assuaged, the J.T. does, in the fullness of time, reveal the contents of the inscription. Albrecht's strategy of temporarily withholding information from the audience thus has more in common with that deployed in Wolfram's *Parzival*, where the audience learns with the hero as he emerges from *tumpheit*. However, in the J.T., the audience lags behind the protagonists: Albrecht's narrator only chooses to cite the text in full at the point of the second public reading at the Arthurian court. In the meantime, the narrative accounts of Sigune's passionate response to her interrupted reading, and of the Arthurian court's enraptured reaction to the first public declamation of the text, both serve to tantalize the audience by revealing the dramatic powers of this addictive and quasi-magical object.

The Brackenseil inscription is ostensibly a love-letter written by Clauditte to Ekunat von Berbester (also known as Ekunat de Silvat), the man whom she has just selected to be her husband and to share her crown. The opening of the letter communicates the essence of her decision in a self-consciously poetological manner. Drawing on the established translation of Ekunat's name as *den wilden von den blu°men* [the wild one of the flowers] (J.T. 1199,2),[12] Clauditte functionalizes both components (*wild* and *blu°me*). The image of the flowers serves not only to stress the moral excellence of Ekunat,[13] but also to draw attention to her own 'geblümten Stil' [florid style]:[14]

> Ich tu°n dir kunt geblu°met   uber alle man ein blu°me
> (J.T. 1876,1).

[Speaking in the geblümten Stil of the *blümer*, I pronounce you to be a flower above all men]

The semantic field of *wild* is wider still.[15] Its immediate association is with the domain of geographical wilderness and specifically with the hunt (be it literal and erotic) which takes place in the wilderness, outside the confined and public spaces of the court.[16] The focus of the hunt is a "wild" (i.e., undomesticated) prey, whose qualities again stand is opposition to the familiar ones associated with the courtly world. By extension, the term *wild* also comes to mean untamed, uncivilized, strange, or simply unusual or novel. Thus the "wild flower" Ekunat is, on the literal level, a hunter dwelling in the wilderness,[17] whereas on the metaphorical level, he is the prey to be tracked down by Gardivias. Once this hunting down has been accomplished, Ekunat becomes the recipient of a message that is *wild* [novel] in form as well as in content. Schmid goes as far as to speak of "eine wilde Wortorgie" [a wild orgy of words]:[18]

> Du eren pflicht geselle,　du wilde blu°me riche,
> in wildez walt gevelle,　send ich dir wilden boten
> und wilden prief mit wilder boteschefte.
> der bot genant Gardivias.　der nam hat richeit vil und tugend krefte.
>
> (J.T. 1882)[19]

[You dutiful companion of honor, you splendid wild flower, into the wild woods I send you this wild messenger and a "wild" [=novel] letter with a "wild"[=novel] message. The messenger is called Gardivias. The name has much splendor and virtuous power.]

Clauditte carefully avoids the somewhat obvious association of wildness with sin or with anarchic, unrestrained behavior. On the contrary, it is suggested that a virtuous man such as Ekunat will be a stranger to wrongdoing (i.e., he will be *wild* in relation to it).[20] By its very nature, however, the leash implies that wildness must, at least on some levels, be subjected to beneficial restraint and to "taming."[21] The fact that Ekunat fails to use the leash to retain ownership of Gardivias suggests that the wildness of both messenger and recipient is not entirely positive. Furthermore, even the much-vaunted wildness of the inscription is not unproblematic, given that the addictive beauty of its medium triggers reckless behavior running entirely counter to its message of controlled moderation. However, these areas of concern are not acknowledged by Clauditte, who seeks, through a rhetorical sleight-of-hand, to eliminate the dangers of all that is wild, exciting, or in any way extreme: the optimistic tenet of her teaching is that these qualities can coexist with, or even flourish under, a regime of ethical restraint. This attitude toward danger and wildness also colors Clauditte's formulation of her aesthetic programme. Staking a bold claim for the formal excellence of her missive, Clauditte explains that she thought it possible to combine divinely sanctioned wisdom with carefully selected elements of pagan seductive beauty:[22]

> so wolt ich hie versigeln in dirre gimme
> salomones witze,　da zu° ein teil, nicht gar, Sirenen stimme.
>
> (J.T. 1875,3–4)

[And so I wanted to seal into these jewels the wisdom of Solomon and a part, although not all, of the voice of the sirens.]

As the narrative goes on to demonstrate, this strategy of using seduction in a good cause is bound to fail: although she wishes only to entice her reader(s) toward virtue, Clauditte does not consider the possibility that in the case of the sirens, beauty and destructiveness are inextricably linked so that it is impossible to borrow the former without risking the latter.[23] Similarly, even the invocation of Solomon's wisdom is not unproblematic, given this figure's susceptibility to carnal pleasures.[24] Ultimately, a love of virtue is not to be inculcated through sensual bedazzlement, but must be founded on clarity of thought and argument.

The real scope of Clauditte's text gradually becomes apparent: it is not so much a love-letter, or even a love-story,[25] as an ethical treatise. Despite the enthusiasm with which she subjects the glossing of Ekunat's name to protracted variation, the personal dimension to the letter is largely confined to the exordium, and when the whole text is viewed with hindsight, the celebration of Ekunat's virtues serves merely to set the tone for its didactic substance, which is inherently aimed at a wider audience. This broader scope has already been suggested by the statement that Clauditte offers *gruᵒz and ler gen aller menschen heile* (J.T. 1873,1) [greetings, and instruction concerning the salvation of all people].[26] Her strophic treatise is structured as follows:

1. Ten strophes on religious obligations (J.T. 1884–1893).
2. Seven strophes on morality and on the senses, including the presentation of the ideal man through a series of animal analogies (J.T. 1894–1900).[27]
3. Ten strophes on *minne* (J.T. 1901–1910).
4. Seventeen strophes on the virtues, presented as a garland of twelve flowers, of which the last one is *minne* (J.T. 1911–1927).

The overall Brackenseil missive is a bipartite object consisting not only of the inanimate inscripted leash, but also of Gardivias, the living and highly active dog to which the leash is attached. The fact that the entire inscription on the Brackenseil may be understood as an elaborate interpretation of the name *Gardivias* (glossed as *huᵉte wol der verte*), underscores the fact that the association of these two disparate entities is by no means accidental or contingent and that the textual significance of the inscription cannot be fully appreciated without reference to the dog.[28]

> Di herzoginne lobesam   las anevanc der mære
> "swie ditz si eins bracken nam,   daz wort ist den werden noch gebere.
> man und wip, die huᵉtent verte schone,
> di fuᵉrent hie der werlde gunst   und wirt in dort diu selde zu lone."
> (J.T. 1191)[29]

[The praiseworthy Duchess read the start of the message: "Although this is a dog's name, the term is still relevant for noble people. Men and women who stay on the proper track enjoy the favor of the world in this life and are rewarded with blessedness in the next life."]

Through the conjunction of dog and inscription, Clauditte claims to be offering both her lover and the world at large a sagacious solution to the long-standing courtly problem of how to obtain the favor of both God and the world.[30] This (somewhat overconfident) claim is all the more striking for the facts that the author is female and is writing in an essentially secular, not to say erotic, context.

However, Albrecht does not seem interested in the psychological and social ramifications of Clauditte's authorship, and so the exceptional authority that she manifests in her writing sits rather uneasily with the conventional and colorless role that she fulfils as 'Minnedame' of Ekunat.

Although the text on the leash is in itself a noteworthy case of female textual activity, the full complexity of Clauditte communicative undertaking only becomes apparent once another material aspect of the Brackenseil—namely the jewels—is taken into account. Just as the overall Brackenseil missive is a bipartite object (dog and inscripted leash), so the leash inscription too may be regarded as bipartite, with two parallel discourses: that of the words, and that of the jewels that make up the words. In formulating her didactic treatise, Clauditte is indeed an author, producing a normal, first-language text; but in selecting the jewels and placing them in an appropriate arrangement, she works more like a compiler, excerpting choice second-language truths from the great library of creation.[31] That the jewels are fundamental to her communicative undertaking, and should not be dismissed as contingently decorative, is made clear by her assertion in J.T. 1875,3–4 (quoted above), where she speaks of sealing the wisdom of Solomon and the voices of the sirens into the jewels themselves. It is therefore to be assumed that Clauditte has taken overall responsibility for the material form of the missive, even if she has not crafted the leash herself.[32]

In communicative terms, the Brackenseil inscription is a disaster: not only are the lessons that it sets out are not assimilated, but, as an object, it triggers widespread conflict and destruction. Whilst the inevitability of this failure can be analyzed from various angles, it seems fair to say that the first-language treatise is not, in itself, particularly at fault. It constitutes largely unexceptionable good advice (even if a strict ascetic might take issue with Clauditte's naive attempt to please both God and the world by presenting *caritas* and courtly love as a single ethical continuum). Furthermore, as this advice is formulated clearly and cogently, there is nothing to prevent an ethically receptive reader of the J.T. from responding positively to the didacticism of strophes J.T. 1884–1927. The fact that so few intradiegetic readers do so is down to two basic factors: first, the material complexity of the Brackenseil, and secondly, the moral and intellectual inadequacy of virtually all its potential readers.

While extradiegetic readers of the J.T. can contemplate words on a page at their leisure, potential intradiegetic readers of the Brackenseil have to contend both with the pairing of the leash and the dog, and with the tensions between the words and the jewels (i.e., between first-language and second-language discourse). These two features may be central to the overall construction of Clauditte's missive, but between them they effectively render the text itself unreadable.

Gardivias is mainly a practical obstacle to comprehension, both in the obvious sense that it runs away with the leash that Sigune is trying to read, and in the more indirect sense that it constitutes a nonhuman, and therefore inadequate, messenger. As Wenzel notes, even in the cases of literate recipients, written missives were liable to cause misunderstandings, and therefore the messenger retained an important function "als vermittelnder Botschafter und Nachrichtenträger" [mediating ambassador and bearer of news].[33] Clauditte's choice of Gardivias not only deprives the rather unperceptive Ekunat of the kind of interpretative guidance that he might have found useful, but also sends out a very mixed message: the dog's nonmoral and irrational nature being entirely at odds with the ethical stringency promoted in the treatise. It is almost as confusing as if Clauditte had sent her beloved a rabbit bearing the motto "Be Chaste."[34] Indeed, whereas in this hypothetical case, a respectable moral reading might still be obtained provided that the rabbit is taken as an illustration of how not to behave, the paradigm of the negative *exemplum* could not be invoked in the case of Gardivias, since the textual glossing of his name explicitly discourages any contrastive reading of beast and leash.

Nonetheless, the two conjoined items clearly do not form a cohesive whole. Their fundamental incongruity is highlighted even in *Titurel*, when Wolfram's narrator playfully asks the audience to guess which of the two he would prefer, if he had to choose:

> Smaragede wâren die buochstabe,   mit rubînen verbundet.
> adamante, krisolîte,   grânât dâ stuonden. nie seil baz gehundet
> wart, ouch was der hunt vil wol geseilet.
> ir muget wol errâten, welhez ih   dâ næme, op wære der hunt dergegene teilet.
>
> (*Titurel* 147)

> [The letters were emerald, bound together with rubies. There were diamonds, chrysolites, garnets. No leash was ever matched more appropriately to a dog, while the dog was also leashed most worthily. You might well guess which of them I would take, if the dog were parted from the leash.]

Notwithstanding the narrator's own previous assertion in *Titurel* 145 that he would prefer the leash to the dog,[35] Liebertz-Grün argues that the "right" answer to the riddle posed in *Titurel* 147 must be the living dog, on the grounds that the dog embodies that active hunt for literary meaning that the readers of an open-ended work such as the *Titurel* are expected to undertake, while the luxurious leash represents the less intellectually challenging model of a text that is closed and complete.[36] This reading is consistent with the modern approach to *Titurel* as "eher ein Geschichtsbaukasten als ein Geschichte." [not so much a narrative as a set of building blocks for constructing a narrative.][37] By contrast, although Albrecht incorporates this same question into the J.T., it would be inconceivable to transfer Liebertz-Grün's answer to this new context, given that Albrecht's stated objectives in composing the J.T. are precisely narrative closure and completeness. The fact that Albrecht expands the basic contents of *Titurel* 147 into two strophes, the second of which focuses exclusively on the splendors of the leash, make the priorities of the J.T. quite clear:[38]

> Smarac warn di bu°chstaben,   mit rubin verpundet,
> mit gewier uf golt erhaben.   iz enwart nie seile baz gehundet.
> nu was ouch der hunt vil wol geseilet.
> wederz ich da neme,   daz riet ein kint obiz mir wer teilet.
>
> Dyomande, crisolde,   torkoiten und sardine,
> jochant, granat uf golde   verwieret, und ander manic in liehten schine,
> der lac vil dar uf mit kraft von grozen.
> von edelkeit der steine   kund dem seil an richeit nicht genozen.
>
> (J.T. 1188–1189)

[The letters were emerald, bound together with rubies, set in gold with the purest fastenings. No leash was ever matched more appropriately to a dog. Now the dog too was leashed most worthily. A child could guess which of them I would take if it were made available to me.

Diamonds, chrysolites, turquoises and sards, jacinths, garnets set in gold, and many others, shining brightly: these were all present on it, wielding great power. Given the nobility of the stones, the leash could not be equalled in magnificence.]

For Albrecht, the matter of the choice between dog and leash is so clear-cut as to be trivial: it is not, as in Liebertz-Grün's reading of Wolfram's strophe, a genuine challenge put to the audience, but is instead presented as a question which any child might answer correctly. While the Brackenseil inscription in the J.T. does not in any way amount to a prototype of textual perfection, it derives its essential value from the fact that it clearly and firmly articulates certain points of ethical doctrine. These points are not inherently elusive and their assimilation need not necessarily involve the audience in any kind of chase or quest.

The fact that a chase nonetheless becomes necessary is entirely a function of the coupling of the fixed text and the anarchic dog. Despite this dog's nobility, and despite the fact that it has been given a name that links it to the contents of the Brackenseil text, Albrecht's Gardivias is not a positive symbol of the hunt for literary meaning and coherence. Instead, its unchecked rushing stands in diametrical opposition to the message of the inscription, which, as Haug as pointed out, may be summarized "die Beherrschung der Sinne und Körperteile" [controlling the senses and the body].[39] It is noteworthy that in his adaptation of *Titurel* 158—

Sît er von der wilde   hiez, gegen der wilde
si sante im disen wiltlîchen   brief, den bracken, der walt unt gevilde
phlac der verte, als er von arte solte.
ouch iach des seiles schrift, daz si   selbe wîplîcher verte hüeten wolte.

[Since he was named after the wilderness, she sent to him in the wilderness this "wild" missive: the hound which stayed on the proper track through woods and fields, in accordance with its nature. The writing on the leash also said that she herself would remain on the track proper to a woman.]—

Albrecht alters the third line, so that it is now Ekunat, not Gardivias, who is said to pay proper attention to his own *verte*:

Sit er von bluᵒmen wilde   der werde was genennet,
durch daz si niht bevilde.   si tet im wilde wort und werk erkennet.
do huᵒt er siner verte, als er solde.
Clauditte was ouch jehende,   daz si wiplicher verte huᵉten wolde.
(J.T. 1200)

[Since he was called the wild and noble one of the flower, she was content to make this gift. She revealed to him "wild" words and deeds. He then stayed on the track, as he ought to. Clauditte also said that she intended to stay on the track proper to a woman.]

Albrecht's removal of this positive endorsement of Gardivias' behavior indicates a fundamental shift in attitude toward the significance of the animal. Whereas Wolfram takes the line that when Gardivias rushes off on the scent of prey, it is doing precisely what a hunting dog ought to be doing,[40] Albrecht focuses on the way in which it evades the control of its owner. His addition of the detail that the leash is soon caught up in a thorn bush (J.T. 1292–1293), where Tschinotulander might easily have found it, had he only carried on slightly further (J.T 1292,4), serves to enhance the impression of Gardivias as careless and inattentive to its own *verte*.[41] Within Albrecht's scheme, the elegant hunting-dog's "hijacking" of the text therefore symbolizes the way in which thoughtlessness, secularity, and self-indulgence are detrimental to the dissemination of ethical doctrine and ultimately to virtuous living.

When the Brackenseil is finally retrieved from the errant dog, it becomes clear that the jewels in fact impede comprehension in a much more fundamental way than did Gardivias. As noted in the previous chapter, jewels in the J.T. function on two distinct levels: they are not only bearers of meaning (second-language discourse), but also incorporate certain quasi-magical powers (the power of a particular stone being loosely related to its meaning). Finckh argues against seeing any hermeneutic opposition between the words and the stones: the divinely ordained meaning of the stones coheres with that of the text and strengthens its impact rather than competing with it.[42] The fact that the Brackenseil inscription transmits parallel layers of discourse is therefore not unduly problematic in itself, although the complexity of such a communicative framework clearly places a heavy interpretative burden on the recipients. However, while a perfect reading would require full engagement with the jewels as well as with the words, a recipient who fails to read the jewels correctly might still understand and assimilate the words perfectly well. The real difficulty arises when the powers of the jewels come into play, affecting recipients in an immediate, nonintellectual way that is somewhat at odds with the normal approach to reading as a process of acknowledging the established relationship between *signum* and *res*.

Strohschneider has drawn attention to the topos of the "exceptional" text that does not function (or does not function primarily) in accordance with this normal concept of reading, and might therefore be termed "unlesbar" [unreadable].[43] With such a text, the written word, rather than merely referring to absent *res*, actually functions "als Instrument der Herstellung von unmittelbarer Präsenz" [as an instrument for bringing about an immediate presence].[44] This presence is accessed via the senses, rather than the intellect:

> Es gibt Situationen und Umstände, in denen Sachverhalte von ansonsten semiotischem Status zum Gegenstand von Praxen werden, welche weniger hermeneutisch verfahren als *sinnhafte* Prozesse der Bezugsetzung von Signifikant und Signifikat, sondern welche vielmehr *sinnliche* Akte sind: sensorische Wahrnehmungen und physische Kontakt.[45]

> [There are situations and circumstances in which contents which normally enjoy a semiotic status are subjected to a form of engagement which does not develop along hermeneutic lines (as a series of intellectual processes establishing the link between the signifier and the signified), but instead manifests itself through sensuous acts: sensory perception and physical contact.]

Strohschneider's key examples are drawn from hagiographical literature and concern texts that are presented not just as accounts of particular saints, but as corporeal substitutes for these saints. As the miraculous powers of the hagiographical subject inhere in the materiality of the text, physical contact becomes more important than intellectual assimilation. So, for example, it is claimed in Priester Wernher's life of the Virgin that if a woman wishes to be spared pain in childbirth, she need only hold a copy of this same text in her right hand during delivery.[46] The material form of the text enacts the physical presence of Mary, just as in the eucharist, the hosts do not just signify but actually constitute the body and blood of Christ.

Whilst there are obvious differences between the Brackenseil inscription and the hagiographical texts discussed by Strohschneider, his paradigm of the unreadable, nonhermeneutic text provides a useful model for assessing the impact of the jewels. Although the leash itself is not an object of transcendent sanctity, the jewels do in a sense constitute tangible "reserves" of those same virtues to which they refer hermeneutically, and, to the extent that they infuse anybody around them with short doses of virtuous pleasure, they function in a manner clearly analogous to the hagiographical relics discussed by Strohschneider.

Nonetheless, the J.T. also differs from the texts discussed by Strohschneider in that it problematizes the opposition between the hermeneutic and the nonhermeneutic approach.[47] Priester Wernher may have seen nothing untoward in women using his text as a magical painkiller. Albrecht, however, appears to suggest, not only that the nonhermeneutic experience is intellectually inferior in itself, but also that it will detract from the likelihood of the recipient going on to engage rationally with the text.

This is made particularly clear in the case of the reception of the Brackenseil inscription by the Arthurian court. On the occasion of each public reading of the Brackenseil, it is stated explicitly that the temporary euphoria descending on the listeners is caused primarily by the stones.[48] Admittedly, the narrator also allows for a very limited intellectual aspect to the collective experience, when he points out that the dissemination of Christian doctrine back in the sixth century was so limited that Clauditte's teaching had a novelty value that might not be immediately apparent to the extradiegetic thirteenth-century audience (J.T. 1928).

Rather than seeing the impact of the stones as a purely negative feature, Finckh introduces the ingenious idea that they provide a form of translation, bridging the gap between the austere intellectual contents and the ethically immature members of the court:

Bei seiner Verlesung "übersetzen" die Edelsteine zunächst den Wortlaut des Geschriebenen in eine unmittelbare emotionale Wirkung; später kann darauf ein inhaltliches Verständnis aufbauen.[49]

[As it is read out, the jewels "translate" the wording of the text into an immediate, emotional effect which may serve as basis for a subsequent understanding of the contents.]

Nonetheless, by suggesting that the emotional response to the stones might eventually lead to an intellectual response to the text, Finkch implicitly accepts that dependence on the stones constitutes a lower, or, in those cases where there is no subsequent understanding of the contents, an inadequate form of response. In any case, there is little sign that the court at large will ever be ready for a more challenging response. The narrator's formulation on the occasion of the second public reading is particularly damning and possibly expresses frustration precisely at this lack of progress:[50]

> die vreude der schrifte gie von der steine krefte
> dar uz die buᵒchstab waren.   die liebtens mere dann von meisterschefte.
> (J.T. 1930,3–4)

[The joy produced by the text was caused by the powers of the stones making up the letters. They derived more pleasure from those than from the teaching.]

As far as individual members of the court are concerned, Sigune comes closer than anybody else to representing the ideal reader of Clauditte's text, and yet even her first impassioned response to the Brackenseil is described in a way that leaves wide open the question of the supremacy of the stones versus that of the words. The statement that

> di schrift der edeln steine   ir herzen was ein klamme habende zange.
> (J.T. 1225,2)

[the script consisting of precious stones was like a pair of tongs around her heart.]

is ambivalent as to which is the ultimate cause of her urgent desire.[51] However, as time progresses, she becomes markedly less affected by the jewels. When she is allowed to read the text on her own, she has to read it three times before her spirits are lifted (J.T. 1868–1869). This suggests that there is a cognitive process underlying her joy, and that she, notwithstanding the presence of the stones so close to her body, is less easily swayed than is the Arthurian court, the members of which are brought to a point of ecstasy simply from listening to a public recital of the text. As the narrative progresses, she becomes less and less interested in the physical form of the text (and the related ownership issues),[52] since she has already internalized its meaning: for example, even after she has passed the Brackenseil on to Clauditte and Ekunat, she is still able to integrate parts of the text into her discourse.[53] Sigune's more intellectual, private reading of the Brackenseil also serves effectively to cut her off from the values and attitudes of the court, who have merely listened to the public recital of the treatise without really being affected by it. To that extent, her experience supports Ong's claim that speech unites, whereas script separates, its recipients.[54] In this case, however, the separation of Sigune from the Arthurian court is a positive thing, which the J.T. aims to replicate on a larger scale with its own ideal audience—regardless of whether they read the narrative as normal script on a page or hear it read out to them. After all, given Sigune's relative disinterest in the physical form of the leash, it could be argued that she is the only one of the protagonists to approach the experience of Albrecht's readers, who at least have the option of experiencing the Brackenseil discourse without the distraction of the jewels.

The deepening of Sigune's understanding of the Brackenseil inscription proves that it is possible for an exceptional reader to rise above the blandishments of the jewels and to engage directly with the didactic contents of the treatise. At the same time, it is equally clear that for the average courtly recipient, the composite materiality of the text is an insuperable obstacle to full assimilation. Although the responsibility for these conceptual flaws ultimately lies with Clauditte and her programmatic attempt to make wildness safe and virtue seductive, it is noteworthy that some recipients fare very much better than others, and that gender plays a role in this respect. While the narrator's implicit criticism of the Arthurian court affects all members and is therefore not gender-specific, the narrative also provides a number of crassly inadequate individual male responses to this female-authored text.

All the men involved in the quest for the Brackenseil seem entirely to miss the point of the treatise; and other individual men who come into casual contact with the text fare no better. Parzifal, for example, responds *kraft der steine* [by virtue of the stones] (J.T 5815,1), while Keie—never one to be singled out for soundness of judgment—is guilty of multiple misapprehensions: he first mocks the Brackenseil as a crude hunting object entirely unworthy of Artus' arbitration (J.T. 1480–1482),[55] but then, having realised that there is something truly remarkable about the inscription, suddenly veers to the opposite extreme of fearful suspicion, claiming that:

>   ez ist von loik der lere
> so si diu kunst verwazen,   mit der man nu die reht zunrehte chere!
>   (J.T. 1870.3–4)

[This reflects the teachings of *logica*. May that art be cursed with which one turns right into wrong!]

Of the contenders for the Brackenseil, Ekunat inevitably stands out as its primary addressee and first recipient. On a personal level, he is presented in a far more favorable light than either the boorish Keie or the villainous Orilus, and, if the Brackenseil refrain of *hu͜ete wol der verte* [stay on the track] can also be taken to mean "show concern for your reputation," the narrator's assurance in J.T. 2000,3 (*do hu͜ot er siner verte, als er solde* [he guarded his reputation, as he should]) is undoubtedly true. Nevertheless, Ekunat's world view is entirely secular,[56] and, despite the elaborately positive glossing of his name provided both by the narrator and by Clauditte, the narrative itself offers little to suggest that he is particularly moved by the religiously-oriented didacticism suffusing the message from his beloved.[57] He may be a stranger to wrongdoing (J.T. 1880,1 and 1881,4), but he is equally a stranger to genuine reflection and self-knowledge. His lack of engagement with the text of the Brackenseil is made apparent through his reaction to its loss. Although he realizes that both hound and leash have come into the possession of Orilus, the claim which he initially stakes for the return of his rightful possession refers only to hound (J.T. 1466). His reluctance to mention the leash is ostensibly based on the fear that public knowledge of the inscription might compromise Clauditte. This concern is, however, entirely misplaced (given that the subsequent public readings of the inscription results in considerable praise for Clauditte). It suggests that Ekunat had not fully appreciated the value, and, in particular, the universal relevance of Clauditte's message. Instead, he appears to be blinded by his own embarrassment at the fact that the text reveals *beide ir namen* (J.T. 1470,2) [the names of both of them] and that an aspect of a private relationship is thus inevitably going to become common knowledge. Furthermore, when he does overcome this diffidence and chooses to alert the courtly world to Sigune's interest in the leash, this is done primarily in the context of an (admittedly selfless) favor to a kinsman whose love-life might benefit from this, rather than as the result of a more general reflection on the desirability of disseminating this valuable text. While care should be taken not to take an unduly psychological approach to the narration of Ekunat's actions, it is also conceivable that it is this same sense of embarrassment and funda- mental unease with the Brackenseil that impels Ekunat to take the object into the final battle with Orilus, thereby bringing about its destruction.[58]

The other contenders for ownership of the Brackenseil are equally misguided, although in different ways. As Parshall puts it, "Initially, the leash appears to be coveted for its costly decoration alone, since Teanglis and Orilus wage a mighty battle over it without reading or presumably even noticing the inscription."[59] The inscription is completely wasted on Teanglis who seems to be illiterate in every sense, unable to understand either normal script or the function of natural phe- nomena as second-language signifiers.[60] There is no evidence that the jewels mean anything to him or have any impact beyond arousing mild curiosity. As such, his response is, on the one hand, the most obviously inadequate of all, but on the other hand, it also serves to highlight the opportunities wasted by others who can read but choose not to. As for Orilus, it appears that he brings about precisely that separation of leash and hound that had previously been discussed in hypothetical terms: he keeps the hound for himself, while the leash becomes the property of Jescute (J.T. 1468,3), whose female gender presumably makes her a suitable recipient both of pretty objects and of "feminine" pieces of writing.[61]

Tschinotulander is the most poignantly misguided of the four principal con- tenders. Although his literacy puts him ahead of Teanglis, he has little opportunity to apply this skill to the Brackenseil. Furthermore, even if he had done so, his temperament makes him particularly unreceptive to its message.[62] From the very outset, he has only a hazy conception of what he is looking for: the instructions given to him by Sigune are so rudimentary that he does not even realize, for example, that the text was addressed to Ekunat.[63] His temporary pursuit of the false Gardivias (J.T. 1362–1367) also highlights the erroneous basis of his quest.[64] Sigune may be blamed for some of these early misunderstandings. However, when, at a much later stage, she actually reads the Brackenseil text out loud to him, the problematic nature of his unresponsiveness becomes unmistakable:

Iedoch er uberhorte   di strangen von ir munde
(J.T. 5029,1)

[And yet he did not take in her reading of the leash]

Tschinotulander's fault is that he seeks the Brackenseil simply in order to fulfil his promise to Sigune, without wanting or feeling any need to understand it himself. Even after the first public reading of the Brackenseil, and after Sigune has been allowed to satisfy her craving by reading the text three times in private (J.T. 1869), Tschinotulander has no greater insight into the nature of the text that will define his destiny than do various completely unimplicated members of the Arthurian court:

> Tschinotulander   hie wunderts dirre mære
> und ouch vil manic ander,   welcherleie schrift so ditze wære.
> (J.T.1870,1–2)

[Tschinotulander and many others wondered what this text actually was.]

While Tschinotulander's assessment of the Brackenseil is not so crassly off the mark as is that of Keie, his downfall may be directly related to his failure to assimilate the Brackenseil message of moderation in all things, even in the pursuit of honor.[65] In his foolish refusal to desist from blind service of Sigune, against her wishes (J.T. 1955) and against the advice of the prominent members of the Arthurian court (J.T. 1957), he not only fails to benefit from the sense of the inscription, but also acts in such a way that the Brackenseil in its material form ultimately becomes a catalyst of tragedy.[66]

Section II: The Grail

Although the Brackenseil antics dominate the bulk of the J.T. narrative, they actually take place within a relatively short period of time, enclosed structurally and chronologically within the multigenerational sweep of Grail history set out in the work. Historiography is much more prominent in the J.T. than in Wolfram's narratives: whereas in genealogical terms, Wolfram does not go back any further than to Titurel, Albrecht traces the origins of the Grail dynasty back as far as Troy, and interweaves the notion of *translatio imperii* into his account of this family.[67] He explains in passing how Rome was founded by the Trojan Eneas (J.T. 93)— thereby justifying the rather anachronistic presentation of Titurel as the glory both of Troy and of Rome (J.T. 9,4)—and underscores the political continuity between classical Rome, the Frankish Empire, and the Holy Roman Empire when Parille, the grandfather of Titurel, marries the daughter of Emperor Vespasian, and receives France as a fief (J.T. 115–116).

Salvation history becomes intertwined with *translatio imperii* through the focus on the Grail, which is presented as the original chalice used at the Last Supper and therefore enjoys a more specific historical and material identity than in the works of Wolfram. When Titurel receives this object from the angel, he is instructed to move even further west, to Galicia in Spain, to found the kingdom of Salvaterre (J.T. 297–324). Within this early history of the Grail family, there is thus a subtle shift in emphasis from the conventional *translatio* of political power, to the physical translation of the Grail itself, in which religious authority is concentrated. Albrecht's narrative ends with another physical translation of the Grail, this time in reverse direction, into the kingdom of Prester John. This development is presented as a divine response to the frivolity and sinfulness of Western Christendom, and is consistent with the underlying theme of the failure of Arthurian values, as exemplified by the specific issues raised by the conflict over the Brackenseil.

Although operating on very different timescales, and with little direct causal interaction, the Grail and the Brackenseil thus provide parallel inditements on the Arthurian world. The narrator encourages his audience to note the similarities between these two key textual objects, which, by the end of the narrative, are lost to the Western world. For example, he refers to the construction of a "false" Grail—sharing the physical appearance, but not the sanctity, of the original—which is revered in Constantinople (J.T. 6295). While this "false" Grail has no direct bearing on the narrative, it mirrors the "false" Gardivias chased by Tschinotulander, and thus implies a certain parallelism between the two "real" objects (Brackenseil and Grail), both of which are misunderstood and undervalued.

This parallelism underscores the fact that on one level, these objects have a comparable didactic function: they both teach virtue. That the excellence of their respective messages can be praised in very similar terms may be illustrated through the juxtaposition of the following two passages. In the first one, Titurel speaks of the Grail:

> Wan ich den gral enphie von gote   mit siner hohen krefte.
> der tugende engel was des bote.   (der sie gebenedit der botschefte!)
> der tugend ler was dran geschrieben und orden.
>
> (J.T. 512,1–3)

[When I received the Grail from God, with its great powers, the angel of the virtues was its messenger (and may he be blessed on account of the message). The teaching and *ordo* of virtue was written onto it.]

In the second passage, the narrator speaks of the Brackenseil (referring partly, but not exclusively, to the impact of the jewels):

> ir beider lop daz wart do hoch gemeret,
> Ich mein, des von der wilde   und der magt Clauditten.
> uf erde menschen bilde   in der ersten werld noch in der dritten
> kom nie groᵉzer liep in oren hoᵉre,
> dann an der strangen was geschriben,   und da zu° tugende lere, untugende stoᵉre.
>
> (J.T.1507,4–1508,4)

[The praise of both of them was then greatly enhanced—I mean, of him from the wilderness and of the maiden Clauditte. Nothing was ever heard which caused greater pleasure, either in the first world or in the third, than that which was written on the leash—and which brought with it the teaching of virtue and the destruction of vice.]

Indeed, when the respective destruction and departure of these two didactic objects renders the Western world doubly deprived of moral guidance, it would appear that Albrecht's own narrative aspires to fill this vacuum. In other words, it seeks to provide an extradiegetic solution to an intradiegetic problem, with the excellence of the intradiegetic objects being transferred, or "translated," to the J.T. itself. The claim to salvatory excellence with which the narrator closes the J.T. is certainly comparable to the two statements just quoted about the

Grail and the Brackenseil:

> Nu pru^efet, alle werden,   die wirde dises bu°ches!
> von du^etscher zung uf erden   nie getichte wart so werdes ru°ches,
> daz lib und sele so hoch gen wirde wiset,
> alle, di iz ho^eren, lesen oder schriben,   der sele mu^eze werden geparadiset.
>
> (J.T. 6327)

[Now let all worthy people judge the worth of this book. No poem spoken on earth by a German tongue was ever so full of worthy care that body and soul should strive highly for worthiness, with the result that the souls of all, who hear, or read, or copy it, must attain paradise.]

Nonetheless, while the two inscripted objects are comparable in very general terms, closer consideration of the different ways in which Albrecht handles the respective translations of their contents into his own work will highlight the fundamental opposition between them.

In the case of the Brackenseil inscription, Albrecht appears to understand this task as a process of twofold liberation: first he has to extricate the moral treatise from all those material factors (i.e., the dog and the jewels) which are liable to interfere with its reception and intellectual assimilation; and secondly, he has to isolate it from the secular, eroticizing context of Clauditte's relationship with Ekunat.

The material impediments clearly disappear when the treatise is quoted in its "pure" verbal form separated from the distracting influence of the jewels. Further-more, the ultimate destruction of the Brackenseil highlights its basic frangibility as a further, more long-term barrier to the dissemination of the didactic message. Given the problem of the material transience of script (discussed in chapter 1, section I), the extradiegetic recording of the Brackenseil contents in the J.T. may be viewed as a vital backup, notwithstanding the fact that no single book or manuscript may ultimately be regarded as safe from the ravages of time.

As far as the second stage of liberation is concerned, it is more difficult to disso-ciate the text from the intangible erotic context within which it was composed—with that flawed endorsement of wildness and seduction, from which the dog and the jewels also derived their functions—but the narrator achieves this indirectly, through his repeated demonstration of the failure of erotic love throughout the narrative.[68]

What remains of the Brackenseil after this process of liberation is a competent discourse on the nature of virtue, which will certainly benefit right-thinking read-ers, but which is unlikely to have the spectacular effects of the original leash. The paradox of the Brackenseil is that it derives its mystery and complexity precisely from those material and contextual aspects that also work against the assimilation of its teaching. Once these suspect elements have been stripped away and the com-posite object reduced to a simple text, it becomes clear that the didactic kernel of Clauditte's work is not in itself sufficiently remarkable to account for that claim to excellence which the narrator makes for the J.T. in the final strophe (J.T. 6327; quoted above).[69]

Whereas the *translatio* of the Brackenseil into the narrative ultimately reduces to a transcription of its text, Albrecht appears more interested in the Grail's eucharistic significance than with the actual wording of its texts. Furthermore, in dealing with the Grail, he is much more inclined to draw on the technique of allegorical interpretation, as will be shown below. This difference in strategy is commensurate with the fundamental differences between the two objects: whereas the Brackenseil is a human creation, the Grail is of divine provenance; whereas the Brackenseil no longer exists, the Grail remains intact, albeit inaccessible; and whereas the Brackenseil starts as a composite object with a single fixed text, the Grail is presented as simple object (fashioned from a single jewel, as opposed to the plurality of stones adoring the leash) with multiple, changeable texts. Finally, like the transsubstantiated Eucharist itself, which constitutes the ultimate analogy for Strohschneider's notion of textual immanence (as discussed in section I above), the Grail is unique in that it functions both hermeneutically and nonhermeneutically: although this object does represent a tangible piece of divinity and possesses numerous quasi-magical "special effects," its messages are by no means "unlesbar."

Although critical opinion is divided on the question as to whether Albrecht was familiar with the Joseph of Arimathea legend from the outset of his literary undertaking, or whether he only came into contact with this material as he was approaching completion of his work,[70] there can be little doubt that a strong association of the Grail with the sacraments, and particularly with the eucharist, was central to Albrecht's conception from the start.[71] Huschenbett in particular has drawn attention both to the baptismal imagery in the prologue to the J.T. and to the way in which the Grail temple is presented as a sacristy housing the eucharistic host (J.T. 545–546), concluding that for Albrecht, a vital point of interest was the power traditionally ascribed to the sacramental word(s).[72] Of course, the sacramental words are normally understood as being spoken as part of the celebration of the mass, but for Albrecht, the status of the Grail as a textual object means that the focus inevitably shifts to the power of the written word in all its contexts, literary as well as sacramental. As Huschenbett puts it, Albrecht's Grail is not only a transporter of the word of God in written form,[73] but also an object that stands for the overall power of the written word.[74]

Given that the Grail presumably continues to present its community with fresh texts into a boundless future,[75] it would be impossible for the J.T. to contain a complete record of all that is written on it. Albrecht, however, does not even opt for a partial record. Instead, the mystique and privacy of the communications are respected, the essence of the Grail teaching being reflected, not through direct quotation, but rather in the speeches of Titurel and through the narratorial commentary and exegesis.

While any direct identification of the narrative with the Grail would be inappropriately simplistic, it seems fair to say that the authorial narrator presents his text as the closest substitute available to the audience: it not only constitutes the "best" source of information about the Grail, but, like the Grail with its innumerable *zeichenunge* (J.T. 516,1) [meanings, *significationes*],[76] the text itself also purports to be infinitely interpretable, given the way in which Albrecht's narrator encourages an allegorical approach to the "facts" of the narrative. In both cases, however, the multiplicity of meanings ultimately reduce to one: both Grail and narrative contain *tugent* [virtue] which is the same as God (J.T. 10,2).

In identifying the Grail with the chalice used at the Last Supper, Albrecht is both much more specific and much more open-ended than Wolfram. Although this piece of identification lends the Grail historical and material precision, the technique of allegorization allows him to undertake a metaphorical *translatio* of the Grail, so that it comes to signify something more abstract and diffuse, namely the divine presence in every virtuous Christian. This is made most explicit in the comparison of the Grail temple to each and every human body, which ought to remain pure enough to be worthy of housing its own "grail":

Dem tempel gar geliche   sol sich der mensche reinen.
er bedarf wol zierde riche,   sint daz sich got dar inne wil gemeinen
des menschen sele zu werdem hus genoze.
nein, edel menschen herze,   nu ler den lip di edel tugende groze.

(J.T. 528)

[Man should model himself on the pure temple. He will truly need rich ornamentation, given that God will live inside, as a worthy companion of the human soul. Indeed, noble human heart, now impart the great and noble virtues to the body.][77]

Given this paradox, namely that the Grail is an individual object now located in India and also a divine presence potentially present in every human soul, Albrecht's decision to harness his Grail to the Joseph of Arimathea tradition constitutes more than a move to "correct" Wolfram by making the Christian context of the Grail absolutely clear-cut. Instead, the specifically eucharistic significance of the Grail provides a framework within which this paradox might be analyzed (if not fully resolved) through the use of analogy: just as it is widely understood that the body of Christ, although present locally in heaven, is also spiritually present in the host wherever the eucharist is celebrated,[78] so the fact that the Grail is present locally in the kingdom of Prester John is not inconsistent with its presence within every devout Christian and, more precisely, within every recipient of Albrecht's narrative.

If this analogy is accepted, it follows that the recipients of the Grail-text are to some extent to be seen as forming a congregation or religious community. To that extent, there is a superficial similarity with the community of "noble hearts" who form the ostensible addressees of Gottfried's *Tristan*: a select group that is said to reject the ordinary pleasures of the world in favor of the emotional anguish of *minne* and who ingest the sad love-story of Tristan and Isolde as though it were the eucharist.[79] Nonetheless, unlike these noble hearts, Albrecht's literary congregation is in no way morally subversive or committed to values incompatible with those of the Church. The Grail's opposition to secular love is unambiguous and, to the extent that the "ideal" readers of the J.T. resemble the noble hearts in rejecting the pleasures valued by ordinary people, this will be a reflection precisely of the way in which they have accepted those higher standards of ascetic virtue that are associated intradiegetically with Titurel and with the community which he heads.

Albrecht's technique of stressing the eucharistic nature of the Grail(-text) in order to construct a literary congregation of readers complements his elaborate discussion of the sacrament of baptism in the prologue to the J.T.: this baptismal imagery, which will be discussed in detail in section III of chapter 5, not only supports Albrecht's fundamental program of "christening" (i.e., christianizing) the genre of Arthurian romance,[80] but also serves to "christen" the audience and thereby to enhance the sense of spiritual community between its individual members. The written word is thus intended to unite the true recipients, even as it divides them from those who do not read the text at all, or who read it wrongly.

There is, however, one important difference between Albrecht's metaphorical appropriation of the two sacraments. The eucharistic, Grail-centred, analogies entail a high degree of moral homogeneity. The Grail sets the standards and the would-be human recipients of the Grail have to strive to make themselves worthy, or else be rejected: at worst, the Grail will punish with death and at best it will simply depart, rather than tolerate impure receptacles or surroundings. The discourse on baptism is less extreme, focusing as it does on the ways in which water cleanses and makes the impure pure again. Furthermore, as will be shown in chapter 5, the quasi-scientific properties of water are also expounded in a manner that invites poetological interpretation, with particular reference to the ways in which it is possible for a text to accommodate (although not to endorse) alternative world views.

The principal dissenting voice in the J.T. is of course that of 'Wolfram,' the problematic primary narrator who is presented as being "stuck" in the secular ethos supposedly characteristic of *Parzival* and who retains his faintly subversive tone throughout. In exploring these wider ramifications of the notion of sacramental writing, the second half of this monograph will move away from the intradiegetic level in order to focus, in chapter 4, on the opposition between the two narrators, and then, in chapter 5, on the question of how the J.T. positions itself in relation both to other specific literary texts (including those of the historical Wolfram), and to the written word more generally.

PART II

THE NARRATORS AND THE AUTHOR

CHAPTER 4

'ALBRECHT,' 'WOLFRAM,' AND VROU
AVENTIURE: ARGUING WITH THE TEXT

In the J.T., the themes of authorship, narration, and narrator–identity are handled in a manner that is unusually complex, even by the standards of classical Arthurian romance. Following Haug, it has become commonplace to recognize a link between the transition from Mündlichkeit to Schriftlichkeit and the emergence of a self-consciously fictional form of narration (such as is exemplified by the model of Arthurian romance established by Chrétien de Troyes).[1] As Schaefer points out, the transition to the written medium lends a certain artificiality to the construction of even the most basic narrator-role:

> War der Rhapsode noch wahrhaft das Medium der Erzählung, wird mit der wachsenden Schriftlichkeit die Medialität des Erzählers nun zusehends inszeniert, weil das graphische Medium ihn eigentlich nicht meht braucht.[2]

> [While the rhapsodist had truly constituted the medium of the narrative, the rise of 'Schriftlichkeit' (textual culture) means that the medial role of the narrator is now visibly being staged, because the written medium does not really require him any more.]

Of course, the opposition between Mündlichkeit and Schriftlichkeit is not an absolute one, either theoretically or in terms of cultural practice.[3] Given the near ubiquity in the twelfth and early thirteenth centuries of the pattern whereby an audience receives a written Arthurian romance aurally through the mediation of a reciter or performer,[4] it seems likely that in these cases, the construction of the narrator-role is effected not only within the text, but also on the performance level, the narrator's address to the implicit or fictional audience mirroring the performer's engagement with the actual audience present on a given occasion.[5] Furthermore, on the textual level, this illusion of real-time oral interaction may be strengthened in various ways, such as through the inclusion of dialogues between the narrator and various abstract personifications (e.g., vrou Minne or vrou Aventiure).[6] As will be argued later in this chapter, the dialogic intervention of these figures may also serve to usurp the authority of written sources and thereby to contribute further to a medially anachronistic skewing of the narrative situation.

An additional complication arises from the fact that, notwithstanding the fundamental theoretical distinction between narrator and author, many Arthurian romances, including Hartmann's *Iwein* and Wolfram's *Parzival*, endow the narrator with the name of the historical author, thereby engendering the separate illusion that narrator and author are identical. Whilst the traditional solution to this problem is to think in terms of the narrator temporarily assuming the "mask" of the author, Unzeitig prefers to speak of this as a rhetorical manifestation of the presence of "der Autor im Text" [the author in the text]: on her account, the passages apparently identifying the narrator constitute "ein sprachlich realisiertes Autorbild, das sich mit dem Autornamen verbindet" [a verbally constructed author portrait, which is associated with the name of the author].[7] Such an "Autorbild" (or authorial signature, to use another of Unzeitig's metaphors) is not to be interpreted "als biographischer Verweis auf den 'realen' Autor" [as a biographical reference to the historical author], but rather as "Repräsentation des Autors und seiner Autorschaft" [a representation of the author and his authorship].[8]

These theoretical difficulties that beset the interpretation even of those Arthurian romances with only one narrator-figure, are inevitably compounded in the J.T., given that this work features two narrators ('Wolfram' and 'Albrecht') who stand in polemical opposition to each other. It can be argued that the construction of each of these narrator-figures introduces different elements of an authorial presence into the text: the narrator named 'Wolfram' constitutes a representation of the literary achievements of the historical Wolfram von Eschenbach, whilst the closing references to 'Albrecht' serve as an authorial signature highlighting that which has been achieved specifically in the J.T. (as opposed to in *Parzival*).

This chapter will examine the literary functions and implications of this narratorial doubling, with particular reference to 'Wolfram's' dialogic interaction with the personified vrou Aventiure. The discussion will therefore be directed toward the tension existing between, on the one hand, the notion of the text as a specific written output, and, on the other hand, that of *aventiure* as a quasi-allegorical entity existing independently of any written version. The chapter will also highlight the way in which the relationship between 'Wolfram' and vrou Aventiure is conceived as changing over time and hence as possessing a narrative dynamic of its own. Finally, the chapter will propose a sapiential reading of the figure of vrou Aventiure, which will in turn provide the basis for the analysis in chapter 5 of 'Albrecht's' justification of his own deployment of the written medium.

In J.T. 5961, the audience of the J.T. is presented with a striking new perspective on the identity of the now familiar narrator, when 'Albrecht' suddenly introduces himself in the role of an author who has been let down by his patron:

> Die aventiure habende   bin ich, Albrecht vil gantze,
> von dem wal al drabende   bin ich, sit mir zebrach der helfe lantze
> an einem fursten, den ich wol kunde nennen:
> in allen richen verren,   in duᵉtschen landen moht man in erkennen.

[I, Albrecht, control this tale in its entirety. I am trotting away from the battle-field, since the lance of financial assistance was broken for me by a prince whom I could easily name; he is known in the most remote kingdoms of the German lands.][9]

Until that point, the narrative voice has been associated with the name of 'Wolfram von Eschenbach.' Not only has the speaker been addressed as such by vrou Aventiure,[10] but his personality and frame of reference are clearly modeled on the narrator created by the historical Wolfram. Nonetheless, 'Wolfram never assumes such a clearly articulated authorial role as does 'Albrecht,' who, in this strophe, engages with historically attestable patrons and implicitly takes overall responsibility for the production of a tangible written product. Whilst 'Albrecht' thus implicitly places himself in the same universe as that of the audience, the same is not true of 'Wolfram.' Notwithstanding the fact that the audience would have acknowledged the historical reality of Wolfram von Eschenbach, and the geographical reality of his provenance (e.g., by recognizing that Eschenbach is very close to Pleinfeld),[11] the narrator 'Wolfram' is still kept at one remove from the world of the audience: even while the story is still being presented as "his," 'Wolfram' is not explicitly associated with the practical difficulties of an authorial career (e.g., funding problems).[12] Instead, he simply constitutes a familiar speaking voice that has been resurrected by the historical Albrecht in order to underscore the differences in moral outlook between the J.T. and the works of the historical Wolfram. Rather than perceiving 'Wolfram' as actively writing another book, we are therefore encouraged to focus on his emotional and moral reactions to the narrative that is being funnelled through him by vrou Aventiure. The chain of command is thus clear: 'Albrecht' controls *aventiure* [J.T. 5961,1] and vrou Aventiure dominates 'Wolfram.' Indeed, given the vividness with which he is characterized and given that the flow of the narrative impacts him more than he impacts it, 'Wolfram' effectively functions as just another flawed protagonist (albeit existing in a different narrative universe from that of Titurel and Tschinotulander).

The J.T. is fundamentally critical of the historical author Wolfram von Eschenbach. While the very fact that Albrecht obviously finds it worthwhile to engage with the work of the historical Wolfram may of course be seen as a compliment of sorts, it is worth reiterating the fact that the J.T. does not openly present itself as what it actually is, namely the completion by another person of Wolfram's fragmentary *Titurel* project. To that extent, it diverges markedly from the stance adopted in the so-called *Verfasserfragment* (Vf), a text that Lorenz describes as "eine Art Bewerbungsgedicht" [a kind of versified funding application] addressed to Ludwig II.[13] In the Vf, Albrecht, now speaking in his "own" authorial voice, acknowledges the separate existence of *Titurel*, supposedly left unfinished when Wolfram died:

<Her Wolfram, der durch prisen die mær alsus> enborte
Titurel dem wisen, di tschionatvlander angehorte
vnd sigvne. owe daz er niht lebende
was, vntz er werdeclichen wer der aventivre ein ende gebende!

(Vf 1)[14]

[Lord Wolfram, who raised up in praise of the wise Titurel this tale pertaining to Tschinotulander and Sigune—alas that he did not live long enough to bring the narrative to a worthy end!]

By contrast, until the very late introduction of an author-narrator called 'Albrecht,' the J.T. has ostensibly been presented as the output of 'Wolfram,' the narrator of *Parzival* and *Willehalm*, who was now, at least in part, going over old ground in order to address previous shortcomings. Strohschneider's dictum, "daß der Rang desjenigen Dichters, dessen Werk man zu vollenden unternimmt, aus der Fortsetzerperspektive nicht zur Diskussion steht" [that one cannot question the status of that poet whose work one is completing],[15] therefore does not apply in this case. On the contrary, contesting the status of Wolfram von Eschenbach might be regarded as the central concern of the J.T.

In the Vf, Albrecht not only defends himself against the charge of being presumptuous for even attempting to complete the fragments produced by the historical Wolfram,[16] but also against the implicit, but well-deserved accusation that his mode of completion constitutes an attack on his precursor. With touchy hyperbole, he insists that he could not have revered the historical author Wolfram more if the latter had been an angel decked out with wings:

> Ich Albrecht niemen swache, daz ist mir immer wilde.
> wer der von eschenbache von himel chomen her in engels bilde
> mit flugen, svnnen var von got bechront,
> sin edel hoh getihte kvnd ich mit lob niht richer han bedonet.
> (Vf 13).[17]

> [I, Albrecht, do not belittle anybody. That is utterly alien to me. Even if the man von Eschenbach had come down from heaven in the form of an angel, bearing wings and crowned by God with the radiance of the sun, I could not have praised his noble and excellent work more elaborately in my own verse than I have already done.]

However, as Albrecht goes on to explain with apparent satisfaction, Wolfram was a mere mortal.[18] Furthermore, he does not accept that the works of the historical Wolfram constitute a standard of unattainable artistic excellence. On the contrary, the Vf explicitly articulates the feasibility of *aemulatio*: that is, of the possibility of outdoing the achievements of earlier poets.[19]

In the J.T., Albrecht constructs a 'Wolfram' who is indeed no angel, and who shares many of the mannerisms and idiosyncrasies that contribute to the individuality of the *Parzival*- and *Willehalm*-narrator.[20] Indeed, the similarity in the self-presentation of the narrators should be seen in the broader context of the numerous stylistic parallels linking the J.T. to the works of the historical Wolfram.[21] Like his earlier self, the 'Wolfram' of the J.T. muses on the relationship between art and *sin*;[22] is ambivalent about the written word, to the point of professing illiteracy;[23] makes passing reference to family members;[24] and presents himself as a lustful, albeit not particularly successful, admirer of the ladies.[25] This last point in particularly significant, given the new, ascetic atmosphere of the J.T., in which such attitudes attract a level of censure unknown in *Parzival*. Furthermore, this narrator seems more flippant and amoral than his "earlier self" ever did. For example, whereas the abduction of women (e.g., by Meljakanz or Clinschor) is treated as a matter of grave concern in *Parzival*, the narrator of the J.T. expresses nothing but admiration for the Moroccans who get away with seizing three hundred ladies:

> ich geb im riche miete,   der mich di selben kunste wolde leren!
> (J.T. 2455,4)

[I would pay a rich reward to anybody who would teach me that same trick!]

However, far from having three hundred ladies at his intimate disposal, this narrator is reduced even to envying Tschinotulander on account of the polite kisses that the latter receives from the *baruc*'s wife and from her ladies-in-waiting.[26] This occasion triggers a curiously poetological complaint from the frustrated narrator, who compares himself to a weaver producing beautiful cloth (i.e., the textual representation of beautiful women), but only ever for the benefit of others:

> Ich, Wolfram, clagen solde.   min schad ist dem geliche,
> als der da uzer golde   und siden wurket kleit vil kosteriche,
> und ims ein elle nimmer wirt zeteile.
> moht ichs ein kleit erwerben,   so worht ich erst alsam der vreuden geile.
> (J.T. 2867)

[I, Wolfram, have something to complain about. My plight is like that of somebody who works precious cloth out of gold and silk, without being allowed to keep even a single roll of it. If I could obtain a garment out of it, I would work with real joy.]

Similarly, the narrator becomes agitated when Tschinotulander has won the right to kiss eighty maidens at the Arthurian court. He goes as far as to ask vrou Aventiure not to name them all, as this will render him overexcited:

> ich vurchte, daz mir etsliche   gevalle so, daz ich nach ir verscheide!
> (J.T. 2290,4)

[I fear that some of them will please me so much that I might die of longing for them!]

As will be shown later in this chapter, vrou Aventiure embodies the strict ascetic code that suffuses the work and to the extent that it is justifiable to impute any degree of psychological verisimilitude to the relationship between the two, one can only imagine the irritation triggered by comments like the one just quoted.

These two passages also highlight the difficulty of positioning 'Wolfram' within the narrative universe(s). 'Wolfram' in his universe has no access to the intradiegetic ladies, but he does not belong to the purely extradiegetic world of the historical Albrecht either. The J.T. is thus to some extent also the story of a character called 'Wolfram,' who possesses a personal and artistic past with which the audience is deemed to be familiar, and which is now being subjected to a sometimes traumatic process of renegotiation and correction. In creating such a character and subjecting him to the ritual humiliation of a literary "groundhog day," there is no doubt that Albrecht is showing a certain disrespect for the image of his historical precursor.

In addition to this foregrounding of thwarted sexuality, whereby the narrator lusts after the characters, the construction of the narrator's 'Wolfram'-identity in the J.T. is principally effected through his quasi-dialogic interaction with a range of addressees, which include not only the implicit audience[27] and the human protagonists within the work,[28] but also two abstract personifications: vrou Minne and the already mentioned vrou Aventiure. Although both the J.T. and *Parzival* accord more prominence to the latter, specifically Wolframian creation, each of these personifications is well-established within Middle High German Arthurian romance and the two may to some extent be seen to overlap in terms of literary function: by providing an alternative perspective on the process of the narration, either of them may serve as the narrator's *alter ego*, potentially encompassing the various roles of instructor, collaborator, and rival.

The Middle High German term *aventiure* is inherently ambiguous, referring not only to the kind of challenges traditionally sought by knights, but also to the kinds of stories that recount the pursuit of such challenges.[29] Thus, in the works of Hartmann, statements along the lines of *ich suoche aventiure* (*Iwein* 525) [I am seeking adventure][30] coexist with quasi-personifications of the term in the second (narrative) sense: *aventiure*, although disembodied, is deemed to possess a voice that speaks to narrator and audience alike, as in the case of *Iwein* 3026: *als diu aventiure giht* [as the story reports].[31] Wolfram famously takes this personifying trend a step further by staging the scene in which the figure of Aventiure (now credited with the title *vrou*) knocks on the narrator's heart at the start of Book 9 of *Parzival*, when the story line is about to revert back to the career of the eponymous hero.[32] However, given the importance generally assigned to love as a thematic and motivating force for *aventiure* (in both senses), there is also a certain logic to the suggestion that Minne personified actually should have a view on how the story ought to be told. The first Middle High German example of a personification challenging the competence of the narrator occurs in Hartmann's *Iwein*, when the narrator challenges vrou Minne as to the implications of the "exchange of hearts" that has supposedly taken place between Iwein and Laudine (for example, how can a man fight bravely if he now has a female rather than a male heart?).[33] While the specific subject matter of the debate may be dismissed as the playful literalization of a single metaphor, the interchange does address wider issues of narratorial authority, given that vrou Minne rejects the version of events presented by the narrator and forces him to revise his account:

> si sprach, und sach mich twerhes an,
> 'dune hast niht war, Hartman.'
> 'vrouwe, ich hân entriuwen.' si sprach 'nein'.
> der strit was lanc under uns zwein,
> unz si mich brahte uf die vart
> daz ich ir nach jehende wart.
>
> (*Iwein* 2981–2987)[34]

[She replied, looking crossly at me. "You have not got it right, Hartman." "Lady, I have." She said, "No." The argument between us lasted a long time, until she convinced me to speak in accordance with what she said.]

In assuming control of the presentation of the narrative, vrou Minne moves outside the intradiegetic domain with which she is traditionally associated (i.e., making people within the narrative fall in love with each other) and comes close to embodying the notion of *aventiure*. This development is further underscored by the fact that she is engaging in dialogue with the extradiegetic narrator.

Wolfram's *Parzival*, by contrast, does not allow vrou Minne to concern herself with the overall truthfulness of the account, or even with the appropriateness of particular metaphors. The creation of a separate vrou Aventiure makes it natural that this new figure, rather than vrou Minne, should be the chosen interlocutor for the narrator, and so, although he also voices quite lengthy apostrophes to vrou Minne, she does not reply.[35] Rather than reflecting on the narrative, she is primarily a figure operating within it: on the authority of *manec min meister* (*Parzival* 532,1) [many of my masters], the narrator playfully endorses the intradiegetic existence of an Ovidian love-goddess who literally sets individual characters "on fire."[36] Thus, although the scope of vrou Minne is not exclusively intradiegetic,[37] there is no sense in which she is granted a poetological role comparable to the one played by her counterpart in *Iwein*. Nonetheless, despite not being endowed with critical faculties in her own right, the figure of vrou Minne still triggers consideration of poetological issues, given that the content of the narrator's apostrophes to her has a bearing on how he relates to his own task. Through his posture of objecting to the operations of love,[38] he effectively expresses serious dissatisfaction with a key element of the story being presented (*aventiure* in the narrative sense). If taken at face value, such a statement has as much bearing on the issues of fictionality and of narrative subjectivity as does the image of vrou Aventiure's entry into the narrator's heart: on what level (if at all) does the narrator actually determine the flow of the story?

Albrecht follows Wolfram in assigning poetological priority to vrou Aventiure over vrou Minne and in showing minimal interest in the dialogic potential of the latter. The J.T. contains one substantial, second-person attack by the narrator on vrou Minne (J.T. 2629–2636), but as in *Parzival*, it remains unanswered. Similarly, although the narrator in the J.T. also addresses vrou Minne on other occasions in order to intercede on behalf of particularly favored protagonists (J.T. 1530,4 and 4294,4 on behalf of Tschinotulander; J.T. 2633,1–3 on behalf on the Christian forces in the Orient), she not only fails to reply, but ultimately appears to have less of a real existence than does her counterpart in *Parzival*: notwithstanding a passing reference made by the narrator to the iconography of the classical arrow-wielding love-goddess (J.T. 4016), vrou Minne exists more as a figure of speech than as an autonomous and self-conscious agent within the narrative universe of the J.T.[39] This reduction in the anthropomorphic status of vrou Minne (by comparison both with Hartmann and Wolfram) is consistent with the text's fundamentally negative evaluation of erotic love, which, as Guggenberger has made clear, is perhaps the main area of disagreement between Albrecht and Wolfram,[40] and which is highlighted on a number of occasions by the ethically authoritative vrou Aventiure. So, for example, the latter specifically rejects the iconography of the Ovidian love-goddess, telling the narrator:

> Wiltu die minne malen,   so bedarftu keiner strale.
>
> (J.T. 4023,1)

[If you want to portray love, you do not need to concern yourself with arrows.]

Such a physical conception of love might be appropriate for heathens who, being unbaptized, are inherently incapable of fathoming the spiritual nature of *ware minn* (J.T. 4029,3) [true love].[41]

Nonetheless, there are respects in which Albrecht's handling of the vrou Aventiure dialogues appears to have been influenced by the earlier writers' presentation of vrou Minne. For example, in the J.T., vrou Aventiure is persistently dismissive to the point of rudeness, as in *swigt ir tor, war tu°t ir iwer sinne* (J.T. 245,2) [Be quiet, you fool, are you mad?] or *Wolfram, du kanst min alzu dicke varen!* (J.T. 266,2) [Wolfram, you stray from me far too often!].[42] Whereas this aspect of her discourse cannot be explained by reference to the dialogue at the start of Book 9 of *Parzival*, in which relations are perfectly amicable, not to say loving,[43] the bluntness of vrou Minne in *Iwein* does provide a rhetorical model:

Do zech mich vrou Minne,
ich wære kranker sinne.
si sprach 'tuo zuo dinen munt:
dir ist diu best vuore unkunt'
   (*Iwein* 3011–3014)

[Then vrou Minne accused me of having lost my senses. She said, "Shut your mouth. You do not know the best way to proceed"]

Similarly, the *Parzival*-narrator's dissatisfaction with the apparent cruelty inflicted by vrou Minne, both intra- and extradiegetically, serves as a precursor to the wider objections formulated by the narrator of the J.T. to vrou Aventiure's supposedly cruel decision to "kill off" Secureiz and Tschinotulander.

Albrecht is strikingly enthusiastic in his deployment of the figure of vrou Aventiure; while she makes only one single (albeit high profile) appearance in *Parzival*, the J.T. features no less than ten separate dialogues between her and the narrator, as well as numerous one-sided apostrophes spoken by the narrator.[44] The broad subject matter of these dialogues may be summarized as follows:

1. J.T. 240–246: on the importance of sexual purity, as opposed to the moral laxity underlying courtly love.[45]
2. J.T. 266: on a detail of the narrative: how can Titurel still be described as a *kint* [child or youth] when he is fifty years old?
3. J.T. 607–611: on whether it is possible simultaneously to possess *gotes hulde* [the favor of God], *selde* [blessedness/good fortune], and *ere* [honor] (as the Grail community apparently does, although Walther von der Vogelweide maintains that this is impossible.)[46]
4. J.T. 665–668: on the pace and direction of the narrative. Is it appropriate for vrou Aventiure to abandon the Grail material in favor of other subject matter (e.g., war)?
5. J.T. 3597–3599: on a detail of narrative technique. Should more attention have been paid to two minor characters, the kings of France and of Navarre?

Is the narrator naive to have apparently forgotten the past misdemeanors of the latter (heathen) king?

6. J.T. 3739–3741 and 3745: on the narrator's weariness and his dissatisfaction with an imminent sorrowful outcome (the death of Secureiz).[47]

7. J.T. 4015–4029: on the opposition between (Christian) *minne* and (heathen) *unminne* and on why *minne* can lead to death in battle.[48]

8. J.T. 5078–5089: on the narrator's dissatisfaction with, and vrou Aventiure's justification of, the imminent death of Tschinotulander.[49]

9. J.T. 5150–5154: on women. Vrou Aventiure protests at the narrator's misogynist assertion that women cry easily and not always sincerely. The narrator points out that he is merely quoting Ovid, that Hartmann painted a worse picture of women and that in any case, some women (such as Sigune) are better than the norm.

10. J.T. 5292–5298: on the direction of the narrative. Is it appropriate to shift focus from the bereavement of Sigune to the predicament of Secundille facing the choice between twenty-five suitors? Vrou Aventiure favors concentrating on Sigune but the narrator wishes to discuss Secundille.

Despite the apparent randomness and triviality of some of the topics addressed, these dialogues all ultimately relate to the interface between didacticism and narrative technique (in other words, between the promulgation of general moral contents, and the appropriate narration of particular "facts").[50] It should be emphasized that the identity of vrou Aventiure is associated uniquely with these particular facts. This is made clear in J.T. 4019–4022. Here, the narrator first reminisces about the way in which this vrou Aventiure has entered his heart as set out in Book 9 of *Parzival* (4019–4020), but then goes on to admit that he has subsequently also played host to a different *aventiure*, namely that of *Willehalm* (4021–4022).[51] The vrou Aventiure appearing in the J.T. is therefore not to be seen as a general goddess of poetry or source of literary inspiration,[52] but as a specific personification of the narrative facts common to *Parzival* and the J.T.[53]

On the most basic level, vrou Aventiure therefore stands for factual accuracy: she is the one who knows what happens next and the narrator openly admits that he derives his information directly from her, as in J.T. 2519,5:

Wie nimt der kampf ein ende?   daz sagt vrou Aventiure.

[How will the battle end? That is for vrou Aventiure to say.]

This technique of factual interrogation of vrou Aventiure is clearly derived from Book 9 of *Parzival*, where the new arrival is greeted with a volley of questions concerning the wellbeing of the hero. In taking this line, the narrators of both works ostensibly play down their own literary contribution (either in terms of creating new facts or in terms of providing a subjective slant on received material): like the audience, they are simply waiting passively to find out what happens next. This idea that the story just "tells itself" is neatly expressed in J.T. 5278,2–4, when the narrator makes common ground with the audience by asking them to join him in making a collective request to vrou Aventiure:

> wie diu magt Sigune chom zu reste
> von ir clage zu der engel singen,
> des biten wir die werden   Aventiur uns an ein ende bringen.

[Let us ask the worthy Aventiure to finish the story about how the maiden Sigune came to rest, moving from a state of lamentation to experiencing the singing of the angels.]

In the J.T., vrou Aventiure not only knows the outcomes, but also determines them. This executive aspect of her role emerges once J.T. 2519 is quoted in full:

> Wie nimt der kampf ein ende?   daz sagt vrou Aventiure.
> wa hin der si gewende,   als Oriluse der arm git di stiure,
> daz hat di aventiur noch gar beslozzen,
> unde wa daz bracken seil beste.   des belibt Sigun an vreuden ungenozzen.

[How does the battle end? That is for vrou Aventiure to say. She is also entirely responsible for the decision as to what turn it is to take when Orilus defends himself, and as to where the Brackenseil is to be found. Therefore Sigune is still bereft of joy.]

In addition to simply knowing and reporting the facts, vrou Aventiure is thus also credited with at least the hypothetical power to alter these facts—a power that brings with it the burden of having to justify the course of events that ultimately becomes fixed within the narrative. The unhappy outcomes in the text are a source of continual conflict between the vrou Aventiure and the narrator, despite the fact that this feature may be thought to contradict the basic identification of this narrator with that of *Parzival*—after all, a narrator who has previously narrated the way in which Parzival comes across Sigune as she is clinging to the corpse of her beloved can hardly be surprised that Tschinotulander does not survive the battle with Orilus. Discussion of the death of Tschinotulander and of other specific outcomes features most prominently in dialogues 6 (J.T. 3739–3741 and 3745) and 8 (J.T. 5078–5089), although the narrator also engages in a wider (futile) campaign to introduce more *vreude* [joy] into the narrative

> wa hin, vrou Aventiur, den wec so ruhen?
> als ich ie zu vreuden   gedenke, so kunnet ir uns von vreuden duhen.
> (J.T. 2688,3–4)

[Where are we going, vrou Aventiure, along this rough road? Just as my thoughts take a happy turn, you manage to push us away from joy.]—

or:

> vrou Aventiur, ir welt nu vreude bannen
> in den herzen, die doch vreude uf erbet.
> (J.T. 4986,2–3)

[vrou Aventiure, you are now trying to ban joy from hearts which have a right to it.]

Notwithstanding the objections of the narrator, she argues that her decisions are not to be regarded as capricious or as hard-hearted, but as informed by two fundamental principles: valid interpretation of moral law and reluctant respect for the admittedly random agency of fortuna within the temporal world.[54]

The uneasy coexistence of these two principles emerges from dialogue 8, when, in response to the narrator's objection to the death of Tschinotulander, she provides two divergent justifications. First, the death of Tschinotulander is said to be just because he was too proud in his pursuit of virtue: nobody should manifest *zevil der ubermaze* (J.T. 5079,4) [too great a lack of moderation] through excessive self-reliance. In other words, the implication is that Tschinotulander dies because he has transgressed against a particular moral law. Secondly, she reiterates the circumstances of the misfortune arising from the loss of the *golt der selden* (J.T. 5087), thereby making the rather different suggestion that he dies because of a chain of events ultimately beyond his control. Although she makes a half-hearted attempt to join these two justifications into one, by saying that somebody who enjoyed as much *selde* as did Tschinotulander ought to have been able to hold on to it (J.T. 5082,1–2), this argument is problematic, given that fortune, at least in the Boethian sense, will sooner or later elude the grasp of all. In any case, both of vrou Aventiure's justifications are underpinned by steely resolution to accept that which is unpalatable and not to be distracted by emotional responses to situations. There is no doubt that she finds the death of Tschinotulander difficult. She feels compassion for him (J.T. 5088,2: *mich jamert siner jugende* [I take pity on his youthfulness]) and acknowledges his many good virtues (J.T. 5088,1). Furthermore, in J.T. 5089,1–2 she not only expresses reluctance to abandon him, but also accepts that she will be vilified on account of his death. Nonetheless, this death cannot be avoided:

> Iz kan sich niht gefu^egen,   daz reht mich dar zu° bindet
> (J.T. 5079,1)

> [It cannot be changed; justice compels me]

The narrator's personal preoccupation with *vreude* [joy] is presented as one manifestation of that 'Wolframian' shallowness which needs to be corrected through the (re)telling of the subject matter under the acerbic tutelage of vrou Aventiure. The 'Wolfram' who likes happy endings, pretty girls, and clear-cut rewards for good fighters is forced to face up to a more austere reality in which moral demands go well beyond those of external courtliness and in which secular happiness is unpredictable, even for the apparently virtuous.

The conceit of vrou Aventiure as an über-narrator speaking through 'Wolfram' privileges the notion of an oral reception of the contents and largely bypasses any notion of engagement with written sources.[55] In Wolfram's *Parzival* there is already a dichotomy between, on the one hand, the image of vrou Aventiure entering directly into the heart of the narrator in order to tell him marvellous stories, and on the other hand, the myth that the narrative is based on perusal of the written word (including both the supposedly faulty version of Chrétien, and the complex and painstaking Grail research undertaken by Flegetanis and Kyot). As Albrecht also subscribes to the transmission myth involving Flegetanis and Kyot, this same dichotomy is imported into the J.T., with knowledge of *aventiure* being, at least in theory, assigned a textual as well as an oral basis:

> Der von Provenzale　　und Flegetanis parlu^e^re
> heidenisch von dem grale　　und franzoys tu°nts kunt vil aventu^e^re.
>
> (J.T. 86,1–2)[56]

[The Provençal and the prophet Flegetanis make many stories about the Grail known to us in the heathen tongue and in French.]

On closer examination, however, it becomes apparent that in contrast with *Parzival* the J.T. very much plays down the importance of Kyot. In the latter work, the mysterious Provençal is primarily seen as a translator (J.T. 86,1–2; 2993,3–4), with no broader influence on the shaping of the narrative. Nor is he cited as the guarantor even of trivial facts: the J.T. contains no equivalent reassurance to that provided in *Parzival* 431,1–2, where it is stated that Kyot himself vouches for the fact that Gawan had breakfast.[57] Albrecht's sole positive innovation with respect to Kyot, namely to associate him with the glossing of certain exotic names (Alberose in 5354; Barbidele in 5355), is consistent with this focus on a narrowly conceived role as translator.[58] Furthermore, to the extent that vrou Aventiure constitutes an embodiment, not only of the facts themselves, but also of the appropriate selection, evaluation, and presentation of these facts, she largely usurps the role occupied by Kyot in *Parzival*, who, according to Wolfram's narrator, not only provided a correct version of the facts, but also gave advice on aspects of the narrative strategy (for example by telling the narrator to withhold information about the Grail until a relatively later point in the text).[59] Given that one tends readily to contrast Wolfram, the promoter of orality over *bu°ch*-culture, with Albrecht, the clerical champion of the written word, it is striking that the J.T. should reduce the status of Kyot in this way, whilst increasing the scope and influence of vrou Aventiure. On one occasion, admittedly, the narrator does refer to a category of facts which, although tangentially relevant to the story, are unknown to vrou Aventiure, because the chronicles have not revealed them to her:

> Di alle wider hinder　　mocht ich niht wol benennen,
> di veter und die kinder,　　so mu^e^st ich di kronik wol bekennen.
> di hatz der aventiure niht entslozzen.
>
> (J.T. 2885,1–3)

[I cannot name all those who came after him, the father and the children. To do so, I would have to know the chronicle well. It has not revealed this to *aventiure*.]

While the reference to *di kronik* coheres with Albrecht's strategy of underpinning the historicity of the narrative,[60] this suggestion of vrou Aventiure's dependency on written sources is curiously at odds with the general impression of her as the ultimate narrative authority. Nonetheless, even this passage, which is exceptional in its foregrounding of written sources, does not mention the figure of Kyot.

The responsibility assumed by vrou Aventiure for matters of aesthetic and moral judgment has consequences for the way in which the J.T. is to be seen as a corrective to *Parzival*. Although it has already been noted that a particular personification of *aventiure* is tied to a particular subject matter (in this case, to *Parzival*/J.T. rather than to *Willehalm*), this principle does not exclude multiple, partially overlapping treatments of this same subject matter, which is precisely what we get with *Parzival* and the J.T. The possibility of multiple narrations of the same material is borne out by Albrecht's formulation

> dirre aventu͞re kere,   si si krump oder slihte
> (J.T. 65,1)

[whether the direction taken by this *aventiure* is crooked or straight].

In other words, the *kere* [narrative or literary direction] of the same *aventiure* might be either *krumb* [crooked], as it supposedly is in *Parzival*, or *sliht* [straight] as in the J.T.[61] However, in either case, the *aventiure* is to be conceived as a woman entirely adorned with moral teaching:

> dirre aventu͞re kere   si si krump oder slihte,
> daz ist nicht wan ein lere.   darumb sol ich si wisen uf di rihte.
> hie vor ist si mit tugenden an gevenget,
> ir houbet, ir brust, ir siten,   ir fu͞ze die sint mit tugenden gar gemenget.
> (J.T. 65)

[Whether the direction taken by this *aventiure* is crooked or straight, the whole thing is nothing but a form of teaching. For that reason I should point her to the straight path. From the outset, she has been swathed in virtues. Her head, her bosom, her sides, her feet are as one with them.][62]

The implication is that if the *kere* is *krumb*, the *lere* which is latent within the narrative material will not be communicated effectively. The J.T. thus constitutes more than just one of the various possible *keren* of the same material: it is presented as the definitive version to which vrou Aventiure lends her authority.

This does raise the question of what, in Albrecht's terms, went wrong last time. If the narrator of *Parzival* did indeed admit the very same vrou Aventiure into his heart (as both he and she seem to agree that he did), then why is the earlier work so flawed, both narratologically and morally? The most natural solution appears to be that on the occasion of her first visit, vrou Aventiure presented him with the facts, but did not provide him with sufficient guidance as to their moral significance, with the result that *Parzival* became tainted with 'Wolfram's' own stubbornly inappropriate attitudes. The Vf can be seen to offer an interesting endorsement of the view that in the works of the historical Wolfram, we do not see enough of vrou Aventiure, either literally or metaphorically. In Vf 16–17, Albrecht compares the *aventiure* of the J.T. to a beautiful woman, saying that it would be deeply unsatisfactory for a man just to catch a glance of her cheek and not to see any more. As the Vf (unlike the J.T.) acknowledges the separate existence of *Titurel*, the analogy in Vf 16–17 could be taken to refer specifically to the fragmentary nature of *Titurel* that is being redressed in the J.T. On the other hand, given the association of vrou Aventiure with *lere*, and given Albrecht's consistently negative attitude to *Parzival*, it could be argued that Vf 16–17 may also be interpreted by reference to that work: although Wolfram had the chance to show us vrou Aventiure in her full didactic splendor, he chose only to give us the most minimal of glimpses. Paradoxically, the moralizing J.T. therefore claims to go further in assuaging its audience's desire for (allegorical) female flesh than does the "immoral" *Parzival*. This eroticizing of moral teaching is part of Albrecht's general strategy of making the virtue *caritas* seem "sexy" by presenting it in terms that one might otherwise associate with secular, or even illicit, love.[63]

In the narration of the J.T., vrou Aventiure assumes a far greater degree of control than did her counterpart in Wolfram's *Parzival*, to an extent that raises questions about the unity of the narratorial voice. On one level, the J.T. explicitly presents itself as Wolfram's *Titurel*, of which entire work 'Wolfram' is supposedly the authorial narrator.[64] On another level, however, it would seem that it is only in the vrou Aventiure dialogues and in certain other excurses that 'Wolfram' speaks unambiguously in his own voice. Otherwise, as Guggenberger would see it, 'Wolfram's' narration is essentially dictated by vrou Aventiure, who in turn transmits the viewpoint of the moralist, Albrecht.[65] While it has been conventional to speak of Albrecht's 'Wolfram'-mask, it may thus, at least in the dialogues, be more appropriate to speak of Albrecht's vrou Aventiure-mask. Of course, there are many portions in the work when the implicit opposition between 'Wolfram' and 'Albrecht' fades into the background. For example, although the prologue to the J.T. contains an extensive paraphrase of the prologue to *Parzival*,[66] combined with statements promising improvement vis-à-vis the earlier work,[67] there is at this point in the text no trace as yet of any tension or discontent on the part of the narrator.[68] Furthermore, as the discussion in chapter 1 of the narrator's references to Ovid has shown, there are occasions when a typically 'Wolframian' (i.e., secular and frivolous) comment can also be taken to represent the position of Albrecht. Finally, whilst the explicit identification of the narrator as 'Wolfram' often serves to highlight the ethical opposition between himself and vrou Aventiure, this is not always the case. For example, in the so-called Kunststrophen (J.T. 499 B–E), when the narrator has just referred to himself in the third person to make the point that he should not be blamed for later textual corruptions—

> her Wolfram si unschuldic,   ein schriber dicke recht unrihtic machet.
>
> (J.T. 499 A,4)

[It should be understood that Lord Wolfram is innocent; a scribe often turns right to wrong.]—

he nonetheless appears to express personal pride in his own capacity to effect appropriate improvements:

> als ich daz ungerihte   an disen lieden han zu rechte gerucket.
>
> (J.T. 499 D,4)

[as I have straightened and corrected that which was wrong with these songs.][69]

Every narratorial *ich*-statement is therefore potentially ambiguous: are we listening to 'Wolfram,' to 'Albrecht,' or to vrou Aventiure? Nonetheless, the ambiguity is not always functional. On many occasions, the contents of the statement matters more than the identity of the *ich* and can be appreciated without precise recourse to the identity of the speaker.

Given that the basic narrative model presented in the text is one whereby the words of vrou Aventiure are funneled through a reluctant 'Wolfram,' there are obvious links to the model of authorship commonly adduced in works of religious revelation in which the human author is presented as a mere tool deployed by God, the ultimate author.[70] To some extent, this is unsurprising, given that in the works of the historical Wolfram, the narrator appears to claim a form of divine inspiration for himself.[71] However, in combining this model of inspiration with the technique of using multiple, potentially ambiguous voices, Albrecht goes well beyond Wolfram: in this respect, at least, the J.T. has more in common with mystical writing (e.g., Mechthild von Magdeburg) than with traditional Arthurian romance.

The domination of 'Wolfram' by vrou Aventiure is made particularly explicit in the first dialogue, when the narrator picks up on what appears to be an earlier statement of hers and asks her for the basis of this claim:

'Ir sagt ouch, daz geuneret   si der touf von minne.
wer hat iuch daz geleret?'

(J.T. 245,1–2)

[You also say that baptism has been dishonored by love. Who taught you that?]

In fact, vrou Aventiure has not, either in the first dialogue or at any earlier stage in the text, made a statement to the effect that baptism has been dishonored by love. The voice that has raised this issue is that of the narrator himself, who, apparently speaking with his own authority in J.T. 226, contrasts the sexual decadence of Christians with the virtue of heathens and Jews, building up to the assertion that *Sus wirt der touf geuneret* (J.T. 227,1) [Baptism is thus dishonored]. The fact that the narrator now apparently needs an explanation for his own previous statement creates the impression that this statement was never really his at all: the story really does "tell itself," with the narrator being reduced to repeating statements that do not necessarily make any sense to him,[72] or with which he actively disagrees. For example, the whole of the first dialogue is occasioned by the narrator's realizing the implication of the strict code of sexual ethics that (s)he has just formulated. He is particularly rattled by the suggestion that courtly love is sinful and therefore detrimental to true knighthood, as he makes clear in the first of many angry protests:

'frow Aventiure, kert widere!   man gihet iuch cleiner volg an dirre lere.

Da mit ist iuch verswachet   ritterschaft unde frowen,
und habet da mit gemachet,   daz wir in lutzel eren kunnen trowen,
die immer reine, ku^esch belibent stæte.
so habt ir si enteret,   und daz u^ech immer stechent valsche græte.'

(J.T. 240,4–241,4)

[Vrou Aventiure, come back! Nobody agrees with you on this. In saying it, you are damaging knighthood and the standing of ladies, and would prevent us from according honorable trust to those who always remain pure, chaste, and faithful. You have thereby dishonored them, so may you always choke on treacherous fish-bones.]

We are thus dealing with an extreme version of the topos of the reluctant narrator. Whilst it is not unusual for narrators of secular works to point out either that the process of narration is by its very nature burdensome, or that particular outcomes may be painful to narrate, this narrator is in the uniquely humiliating situation of having to complete a task that is not only tiring and distressing,[73] but which also involves articulating an ascetic ethos that runs counter to his own world view.

Although vrou Aventiure manages to dominate the narrator through force of argument and personality, there is no definitive sense in which the narrator is ever really won over to her point of view. Of course, given that this distinctive 'Wolfram'-voice is identifiable largely through its articulation of discontent and moral dissent, such a conversion would arguably be difficult to detect. Nonetheless, one could imagine a development whereby 'Wolfram' eventually recants his former errors, and, still in his own distinctive voice, thanks vrou Aventiure for her patience and forbearance. However, not only does no such recantation take place, but we do not even note a fading of the dissident 'Wolfram'-voice that might have provided indirect evidence of this narrator's assimilation of the values of vrou Aventiure. On the contrary, in the dialogues that occur late in the narrative, after the death of Tschinotulander, the defiant narrator has lost none of his energy and even enjoys more autonomy than in the earlier stages. Although there is no final resolution, this resurgence of his 'Wolframian' personality possibly serves as a marker of final compromise: he may have failed to prevent the death of Tschinotulander, but he does score a few small points. In the ninth dialogue, as has already been mentioned, he gets away with invoking Ovid as an authority (notwithstanding vrou Aventiure's stated views on Ovidian love). The tenth dialogue even grants him a rare outright triumph. For once, his wishes for fun to prevail over vrou Aventiure's didacticism: although it is consistent with her rejection of heathen *unminne* not to want to engage at length with Secundille's love-life, he persuades her to do so, on the grounds that Feirefiz, the suitor whom she ultimately chooses, is related to Parzifal and thus important for the story as a whole (including, by implication, the future of the Grail).

The uneasy nature of this working relationship is continually highlighted by expressions of frustration and hostility: he complains of her cruelty and high-handedness, while she focuses on his discourtesy, disrespect, and lack of understanding. Although the didactic slant suggests a connection to the genre of the 'Lehrgespräch' [didactic dialogue] as well as to that of the 'Streitgespräch' [disputation], the reluctance of this pupil is such that he has very little in common with the *discipuli* of closed 'Lehrgespräche' such as the *Lucidarius*,[74] and more with the human protagonists of dialogue texts such as *De consolatione philosophiae* and *Der Ackermann aus Böhmen*, in which a certain clash of outlooks and personalities is central to the overall dynamics.[75]

Like the contestants of many Streitgespräche, 'Wolfram' and vrou Aventiure are codependent, deriving their individual contours and identities only through the articulation of conflict. Neither entity is entirely autonomous: as in any dialogue between a human being and an allegorical authority figure, it is natural to assume that this dialogue is located within the inner space of the human being's psyche and that, at least on one level, he is talking to himself.[76] Furthermore, in this case, the two are also functionally dependent on each other: *aventiure* needs a narrator and vice versa. The conflict under discussion is therefore indebted not only to the image in *Parzival* of the habitable heart, but also to the broad traditions of *psychomachia* and, above all, of debates between body and soul, the latter featuring the inseparable conjunction of two very different entities who regard each other as both friend and foe.[77] On this account, the wise, morally superior, and, above all, intangible vrou Aventiure would fulfil the role of the soul, whereas the more confused and earthy narrator approximates to the body: the mouth or hand who puts the narrative into a form in which it can be received by others. This being said, vrou Aventiure does not just reduce to a part of 'Wolfram,' any more than Philosophy only exists within Boethius, or Death within the Ploughman: all three allegorical entities also reflect a broader reality existing independently of the human interlocutor.

This ambiguity regarding the individuation of these two figures is expressed most clearly through the use of two contrasting metaphorical clusters, both of which relate to the spatial presentation of 'Wolfram' and vrou Aventiure. The first cluster hints that the conjunction between the two figures is so intimate that boundaries of identity becomes blurred and they almost reduce to a single entity. The sense of conjunction is strengthened by the fact that this entity is presented in motion, traveling through a narratological landscape in search of fresh *aventiuren*: space is therefore something that surrounds it as a whole, rather than something that comes between the two conjoined figures. By contrast, the second metaphorical cluster presents the pair from a settled and sedentary angle, with architectural images—including that of the house built by vrou Aventiure—being used to suggest multiple levels of distance and separation within the relationship.

The first cluster, indicating the quasi-physical conjunction of 'Wolfram' and vrou Aventiure, features in dialogue 4. When the narrator protests at the fact that vrou Aventiure seems to be in a hurry to abandon the temple and the Grail in favor of different *meren* [tales], she counters that she is inseparable from him. Where she goes, he must follow:

> Friunt, ich bin hie varende   nicht wan in dinem geleite,
> swie daz du gen mir sparnde   bist din kurteise und din werdicheite.
> (J.T. 666,1–2)

> [My friend, I do not travel other than in your company, even though you are very sparing toward me as far as courtesy and honorable treatment are concerned.]

Here, the narrator's disorientation (J.T. 2688,3–4), his request that they turn back (J.T. 240,4 and 3738,1) and his bitter complaint that vrou Aventiure is leading him astray (J.T. 3732,4) are all to no avail.[78] At this point, one is reminded of a very different partnership of conjoined objects, namely that of hound and Brackenseil. However, whereas Gardivias notoriously runs wild with the text, in complete disregard of the adage *hu^e te der verte*, vrou Aventiure insists that her choice of route is appropriate,[79] even if it leads to war.

The issue of war, first raised in dialogue 4, causes particular difficulty between the narrator and vrou Aventiure. As well as expressing outright distaste for the topic of warfare (e.g., J.T. 4690,1–2), 'Wolfram' also resorts to using traditional topoi of literary inadequacy as a way of marking his unwillingness to cooperate with vrou Aventiure. Thus he claims to be unable to do justice to battle scenes (J.T. 1568,1; 1626,1–3; 4098), complains that *di aventiur* is not giving him proper guidance about what to say (J.T. 4097), and suggests that points of detail are in any case irrelevant:

> Mich wil diu aventiure   urliuges niht erlazen.
> so gib ich ir zestiure,   daz ich mich der umbe rede wol mazen
> kan, die man in strite kondiwieret:
> vergizze ich ir zimiere,   daz wirret niht, si waren rich gezieret.
>
> (J.T. 4617)

> [Aventiure will not let me get away from battles. I can tell her that I am all too able to limit the kinds of descriptions which one gives of battles: they were all richly dressed, so it does not matter if I forget their individual finery.]

In fact, the heraldic beasts adorning the knights are not irrelevant: as has been shown in chapter 2, these beasts can be subjected to allegorical interpretation and therefore form a basis for Albrecht's *lere*. In adopting this sulky stance toward his task of describing warfare, 'Wolfram' is not just being idiosyncratically soft-hearted, but is in fact seeking to sabotage part of the didactic program determined by 'Albrecht' and vrou Aventiure. The theme of the literary discussion of armed conflict may thus be seen as a 'mise en abyme' for the broader ethical and narratological differences between the two.

It is also in this context that architectural metaphors become significant. According to vrou Aventiure (J.T. 667,3), the narrator presents her as a destructive warmonger with an appetite for robbing and stealing. She appears initially to rebut this charge (J.T. 668,4: *des wirt ouch selten hus von mir enzundet* [I also do not burn down houses]), but later acknowledges the necessity of some collateral damage: when the narrator argues that it is wrong to destroy a land that been painfully built up (J.T. 3738,3–4), she retorts that *muren* [rebuilding] can come later, once the *niderbrechen* [tearing down] has been completed. The charge of destructiveness applies not only to the literal course of events (in the sense that vrou Aventiure's decision to introduce armed conflict into the story means that the narrative will inevitably feature damage to property and loss of lives), but also to the allegorical level on which vrou Aventiure's own house constitutes a poetological metaphor for the literary edifice.[80] According to the narrator, this literary edifice stands to suffer on two accounts: intradiegetically through the elimination of key characters, and (as is made clear in dialogue 7) extradiegetically through the destruction of that loving harmony which, as he sees it, is still fundamentally characteristic of his relationship with vrou Aventiure.

The narrator, however, appears to be wrong about the status of this bond with vrou Aventiure. As Hirschberg has noted, the vrou Aventiure in the J.T. differs from her counterpart (or former self) in *Parzival*, in that she no longer chooses to dwell directly in the narrator's heart, but has built herself a separate house, albeit one that is still close enough for her to keep an eye on what he is doing.[81] The narrator, by contrast, still subscribes to the belief that he constitutes her base and that by disagreeing with him, she will ultimately harm herself:

> Sit habt ir iuch geliebet   dem herzen min so vaste,
> swie oft ir von mir schiebet   gemach, iedoch so wolt ich iur ze gaste
> nicht wandel han in mines herzen cluse.
> ob ir mich danne krenket,   dast ein heimsu^{e}ch iwerm swachen huse.
>
> (J.T. 4020)

[Since then you availed yourself extensively of my heart. However often you make life uncomfortable for me, I would not want to lose you as a guest in the cell of my heart. If you damage me there, you will be attacking your own defenceless house.]

Vrou Aventiure does not give in to this kind of blackmail: protagonists are dispensable if the narrative requires it, while the earlier reference that she has made to the separate existence of her own house (J.T.4017,2) preempts the entire argument of J.T. 4020.

The primary function of vrou Aventiure's own house is, as Hirschberg suggests, to create distance between herself and the narrator.[82] He is not an appropriate base for her—indeed, his very failure to notice that she has moved out, and moved on, is in itself indicative of his lack of insight. Given his short-comings, she cannot manage him properly if she is snuggled lover-like in his heart. Similarly, there is no evidence of him having access to her house. As a brief illustration of how the building of an allegorical house can be undertaken in a very different spirit, one need only consider the mystical *In-principio-Dialog*, a harmonious Lehrgespräch in which the master is urged to use the *gezeu^{e}ge* [tools] of dialogue in order to build a spiritual *hav^{e}selein* [little house] for his disciple rather than for himself.[83]

Whilst metaphors of house-building are almost infinite in their variety, the reference to the house of vrou Aventiure does strengthen the thematic link between her and the Old Testament figure of Wisdom, who also, famously, builds a house (in this case, one with seven pillars; cf. Prov. 9.1). As Newman has shown, "the Wisdom of the sapiential books is a powerful, iridescent character: street preacher, prophet, Temple priestess, daughter and counselor or God, creatrix of the world, all-pervading spirit, celestial bride of sages and philosopher-kings,"[84] who becomes incorporated into medieval literature as "the most protean of goddesses."[85] In terms of personality, obvious points of similarity between Wisdom and vrou Aventiure include their authoritative modes of address, didactic nature of their discourse, their itinerant life-styles,[86] and their hostility to loose sexual morals. In particular, Albrecht's strategy of using rhetorical devices (such as personification) in order to make Christian virtue seem more enticing than secular Minne, parallels the way in which Ecclesiasticus "employed the erotic allure of Sophia to compete with the popular hellenistic cult of Isis."[87]

In addition to these similarities in the constructed personalities of the two figures (both are strict and bossy), there is evidence to suggest that Albrecht intended a more fundamentally sapiential reading of vrou Aventiure. In this context, strophe

65 from the prologue (quoted above), which presents the image of a woman entirely bedecked with virtues, has been adduced to suggest that the poet's creation of *aventiure* parallels God's creation of the cosmos.[88] Whilst this strophe certainly makes it clear that Albrecht sees vrou Aventiure as a personification of *lere* as well as merely of narrative facts, a stronger case for a sapiential reading may be made on the basis of a later excursus on the value of literature. Here an explicit connection is made between the moral benefits to be derived from fiction and the part played by Wisdom in the creation of the world:

> Aller selden beste   wirt us kunt von mæren.
> immer vremde geste   wir sam ein vih der ganzen tugende weren.
> sus chenne wir daz ubel und daz guͤte.
> der tumbe tuͦt daz boͤse,   dem guͦten volget ie der witze vruͤte.
>
> 'Ich half den himel machen',   diu wisheit sich des ruͤmet.
> mit seldenrichen sachen   werdent si gekroͤnet und gebluͤmet
> alle, die ir muot nach wisheit stellent.
> zehimel und uf erden   zem besten sich die wisen gesellent.
>
> So sprichet meister være   und meister wider strite,
> ditz si ein lugemære   und tribe niht wan toren zaller zite.
> iz mache herzen irre und ouch unstæte.
> si sint, di selbe liegent   und wurgent mit ir valsche sam die græte.
>
> (2949–2951)

[The essence of blessedness is made known to us through stories. Without them, we would always be like animals, utter strangers to virtue. Through them we know wickedness and goodness. The foolish man acts wickedly, the excellence of good sense always keeps close to the good man.

"I helped to make the heavens," Wisdom says proudly. All those who aspire to wisdom will be crowned and garlanded with the tokens of blessedness. In heaven and on earth, the wise keep the very best company.

Some ill-intentioned and hostile masters claim that this tale is made of lies and will only ever appeal to fools. It supposedly turns hearts wild and giddy. But they are the ones who lie and with their falseness they choke you like a fishbone.][89]

These three strophes present a dense web of associations that blur the boundaries between human and divine creativity. The first and most prominent strand of the argument presents fiction as *integumentum* and implicitly endorses the theoretical framework established by Thomasin von Zirclaria in a much more famous passage.[90] While the J.T. does not go as far as to cast serious doubt on the historical accuracy of its own narrative, this strand of the argument makes it clear that the fundamental "truth-value" of this and other Arthurian *aventiuren* does not hinge on the narrative facts themselves, but rather on the interpretation of these facts. A second strand then suggests a connection between the moral insights communicated through *meren*, and the overall ethos of the sapiential books of the Old Testament, in which direct moral instruction is provided by the personification of Wisdom. Finally, a third strand picks up the Old Testament image of this figure as a creatrix sharing with God the responsibility for the existence of the cosmos.[91]

This overall argument enables Albrecht to foreground the topos whereby literary output is seen as an analogon for the divinely created cosmos. It also provides a crucial link between what might otherwise look like a series of unrelated architectural images: Wisheit forms the structure of the heavens; Wisdom and vrou Aventiure build themselves appropriate houses; the narrator and vrou Aventiure both deploy metaphors of *muren* and *niderbrechen* for their common literary enterprise; Titurel builds a temple that is both a real object and an allegory for the bodies of readers of the J.T. who now house the Grail within themselves;[92] and in the Vf, Albrecht, speaking in his authorial voice, compares his task to that of the builders completing the unfinished basilica of St Mark in Venice.[93]

That is not to say that these various building images map directly on to each other. For example, while it is relatively common to represent the created cosmos as a house,[94] the house built by Wisdom in Prov. 9.1 is traditionally interpreted by reference to the Incarnation,[95] and not by reference to her role as cosmic creatrix. Similarly, it is not entirely clear how vrou Aventiure's own house relates to the broader building project on which she is working together with the narrator; and above all, the building image in the Vf differs from the others by virtue of its focus on the finishing of somebody else's interrupted undertaking. Nonetheless, despite these interpretational mismatches, the architectural imagery in the J.T. points to a distinctive twofold poetological strategy: not only is the production of the text presented (somewhat unremarkably) as an act of cosmological creation, but, more unusually, its guiding principle, vrou Aventiure, is also cast in the mould of Sapientia, the Old Testament dispenser of moral instruction.

This sapiential approach to the term *aventiure* may account for an apparent inconsistency in Albrecht's handling of the Brackenseil. In Wolfram's *Titurel*, it is never made clear what is written on the leash, but the assumption is that the discourse is narrative, not least because Sigune justifies her desire for the retrieval of the leash with the words *da stuont aventiure an der strangen* (*Titurel* 170,1) [there was *aventiure* written on the leash]. In the equivalent scene in J.T., Sigune also invokes the concept of *aventiure*—

> Solch aventiur ist wesende   geschriben an der strangen.
> (J.T. 1215,1)

[such *aventiure* is written on the leash.]—

even though the Brackenseil text is ultimately shown to be non-narrative.[96] Of course, this inconsistency cannot be explained away simply by saying that for Albrecht, *aventiure* means "wisdom" rather than "a story": the young, courtly Sigune is speaking at this point, and we have no reason to suppose that she would use the term *aventiure* in such an unusual manner.[97] On another level, however, the fact that the statement in J.T. 1215,1 only becomes unambiguously true if one mentally replaces *aventiure* with *wisheit*, may be read as a polemical assertion of the pre-eminence of *lere*: if what ultimately makes stories (*aventiuren*) worthwhile is their *lere*, then one could, theoretically, dispense with the narrative material altogether and change the meaning of the term *aventiure* so that it no longer refers to that which is contingent and unnecessary (the facts), but rather to that which is essential (the *lere* itself).

It does not follow from such an assertion of the pre-eminence of *lere* that texts will necessarily be "better" for being non-narrative. As was discussed in chapter 3, the Brackenseil inscription features unexceptionable *lere* but is nonetheless problematic for all sorts of reasons (the erotic context of its composition; the use of the jewels; the association with the hound). In other words, it is clearly authored by the fallible Clauditte herself, rather than having been dictated by vrou Aventiure. The latter is in any case content to work through narrative material, as is made clear by her involvement in the creation of the J.T.

Nonetheless, this raises the fundamental question of how textual *lere* is best disseminated: given the multiple risks and shortcomings affecting the written word, how is Albrecht able to sustain the two key claims made through the narrator(s) to the effect that i) stories generally impart virtue and ii) the J.T. specifically is the greatest of German books, capable of imparting salvation to all who come into contact with it (J.T. 6327)?[98] This problem of establishing the criteria on the basis of which 'Albrecht' believes himself able to distinguish his own text (which he presents as morally and aesthetically effective) from the flawed outputs of the protagonists and of 'Wolfram' will be addressed in chapter 5.

CHAPTER 5

JUSTIFYING THE TEXT: THE POETOLOGICAL PROGRAM

Nu pruᵉfet, alle werden,   die wirde dises bu°ches!
von duᵉtscher zung uf erden   nie getichte wart so werdes ru°ches,
daz lib und sele so hoch gen wirde wiset,
alle, di iz hoᵉren, lesen oder schriben,   der sele muᵉze werden geparadiset.

(J.T. 6327)

[Now let all worthy people judge the worth of this book. No poem spoken on earth by a German tongue was ever composed of such worthy concerns, pointing body and soul so well toward worthiness that the souls of all who hear, or read, or copy it, must attain paradise.]

In ending his work with such a hyperbolic celebration of its salvatory qualities, Albrecht is doing more than merely preconditioning a positive reception: he is making a theoretical claim about the redemptive potential of textuality and hence about the benefits of literacy.

The previous chapters have shown that for the most part, the J.T. promulgates a negative view of human writing, regardless of whether the texts in question are composed by the characters within its own narrative, by canonical authors from classical antiquity, or by the historical Wolfram von Eschenbach. The work offers its recipients a succession of intra- and extradiegetic case studies that cumulatively amount to a blanket condemnation of textual activity on the part of human beings. At best, texts are materially fragile and liable to be lost or misunderstood; at worst, they are morally corrosive. However, even as it engages critically with its own written medium, the J.T. presents itself as the great exception to the norm. This final chapter aims to identify the grounds on which the J.T. seeks to justify the claim that it represents a unique and fundamentally different form of writing.

In order to justify this claim, the J.T. needs specifically to distinguish itself not only from the flawed textual outputs of Clauditte and of 'Wolfram,' but also from the rest of Middle High German literature. Accordingly, section I of this chapter discusses the explicit references made in the J.T. to other literary works and genres.[1]

It is impossible entirely to dissociate the specific 'Wolfram'-polemic from a wider discussion of how the J.T. relates to the genre of courtly Arthurian romance. This is not least because the perceived faults of 'Wolfram' are largely shared by other writers within the same genre: if *Parzival* is unacceptably worldly, despite its distinctive religious element,[2] the same must surely apply to *Erec* and *Iwein*, not to mention *Lanzelet*.[3] However, notwithstanding the fact that the handling of 'Wolfram' ought logically to entail a fundamental repudiation of the genre and its values, the J.T. is ambivalent rather than hostile in its engagement with other courtly romances. On the one hand, it approaches them competitively and even rapaciously (at least as far as the appropriation and reevaluation of protagonists is concerned). On the other hand, however, it seeks to distance itself from them by reference to two criteria: a concern for historicity and an insistence on the importance of the "learned" tradition, particularly with respect to natural phenomena, as the basis for Christian teaching. Given the enthusiasm with which the J.T. presents its audience with points of information about the world and then subjects these points to moral interpretation, one may form the impression that this kind of overt didacticism must constitute the corner stone of any claim to literary preeminence or salvatory potential.

Nonetheless, as will be pointed out in section II, it is surprisingly difficult to distil the didactic essence of the work from the body of narrative complications and narratorial digressions. Although on one level, the work operates with a straightforwardly reductionist morality ("Be pure," "Shun the world," etc.), it also appears to celebrate the splendor of the Arthurian world and promises to impart its audience with courtly values. The assessment of Tschinotulander is particularly problematic: is he a model of virtue to be emulated, or does he encapsulate the shallow and secular stance that characterizes many of the courtly characters?

To some extent, of course, the interpretative open-endedness of the J.T. is a feature that it shares with many postclassical Arthurian romances. As Haug has pointed out, the interpretational framework of symbolic structure is no longer applicable to postclassical romances that have dispensed with the central crisis suffered by the hero—with the result that individual scenes become ambivalent, interpretable on their own terms in a variety of different ways, rather than by reference to the crisis, as would have been the case in earlier texts.[4] For this reason alone, the career of Tschinotulander will be more difficult to interpret than that of Erec or Iwein. However, whereas according to Haug, the J.T. addresses this interpretative deficiency through the imposition of a new, moralizing framework onto the *aventiure*,[5] this study will argue that this is only one part of the literary process: the J.T. certainly moralizes, but it also appears to take an almost perverse pleasure in undercutting its own didactic program through the use of spurious promises, ambiguous exempla,[6] and the voice of an unreliable narrator. This should not be taken as evidence of incompetent teaching, but rather as a recognition of the limits of didacticism: whilst didactic intentions are regarded as valuable and as serving to some extent to lift the J.T. above its rivals, it does not follow that Albrecht regards such intentions as sufficient to actualize the full positive potential of the written word.

Instead of basing its special claim purely on the didactic intentions of the authorial persona, the J.T. does so by recourse to the divine: only God's involvement in the authorial project can "redeem" the fallibility of the written word so as to make a text capable of effecting a lasting and beneficial impact on its recipients. An argument of this kind is inevitably predicated on the assumption that the authorial intentions are in any case impeccably devout (since God is unlikely to wish to work through, for example, an Ovidian reprobate), but it is important to note that the success of the project is not attributable only to the authorial state of mind.

As section III will show, Albrecht's harnessing of the divine works on the level of poetological metaphor rather than on that of pseudo-autobiography: whilst his authorial persona does not make any claims to have received divine inspiration or revelation, certain bold parallels are drawn between the way in which he operates through his text and the ways in which God engages with humankind through the creation and through the sacraments.

Poetological analogies with the creation and with the sacraments form the two stages of Albrecht's argument. Whilst general analogies between the creative output of God and poet are conventional in the Middle Ages, this topos receives a particular twist in the J.T., given the cosmological and poetological status of the Grail temple within the narrative. The implication is that just as God and Titurel work in unison to produce the temple—a physical object representing the whole world—so God and the authorial narrator work together to produce the text, a microcosmic representation of the universe. Here, the heathen figure of Khusro,[7] whose architectural representation of the cosmos seeks to challenge God, provides a useful contrast both to Titurel and to the authorial narrator.

In the context of such a model of an authorial partnership between God and human agent, the J.T.'s use of two narrators (one morally irreproachable, the other less so) is unusual and potentially problematic. Whilst the opposition between the worldly 'Wolfram' and the pious 'Albrecht' underscores the fact that the latter is indeed worthy of forming part of a joint undertaking with God, a proper explanation of how 'Wolfram' too might be accommodated within the poetological model can only be provided by reference to Albrecht's conception of sacramental writing and to his willingness to create new analogies based on the interpretation of natural phenomena.

Section I: The Position of the J.T. in MHG Literature

The fact that the closing strophe of the J.T. includes a specific reference to the German language (J.T. 6327,2) not only signals a desire to mark the position of the J.T. within Middle High German literature but also directs the audience to approach the work with a particular awareness of intertextual relationships. To some extent, this directive is redundant: given the central importance played by complex manipulation of the narrator based on Wolfram von Eschenbach, any recipient who has not been reading the work "against" *Parzival* will have missed the point so entirely that no last-minute hint will make the slightest difference. However, the blanket reference to works composed in the German tongue suggests that the basis for comparison and contrast extends well beyond the works of Wolfram, or even those of other well-established Arthurian authors.

The case for examining the way in which the work positions itself within a wider system of vernacular literary expression is supported by the fact that J.T. makes explicit reference, not only to Arthurian figures and models, but also to authors and protagonists associated with more remote genres, such as the lyric, the *chanson de geste* and the heroic epic. The assessment of these references is further complicated by the fact that the narration is mediated almost entirely by 'Wolfram.' Given that extensive intertextual cross-referencing is a hallmark of the work of the historical Wolfram, the question arises as to whether similar practices in the J.T. should not be seen primarily as the evocation of a Wolfram-mannerism, rather than as evidence of Albrecht's own reflection on how the J.T. relates to the Arthurian tradition or even to other genres. For example, when 'Wolfram' taunts his predecessor Hartmann on the occasion of Erek's defeat at the hands of Tschinotulander—

Her Hartman von Owe,   nu sprecht, daz iu gevalle
Enite iur werden vrowe,   der dienær mu°z hie slichen sam si alle
(J.T. 4596,1–2)

[Lord Hartmann von Aue, now say how pleased you are with Enite, your noble lady, whose servant now has to slink away like the rest of them]—

even the rhyme *Owe/vrowe* echoes the opening of the famous apostrophe to Hartmann in *Parzival*, in which the narrator goes on to threaten to slander his rival's characters (especially Enite and her mother) if the new hero Parzival is not welcomed at the Arthurian court:

mîn hêr Hartman von Ouwe
vrou Ginovêr iuwer vrouwe
und iuwer hêrre der künc Artûs,
den kumt ein mîn gast ze hûs.
(*Parzival* 143,21–24)

[My lord Hartmann von Aue, your lord and lady, King Artus and Queen Ginover, will be receiving in their house a new arrival sent by me.]

Although the J.T. never goes as far as to launch a personal attack on Enite,[8] figures such as Erec and Laudine, who have already been singled out for criticism in *Parzival*, are treated with blunt hostility. In *Parzival* 134,12 the achievements of the absent Erec are indirectly relativized through Orilus' boast of having defeated the latter at Karnant.[9] However, the J.T. goes further in that it actually shows the defeat and disgrace of Hartmann's heroic knight: once on the bridge that form a test of virtue, and once when he is misguidedly fighting with Orilus against the forces of Artus.[10] In both cases, there is a clear-cut opposition between him and the victorious Tschinotulander. Similarly, whereas in *Parzival*, Laudine's willingness to take Lunete's faithless advice is merely criticized in a narratorial aside (J.T. 436,4–10), the J.T. provides Laudine with an intradiegetic erotic prehistory that supports the view that she is lacking in *triuwe*. Although Laudine is initially presented as the beloved of Yblet (J.T. 1344), no more is heard of this association after he has been defeated by Tschinotulander. Instead, her name is shortly afterward linked with that of Ascalun (J.T. 1644), who will ultimately be defeated and killed by Iwein (as J.T. 1645 reminds us). This detail implicitly underscores Laudine's flightiness, as manifested in her readiness to move on from the weaker to the apparently stronger man. Finally, toward the end of the work, the moral inadequacy of Laudine is presented as an undisputed fact, to be evoked in the ninth dialogue with vrou Aventiure: when the latter berates 'Wolfram' for his apparent misogyny, he defends himself with the claim that Hartmann's creation of Laudine constitutes a far greater slur on womankind (J.T. 5151–5153), notwithstanding the fact that Laudine's "badness" has been enhanced through additional narrative details that are unique to the J.T.

Just as this strategy of discrediting the characters of Hartmann may be seen as an amplification of the narratorial stance adopted in *Parzival*, so many of the references to non-Arthurian works also reflect the readiness of the historical Wolfram to integrate a common literary frame of reference into the implicit dialogue between narrator and audience. When the experiences of Witege are cited as a standard of suffering (J.T. 3408,4), this matches equivalent short allusions in *Parzival* and in *Willehalm*,[11] while invocations of Heinrich von Veldeke (as an expert on love), and of the Spruchdichter Walther von der Vogelweide (as a moral authority) also have their approximate counterparts in that work.[12] Similarly, the reference to *Runzevale* (J.T. 1711,1) should be understood within the context of the *Willehalm* complex: the *Rolandslied* is being evoked in its function as a pre-text for Wolfram, rather than as a representative of a different genre.

Nonetheless, the function of intertextual references goes beyond that of endowing the narrator with recognizable 'Wolfram'-features, or even that of demonstrating the credentials of the protagonists. It follows logically from the strongly Christian, ascetic orientation of the J.T. that this text should ultimately position itself in opposition, not only to its immediate Arthurian predecessors, but to all worldly literature. As far as the Arthurian material is concerned, there is indeed ample evidence pointing to Albrecht's subversion of the traditional courtly romance, both on the level of narrative facts (e.g., Artus and Ginover ultimately leave the courtly world behind in order to enter the monastic life) and on the level of interpretation (see for example the allegorization of Arthur's May-time celebrations discussed in chapter 2, section II). At the same time, Albrecht's engagement with the genre is also marked by a certain ambivalence of purpose: whilst his ultimate aim may involve the effective dismantling of the genre, there is also a level on which he seems concerned to outperform his rivals on their own terms. His predicament is comparable to that of the author of *Der saelden hort*, another work that sits on the cusp of secular and religious writing. Despite being informed by a strict ascetic ethos commensurate with its subject matter, this text explicitly aspires toward a courtly style of writing which, by outshining that of *Wigalois* and *Tristan*, will make spiritual contents palatable for a worldly audience.[13]

Many of Albrecht's intertextual references are subordinated to this purpose of presenting the J.T. as a "bigger and better" Arthurian romance. A primary strategy involves the appropriation of figures from other works: these figures may only play a very peripheral part in the J.T., but the fact that Yblis (from *Lanzelet*) or Larie (from *Wigalois*) appear at all implies that the source works have in a sense been colonized and subordinated into the larger-scale project of the J.T. Similar considerations may explain the fact that in the J.T., unlike in *Parzival*, Erek, Enite, and Laudine are in fact fully integrated minor characters with "walk-on" parts. In J.T. 1745,4, Albrecht also expands the intradiegetic Arthurian world to include the Amelungen and the Huns familiar from the heroic epic, thereby taking a small but decisive step toward that syncretic approach to genre that characterizes later romances in general,[14] and of which the *Göttweiger Trojanerkrieg* constitutes an extreme example.[15]

The appropriation of characters from other works also plays an important part in establishing relative chronologies and thereby contributes to the sense of historicity underpinning the J.T.[16] To some extent, a concern with chronological detail, and ultimately with historicity, is fundamental to the overall development of the Arthurian tradition. As Green has argued, the evolution of the fictional Arthurian world may have been driven by *horror vacui* regarding the gaps (which Green calls "weiße Flecken" or blank spots) in earlier romances and ultimately in historical accounts.[17] A passing reference by Geoffrey of Monmouth to a twelve-year period of peace within the Arthurian reign triggered a sequence of responses: Wace first introduced the notion of what one might call recreational chivalry; Chrétien invented further specific incidents that might have happened in that time; Hartmann addressed certain gaps within Chrétien's narratives and Wolfram reacted in a similar way to Hartmann.[18] Whilst Green does not mention the J.T. in this context, Albrecht's overall project of tidying up the loose ends in *Parzival* fits this pattern exactly, with the comprehensive appropriation of courtly characters into the J.T. contributing to the imposition of an overarching chronological order on the genre. For example, Tschinotulander's first appearance at Arthur's court can be pinpointed in relation to Hartmann's works: it happens after the marriage of Erec and Enite, but before Laudine has even been betrothed to Ascalun. In view of this, and of the erotic prehistory ascribed to Laudine, the J.T. may be seen to serve as a prequel, not only to *Parzival*, but also to *Iwein*. This may in turn be read as further evidence of Albrecht's attempt to absorb earlier works into his own larger-scale undertaking.

However, notwithstanding the way in which the genre as a whole is ultimately rooted in history, an explicit commitment to historicity is also one of the key ways in which Albrecht seeks to distinguish his work from all other Arthurian texts written in German.[19] One aspects of this commitment relates to the presentation of the Grail family. *Parzival* already highlights the importance played by chronicles in the Grail researches undertaken by Kyot.[20] The J.T., however, is more thorough and far-reaching in its historical anchoring: by tracing the Grail family back as far as Troy, it establishes a intergeneric link to the 'Antikenroman' and to historiographical texts that focus on concepts of *translatio*. Furthermore, as will be argued in section III, Albrecht also appears to draw on Otte's *Eraclius*, a historicizing work recounting the way in which the Emperor Heraclius wins back the Cross from the Persian King Khusro and restores it to Jerusalem.[21] Albrecht's interest in history may also be illustrated by reference to his perspective on Arthur. In one striking passage, it is maintained that all other (fictional) German works have misrepresented Artus and that the proper account survives only in Latin chronicles:[22]

Swie lutzel man iz sagende   si in duᵉtscher schrifte,
so pflac er unversagende   ellenthaftes mu°ts, er wunder stifte.
ein roᵉmisch keiser lak von im erstorben
an risen und ane tracken: daran hat Artus wirde vil erworben.

Der die bu°ch der hugede   lesen wil latine,
der hatz fur kein getrugede.   die sagent war vil mange wirde sine,
kronik zeBritanje und Kornevale.
von dannen was er burtik,   von vater und von mu°ter sunder twale.
                              (J.T. 4077–4078)

[However little is said of this in German texts, he was ceaselessly courageous and wrought wonders. A Roman emperor lay dead by his hand, without any giants or dragons being involved. Artus earned great honor from this.

Whoever is prepared to read the "books of memory" in Latin will know that this is no deception.[23] Without hesitation, they tell his many honors, these chronicles of Brittany and Cornwall, whence he was born and of his father and mother.]

By thus rejecting the traditional notion that the Arthurian world is one of forests, dragons, and giants, the J.T. presents itself as a corrective to those works in which Artus' domains are bordered by various kinds of otherworlds, and Artus himself serves as a static arbiter of courtliness. Instead, Albrecht presents him (for all his other faults) as a dynamic military leader engaged in conflict with the political reality of Roman Empire.

The implicit suggestion in J.T. 4077,4 that giants and dragons are somehow historically unsound may seem surprising in a work that abounds with anthropological and zoological exotica and in which even emblematic dragons appear to possess some of the powers of their real equivalents.[24] However, Albrecht's objection relates not to giants and dragons *per se*, but rather to the context in which they are presented. In the J.T., exotic creatures provide Albrecht the opportunity both to display his knowledge of scientific *realia*, and to subject them to Christian interpretation. With the possible exception of the works of Wolfram, such a dual approach runs counter to the ways in which monsters and monstrous peoples are normally functionalized in Middle High German narratives: even in the works of Hartmann, in which giants and dragons represent the evil that the hero must overcome, their symbolic value is largely dependent on their position within the narrative, without any discussion of the scientific basis of their existence or any general Christian reflections on their function within creation. In short, these creatures are presented within a popular, vernacular tradition, rather than a learned, Latin one, paying implicit tribute to authorities such as Pliny, Solinus, and Isidore. On the basis that history, science, and allegory form a seamless continuum, the J.T. claims to transcend all works that incorporate exotic *realia* without appropriate discussion.

This view is borne out by J.T. 3364, in which Siegfried's bathing in dragon's blood forms the basis for a polemical rejection of the truth-value of the heroic epic:

> So singent uns die blinden,   daz Sifrit hurnin were,
> durch daz er uber winden   kund ouch einen tracken vreisebære,
> von des bluᵒte wurd sin vel verwandelt
> in horne stark fur wapen.   di habent sich der warheit missehandelt.
>
> (J.T. 3364)

[So the blind ones sing to us that Siegfried became scaly from the fact that he was able to slay a fierce dragon; his skin was changed by its blood into strong horn-like scales which served in place of armor. Those who say this have not told the truth.]

If read in isolation, this strophe might give the impression that the speaker[25] is rejecting the story of the Siegfried's impenetrable dragon-skin simply on the grounds that it is unrealistic, just as the narrator of Gottfried's *Tristan* rejects the story of the swallow bringing a strand of Isolde's golden hair from Ireland to Cornwall.[26] In fact, Albrecht simply wishes to promote an alternative, "learned" account of how one might acquire dragon-skin. The subsequent strophes explain exactly how this is to be achieved: Radoltz of Kanias (a heathen fighting on the side of Secureiz) experiments with a particular root and after initially feeding it to his children without any result, discovers that if he and his wife eat it, any children that they subsequently beget—and the further descendants of these children—will indeed have the desired protective skin, as well as a green coloring and a distorted voice.[27] Whilst this story is no less fanciful than that of Siegfried bathing in dragon's blood, the context is very different. The motif of contact with dragon's blood, either through drinking or bathing, is associated in the heroic epic with individual achievement and hence with the acquisition of individual privileged prowess. By contrast, the motif of the herb has a quasi-biblical (and quasi-scientific) resonance, echoing the accounts of how entire populations of semi-human monsters were generated as a result of the disobedience of the daughters of Adam, who consumed a herb against his advice.[28] As Wegner notes, these monstrous peoples have a particular place within the divine order: "An ihnen zeige sich, so Augustinus, die göttliche Macht über die Natur des menschlichen Körpers: schließlich sind auch die monströsen Wesen auslegbare Zeichen im 'Buch der Natur.'"[29] [According to Augustine, they testify to the power wielded by God over the human body: after all, even monstrous creatures constitute interpretable signs in the "Book of Nature"]. The potential interpretability of such populations clearly holds a particular appeal for Albrecht: his decision to combine the genesis of one such population with the rejection of the Siegfried story constitutes a unique and original claim for the superiority of his particular brand of Arthurian romance (in which science serves as a basis for Christian teaching), over the predominantly secular and hermeneutically one-dimensional heroic epic that focuses on the one-off achievements of mythic individuals.

Although this particular approach to the *realia* of the natural world distances the J.T. equally from the works of Hartmann and from the heroic epic, it could be argued that Wolfram is no less fascinated than Albrecht by this kind of subject matter. Indeed, the story of Radoltz's attempts at genetic engineering may even be understood as a conflation of two separate passages from the works of Wolfram. On the one hand, the herb comes from *Parzival*, in which the daughters of Adam are presented as the ultimate cause of the peculiar appearance of Cundrie, Malcreature, and other inhabitants of the lands of Secundille.[30] On the other hand, the notion of an entire population covered in dragon-scales derives from *Willehalm*.[31] However, whilst there is a certain compassionate regret on the part of the *Parzival*-narrator for the distortion of the human form,[32] there is little judgment or overt didacticism in any of Wolfram's passages. By contrast, these qualities are abundantly present in the J.T., as it presents its own final twist to the anecdote about the origins of the scaly people: it turns out that the loss of humanity sustained by the children of Radoltz is in fact not even outweighed by the attainment of military effectiveness, since the heat of the battle actually causes the scales to melt (J.T. 4173). This failure of heathen cleverness illustrates the point that God is ultimately in charge of nature, lending a particular resonance to the term *wurtz* in line 2:

> Gelucke, selden lune   leit an got aleine.
> heil und ouch fortune,   sterne, wurtze, wort und ouch gesteine,
> die habent kraft niht wan von des krefte,
> der kraft an allen dingen   was gebnde, do ers schu°f mit meisterschefte.
> (J.T. 4207)[33]

[Good luck and the favor of fortune are all attributable to God. Blessedness and fortune, stars, herbs, words, and stones: these have no power other than from his power who gave power to all things, when he created them with mastery.]

The episode also underscores the fundamental opposition between the heathen and the Christian approach to the world.[34] Although the heathens' knowledge of science in superior to that of the Christians, they lack the proper framework that would allow them to benefit from the information at their disposal.[35] This principle is also borne out by the part played by Tschinotulander's salamander shield: the scientific expertise and the well-intentioned advice of the heathen masters who have crafted this item are not sufficient to prevent it from turning into a destructive force. In short, although many romances (and some heroic epics) are marked by a basic desire to entertain an audience with accounts of the magical and the fantastical, Albrecht's scientific approach stands out, both on account of the exuberant detail of the natural *realia*, and on account of the way in which these are systematically relativized: whilst on one level, the J.T. purports to teach its audience about the inner workings of the natural world, it is made clear that this information is only of value within the context of the Christian religion. This in turn raises the wider question, to be addressed in section II below, of the way in which the J.T. functionalizes its own didacticisim.

Section II: Albrecht's Didacticism (*lere*)

Almost all medieval literature is in some sense didactic. Whilst the balance between the Horatian functions of *delectare* [being beautiful] and *prodesse* [being useful] may differ from work to work, it is difficult to identify any text from which the second of these is entirely absent. Brüggen has argued that as far as the didactic quality of literature is concerned, one is dealing with a continuum of possibilities and gradations that cuts across genre and makes it impossible to distinguish absolutely between the "Gebrauchstext, der unmittelbar zweckhaftem Handeln dient" [the manual, which is directly concerned with purposeful action] and the "poetische[n], ästhetisch-fiktionale[n] Text, der seinen Gegenstand selbst konstituiert" [the poetic, aesthetically oriented fictional text, which constitutes its own subject matter].[36] As she sees it, these two textual categories should only serve as notional topographical poles: they may be of assistance when it comes to identifying the relative positions of actual works, but in their absolute form, they constitute empty sets.

Brüggen's conclusions are particularly appropriate to the J.T., given that we are dealing with an Arthurian romance—a genre traditionally regarded as quintessentially "poetisch" and "ästhetisch-fiktional"—which nonetheless accords overt and quite exceptional importance to the promulgation of *lere*.[37] The supposed accessibility of the *lere* transmitted in this version of the *aventiure* is presented as one of the key ways in which the J.T. constitutes an improvement on *Parzival*:

> Ob sinnericher stiure   dise mær iht walten?
> si tuᵒnt sich niemant tiure,   si nennent sich den jungen zuo den alten.
> und mugen sich die tumben gar gesellen?
> durch sinneriche lere   muᵒz ich di wilden mær hie zam gestellen.

(J.T. 59)

[Do these tales contain anything of wise direction? They do not hold themselves aloof from anyone, they address young and old alike. And may the foolish ones join in at all? I must tame the wild tales here by means of wise instruction.]

The narrator's programmatic statement in J.T. 65,1–2 that *Dirre aventuᵉre kere . . . ist nicht wan ein lere* [the direction taken by this *aventiure* is nothing but an education] highlights the fact that instruction (in the broadest sense) is going to be a central theme of the work.[38]

In terms of didactic contents, the J.T. essentially features two separate categories: points of information (be they historical or scientific) and behavioral imperatives. We have already seen that the text devotes considerable energy to the exposition of various types of factual information about the constitution of the world, with the result that critics often compare it to a thesaurus, compendium, or encyclopedia.[39] It also commemorates many of the important figures, such as Hippocrates, Galen and Avicenna, *di von nature / ie gelasen vruᵒ und spate* (J.T. 1790,1–2) [who studied natural science continuously]. Nonetheless, just as the scientific information possessed intradiegetically does not benefit the heathen protagonists, so the value of the information imparted to the audience of the J.T. is contingent on its interpretative framework: *realia* are only of interest to the extent that they yield some form of moral lesson, which may either take the form of a straightforward translation from second to first language (according to the model that the sapphire signifies chastity), or of a more diffuse discussion of how a Christian ought to relate to the wonders of the natural world. However, even on this level, the transmission of factual information and associated allegorical interpretation cannot be divorced from the fictional nature of the work. This has been shown in chapter 2, in the context of Albrecht's allegorical interpretation of made-up composite beings such as the chimera.[40] Similarly, when Tschinotulander unwisely ignores the heathen experts who advise against taking the salamander shield out to sea, the story line is designed not only to affirm the intrinsic usefulness of scientific knowledge (e.g., of the fact that the elements of fire and water are hostile to each other) and to warn against headstrong behavior, but also, as Finckh has shown, to draw analogies between the balance of the elements in nature and the equivalent balance within the human soul.[41]

As far as behavioral imperatives are concerned, these arise partly out of the discussion of *realia* (as has just been shown) and partly out of consideration of the behavior of figures in the work. However, notwithstanding the promise of inclusiveness made in J.T. 59, the J.T. does not make it easy for its audience to learn from the narrative. The recipients are constantly required to negotiate ambiguous and conflicting value systems, whilst being given very little encouragement from the story line itself as to the feasibility of improvement through *lere*. Given that it abounds with individuals who fail truly to assimilate the didactic material that is presented to them—be it the members of the Arthurian court in their reception of the Brackenseil or the 'Wolfram'-narrator in his conflict with vrou Aventiure—the text is so pessimistic in outlook that it actually undercuts its own didactic programme.

To some extent, there is an argument for reading the instances of missed learning opportunities simply as negative exempla: the fact that the protagonists do not learn does not necessarily mean that learning is impossible, but should in fact inspire the audience to want do better. As in earlier courtly romances, the basic facts of the story provide scope for reflection, in the sense that the ultimate success or failure of particular protagonists provides a judgment on the type of behavior associated with these individuals: for example, the demise of Tschinotulander suggests that the values that he represents are to some extent dangerous and problematic. This kind of judgment also works on a collective level: the effective disintegration of the Arthurian court at the end of the work, combined with the translation of the Grail to the East, offers a clear moral verdict on the lifestyle enjoyed by this group of people.

However, in the J.T., the audience is confronted with the challenge of assessing, not only the bare facts, but also the plethora of different voices trying more or less successfully to formulate a moral code. Intradiegetically, the key didactic voices are those of Titurel (the 'Thronrede' [throne speech, J.T. 500–603]) and Clauditte (the Brackenseil), whilst the Grail constitutes a more impersonal normative authority: for example, the audience learns to distrust erotic love not only because of the unhappy destiny of Sigune and Tschinotulander, but also because the Grail is particularly intolerant of such behavior within its own community.[42]

Furthermore, it is the narratorial mediation of the narrative facts that presents the greatest obstacle to the unambiguous dissemination of *lere*. Of course, the J.T. is not the first German text to functionalize the tension between the ostensible verdict articulated by a narrator figure and the implicit verdict that may be extrapolated from the facts,[43] but the marked absence in this work of any single (let alone authoritative) narratorial voice does create particular difficulties for the audience. Whilst there is little doubt in the actual dialogues that the audience is supposed to heed vrou Aventiure rather than 'Wolfram,' this clarity does not extend to other parts of the texts in which one is often left wondering whether the narrator is mediating the correct views of vrou Aventiure or speaking in his own unreliable capacity. For example, the suggestion that Sigune constitutes an image and *exemplum* of maidenly honor (J.T. 2560,1) is not necessarily consistent with her willingness to strip for Tschinotulander,[44] and may ultimately have to be explained as a manifestation of 'Wolfram's' moral laxity, even though the 'Wolfram'-identity of the narrator is not otherwise highlighted at this point. Nor is this a one-off case of ambiguous exemplarity. Instead, the assessment of courtly characters and of courtliness itself is the central problem for which the text provides no easy answer—or rather, for which it deliberately provides at least two mutually exclusive answers. 'Wolfram' and vrou Aventiure are not the only ones to disagree about what (if anything) is wrong with Tschinotulander, whose indisputably outstanding chivalric achievements are not sufficient to protect him either from bad luck or from the charge of *unmaze* [immoderate behavior]. As Finckh has shown, this issue has divided critics into two broad camps, according to whether they regard him as a positive exemplary figure (e.g., Parshall, Haug, Schmid), or as an illustration of the failures of the Arthurian world and its values (e.g., Guggenberger, Wegner, and to some extent Finckh herself).[45] Most importantly, the text contains so much conflicting material that it is almost impossible to defend either of these critical positions:

> Es zeigt sich also, daß die gegensätzlichen Positionen der Forschung bezüglich der Bewertung von Tschinotulanders ritterlichen Eigenschaften eine Basis im Text selber haben. Da die Haltung des Erzählers zwischen moralischen Bewertungssystemen changiert und teils christliche, teils ritterliche Maßstäbe anlegt, erscheint die ins Extrem getriebene Ritterlichkeit des Helden an manchen Stellen des Textes als bewunderungswürdiges Ideal, an anderen als Verblendung. Je nachdem, auf welche Passage man sich beruft, kommt man so zu sehr unterschiedlichen Ergebnissen.[46]

> [So it turns out that the opposing positions adopted by critics regarding the assessment of Tschinotulander's knightly qualities do have a basis in the text itself. Since the attitude of the narrator oscillates between different systems of moral evaluation, in part adopting Christian standards and in part knightly ones, the extreme knightliness of the hero sometimes appears as an admirable ideal, and at other times as moral blindness. One may thus reach very different conclusions, depending on which passages are considered.]

Even if one does, unlike Finckh, take account of the particular problems arising from the cultural clash between the courtly figure of 'Wolfram' and his ascetic opponents (vrou Aventiure and 'Albrecht'), the fundamental difficulty highlighted by this passage still stands.

Whilst this monograph takes the line that there is, on balance, more evidence in the text to support a negative interpretation of Tschinotulander and of all that he stands for, it cannot be denied that, for a supposedly anticourtly work, the J.T. goes a long way toward celebrating knighthood and aristocratic good breeding. For example, the Grail community pleases God through its chivalric activities (e.g., jousting), while other aspects of courtly behavior are also considered sufficiently important for the Grail temple to be adorned externally with written prescriptions concerning aristocratic gesture and discourse (J.T. 575–580).

Furthermore, an implicit endorsement of traditional knightly values follows not only from the narrative importance accorded to combat in all contexts (Arthurian as well as Grail-related), but also from the hyperbolic praise frequently heaped on Tschinotulander by protagonists and narrator alike.[47]

Finally, and most surprisingly, courtliness is one of the areas in which the J.T. purports to provide its audience with explicit instruction. This claim is made as part of a longer poetological excursus (J.T. 2947–2962),[48] ostensibly triggered by the narrator's irritation at those who reveal their lack of appreciation of *gu°ter mer* [good tales] and of *gu°ter witze* [good sense] by asking premature questions during the recital of a narrative (J.T. 2947–2948). After a complicated defense of the moral importance and truth-value of fiction (J.T. 2949–2951),[49] the narrator turns to the concrete situation of the aristocratic (implicit) audience, pointing out that those who are to possess and control great territories require *witzen* [wit, intelligence]. This is a broadly conceived quality that has previously been associated at least in part with literary taste (J.T. 2957). Then follow the strophes engaging directly with the promulgation of courtliness:

> Swer ritterlich geverte   sol ritterlichen triben
> in schimpf und ouch in herte,   der sol daz nimmer gerne lan beliben,
> ern ho°re da von lesen, sagen, singen.
> daz git im kunst und ellen   noch mere dann mit toren gampel ringen.
>
> Sprechen und gebaren   mit hovschen siten riche,
> des sol man gerne varen,   daz man zu hove kunne hoveliche
> werben gen den herren und den vrowen.
> erdaht durch tugende schulde   wart diutscher bu°ch mit triwen unverhowen.
> (J.T. 2958–2959)

[Whoever is to partake in knightly activities in a properly knightly manner, be it for recreation or in earnest, should never like to go for long without hearing people read, speak, and sing on the subject. This will give him knowledge and strength, more so than engaging with the pranks of fools.

One should willingly strive toward speaking and behaving nobly, with courtly manners, to gain the favor, in a courtly way, of lords and ladies at court. German books were devised for the sake of virtue, on the basis of unconstrained loyalty.]

The argument culminates with the promise that:

> alle werde lu°te   werdent des hie vil wol under wiset.
> (J.T. 2961,4)

[All worthy people will here receive full instruction in this matter.]

Although strictly speaking these passages relate to the general potential of literature for teaching *ritterlich geverte* [knightly conduct], the poetological context makes it reasonable to interpret them as highlighting the didactic scope of this particular piece of literature.

Nonetheless, this promise of instruction is somewhat disingenuous. First, the J.T. does not provide the information that would be necessary for teaching the detail of aristocratic life. The text does neither give specific advice on, for example, how to behave at table, nor does it recount what is actually written on the outside of the Grail temple. Any practical instruction in courtliness is inevitably indirect and limited to the hints that a reader might pick up regarding the specifics of clothing and of related areas of material culture, or regarding the elegant discourse of figures such as Sigune and Ekunat (complete with Ovidian references).[50] However, even if the J.T. cannot be characterized either as a 'Tischzuht' [guide to table manners] or as a 'Fürstenspiegel' [mirror of princes], it does at least pay homage to the principle that such information would be worthwhile and would constitute suitable subject matter for a literary text.

Secondly, the J.T. promotes courtliness only in a special, limited sense. Whilst J.T. 2957–2959 do indeed imply that literature might be of practical benefit in the pursuit of worldly success, the subsequent strophe in the excursus makes it clear that literature is ultimately about the acquisition of virtue, rather than of courtly polish:

> Tugende, manheit jehende   ist man den hohen werden
> di wilent waren spehende   niht wan daz si werdicheit begerden.
> manheit, triwe, zuhte, maz und milte,
> der vrowen zuht mit kuᵉsche,   ir beider wirde sich hie mit hohe zilte.
>
> (J.T. 2960)

[One ascribes virtues and manhood to the high-ranking worthy ones who, in times past, cared for nothing save attaining worthiness. Virility, loyalty, breeding, moderation, and generosity, womanly breeding together with chastity—with these, the worthiness of both sexes aimed high.]

A similar, slightly deceptive shift in values becomes apparent in a later excursus endorsing the practical benefits of the written word. In J.T. 5279–5294 the narrator discusses the value of learning for the different classes of individuals, including clerics, scholars, aristocrats, the aged, the wealthy, poets, knights, and peasants.[51] Again, the argument is adduced that, notwithstanding his physical prowess, a knight will fail in his appointed role if he lacks *kunst* and *meisterschaft*, qualities that are closely associated with literacy:[52]

> Es lit an aller kunste   meisterschaft mit sinne.
> ein ritter werder gunste   wirt, und wil er dienen werder minne.
> kraft und ellen ist gen wird ein stiure,
> und ist er kunste sunder,   im mac wol ritters wirde werden tiure.
>
> (J.T. 5286)

[All *kunste* combine *meisterschaft* with good sense. A knight acquires worthy favor if he chooses to serve a worthy love. Power and strength are of some help in attaining worth—but if he is without *kunst*, knightly worthiness will elude him.]

However, the formulation *dienen werder minne* [to serve a worthy love] provides the clue to the fact that the narrator is not talking about the kind of familiar knightly activity that would involve courtly love service.[53] Instead, when the J.T. claims to offer advice about how to achieve knightly excellence or courtly renown, it is really offering instruction in ascetically oriented Christian virtue and promoting a code so strict that it is difficult to see how it might be realized in a secular setting. This disingenuousness is partly, but not entirely, a question of definition: Albrecht oscillates between using abstract terms in the way that they are ordinarily used in courtly literature, and using them with the stricter, more moral meaning which he believes that they ought to have,[54] with the result that courtliness, together with its component values such as *minne*, may simultaneously be celebrated and denigrated. Whilst paradoxes of this kind are not unknown in other forms of courtly writing, Albrecht's decision effectively to redefine a key concept in some contexts (but not in others) undeniably introduces a further level of difficulty for the recipients.

Finally, whilst the presentation of Grail-figures and Grail-values is generally less ambiguous than that of the Arthurian world, the assimilation of *lere* from even these sections of the work is beset with difficulty.

On the one hand, the narrator hammers home the point that the audience is supposed to imitate virtuous protagonists such as Titurel:

wil er im selben sælde und vrowen ere
zu beiden siten koufen,   so tu° sam Tyturel nach dirre lere.
(J.T. 237,3–4)

[If a man wants to obtain blessedness for himself and to preserve the honor of women, let him act like Titurel, in accordance with this teaching.]

Titurel himself presents his own life in similar terms, when he opens the Thronrede with a celebration of his chivalric past, tellingly formulated *zelere, nicht zu ru°me* (J.T. 504,4) [in the interests of *lere*, not out of boastfulness]. On this occasion, the striking overlap in the didactic intentions of the protagonist and of the narrator is such that it breaks down the distinction between the intradiegetic and extradiegetic worlds: the two separate audiences effectively merge, the readers joining the Grail community as the primary addressees of the Thronrede.

On the other hand, even though Titurel is as consistent and reliable an exemplary figure as any in the text, the didactic use even of this figure is not without ambiguity. In this case, the difficulty does not relate to any dubious deeds actually committed by Titurel himself, but rather to the narrator's practice of linking his protagonists to a wider network of exemplary or illustrative figures derived from history, mythology, or the Bible.[55] In the case of Titurel, an equivalence is posited between him and Solomon (J.T. 210,3–4) which, on the face of it, seems reasonable: like Solomon, Titurel builds a temple, and like Solomon, he is splendid, wise, and favored by God. Solomon's praise of God's creation is highlighted in J.T. 284, reinforcing the positive evaluation of the Old Testament figure. However, there are darker sides to Solomon. In J.T. 1761, he is presented in entirely negative terms as a 'Minnesklave' [slave of love] alongside Samson and David. In J.T. 108, by contrast, he is invoked as an ideal comparator for the narrator and hence as a figure sufficiently wise to deal with the challenges of mediating the narrative. However, the other exempla of ideal wisdom mentioned in the strophe include not only Aristotle and Heraclius,[56] but also *Ovidius*—that very incorporation of literary lechery from whom the virtuous Titurel recoils in disgust (J.T. 190). Of course, one might seek to bypass this problem by saying that the medieval Solomon was a multifaceted figure,[57] whom Titurel resembles in some respects but not in others. Nonetheless, Albrecht clearly functionalizes the incongruities within the Solomon-tradition. It would have been perfectly possible for him to take a one-dimensional approach to Solomon, using him to signify either wisdom or uxoriousness: indeed, as there are many other 'Minnesklaven' in the medieval catalogues, it might have made sense to use the temple-building Solomon exclusively as a comparator for Titurel. Similar considerations apply to the figure of Ovid, as has already been discussed in chapter 1: if the aim of the author were simply to give examples of "the erotic writer" and of "the moralizing writer," it might have been more effective to use two different individuals. The fact that Albrecht chooses, not only to draw attention to the entire complex personae of both figures, but also to incorporate them both into an implicit chain of equivalences, serves deliberately to highlight their ambiguity as ciphers and to draw attention to the spuriousness of such comparative chains: If i) x is virtuous and worthy of imitation, ii) x is like y, and iii) y is like z, should it not follow that iv) y and z are also worthy of imitation? The fact that this clearly does not follow within the literary context of the J.T. underscores the fact that exempla and comparators, far from facilitating immediate and compelling communication, are inevitably part of that regressive and ambivalent "web of signs" that Augustine sees as underlying all human discourse.[58] Even if instruction and virtue are fundamental to this whole *aventiure* (as suggested in J.T. 65), they are not readily distilled from the morass of narrative events and descriptions. Whilst the story line may be regarded as passing a judgment of sorts on the protagonists (as has already been discussed), the interpretation of this judgment is inevitably subjective and open-ended. Chosen protagonists are apparently promoted as models to be copied and imitated, but the ease with which virtue and vice can be linked through comparative exempla draws into doubt the validity of mapping one life onto another—and hence of learning from literary antecedents.

The J.T. is thus a work which problematizes its own medium: the text is ambiguous, not only as to precisely what didactic contents it purports to relay, but also as to the ultimate feasibility of writing fiction for these purposes. Accordingly, whilst the deliberate foregrounding of didactic intent may on one level be seen as a key stratagem by means of which Albrecht seeks to elevate his work above other Middle High German narratives, it does not follow that a commitment to *lere* is in itself sufficient to rescue the J.T. from the more fundamental limitations of the written word (outlined in chapter 1). To revert to Brüggen's notional topographical poles—it is precisely by posing as a "Gebrauchstext, der unmittelbar zweckhaftem Handeln dient" that the J.T. ultimately emerges as a self-referential, "poetische[r], ästhetisch-fiktionale[r] Text."

This feature may make it more interesting to the modern reader, but does not take one any further in establishing the basis on which the text's claim to salvatory status might be based. To put it differently: Albrecht's commitment to historical truth and to *lere* (particularly regarding Christian virtue) may go some way toward differentiating his work both from the Brackenseil and from other Middle High German texts, but it does not exempt it from the inherent fallibility of these texts. Indeed, asceticism cuts both ways: it may make the enterprise more morally respectable, but, as has already been suggested in chapter 1, the same ascetic tradition that underpins the worthy moral values of the book also entails a fundamentally pessimistic evaluation of the written word and therefore precludes the promulgation of any model of literary communication characterized by immediacy and transparency. If this impasse is to be sidestepped, the case for the supposed excellence and efficacy of the text ultimately has to be made on quite a different basis.

Given that on Albrecht's own terms, neither historicity nor didacticism would in themselves suffice for his purpose of producing a flawless text, further consideration has to be given to the way in which authorial intent is embedded in the poetological program and to the interpretational quantum leap that this program poses for the audience.

At first sight, it may seem as though the model of allegorical interpretation may in itself provide the key to the supposedly special status of the J.T., at least within Middle High German narrative writing.[59] After all, Albrecht's enthusiasm for the allegorical interpretation of *realia* is unusual within an Arthurian romance and in the poetological excursus mentioned above, the narrator does appear to offer explicit support for the *integumentum* model, according to which fiction may be literally false but morally true.[60]

On closer inspection, however, the allegorical interpretation offered in the J.T. is to a very large extent tied up with the kind of didacticism that has already been discussed. The model of *integumentum* (at least as realized in this work) does not go beyond the point made in the previous section, namely that even a made-up story should be regarded as true to the extent that it offers an instructive verdict on the behavior of its protagonist. The J.T. is clearly not conceived along the same kinds of allegorical principles as, for example, Alan of Lille's *Anticlaudianus*, in which both the points of detail and the entire narrative flow are to be understood as signifying something distinctively different from that which is being stated on the literal level. As for the allegorical interpretation of *realia*, Albrecht's practice of explaining the hidden significance of objects serves on most occasions to impart specific points of scientific and moral information, rather than to encourage the audience to think of the whole narrative as operating with multiple levels.[61] Only seldom is the technique of allegorical interpretation used poetologically, in the sense of saying something about the way in which the text is intended to function.

It is noteworthy that the one striking example of poetological allegory—when the temple is interpreted as a model for the way in which the audience should internalize and "house" the Grail text (J.T. 528)—should be based on a sacred rather than on a secular aspect of the intradiegetic world. After all, the hierarchical subordination of the Arthurian world to that of the Grail is clearer in the J.T. than even in *Parzival* and even though the bulk of the narrative is concerned with the career of somebody who was not chosen for the Grail, Tschinotulander's story is framed, literally and thematically, by the story of the Grail and its community. Indeed, the short answer to the question of how Albrecht sees his text as being "better" than other Middle High German works would simply highlight the subject matter: *Parzival* and the J.T. both transcend those works that do not mention the Grail at all, but the J.T. transcends *Parzival* because it gives a more detailed and supposedly more correct account. Whilst this short answer is too simplistic in itself, it does draw attention to the key status in the text of the Grail specifically and of the sacred domain more generally and raises the question of the way in which this concern with the sacred manifests itself on a poetological level.

Section III: The Creation and the Sacraments: Poetological Analogies

In the J.T., the Grail possesses both cosmological and sacramental associations: whilst the ceiling of its temple is decorated in such a way as to replicate the night sky, the object itself is linked historically to the institution of the Eucharist. Given the inscripted nature of both Grail and temple,[62] together with the parallelism between Grail and text established in J.T. 528, it is legitimate to interpret these associations poetologically. The implications of this for the status of the literary work are far-reaching: on the one hand, Albrecht presents his act of literary creation as an acceptable imitation of God's creation of the cosmos, whilst on the other hand, the notions of sacramental transformation and of sacramental efficacy provide a framework that he can set against the ascetic notion of the deadness of script.

In the Middle Ages, attempts on the part of human beings to imitate God's cosmic act of creation were often viewed with deep suspicion. The inappropriateness of such attempts was commonly illustrated by reference to the failure of overambitious architectural projects: whilst the Tower of Babel remains the archetypal biblical example of an attempt to penetrate the heavens, Herweg has drawn attention to the way in which the cosmologically themed throne-room of the Persian King Khusro (Cosdras)—complete with sun, moon, and stars inlaid into the ceiling, and a device for producing rain and wind—was presented in medieval literature as a "post-figuration" of the Tower of Babel.[63] Here, the proud heathen king, who has effectively styled himself as God the Father by taking up position at the centre of his own creation, eventually receives his due punishment at the hands of the Christian Emperor Heraclius.[64] The architectural folly of Khusro is not only repudiated explicitly in the *Kaiserchronik* and in Otte's *Eraclius*, but also colors the approach taken to extravagant building projects in many courtly works (the buildings belonging to Clinschor in *Parzival* being a case in point). However, Herweg argues that in this respect, the Grail temple in the J.T. constitutes a notable exception: notwithstanding the unmistakably cosmological styling of the building, the project is presented in entirely positive terms. The difference lies partly in the devout attitude of Titurel, its builder, and partly in the fact that it is God himself who provides the directions as to structure and ornamentation.[65]

Herweg's observations on the Grail temple lend themselves to further poetological interpretation, in the sense that the permissible cooperation of God and

Titurel mirrors an equivalently valid cooperation between God and poet in an undertaking that might otherwise have been problematic.

The notion that the involvement of God might be necessary in order to exempt the project from charges of *superbia* is supported by the way in which the prologue handles the topos of the poet as creator. Initially, the prologue appears to favor a model according to which the poet works alone, in imitation of God. Whilst critics such as Finckh and Hahn possibly go too far in positing a direct and specific equivalence between God's creation of *tugent* (J.T. 9) and Albrecht's "creation" of a vrou Aventiure who is bedecked with virtue (J.T. 65),[66] there can be no doubt either as to the general cosmological orientation of the prologue, or as to the suggested parallelism between the *getichte* [creation, opus, poem] of God (e.g., J.T. 3,1) and of the poet.[67]

Formulations of this kind are of course not necessarily controversial or in need of justification. On the contrary, to the extent that they highlight the difference between the creative achievements of God and poet, they constitute *humilitas*-topoi which are familiar from prologues to wide variety of Middle High German texts.[68] Nonetheless, there are two reasons why precisely these topoi might require more detailed consideration in the case of the J.T. First, there is the tension (already highlighted) between Albrecht's generally pessimistic approach to the status of writing and the idea that it is appropriate to compare his work to God's act of creation. Secondly, the quantity of scientific detail in the J.T. is such that the idea of a literary re-creation of the cosmos reads as more than a mere rhetorical flourish. Just as Herweg argues that the temple should be regarded as an architectural encyclopedia, so the work as a whole is encyclopedic in nature. Indeed, it may almost be regarded as a would-be forerunner of the book destroyed by Brandan: a quasi-magical text that contains all the marvels of the universe.[69] That the authorial basis for so unusually bold an undertaking should require some justification seems entirely reasonable.

The prologue provides a careful formulation of the human writer's position vis-à-vis the divine creator. Although the speaker makes it clear that he does not seek to compete with God, and accepts that the wonders of God can never be adequately praised (J.T. 68–69), he argues that it is acceptable to articulate at least a partial celebration of these, whilst according appropriate credit to God,

> der dise aventuͤre   tuot erkant geschehen und noch geschehende.
>
> (J.T. 70,4)
>
> [who has made, and still makes, this *aventiure* known.]

Responsibility for the J.T. therefore rests with God as much as with 'Albrecht.'

The building of the Grail temple therefore not only provides an unusual example of acceptable and didactically effective cosmological architecture, but also endorses a particular model of joint authorship, whereby the broad direction (and seal of approval) comes from God, whilst the detailed decisions, together with the labor, is undertaken by the human partner. As Minnis has shown, this model of religious authorship emerges in the course of the thirteenth century and as distinct from the earlier model, whereby God is entirely responsible for the revelatory work, using the human partner as a scribe or mouthpiece.[70] This earlier model is to some extent reflected (or even parodied) in the troubled working relationship between vrou Aventiure and 'Wolfram,' when she effectively puts the words into his mouth to make him to tell the story in a way that he would not have chosen himself. By contrast, the authorial narrator 'Albrecht' is a temple builder on a par with Solomon and Titurel, responding to direction rather than to dictation.

The notion that the narrator is presenting his own literary building project in opposition to that of Khusro is also borne out by the two references to Heraclius, the nemesis of the proud heathen king (J.T. 108 and J.T. 331). The second of these strophes has already been discussed in the previous section, in the context of the analogies drawn between Solomon, Ovid and the narrator. Although the J.T. makes no explicit reference to the Khusro story, the cosmological and mechanical splendors of the Grail temple are so striking that it seems reasonable, not just to endorse Herweg's view that this building constitutes a moral inversion of the Khusro-hall, but also to build the figure of Heraclius into the poetological insights that follow from this.

On the face of it, the references to Heraclius are simply recycled from *Parzival*. Whilst it is thought that Wolfram knew Otte's *Eraclius*, which covers the full spectrum of Heraclius' career, culminating in his regaining of the Cross that had been stolen by Khusro, *Parzival* itself does not allude directly to this final, historiographical portion of the work. Instead, Wolfram's narrator bases his single reference (*Parzival* 773,23) on an earlier section of Otte's work, in which the eponymous hero consolidates his position at court of the Emperor Phocas on the basis of his skill in assessing the true merits of gemstones, horses, and women.[71] *Parzival* evokes the first of these areas of expertise, when *Eraclîus* (also called *Ercules*),[72] *Alexander*, and *Pictagoras* are listed as examples of individuals who would be better able than the narrator to explain the properties of the stones adorning the armor of Feirefiz. In the second of his two references to Heraclius (J.T. 331), Albrecht follows this *Parzival* passage quite closely: although there is no mention of Alexander, *Pitagoras* and *Hercules* are presented as experts on precious stones who might have described a particular object more successfully than the narrator: *di waren jehende hie mit meisterschefte* (J.T. 331,4) [they spoke with mastery on this matter]. The only important difference is that the object in question is not a piece of relatively unimportant armor, but the Grail temple itself, which occupies a crucial symbolic role within the text. At the very least, the fact that the J.T. presents Heraclius as potentially capable of interpreting the Grail temple implies not only that he would have something to say about the individual stones, but also that he would appreciate the ethical difference between this building and that of Khusro. Furthermore, to the extent that the Grail temple constitutes a metaphor for the text as a whole, the hypothetical competence of the authorities takes on a more general literary and moral dimension.

The broader literary significance of Heraclius in particular has already been established in J.T. 108, a strophe that introduces four potential comparators for the narrator. Here the issue at stake is not the interpretation of precious stones, but the narration of the history of the Grail dynasty. To emphasize the difficulty of the narrative material, the narrator wishes for the wisdom of Aristotle and Solomon, while conceding that even Ovid and Heraclius might find the task challenging:

> Wirt diu wurtz ie bernde   stam, und der stam dann este,
> wa wer ich dann der wernde,   an lip, an kunst, an witzen also veste
> sam Aristotel und Salamon der wise?
> Ovidius und Ercules,   ich wen, in gar zerunne an disem prise.
>
> (J.T. 108)

> [If the root ever produces a trunk, and the trunk then branches, how will I then cope, without the strength, without skill, without wits as sharp as those of Aristotle and the wise Solomon. As for Ovid and Heraclius, I believe that even they would be exhausted by the amount of praise required.]

The panel of authorities in this strophe is in many ways a strange one: whilst all four figures have an obvious claim to wisdom, their intellectual excellence is in every case undermined by a certain moral ambiguity. The paradoxical profiles of Solomon (wise temple builder and 'Minnesklave') and of Ovid (moralist and erotic writer) have already been discussed. Aristotle's heathen status is potentially problematic,[73] as is the famous story of his humiliation at the hands of Phyllis.[74] Finally, whilst Heraclius is personally blameless, his advice on the subject of women is less reliable than on the subject of stones and horses: in Otte's text, the apparently flawless bride whom he selects for the Emperor Phocas soon succumbs to adultery. Admittedly, Otte takes a remarkably generous stance toward this errant woman, ascribing the cause of her behavior entirely to the unreasonable jealousy of Phocas, and arguing that the failure of the marriage did not undermine the validity of Heraclius' recommendation. Nonetheless, if (as seems likely) Otte's work does indeed constitute an intertext for this strophe, one can safely assume that Albrecht would take a different view of adultery: for him, the bottom line must be that even if Heraclius was right about stones, he was wrong about women.

What, then, might be the function of this paradoxical panel? One might seek to explain it specifically by reference to the predilections of the 'Wolfram'-persona: a worldly, slightly lecherous narrator might naturally gravitate toward similarly unreliable comparators, even as he is formulating his variation on the 'Unfähigkeitstopos' [topos of literary inadequacy]. However, as the comparators are ambiguous, rather than unremittingly sleazy, it could be argued that their combination of towering excellence and venal fallibility matches, not the individual profile of 'Wolfram' himself, but the combined profiles of 'Wolfram' and 'Albrecht,' the two narrators whose diverging agendas potentially pull the story in different directions. For such a sustained act of mixed narration, a panel of morally indeterminate authorities is not inappropriate.

Albrecht's idiosyncratic practice of operating through two narrators clearly adds a complicating layer to the previously suggested model of joint authorship involving both God and human being. One could argue that the advantage of his using two ethically polarized figures is that it preserves the authorial narrator from the kind of moral indeterminacy that is otherwise associated not only with the authority figures just discussed, but also with the act of writing more generally: because the fallibility of the flesh is concentrated in the figure of 'Wolfram,' his ultimate opponent 'Albrecht' is effectively absolved from such charges. The devout intent of the authorial narrator is thus beyond doubt.

As the text is very largely narrated by 'Wolfram,' there is no doubt that his values and personality do shine through, even as vrou Aventiure tries to control him on behalf of 'Albrecht.' To that extent, the work is deliberately flawed: it not only thematizes the fallibility of the written word by reference to other texts, but also by reference to itself. It follows from this that not every line or strophe is to be thought of as being divinely inspired, or even directed: points of detail are negotiated between Wolfram and vrou Aventiure. Instead, the supposed greatness of the J.T. hinges, not on the rigid exclusion of inappropriately worldly material and viewpoints, but rather on the successful containment of these within the strictures of the religious framework established by God and by 'Albrecht.' Of course, diversity of outlook is not actually encouraged: there is no sense in which the perspective of 'Wolfram' is presented as equally valid to that of vrou Aventiure. Nonetheless, the fact that the historical Albrecht chose to merge his moral and spiritual encyclopedia with the fictional world of Wolfram (just as 'Albrecht' chooses to narrate jointly with 'Wolfram') is in itself a strong statement about the potential redeemability of fiction. Admittedly, as has been argued in chapter 4, 'Wolfram' is effectively a sullen victim and should not be regarded as a partner in the creative undertaking shared between God and 'Albrecht,' the authorial narrator. However, the use that 'Albrecht' makes of 'Wolfram' underscores the fact that, given divine direction and an appropriately devout stance on the part of the primary human agent, all sorts of potentially suspect acts of creativity are absolved from criticism, be it the construction of buildings and texts that replicate the natural world, or the apparent celebration of courtliness, or the charting of a love-relationship steeped in secular values.

The second strand of Albrecht's poetological argument hinges on parallels between text and sacrament. On the intradiegetic level, it is the Grail's historical association with the eucharist that provides the crucial link between cosmology, sacrament, and text. As has been discussed in chapter 3, this link allows Huschenbett to suggest that Albrecht's Grail text, as well as his intradiegetic Grail, exemplifies the transformative power of eucharistic language.[75] By contrast, on the narratorial level it is the sacrament of baptism rather than that of the eucharist that is subjected to poetological interpretation, as the prologue focuses on the substance water in its cosmological and sacramental contexts.[76]

In the case of baptism, the theme of transformation is obviously less striking than in the case of the eucharist: whereas transsubstantiation of the hosts is central to the eucharist, the water used in baptism is not deemed to undergo any change in itself. Whereas the eucharist therefore constitutes an attractive model for the way in which a fallible, secular text might, by the grace of God, be transformed into something different even as it is being articulated (i.e., simultaneously playing the part both of eucharistic host and of eucharistic utterance), baptism does not provide a basis for precisely the same poetological analogy. However, even if the material substance used in baptism remains unchanged, baptism is deemed to share with the eucharist— as with the other sacraments—the capacity to effect a profound transformation in the recipients.[77] This point constitutes the key to a poetological interpretation of any of the sacraments: the J.T. aspires to the "sacramental" in the sense of being able to effect a permanent impact on its readers (in contrast, for example, to the nonsacramental language of the Brackenseil).

Furthermore, the prologue effectively compensates for the absence of any spectacular material change in baptismal water by invoking quasi-miraculous examples of the transformation of water in the natural world. Overall, as will be argued here, baptism is handled in such a way in the prologue as to provide the basis for a more subtle poetological analogy than does the eucharist in the narrative itself.

The prologue presents water as one of the building blocks of the created universe (on par with fire, air, and earth). However, water is also assigned a predominant role amongst the elements, partly because it can overpower any of the others,[78] and partly because it possesses a religious significance not shared by the others. Water forms the substance of penitent tears and plays a key part within the sacrament of baptism, where its literal cleansing function is spiritualized.[79] Furthermore, the fact that there are different kinds of bodies of water (J.T. 29,1: *ein se, ein vluz, ein brunn* [a lake, a river, a well]) is used as the basis for a trinitarian analogy seeking to explain how something can be threefold and yet one.[80] We are thus presented with a chain of associations reaching from the natural world of the elements to the sacrament of baptism to divine revelation regarding the Trinity.[81] This chain in turn underpins the viable dissemination of religious instruction through the medium of the written word underscoring the way in which water and text (*schrift*) both play a part in keeping human beings clean:

> Ein got, din nam gedriet,   und doch ein got aleine!
> din tot sus tuot gefriet   den menschen gar vor allen sunden reine.
> durch daz so leret uns diu schrift mit flize,
> daz wir gar ungemeilet   behalten wol di selben wat so wize.
>
>   (J.T. 32)

[One God, your name threefold and still just one God! Your death thereby freed mankind entirely from all sins. As a result, scripture teaches us assiduously how to preserve the same pure white raiments free from stain.]

Whilst *diu schrift* in line 3 refers primarily to the Holy Scripture, the statement may also be extended to other forms of writing: the spiritual effectiveness of any scriptural activity is ultimately dependent on God's willingness to engage with humankind, either through the incarnation and the sacraments, or through joint literary projects of the kinds under discussion.[82] The prologue repeatedly stresses God's own reliance on language, both in the context of creation—

> sint er mit siner worte kraft hiez werden
> himel, stern, loup und gras,   visch, vogel, wurme, tier und erden.
>   (J.T. 33,3–4)

[Since he called into being through the power of his words the heavens, stars, foliage and grass, fish, birds, worms, beasts, and the earth.]—

and of the sacraments:

> Noch alsust kreftliche   sint sine wort gesterket,
> daz er gewalticliche   den touf mit sinen worten sus beserket
> (J.T. 34,1–2)

[His words are strengthened with so much power than he, in his might, has encased baptism with his words]

The sacramental power of language is also reiterated in a later strophe, which warns against ascribing any special status to water itself (as the heathens might do). The power lies not in the element itself, but in the transformative power of language:[83]

> Durch daz si nieman jehende   dem wazzer heilikeite,
> e daz si im geschehende   von priester si und e er iz beleite
> mit worten, di von recht da zuᵒ gehoᵉrent.
> von worten sacramenta   gewinnent kreft, di uns zu got enboᵉrent.
> (J.T. 44)

[For that reason, let nobody ascribe sanctity to water before it has received this quality from the priest and before he has pronounced over it the appropriate words. Sacraments derive power from words which take us to God.]

So far, there has been little discussion of the ways in which the water itself might change. In J.T. 44, the *worte* in question bring about a change in the candidate for baptism rather than in the element water, which remains unchanged, both with respect to its substance and to its state. Similarly, the trinitarian analogy quoted above requires the audience to think about water in its familiar liquid state. Nonetheless, fact that water exists in several different states is not ignored by the prologue and plays a central role in the poetological argument.

Rather than seeing the transition of water from the liquid to the solid state in terms of a natural and predictable response to a change in temperature, the prologue presents this as a quasi-miraculous manifestation of the grace of God. The effect of this is to introduce a moral hierarchy of states: although the baptismal and trinitarian discussion in J.T. 27–36 would not have made sense without a positive interpretation of water in its liquid form, the suggestion from J.T. 37 onward is that the solid state, being the result of divine intervention, constitutes a definite improvement on the merely "natural" liquid state. The first illustration of such divine intervention relates to the way in which frozen bodies of water become traversable:

> Got machet brucke herte   uz wazzer dem vil weichen
> und straz der wagen verte.
> (J.T. 37,1–2)

[Out of the softest water God makes hard bridges and roads for carts to traverse.]

The second illustration relates to two special, water-based stones: the crystal and the so-called *enidorium*.[84] These two stones constitute the key to a poetological analogy which, unlike that based on the eucharist, is specifically able to accommodate the particular complexities of the 'Wolfram' / 'Albrecht' relationship.

The crystal is said to form from the impact of fire (i.e. lightning) on water that has collected in rocky outcrops, where it is otherwise shielded from sunlight, wind, or rain (J.T. 38). However, rather than regarding this as a purely natural phenomenon, the prologue once again stresses God's direct involvement in the transformation. The genesis of the crystal is then interpreted allegorically to signify the moral transformation of the believer who becomes fixed (i.e., "crystallized") in his devotion to Christ:

> Der nam krist sælden riche   mir sæliclich gevellet.
> ir cristen an geliche   schaffet, daz ir zu Kriste u^ech kristellet,
> daz u^ech chein hitze, wint noch wazzers unde
> von Kriste icht vertribe!   so habt ir kristen Krist mit stæte kunde.
>   (J.T. 39)

> [The most blessed name "Christ" delights me. You Christians should similarly ensure that you become crystallized in relation to Christ, so that no heat, wind, or wave might drive you from him at all! Then you Christians will know Christ permanently.]

The following strophes set out the allegorical meaning of those natural forces that threaten the crystal: the wind signifies pride, and heat lust, while the greed of water (the liquid state of which is now interpreted very negatively) is such that this can sweep Christians away to hell.

By contrast, the mysterious stone enidorium is more robust, even though it, like the crystal, results from a particular fusion of water and fire (J.T. 45). The enidorium's nature is remarkable for two reasons. First, it serves as a source of water, although there is no "natural" explanation as to how the water entered it in the first place; and secondly, it is not diminished or eroded by the fact that water constantly flows out of it:

> Enidorium diezen   sicht man zu allen stunden
> und wazzer dar uz vliezen,   und wirt an siner gro^ez nicht minner funden.
> der stein hat solche kraft von got besunder.
> von wannen daz wazzer vliuzet,   in den stein, daz ist von got ein wunder.
>   (J.T. 41)

> [One always sees the enidorium swollen, with water seeping out of it, and yet its size never diminishes. The stone has been granted this special property from God, for the question of where the water flowing into the stone comes from is indeed a miracle from God.]

In exegetical literature, the water issuing from the enidorium is generally interpreted *in bonum partem*, as signifying the infinite flow of mercy from God or Mary.[85] However, given the close connection between the crystal and the enidorium in the J.T., it seems reasonable to assume that the liquid state is still being presented as morally suspect. Accordingly, the fact that the enidorium retains its solid shape despite being in contact with water gives it an advantage over the more vulnerable crystal.

Whilst no explicit connection is drawn between these two stones and Albrecht's literary enterprise, the prologue context, with its overall foregrounding of the power of language, makes it appropriate to consider the possibilities offered by a poetological interpretation. More specifically, J.T. 68,3 invokes all the *wunder* of God (which must include the two stones in question) in a plea that he might intervene to assist the speaker who is *kunstlos, an meisterschefte . . . der schrifte* (J.T. 68,2) [unskilled, without mastery of the written word].

The crystal lends itself to a poetological argument for a number of reasons. First, crystal is a substance that features prominently in the later description of the Grail temple.[86] Secondly, there is a tradition of using the crystal as a token of the aesthetic evaluation of language, the reference to Hartmann's *cristallînen wortelîn* [little crystalline words] in the literary excursus to Gottfried's *Tristan* being the most famous vernacular case in point.[87] The etymology for the crystal suggested in J.T. 39 (*Krist / kristellen*) is in any case associated loosely with the question of the meaningfulness of language that was discussed in chapter 2: whilst so many of the etymologies set out in the J.T. are deliberately spurious, the direct invocation of the name of Christ suggests that this one has a uniquely solid basis. More generally, the strophe may be taken to suggest that whereas weakness, sin, and "liquidity" are the norm not only for human beings, but also for the texts that they produce, exceptions are possible: given the right circumstances and the assistance of God, a text may crystallize just like a human soul. As far as texts are concerned, the solidity of the crystal suggests not only moral excellence, but also material durability: a crystallized text may be deemed to be divinely protected from those risks of destruction and obliteration that were discussed in chapter 1.

The crystal thus provides a general metaphor of how a text might transcend the shortcomings usually associated with the written word. However, as it is made clear that the crystal is still in some ways fragile, requiring absolute isolation from any hints of pride and lust, there is a potential question mark as to whether a text set largely in the Arthurian world—and narrated through, if not by, a figure such as 'Wolfram'—is really capable of undergoing the transformation in question.

Here the alternative model offered by the enidorium becomes relevant. This stone, formed by the same noble fusion of water and fire as is the crystal, retains its unquestionably solid state despite being permeated by water, just as the J.T. is permeated by the values, and indeed the language, of 'Wolfram.'

The central aspect of this analogy is the coexistence of the solid and the liquid forms within the enidorium: the fact that contact with water does not damage this stone illustrates the capacity of the J.T. to incorporate 'Wolfram' and all that he stands for without suffering moral detriment. At the same time, the question of causative priority must also be addressed. Whilst the enidorium functions as a source of water, one obviously cannot say that the J.T. is the "source" (in the standard literary sense) of *Parzival*. At the same time, the J.T. is a source in the sense that it gives its readers (partial) access to *Parzival*: after all, the presentation of the two stones, and indeed the whole exposition of the marvels of the element water, is embedded within a paraphrase of part of the prologue to *Parzival*.[88] This illustrates both the extent to which 'Wolfram' flows through the text, and the extent to which the J.T. has become more "solid" than *Parzival*. Finally, it is fair to say that 'Albrecht,' as the ultimate human controller of the narrative, does have causative priority over 'Wolfram.' Accordingly, this enidorium constitutes a remarkably apt metaphor for the way in which the J.T. thematizes, and to some extent exemplifies the inevitability of moral and literary inadequacy, whilst at the same time ultimately exempting itself from these charges.

CONCLUSION

In its handling of literacy and textuality, the J.T. negotiates a balance between two apparently opposing traditions. On the one hand, Albrecht draws on an ascetic tradition that denigrates the written (as opposed to the spoken) word as corporeal, residual, and inanimate. Just as the J.T. takes an ascetic stance on carnality in general, so does it implicitly associate writing with the body, with imperfection and ultimately with death—the inscriptions on the body of the doomed Tschinotulander making this connection particularly clear. On the other hand, Albrecht's work also endorses the topos of God as a writer and of the universe as an interpretable script with which human beings have a duty to engage intellectually. Accordingly, although the J.T. argues that literacy—understood in the broadest possible sense—is essential if one is to live properly, the work is also fundamentally concerned with highlighting the difficulties inherent in the process of reading.

This overall subject matter is inevitably self-referential intended to encourage the recipients of the text to compare the protagonists' textual engagement with the way in which they themselves approach the J.T. Whilst virtually all Middle High German narratives require the audience to pass some form of judgment on the overall actions of the protagonists, the J.T. is relatively unusual in that it requires its audience specifically to "read the readers," in the sense of passing judgment on the adequacy or otherwise of their textual engagement. At the same time, the J.T.'s adaptation of narrative material from the works of the historical Wolfram von Eschenbach, together with the its polemical appropriation of 'Wolfram' as a narrator, means that the recipients of the J.T. are also forced to form a view on the appropriateness of Albrecht's "reading" of Wolfram.

The texts confronting the protagonists of the J.T. range from the most mundanely pragmatic documents to the Brackenseil, the Grail, and the ubiquitous yet often misunderstood "book" of God's creation. That Albrecht thinks in terms of a textual continuum extending from the routine correspondence of the Arthurian court to the universe itself is made clear by the ways in which the Brackenseil and the Grail occupy intermediate positions on the cusp of the human and the divine. Although one is clearly human in provenance and the other divine, each uses textual elements normally associated with the other domain. For its full impact, the Brackenseil depends on the impact of the jewels that form part of God's second-language discourse, while the Grail, for all its sanctity, does not shy away from using ordinary human script in its communications. Nonetheless, despite this suggestion of a broadly conceived textual continuum, there is an unmistakable hiatus, or even disjuncture, between the Brackenseil and the Grail: the latter is flawless, but the former, although marked by good intentions, is as fallible as it author and may be seen as representative of the short-comings of all human writing. As the vast majority of texts confronting the protagonists are authored by other human beings, the narrative constitutes an extended discourse on how to deal most appropriately with a category of objects that is essentially problematic, yet also fundamental for anybody wising to survive and to flourish within the culture depicted.

There is a certain ambivalence in the J.T. regarding the level at which the cultural attainment of the protagonists is pitched. On the one hand, levels of education seem to be high: virtually everybody is able to read and the members of the Arthurian court reveal a strong textual orientation. They not only find written documentation psychologically reassuring, but also choose to express their sense of their own elite sophistication through the use of inscriptions on armor and clothing and through the inclusion of classical references in their conversation. To that extent, they may be regarded as representative of the thirteenth century, in which expressions of unease at an increasingly facile engagement with writing were common. On the other hand, however, Albrecht stresses the fact that the events of the narrative are actually set in a more backward age, around 500 A.D., when the population as a whole was less well taught and sophisticated. Specifically, they are said to be unfamiliar with the kind of competent pastoral and didactic care that Albrecht associates with his own time. The fact that the Arthurian community is so easily bedazzled by the public readings of the Brackenseil at least partly due to the fact that they had never before experienced a comparable moral treatise. Similarly, their obsession with other forms of textuality is also presented as misguidedly naive: the facts of the narrative demonstrate that the trust in the supposed clarity and solidity of written documentation is misplaced, while the fashion for inscriptions and quotations is associated with an excessively secular mindset.

The events surrounding the Brackenseil illustrate a number of issues relating to literacy and textuality. Just as in the case of everyday documents, the J.T. expresses an aversion to the use of texts for purposes of self-promotion and entertainment, so in the case of the Brackenseil, the protagonists' half-hearted engagement is handled disapprovingly. Furthermore, this disapproval is gender-specific: the men most actively involved in the quest for the inscribed leash are neither literate (given that they have no desire to read and assimilate its contents) or even particularly textual in orientation (given that they are more interested in possessing the hound and see the leash as a trinket to be handed on to a woman). By contrast, even Jescute, the most inadequate of the female claimants, actively desires ownership, whereas Clauditte and Sigune are to be taken seriously as representative of the roles of writer and reader.

Despite the fundamentally good advice set out in the Brackenseil, Clauditte's authorship is complicated by her attempts to be rhetorically seductive (both in relation to Ekunat, the man she loves, and to a wider readership) and by the use of jewels in forming the script. The jewels possess not only a second-language meaning of their own, which is potentially at odds with the first-language meaning of the words chosen by Clauditte, but they also exert their natural powers to cast a temporary spell over anybody who comes into contact with the Brackenseil.

Whilst the jewels form part of God's creation and are therefore not inherently bad, the J.T. disapproves of the way in which it has become possible for the materiality of the text to override the verbal contents. Reading is ultimately presented in the J.T. as a slightly austere intellectual quest, engaging the readers' mental faculties rather than their senses. Whilst it would not necessarily have been undesirable for a reader to engage intellectually with the jewels, mapping out the second-language meaning of each and every one, the response of the Arthurian court is purely passive and pleasure oriented: moral teaching has become packaged as entertainment, with the jewels providing the court with a cheap experience of being uplifted. It should be stressed that the communal nature of the reading is not a decisive factor here: the passivity of the courtiers derives from their mental stance, not from the fact that they are listening rather than running their eyes over the text. In theory, at least, adequate reading should be achievable even if based on an aural reception of the text. On the other hand, the fact that Sigune constitutes the only adequate recipient of the Brackenseil, underscores the fact that private reading is more likely to be conducive to an intellectual response.

Although it has sometimes been argued that the Brackenseil, with its seductive beauty and virtuous message, constitutes a metaphor for Albrecht's aspirations for his own text, this suggestion does not take account either of Clauditte's problematic methodology (arising from her mixed motivation) or of the fundamental ineffectiveness of the Brackenseil (which is destroyed without its message having made any serious impact on the world). The writing on the Grail offers a far more appealing model of textual efficacy. Of course, merely recognizing in a very general way that God is a better writer than Clauditte does not take one very far in developing a cogent model of human authorship. However, the specifically eucharistic nature of the Grail provides Albrecht with the opportunity to develop a notion of sacramental writing based on a partnership of God and human being. Just as the words spoken by the celebrant of a sacrament are endowed with a power and efficacy going far beyond their ordinary connotation, so the implicit suggestion is that the J.T. is not only eucharistic in subject matter, but also—with the help of God—in impact. Like the body of Christ, which is present both in heaven and on every altar where communion is celebrated, so the Grail is present both in India and within every adequate recipient of the J.T. Furthermore, the sacramental understanding of the function of the J.T. hinges not only on the eucharistic nature of the Grail, but also on the discussion in the prologue of the cleansing nature of baptism. Notwithstanding the fact that sacramental ritual is fundamentally oral in nature, and notwithstanding the widespread association of script with death and the flesh, the implicit contention of the J.T. is thus that under certain circumstances, writing—and fiction at that—need not be debarred from the domain of the sacral.

However, if this cleansing and transformative impact of the J.T. is to be stronger than, and fundamentally different from the spell cast by the Brackenseil, the readers must be more actively engaged on the interpretative quests than were the members of the Arthurian court. Accordingly, they are not only confronted with multiple levels of signs—letters, words, names, objects, and narrative facts—but are also constantly reminded of potential interpretative challenges and pitfalls.

The fictionality of the work constitutes one such challenge. To a large extent, the universe of the J.T. is designed to replicate the real world: the text not only stresses its own historicity (in contrast to other Arthurian romances), but also aspires to encyclopedic completeness in the presentation of natural phenomena. The recipients may thus be lulled into the belief that interpreting the J.T. is a good approximation—or even a short cut—to interpreting the book of God's creation. However, the text also contains numerous reminders of the difference between archetype and image. For example, the narrative world of the J.T. not only contains hybrid creatures of Albrecht's own invention but subjects these to the kind of allegorical interpretation normally reserved only for the constituent parts of the real "book of nature." Similarly, through the playful use of etymologies and name-switching, attention is drawn to the constructed, "textual" nature of the protagonists themselves. Finally, the mediated nature of the narrative introduces a barrier between the audience and the intradiegetic world—for example, attention is drawn to the linguistic difference between what the protagonists supposedly said (in French) and what the audience is told (in German) that they said.

Overall, this conceded divergence of the fiction from reality gives scope for *integumentum*-style reflection on the didactic function of made-up tales and for a sapiential interpretation of vrou Aventiure, the allegorical guardian of the narrative facts and of the *lere* associated with these. However, whilst the J.T. regularly insists on the importance of *lere* within its program, the precise nature of the didactic contents supposedly being promulgated is deliberately shrouded in ambiguity. Here, a major contributory factor is the plurality of voices mediating the narrative and the very different moral codes associated with 'Wolfram' on the one hand, and with 'Albrecht' and vrou Aventiure on the other.

Whereas the views ascribed to 'Wolfram' are vigorously denigrated by his opponents, 'Wolfram' himself is never entirely silenced, with the result that the J.T. may be regarded as an exercise in the containment of divergent world views. The prologue's quasi-scientific discussion of water provides a useful poetological analogy for the relationship between the two narrators. In its description of how water may miraculously solidify to form stones, the prologue takes two examples, the crystal and the porous enidorium. In the case of the crystal, the transition of the water from the liquid to the solid state constitutes a general image for the way in which divine assistance might render a text "solid," both literally (in the sense of being indelible) and morally. By contrast, the enidorium, a solid stone that is nonetheless permeated with flowing water, illustrates the nature of the complexities of the interaction between 'Albrecht' and 'Wolfram.' Just as the solidity of the enidorium is permeated by fluid water, so the J.T. loses none of its God-given "solidity" despite being permeated by the voice and views of 'Wolfram.' Indeed, just as it is the presence of water that makes the enidorium unique amongst stones, so it is the tension between 'Albrecht' and 'Wolfram' that provides the audience with a worthy and lasting interpretative challenge.

NOTES

Introduction

1. Walter Haug, *Literaturtheorie im deutschen Mittelalter. Von den Anfängen bis zum Ende des 13. Jahrhunderts*, 2nd edn. (Darmstadt: Wissenschaftliche Buchgesellschaft, 1992) provides a compelling overview.

2. Hartmann von Aue, *Iwein* 54–59, ed. Ludwig Wolf based on the text by Georg Friedrich Benecke and Karl Lachmann, 7th edn., 2 vols. (Berlin: de Gruyter, 1968) suggests that it is better to hear stories about Arthur than to have experienced his reign firsthand. Thomasin von Zirclaria, *Der Wälsche Gast* 1121–1126, ed. Heinrich Rückert, Bibliothek der gesamten deutschen National-Literatur 30 (Quedlinburg: G. Basse, 1852); reprinted with a foreword and index by Friedrich Neumann, Deutsche Neudrucke: Texte des Mittelalters (Berlin: de Gruyter, 1965) addresses the truth-value of fiction: *ich schilt die âventiure niht, / sit uns ze liegen geschiht / von der âventiure rat, / wan si bezeichenunge hât / der zuht und der wârheit: / daz wâr man mit lüge kleit.* [I do not criticize stories on account of the fact that they impel us to tell lies, for they signify breeding and truth: that which is true is clothed with lies.] On fiction as *integumentum* [a layer of lies concealing an inner moral truth], see also Harald Haferland, *Höfische Interaktion. Interpretationen zur höfischen Epik und Didaktik um 1200*. Forschungen zur Geschichte der älteren deutschen Literatur 10 (Munich: Fink, 1989), pp. 14–18; Haug, *Literaturtheorie*, pp. 228–240; Gertrud Grünkorn, *Die Fiktionalität des höfischen Roman um 1200*, Philologische Studien und Quellen 129 (Berlin: Erich Schmidt, 1994), pp. 52–60 and 193–194; and Christoph Huber, "Zur mittelalterlichen Roman-Hermeneutik: Noch einmal Thomasin von Zerklaere und das Integumentum," in *German Narrative Literature of the Twelfth and Thirteenth Centuries. Studies Presented to Roy Wisbey on his Sixty-fifth Birthday*, ed. Volker Honemann (Tübingen: Nimeyer, 1994), pp. 27–38.

3. For the ways in which Middle High German texts thematize the nature and extent of their dependence on French or Latin sources, see Carl Lofmark, *The Authority of the Source in Middle High German Narrative Poetry*, Bithell Series of Dissertations 5 (London: Institute of Germanic Studies, 1981), especially pp. 48–87. In the twelfth century, the most striking indication of a sense of literary canon in Middle High German is found in the catalogue of narrative and lyric poets in Gottfried von Straßburg's *Tristan* 4621–4820, ed. and German trans. Rüdiger Krohn based on the text by Friedrich Ranke, 3rd edn., 2 vols., Universal-Bibliothek 4471–4472 (Stuttgart: Reclam, 1984). For the further development of the concept of authorship during the thirteenth century, see Sebastian Coxon, *The Presentation of Authorship in Medieval German Narrative Literature 1220–1290* (Oxford: Oxford University Press, 2001).

4. In Middle High German Arthurian romances, an implicit sense of what is now called "genre" is created through narratorial discussion of the stock figure of Arthur: a narrator may speculate as to the expectations of the audience, or contrast his own approach to this figure with those found in other texts. Often the point of such comments is to suggest that Arthur is in fact less ideal than might be expected, and that other texts have been simplistic is failing to stress this. See Bernd Schirok, "*Artûs der meienbære man–Zum* Stellenwert der 'Artuskritik' im klassischen deutschen Artusroman," in *Gotes und der werlde hulde. Literatur in Mittelalter und Neuzeit. Festschrift für Heinz Rupp zum 70. Geburtstag,* ed. Rüdiger Schnell (Bern: Francke, 1989), pp. 58–81; Klaus Grubmüller, "Die Konzeption der Artusfigur bei Chrestien und in Ulrichs *Lanzelet:* Mißverständnis, Kritik oder Selbständigkeit? Ein Diskussionsbeitrag," in *Chrétien de Troyes and the German Middle Ages,* ed. Martin H. Jones and Roy Wisbey, Arthurian Studies 26 (Cambridge: D.S. Brewer, 1993), pp. 137–149. For Albrecht's contribution to this critique, see chapter 1, section I and chapter 2, section II of this monograph. For Wolfram von Eschenbach's polemical uses of intertextuality, see Christine Wand, *Wolfram von Eschenbach und Hartmann von Aue: Literarische Reaktionen auf Hartmann im "Parzival,"* 2nd edn. (Herne: Verlag für Wissenschaft und Kunst, 1992); and Ulrike Draesner, *Wege durch erzählte Welten. Intertextuelle Verweise als Mittel der Bedeutungskonstitution in Wolframs "Parzival,"* Mikrokosmos 36 (Frankfurt am Main: Peter Lang, 1993). For a useful overview of the concept of intertextuality more generally, see also Klaus Ridder, *Mittelhochdeutsche Minne—und Aventiureromane: Fiktion, Geschichte und literarische Tradition im späthöfischen Roman: "Reinfried von Braunschweig," "Wilhelm von Österreich," "Friedrich von Schwaben,"* Quellen und Forschungen 12 (Berlin: de Gruyter, 1998), pp. 37–47.

5. See Dennis Howard Green, *Medieval Listening and Reading: The Primary Reception of German Literature 800–1300* (Cambridge: Cambridge University Press, 1994).

6. Wirnt von Grafenberg, *Wigalois* 1, ed. Sabine Seelbach and Ulrich Seelbach based on the text by J.M.N. Kapteyn (Berlin: de Gruyter, 2005).

7. Heinrich von Veldeke, *Eneasroman: Mittelhochdeutsch—Neuhochdeutsch,* Universal-Bibliothek 8303, ed. and trans. Dieter Kartschoke based on the text by Ludwig Ettmüller (Stuttgart: Reclam, 1989). Passages highlighting the literacy of the protagonists include 1530–1534, 10624–10627, 10789–10808. Cf. Henning Wuth, "*was, strâle* und *permint.* Mediengeschichtliches zum Eneasroman Heinrichs von Veldeke," in *Gespräche—Boten—Briefe. Körpergedächtnis und Schriftgedächtnis im Mittelalter,* ed. Horst Wenzel, Philologische Studien und Quellen 143 (Berlin: Erich Schmidt, 1997), pp. 63–76.

8. Wolfram von Eschenbach, *Parzival* 115.25–116.3, ed. Eberhard Nellmann, 2 vols., Bibliothek des Mittelalters 8.1–2 (Frankfurt am Main: Deutscher Klassiker Verlag, 1994).

9. Wolfram von Eschenbach, *Willehalm* 2,19–20, ed. Joachin Heinzle (Tübingen: Niemeyer, 1994). The narrator of *Willehalm* shares the personality and mannerisms of his *Parzival*-counterpart. The fact that he specifically incorporates authorship of *Parzival* into his identity (*Willehalm* 4,19–20) encourages the audience to regard the two narrators as a single figure. By contrast, in Wolfram's *Titurel,* the narrator is much more withdrawn and less inclined to impart personal information about himself.

10. For a survey of interpretations of the apparent claims to illiteracy, see Wolfram von Eschenbach, *Parzival,* ed. Nellmann, 2:517, and Joachim Bumke, *Wolfram von Eschenbach,* Sammlung Metzler 36, 7th edn. (Stuttgart: Metzler, 1997), pp. 5–8 and p. 25. It should be noted that these enigmatic claims do not stop Wolfram from operating with a complex configuration of written authorities in *Parzival:* Wolfram's

actual source, Chrétien de Troyes, is said to have told the tale incorrectly (827,1–2), by contrast with the invented authority Kyot (827,3–4), whose wide-ranging research supposedly included both the chronicles of the house of Anjou (455,2–24) and the astronomical writings of the heathen Flegetanis (454,9–455,1).

11. Albrecht Hagenlocher, "Littera Meretrix. Brun von Schönebeck und die Autorität der Schrift im Mittelalter," *Zeitschrift für deutsches Altertum und deutsche Literatur* 118 (1989): 131–163.

12. Brun von Schönebeck, *Das Hohe Lied* 953–956, ed. Arwed Fischer, Bibliothek des Litterarischen Vereins in Stuttgart 198 (Tübingen: Litterarischer Verein, 1893). For the importance of Wolfram for Brun, see Annette Volfing, "The Song of Songs as Fiction: Brun von Schönebeck's *Das Hohe Lied*," in *Vir ingenio mirandus. Studies Presented to John L. Flood*, ed. William Jones, Göppinger Arbeiten zur Germanistik 710 (Göppingen: Kümmerle, 2003), pp. 137–154.

13. *Albrechts [von Scharfenberg] Jüngerer Titurel*, ed. Werner Wolf (I–II,2) and Kurt Nyholm (II,2–III,2), 5 vols. (I; II,1; II,2; III,1; III,2), Deutsche Texte des Mittelalters 45, 55, 61, 73, 77 (Berlin: Akademie-Verlag, 1955–1992). Very little is known about the identity of Albrecht. It was previously assumed that this Albrecht was identical with Albrecht von Scharfenberg, a figure associated with a work on Merlin and with various other texts. Hence the first three volumes of the critical edition (ed. Wolf) name Albrecht von Scharfenberg as the author of the J.T. However, whilst it cannot be entirely ruled out that these two shadowy authors are one and the same, there is very little positive evidence supporting the assumption. Accordingly, the last two volumes (ed. Nyholm) simply present J.T. as the work of Albrecht. For further discussion of this issue, see Dietrich Huschenbett, "Albrecht von Scharfenberg," in *Die deutsche Literatur des Mittelalters. Verfasserlexikon*, ed. Kurt Ruh, 2nd edn., 10 vols. (Berlin: de Gruyter: 1978–1999), 1:200–206.

14. The complexities of the manuscript tradition are such that there remains some doubt as to the exact number of strophes forming part of the J.T. The work is represented by eleven more or less complete manuscripts, forty-five fragments, and one early print: these fall into two distinct recensions, of which the first (I) forms the basis for the critical edition. The second recension (II) is regarded by Kurt Nyholm, "Pragmatische Isotypien im 'Jüngeren Titurel.' Überlegungen zur Autor-Hörer/ Leser-Situation," *Wolfram-Studien* 8 (1984): 127 [120–137] as a *lectio facilior*, not least because it simplifies the narratorial situation by omitting strophe 5961, with its crucial reference to 'Albrecht.' The critical edition runs to 6327 numbered strophes but also includes certain additional strophes. These blocks of additional material include: 1) a forty-two-strophe *Marienlob* [praise of Mary] inserted after J.T. 439; 2) six strophes on the nature of dragon-people inserted after J.T. 3363; 3) eighteen further closing strophes inserted after J.T. 6327; 4) the so-called "Hinweisstrophen" [reference strophes] (J.T. 449 A and 1172 A) and "Kunststrophen" [poetological strophes] (J.T. 499 B–F). With the possible exception of J.T. 1172 A (for which see n30 below), the Hinweisstrophen and Kunststrophen are generally regarded as forming part of the J.T. The authenticity of the other additional strophes is more dubious, although Kurt Nyholm, *Studien zum sogenannten geblümten Stil*, Acta Academiae Aboensis, ser. A, Humaniora 33.2 (Åbo: Åbo akademi, 1971), pp. 53–56 does regard the *Marienlob* as the work of Albrecht. For an overview of the manuscript tradition, see Dietrich Huschenbett, "Albrecht, Dichter des 'Jüngeren Titurel," in *Die deutsche Literatur des Mittelalters. Verfasserlexikon*, ed. Kurt Ruh, 2nd edn., 10 vols. (Berlin: de Gruyter: 1978–1999), 1:161–163 [1:158–173]; for a more detailed discussion, see the introduction to the critical edition (I:xliv–cviii); and also

Walter Röll, *Studien zu Text und Überlieferung des sogenannten Jüngeren Titurel*, Germanische Bibliothek, reihe 3, Untersuchungen und Einzeldarstelllungen (Heidelberg: C. Winter, 1964). A further important companion document to the J.T.—not included in the critical edition—is the so-called "Verfasserfragment" (Vf), which is most readily accessible in the transcription by Andrea Lorenz, *Der Jüngere Titurel als Wolfram-Fortsetzung. Eine Reise zum Mittelpunkt des Werks*, Deutsche Literatur von den Anfängen bis 1700 36 (Bern: Peter Lang, 2002), pp. 68–72. In this text Albrecht, rather than operating with a 'Wolfram'-mask, represents himself as an author reacting to the work of Wolfram. The Vf is discussed in chapter 4 of this monograph.

15. Other Middle High German texts may also be regarded as significant pre-texts for the J.T., as will be discussed in chapter 5, section I. For the particular importance of Wolfram's *Willehalm* for the J.T., see Lorenz, *Wolfram-Fortsetzung*, pp. 303–316.

16. As very little is known about the life of Albrecht, (cf. n13 above and Lorenz, *Wolfram-Fortsetzung*, pp. 109–129), the dating of the J.T. is based largely on internal evidence: for example, as the J.T. 2997 refers obliquely to Richard of Cornwall as being alive, it seems likely that at least half of the work was extant by his date of death (April 2, 1272). The second Hinweisstrophe (J.T. 1172 A), which refers to a master picking up Wolfram's *Titurel* fragments fifty years later, appears also to suggest that the J.T. was composed in the late 1260s and early 1270s. However, the status of this strophe is problematic, as will be discussed in n30 below. The Vf itself can be dated more precisely as it refers indirectly to the attempt of the Wittelsbacher Ludwig II (1253–1294) to become Deutscher König: this would place it between April 2, 1272 (the death of Richard of Cornwall) and October 1, 1273 (the election of Rudolph of Habsburg). However, attempts to date the J.T. by reference to the Vf (on the grounds that the assertion of Albrecht's authorship in the latter text must have coincided chronologically with the introduction of 'Albrecht' into the J.T. in strophe 5961) have now been discredited (cf. Lorenz, *Wolfram-Fortsetzung*, p. 120). Finally, the date of death of the Franciscan preacher Berthold von Regensburg (December 14, 1272) has also been suggested as a *terminus ante quem* for the J.T., given a number of verbal parallels between the J.T. and the German sermon material ascribed to Berthold, the most striking of which relates to the allegorical interpretation of the planets in J.T. 2803–2805 and the Berthold sermon *'Von den siben planêten'* (Berthold von Regensburg, *Vollständige Ausgabe seiner deutschen Predigten*, ed. Franz Pfeiffer and Joseph Strobl, 2 vols. (Vienna: Braumüller, 1862–1880), 1:48–64. However, as Walter Röll, "Berthold von Regensburg und der 'Jüngere Titurel,'" *Wolfram-Studien* 8 (1984): 67–93 argues convincingly that Albrecht was drawing on Berthold (rather than the other way around), there is no reason to suppose that passages such as J.T. 2803–2805 must have been composed before the death of Berthold. See also Lorenz, *Wolfram-Fortsetzung*, pp. 131–135.

17. Most strikingly, Ulrich von dem Türlin's *Arabel* (previously know as *Willehalm*) is a prequel to Wolfram's *Willehalm*, whilst Ulrich von Türheim's *Rennewart* is a sequel to the same text. Note also the various attempts to continue Gottfried's *Tristan* (Ulrich von Türheim; Heinrich von Freiberg; *Tristan als Mönch*). On the *Tristan* material, see Peter Strohschneider, "Gotfrid-Fortsetzungen. Tristans Ende im 13. Jahrhundert und die Möglichkeiten nachklassischer Epik," *Deutsche Vierteljahrschrift für Literaturwissenschaft und Geistesgeschichte* 65 (1991): 70–98; on literary continuation more generally, see Lorenz, *Wolfram-Fortsetzung*, pp. 23–53. Of course, many Middle High German "classics" also suggest temporal, or even causal connections between the events that they describe and the events set out in other works. For

example, as Arthurian romances are typically understood to share a common narrative universe, it is easy for a narrator to "date" his events by reference to events in earlier works of the same genre. Thus the events of Hartmann's *Iwein* explicitly take place after those of Hartmann's *Erec* and are affected by these (cf. *Iwein* 2791–2798). Similarly, the genealogical links set out in Wolfram's *Willehalm* are such that this work may be seen as continuing the religious conflict described in Pfaffe Konrad's *Rolandslied*; for these links, see Jeffrey Ashcroft, *"dicke Karel wart genant*: Konrad's *Rolandslied* and the Transmission of Authority and Legitimacy in Wolfram's *Willehalm*," in *Wolfram's "Willehalm": Fifteen Essays*, ed. Martin H. Jones and Timothy McFarland (Rochester, NY and Woodbridge, Suffolk: Camden House, 2002), pp. 21–43. See also chapter 5, section I of this monograph for the way in which the J.T. positions itself temporally with respect to works other than *Parzival*.

18. On the overall phenomenon, see Hedda Ragotzky, *Studien zur Wolfram-Rezeption. Die Entstehung und Verwandlung der Wolfram-Rolle in der deutschen Literatur des 13. Jahrhunderts*, Studien zur Poetik und geschichte der Literatur 20 (Stuttgart: Kohlhammer, 1971). Note in particular the presentation of 'Wolfram' as a protagonist within the riddle contests ('Rätselspiele') of the *Wartburgkrieg*: here he engages in conflict with Klingsor, a figure based nominally on one of "his" own characters from *Parzival* (Clinschor). For general information on this part of the 'Wartburgkrieg,' see Burghart Wachinger, *Sängerkrieg. Untersuchungen zur Spruchdichtung des 13. Jahrhunderts*, Münchener Texte und Untersuchungen 42 (Munich: Beck, 1973), pp. 83–89; and the same author, "Wartburgkrieg," in *Die deutsche Literatur des Mittelalters. Verfasserlexikon*, ed. Kurt Ruh, 2nd edn., 10 vols. (Berlin: de Gruyter: 1978–1999), 10:746–750 [10:740–766]. For literary parallels between the *Wartburgkrieg* and the J.T., see Lorenz, *Wolfram-Forsetzung*, pp. 138–141.

19. The J.T.'s model of using a 'Wolfram'-narrator is also taken up by the *Göttweiger Trojanerkrieg* (dated ca. 1270–1300) and by Johann von Würzburg's *Wilhelm von Österreich* (dated 1314). In the latter work, the narrator even switches from calling himself 'Wolfram' to calling himself 'Albrecht,' by analogy with the J.T. See Cora Dietl, *Minnerede, Roman und historia. "Der Wilhelm von Österreic" Johanns von Würzburg*, Germanistische Forschungen N.F. 87 (Tübingen: Niemeyer, 1990), pp. 268–272.

20. For an overview of Arthurian romance in German, see Volker Mertens, *Der deutsche Artusroman*, Universal-Bibliothek 17609 (Stuttgart: Reclam, 1998); Martin H. Jones and Roy Wisbey (eds.), *Chrétien de Troyes and the German Middle Ages*, Arthurian Studies 26 (Cambridge: D.S. Brewer, 1993); William Henry Jackson and Silvia Ranawake (eds.), *The Arthur of the Germans: The Arthurian Legend in Medieval German and Dutch Literature* (Cardiff: University of Wales Press, 2002). For the development of Grail literature in a European context, see Richard Barber, *The Holy Grail. Imagination and Belief* (London: Allen Lane, 2004). For German Grail romances, see Volker Mertens, *Der Gral: Mythos und Literatur*, Universal-Bibliothek 18261 (Stuttgart: Reclam, 2003).

21. *Parzival* 114,12.

22. *Parzival* 138–141 and 249.

23. Whilst the *Nibelungenlied*-strophe consists of four long lines each separated by a cesura, the *Titurel*-strophe follows the pattern 4+4a / 4+6a / 6b / 4+6b, with no cesura in the third line. The J.T.-strophe represents a further refinement of the *Titurel*-strophe, in that it includes internal rhymes in the first two lines (4a+4b / 4a+6b / 6c / 4+6c). Cf. Mertens, *Artusroman*, p. 286; also Wolfram von Eschenbach, *Titurel. Text—Übersetzung—Stellenkommentar*, ed. Helmut Brackert and

Stephan Fuchs-Jolie (Berlin: de Gruyter, 2003), pp. 21–23 for metrical details and for discussion about the thematic connections between *Titurel* and the *Nibelungenlied*.

24. A synopsis of the events relating to the Brackenseil is provided in chapter 3, section I.

25. *Parzival* 141,16.

26. Note the spelling of the hero's name. The names of the protagonists of the J.T. are given as listed in the index at the end of the critical edition (III,2:490–600). Some of these spellings differ from the forms associated with the works of Wolfram. Thus Tschinotulander, Gamuret, Jescute, Parzifal, and Klinschor are characters in the J.T., as opposed to Wolfram's Schionatulander, Gahmuret, Jeschute, Parzival, and Clinschor. Similarly, the mountain on which the Grail temple is located is called Munt Salvasch in the J.T., as opposed to Wolfram's Munsalvæsche.

27. On this account, Tschinotulander's death is attributable partly to bad luck, and partly to his immoderate pursuit of courtly renown. Cf. chapter 4.

28. *Parzival* 478,8–484,8.

29. Cf. Lorenz, *Wolfram-Fortsetzung*, pp. 320–322.

30. The editors of the critical edition believed that the function of the so-called Hinweisstrophen (J.T. 499 A and 1172 A) was precisely to acknowledge the start of the *Titurel*-fragments embedded within the J.T., and that the Kunststrophen (J.T. 499 B–F; so called because they contain poetological reflection) fitted into this same context —notwithstanding the fact that the manuscripts within the first recension (on which the critical edition is based) in fact place the strophes now identified as J.T. 499 A–F after J.T. 919 (rather than after J.T 499) and do not include J.T. 1172 A anywhere. The presentation of these strophes in the edition has been challenged by Thomas Neukirchen, "*krumb* und *sliht*. Über die sogenannten Hinweis- und Kunststrophen im Überlieferungszweig I des 'Jüngeren Titurel,'" *Zeitschrift für deutsches Altertum und deutsche Literatur* 132 (2003): 62–76. He questions the appropriateness of including J.T. 1172 A at all (given that it is only transmitted in the second recension) and of moving J.T. 499 A–F away from the context in which the manuscripts place them and in which they make sense. Neukirchen's argument is central to the question of how the J.T. positions itself with respect to *Titurel*, but also highlights the complexities of the manuscript tradition. Cf. nn14 and 16 above.

31. On the prestige of the J.T., see the fourteenth-century lyrical and didactic poet Hugo von Montfort, Song 15.43, *Das poetische Werk. Texte—Melodien—Einführung*, ed. Wernfried Hofmeister (Berlin: de Gruyter, 2005), p. 54: *Ich hán ain búch gelesen, / aller tewtsch ain blúm / (das mag nicht anders wesen), / genant 'Títterel', ist es sunder rúm.* [I have read a book called *Titurel* which is, indisputably and without any exaggeration, the flower of all German writing.] As song 15 refers to events from the J.T. that do not occur in *Titurel* (e.g., Ekunat's killing of Orilus; the translation of the Grail to India), Hugo is clearly using the name *Titurel* to refer to Albrecht's work. In the fifteenth century, Jakob Püterich von Reichertshausen also speaks proudly of the fact that he possesses a copy of the J.T.: *Ich hab den Titurel, / das haupt ab teutschen puechen* (*Ehrenbrief* 100,1–2, ed. Fritz Behrend and Rudolf Wolkan (Weimar: Gesellschaft der Bibliophilen, 1920) [I own the *Titurel*, the greatest of German books].

32. For example, August Wilhelm Schlegel, *Geschichte der deutschen Sprache und Poesie. Vorlesungen an der Universität Bonn seit dem Wintersemester 1818–1819*, ed. Joself Körner, Deutsche Literaturdenkmale des 18. und 19. Jahrhunderts 147 = 3. Folge 27 (Berlin: B. Behr, 1913), p. 121.

33. Wolfram von Eschenbach, *Werke*, ed. Karl Lachmann (Berlin: Georg Reimer, 1833); 6th edn. (Berlin: de Gruyter, 1926), p. XXIX.

34. Karl Rosenkranz, *Über den Titurel und Dantes Komödie* (Halle: Reinicke, 1829), p. 53. Cf. Karl Lachmann, "Titurel und Dante," (review of Rosenkranz, *Über den Titurel*), *Hallische Allgemeine Literatur-Zeitung* 238 (1829): 351–357.

35. Conrad Borchling, *Der jüngere Titurel und sein Verhältnis zu Wolfram von Eschenbach* (Göttingen: Dieterich'sche Universitäts-Buchdruckerei, 1897) also consistently stresses the apparent dependence of Albrecht on Wolfram. For a more detailed survey of early critical responses and for the extent to which Lachmann's personal dislike of the J.T. was allowed to set the tone for the next hundred years, see Lorenz, *Wolfram-Fortsetzung*, pp. 53–62.

36. Notably, Hanspeter Brode, *Untersuchungen zum Sprach- und Werkstil des "Jüngeren Titurel" von Albrecht von Scharfenberg*, Dissertation (Freiburg in Breigau, 1966); Ragotzky, *Wolfram-Rezeption*, pp. 93–141; Klaus Zatloukal, *Salvaterre. Studien zu Sinn und funktion des Gralsbereiches im "Jüngeren Titurel,"* Wiener Arbeiten zur germanistischen Altertumskunde und Philologie 12 (Vienna: Halosar, 1978); Dietrich Huschenbett, *Albrechts "Jüngerer Titurel." Zu Stil und Komposition*, Medium Aevum: Philologische Studien 35 (Munich: Fink, 1979); with particular reference to sexual ethics, Herbert Guggenberger, *Albrechts Jüngerer Titurel: Studien zur Minnethematik und zur Werkkonzeption*, Göppinger Arbeiten zur Germanistik 566 (Göppingen: Kümmerle, 1992); and Lorenz, *Wolfram-Fortsetzung*.

37. Michael Curschmann, "Das Abenteuer des Erzählens. Über den Erzähler in Wolframs 'Parzival,'" *Deutsche Vierteljahrschrift für Literaturwissenschaft und Geistesgeschichte* 45 (1971): 627–667. Kurt Nyholm, "Pragmatische Isotypien," 136 dismisses the view that the J.T. was intended to be understood as the work of the historical Wolfram, and argues instead that the various riddles and games of disguise built into the narratorial situation in the J.T. would have been comprehensible to the original audience.

38. Werner Schröder, *Wolfram-Nachfolge im "Jüngeren Titurel": Devotion oder Arroganz*, Frankfurter wissenschftliche Beiträge 150 (Frankfurt am Main: Klostermann, 1982).

39. Georg Gottfried Gervinus, *Geschichte der deutschen Dichtung*, 5th edn., 5 vols. (Leipzig: W. Engelmann, 1871–1874), 2:161 compares the J.T. to a fruit that is not only tremendously difficult to peel, but also has a bitter taste.

40. Ulrich Wyss, "Den 'Jüngeren Titurel' lesen," in *Germanistik in Erlangen. Hundert Jahre nach der Gründung des Deutsche Seminars*, ed. Dietmar Peschel, Erlanger Forschungen, Reihe A, Geisterwissenschaften 31 (Erlangen: Universitätsbund Erlangen-Nürnberg, 1983), p. 95 [pp. 95–113].

41. Guggenberger, *Minnethematik*; Lorenz, *Wolfram-Fortsetzung*; Volker Mertens, "Wolfram als Rolle und Vorstellung. Zur Poetologie der Authentizität im 'Jüngeren Titurel,'" in *Geltung der Literatur. Formen ihrer Authorisierung und Legitimierung im Mittelalter*, ed. Beate Kellner and others, Philologische Studien und Quellen 190 (Berlin: Erich Schmidt, 2005), pp. 203–226.

42. The terms "intra-" and "extradiegetic," referring respectively to that, which exists inside and outside a particular narrative world, form part of the narratological terminology developed by Gérard Genette, *Narrative Discourse. Translation of "Discours du récit," a portion of Figures III*, trans. Jane E. Lewin (Ithaca: Cornell University Press, 1980). For a helpful summary and elucidation of Genette's terminology, see also Ludger Lieb and Stephan Müller (eds.), *Situationen des Erzählens. Aspekte narrativer Praxis im Mittelalter*, Quellen und Forschungen 20 (Berlin: de Gruyter, 2002), pp. 7–8, n23.

43. Adolf Muschg, *Der Rote Ritter. Eine Geschichte von Parzivâl* (Frankfurt am Main: Suhrkamp, 1993), p. 648. This imaginative modern novel retells Wolfram's narrative with considerable elaborations.

44. The miraculous properties of Wolfram's Grail are listed by Bumke, *Wolfram*,
    pp. 107–113. The main differences between Wolfram's Grail and Albrecht's Grail
    are summarized by Zatloukal, *Salvaterre*, pp. 233–236.

45. The Grail reveals the names of those who are summoned to its community. For the
    minor differences as to how this procedure operates in the J.T. as opposed to in
    Parzival, see Guggenberger, *Minnethematik*, pp. 88–92, who points out that whereas
    the decisions set out on Wolfram's Grail seem to be entirely inscrutable, Albrecht's
    Grail is more transparent in its selection criteria, summoning anybody who lives
    according to its strict moral code. Albrecht also grants the Grail a further level of
    selectivity as to its addressees, in that it is able to command its own physical removal
    from one cultural environment (Salvaterre in Galicia) and its translation to another
    (the land of Prester John in the East).

46. See J.T. 443,2–3, when the Grail commands the marriage of Titurel to Richaude:
    iwer zweier geburt ich also schribe / daz ir ein ander sit mit rehte nemende. [I record the
    births of both of you, so that you might properly take each other in marriage.]

47. J.T. 579,4: *Alsus der gral was sagende allez mit der schrifte sunder stimme.* [The Grail said
    everything in writing, without using a voice.] There is, however, a tradition of
    ascribing speech even to ordinary written documents. As well as the speaking book
    at the start of *Wigalois* (see n6 above), note also the speaking letter in *Parzival* 78,20:
    ein brief sagt im daz maere [a letter pronounces the news to him]. For the notion of a
    letter as a "sprechende Instanz" [speaking authority], see Horst Wenzel, "Boten und
    Briefe. Zum Verhältnis körperlicher und nicht-körperlicher Nachrichtenträger," in
    Gespräche–Boten–Briefe. Körpergedächtnis und Schriftgedächtnis im Mittelalter, ed. Horst
    Wenzel, Philologische Studien und Quellen 143 (Berlin: Erich Schmidt, 1997),
    p. 97 [pp. 86–105]. For speaking texts more generally, see Michael Clanchy, *From
    Memory to Written Record. England 1066–1307*, 2nd edn. (Oxford: Basil Blackwell,
    1993), pp. 253–256. Clanchy, *Memory*, p. 253 quotes John of Salisbury's claim
    (*Metalogicon* I.13, ed. J.B. Hall and K.S.B. Keats-Rohan, Corpus Christianorum,
    Continuatio Mediaevalis 98 (Turnhout: Brepols, 1991), p. 32) that *Litterae . . .
    frequenter absentium dicta sine uoce loquuntur* [Often letters of the alphabet articulate
    voicelessly the utterances of the absent.]

48. Flegetanis' ability to read about the Grail in the stars (*Parzival* 454,21–23) constitutes
    one of many examples of the interpretability of the natural world in that work—an
    approach that Albrecht builds on in the J.T. For Wolfram's presentation of the
    cosmos more generally, see Wilhelm Deinert, *Ritter und Kosmos im Parzival. Eine
    Untersuchung der Sternkunde Wolframs von Eschenbach*, Münchener Texte und
    Untersuchungen 2 (Munich: Beck, 1960).

49. The link between the Grail and the Last Supper is only made explicit in J.T. 6293;
    and its association with the legend of Joseph of Arimathea in J.T. 6296.

50. Titurel makes it clear that although the raw material for the Grail came from heaven,
    this material was then subjected to human craftsmanship: *Ein schar den gral uf erde bi
    alten ziten brahte. / ein stein in hohem werde. man eine schuzzel druz da wurken dahte.*
    (J.T. 6292,1–2) [A host of angels brought the Grail down to earth a long time ago.
    This was a stone of great value. It was decided to make a cup of out it.]

51. For detailed discussion of the Grail temple, see Gundula Trendelenburg, *Studien zum
    Gralraum im Jüngeren Titurel*, Göppinger Arbeiten zur Germanistik 78 (Göppingen:
    Kümmerle, 1972); Karen-Maria Petersen, "Zum Grundriß des Graltempels," in
    Festschrift für Kurt Herbert Halbach zum 70. Geburtstag, ed. Rose Beate Schäfer-
    Maulbetsch, Göppinger Arbeiten zur Germanistik 70 (Göppingen: Kümmerle,
    1972), pp. 271–306; Zatloukal, *Salvaterre*, pp. 158–230; Finckh, *Minor Mundus*,

pp. 344–366; Richard Barber and Cyril Edwards, "The Grail Temple in *Der Jüngere Titurel*," *Arthurian Literature* 20 (2003): 85–102; Britta Bussmann, "Mit *tugent* und *kunst*. Wiedererzählen, Weitererzählen und Beschreiben in Albrechts Jüngerem Titurel," in *Übertragungen. Formen und Konzepte von Reproduktion in Mittelalter und Früher Neuzeit*, ed. Britta Bussmann and others, Trends in Medieval Philology 5 (Berlin and Ney York: de Gruyter, 2005), pp. 437–461.

52. Ruth Finckh, *Minor Mundus Homo. Studien zu Mikrokosmos-Idee in der mittelalterlichen Literatur*, Palaestra 306 (Göttingen: Vandenhoeck and Ruprecht, 1999), pp. 326–378 sees the construction of interpretable key objects within the narrative framework as central to Albrecht's didactic program. In particular, she focuses on the Grail temple and on Tschinotulander's salamander shield as key objects that are largely or entirely of Albrecht's own invention. However, whilst the Grail temple features certain written inscriptions (as will be discussed in chapter 1 of this monograph), the salamander shield is not textual in this sense: its significance is deduced entirely through the interpretation of natural phenomena (cf. chapter 2, section II of this monograph).

53. When the opposition between the voice of 'Wolfram' and that of 'Albrecht'/vrou Aventiure is not functionalized, this study will, for convenience, simply speak of "the narrator" as though there were one such single figure.

54. Other passages presenting the text as a *buᵒch* [book] include J.T. 5960,4, 5988,2, and 5990,1. However, this 'Wolfram' also fleshes out his role with protestations of illiteracy (e.g., J.T. 68,2) similar to the ones made by the narrator in the works of the historical Wolfram. For further discussion, see chapter 4.

55. This strophe ends by expressing hope of salvation for all *di iz hoᵉren, lesen oder schriben* (J.T. 6327,4) [who hear, read, or copy it]. For the ambiguity in the presumed mode of reception of the J.T., see Green, *Medieval Listening*, pp. 81, 93, 142, and especially p. 209: "the author supplied a range of pointers to an acoustic reception and little for reading, but stresses the written dimension of his work and links this explicitly with a double formula." Examples of this "double formula" include J.T. 1663,1 (*Swer hie nu vreude si lesende oder hoᵉre an disem buᵒche* [whoever reads or hears about joy in this book]) and J.T. 6077,4 (*diez lesen oder hoᵉren, oder der iz sag oder in dem done singe* [those who read it or hear it, or who recite or sing it in the proper tune]).

56. Thomas Aquinas, *Summa Theologiae*, ed. Thomas Gilby, 61 vols. (London: Blackfriars, 1963–1980), 3a, 66.5.ad 3, 57:24.

1   Literacy and Textual Culture: Letters, Lettering, and Literature

1. Brian Stock, *The Implications of Literacy. Written Language and Models of Interpretation in the Eleventh and Twelfth Centuries* (Princeton: Princeton University Press, 1983), p. 6. For the nature of the "illiteracy" of Teanglis of Talimon, the knight who is unable to read the Brackenseil, see chapter 3. Note that Tschinotulander stresses his own literacy in the context of the Brackenseil (J.T. 1213).

2. Stock, *Literacy*, p. 7. Note also the distinction made by Mary Carruthers, *The Book of Memory. A Study of Memory in Medieval Culture* (Cambridge: Cambridge University Press, 1990), p. 11 between literacy and literary culture: "As a concept, literacy privileges a physical artefact, the writing support, over the social and rhetorical process that a text both records and generates." In Carruthers' terms, "textualiztion" (like its synonym "familiarization") refers to the process of collective assimilation within a literary culture: it represents the "institutionalization of a story through *memoria*" (p. 12).

3. In the J.T., the principal linguistic barrier to be crossed, both in speech and writing, is that between French and Arabic, the principal language of the heathens. In general, the heathens are presented as more linguistically versatile than the Christians. The heathen *baruc* Ackerin, for example, writes to Tschinotulander in French (J.T. 5900,3). Tschinotulander implicitly highlights his knowledge of Arabic culture (if not of Arabic language) when he tells Sigune that he never heard of a leash being inscripted, either in French or in Arabic (J.T. 1213). In the equivalent strophe in *Titurel* (169,2), Schionatulander mentions *brieve, buoch, en franzoyse* [letters and books in French], but makes no reference to Arabic. Explicit references to competence in Latin are rarer, although traditional instruction in *grammatica* plays a part in Titurel's upbringing (J.T. 184,3: *an der grammatik wart er schier vol varnde* [he soon made good progress with *grammatica*]) and many protagonists express familiarity with Latin literature, as is discussed in section III of this chapter. For the presentation of linguistic diversity and multilingualism in Wolfram's *Willehalm*, see Kathryn Starkey, *Reading the Medieval Book. Word, Image, and Performance in Wolfram von Eschenbach's Willehalm*, Poetics of Orality and Literacy (Notre Dame: University of Notre Dame Press, 2004), pp. 23–46; on the plurality of heathen languages in *Willehalm*, see Paul Kunitzsch, "Caldeis und Côati," *Deutsche Viertaljahrsschrift für Literaturwissenschaft und Geistesgeschichte* 49 (1975), 372–377.

4. Timo Reuvekamp-Felber, "Briefe als Kommunikations- und Strukturelemente in der 'Virginal'," *Beiträge zur Geschichte der deutschen Sprache und Literatur* 125 (2003): 57 [56–81].

5. For a useful overview of critical positions, see Dennis H. Green, "Terminologische Überlegungen zum Hören und Lesen im Mittelalter," in *Eine Epoche im Umbruch. Volkssprachliche Literalität 1200–1300*, ed. Christa Bertelsmeier-Kierst and Christopher Young (Tübingen: Niemeyer, 2003), pp. 1–22. For the coexistence of oral and written culture (including, for example, the public reading of letters as a formal reenactment of the underlying dialogic situation), see Wenzel, "Boten und Briefe," in *Gespräche–Boten–Briefe*, pp. 86–105.

6. Rolf Köhn, "Latein und Volkssprache, Schriftlichkeit und Mündlichkeit in der Korrespondenz des lateinischen Mittelalters," in *Zusammenhänge, Einflüsse, Wirkungen. Kongressakten zum ersten Symposium des Mediävistenverbandes in Tübingen 1984*, ed. Joerg Fichte (Berlin: de Gruyter, 1986), pp. 340–356 argues that the literary representation of private reading would not have reflected actual practices before the thirteenth century: in the earlier Middle Ages, a letter would have been written down in Latin by a scribe (who might have had to translate the contents relayed to him orally by a "sender" who did know Latin). The letter would then be read out (and, if necessary, translated back into the vernacular) for the benefit of the addressee(s).

7. For the function of letters within postclassical narratives, see Helmut Brackert, "*Da stuont daz minne wol gezam*. Minnebriefe im späthöfischen Roman," *Zeitschrift für deutsche Philologie* 93 (1974): 1–18; also Karina Kellermann and Christopher Young, "You've got mail! Briefe, Büchlein, Boten im 'Frauendienst' Ulrichs von Liechtenstein," in *Eine Epoche im Umbruch. Volkssprachliche Literalität 1200–1300*, ed. Christa Bertelsmeier-Kierst and Christopher Young (Tübingen: Niemeyer, 2003), pp. 317–344.

8. The designation "briefwütig" is applied to the author of the *Virginal* by Dietmar Peschel-Rentsch, *Pferdemänner. Sieben Essays über Sozialisation und ihre Wirkungen in mittelalterlicher Literatur*, Erlangen Studien 117 (Erlangen: Universitätsbund Erlangen-Nürnberg, 1998), p. 193 On the importance of letters in the *Virginal*, see also Uta Störmer-Caysa, "Die Architektur eines Vorlesebuches. Über Boten, Briefe und

Zusammenfassungen in der Heidelberger 'Virginal'," *Zeitschrift für Germanistik* N.F. 7 (2002): 12–24. For the proliferation of letters in Johann von Würzburg's *Wilhelm von Österreich*, a work that is influenced by the J.T., see Dietl, *Minnerede*, pp. 83–93. For the Alexander-material, see Christine Wand-Wittkowski, *Briefe im Mittelalter. Der deutschsprachige Brief als weltliche und religiöse Literatur* (Herne: Verlag für Wissenschaft und Kunst, 2000), p. 39.

9. Wand-Wittkowski, *Briefe*, pp. 336–352 provides a catalogue of letters featuring in Middle High German narrative texts.

10. Christian Kiening, *Zwischen Körper und Schrift. Texte vor dem Zeitalter der Literatur* (Frankfurt am Main: Fischer, 2003), pp. 20–21.

11. For the use of *schriben* to refer to the formulation of an authoritative oral statement, see J.T. 2546,1 (*Ein ander wort zem grale der engel hat geschribene* [the angel said one more thing about the Grail]); for the use of the term to refer to a strongly felt opinion, see J.T. 617,2 (*gen werdicheit ichz schribe* [I ascribe this to moral worthiness]). Note also the quasi-metaphorical use of the verb *schriben* in *Parzival* 752,20 when Feirefiz, reunited with his brother Parzival, exclaims in delight *Jupiter, diz wunder schrîp* [Jupiter, record this marvel]. The implication here is not only that the reunion is remarkable and worthy of record, but also (more fundamentally) that facts are validated through the production of written records.

12. Here the Brackenseil constitutes an important exception: although it is ostensibly addressed only to Ekunat, it contains a number of general formulations would be out of place in a purely private love-letter. Cf. chapter 3, section I.

13. For further discussion of the reception of Ovid by the protagonists, see section III of this chapter.

14. In J.T. 2603,1–2, the narrator wonders why the heathens, who are skilled in the arts, should be spiritually misguided. He goes on to compare the heathens to performing animals: apes (J.T. 2603,4), dogs (J.T. 2604,1), and talking birds (J.T. 2604,2). The pagan Greeks are condemned in similar terms in J.T. 837–838, notwithstanding the fact that they are credited with discovery of all the arts (J.T. 838,4). Nonetheless, morally excellent heathens (such as Secureiz) do feature in the J.T.; on this point, see Lorenz, *Wolfram-Fortsetzung*, p. 169; Finckh, *Minor Mundus*, p. 343.

15. Occasionally, the narrator equates *diu schrift* with the Bible (e.g., J.T. 32,3; 368,2). However, the term is also used indiscriminately to refer to all other forms of writing.

16. Deut. 4.1: *Audi, Israel, praecepta vitae, et scribe ea in corde tuo.* [Listen, Israel, to the precepts of life and write them in your heart.]

17. Ackerin, for example, knows about Christ through hearsay rather than from reading Scripture—and is puzzled by what he hears (J.T. 3619,1). However, for the sake of Tschinotulander, he is resolved to honor Christ, even if he cannot worship him (J.T. 3621).

18. In the earlier stages of the narrative, God's commandments are received orally, through the mediation of an angel (J.T. 161,4; 271,2), but once the Grail has been entrusted to Titurel, it becomes the chief conduit for the word of God. For example, it is the Grail which promises that Anfortas' suffering will be relieved when a knight asks the right question unprompted (J.T. 5270) and which commands the journey to the East (J.T. 6068). As in *Parzival*, it also lists the names of those who are chosen to belong to its community (J.T. 520–521). However, Guggenberger, *Minnethematik*, pp. 88–89 argues that the J.T. operates with objective selection criteria (based on the personal virtue of potential members), thereby allowing the Grail less scope for apparently idiosyncratic decisions than was the case in *Parzival*.

19. The messages appearing on the Grail are also to be regarded as spiritual sustenance. Under the new regime following the death of Titurel, the Grail no longer provides food for its community, but continues to reveal written directions (J.T. 6307,1–2).

20. For the notion that some letters originate in heaven, see L. Böer, "Briefe," in *Marienlexikon*, ed. Remigius Bäumer and Leo Scheffczuk, 6 vols. (St Ottilien: Eos, 1988–1994), 1:588–589 [1:584–589].

21. Exod. 31.18. For the view that God's authorship of the Tablets lends sanctity to the act of writing, see Ernst Robert Curtius, *European Literature and the Latin Middle Ages*, trans. Willard R. Trask (London: Routledge and Kegan, 1953), pp. 314–315. For articulation of the idea that the "Book of Life" was written by God, see Exod. 32.22, Ps. 68.29, and Ps. 138.16, as well as the discussion by Curtius, *European Literature*, pp. 311 and 318–319. There are references to the "Book of Life" in J.T. 634,3 and 998,4: this written list of those who obtain salvation serves as a heavenly counterpart to the Grail which also records the names of those who can expect to obtain salvation (J.T. 272,2; 2544,3–4).

22. For surveys of this topos, see Curtius, *European Literature*, pp. 319–326 and Jesse M. Gellrich, *The Idea of the Book in the Middle Ages. Language Theory, Mythology, and Fiction* (Ithaca: Cornell University Press, 1985), pp. 29–50.

23. Alan of Lille, *De incarnatione Christi rhytmus perelegans* (second version) 1–3, PL 210:579 [210:579–580]: *omnis mundi creatura / Quasi liber, et pictura / Nobis est, et speculum.* [Every creature in the world is like a book, and like a picture and a mirror for us.]

24. Walter J., Ong, *Orality and Literacy. The Technologizing of the Word* (New York: Routledge, 1982, reprint. 2002), p. 74.

25. This dual aspect lends a particular complexity to the reading of an item such as the Brackenseil, which is a conventional text in the sense that it consists of letters and words, but which also happens to be fashioned out of materials that are themselves open to independent interpretation.

26. Note the celebration of God's cosmic *getihte* (J.T. 3,3) in the prologue to the J.T. For further discussion, see chapter 5, section III.

27. Geoffrey Galt Harpham, *The Ascetic Imperative in Culture and Criticism* (Chicago: University of Chicago Press, 1987), p. 6. Ong, *Orality and Literacy*, p. 80 also comments on the association of writing with death, noting that "The paradox lies in the fact that the deadness of the text, its removal from the living human lifeworld, its rigid visual fixity, assures its endurance and its potential for being resurrected into limitless living contexts by a potentially infinite number of living readers."

28. Harpham, *Ascetic Imperative*, p. 6: "Even God's writing requires phonemic redemption; even Scripture requires the mediation of Christ."

29. Martin Irvine, *The Making of Textual Culture. 'Grammatica' and Literary Theory 350–1100* (Cambridge: Cambridge University Press, 1994), p. 188.

30. Augustine, *Confessiones* 13.15, ed. Lucas Verheijen, Corpus Christianorum. Series Latina 27 (Turnhout: Brepols, 1981), p. 251.

31. For example, Artus advises Ekunat to write letters to his vassals in Kanadik and Berbester, calling for their military support (J.T. 4623,2–3). Similarly, the Babylonian brothers give instructions to summon their vassals by means of letters (J.T. 853,1). See n33 below for Artus' correspondence with the King of Morocco about the abduction of the three hundred ladies from his court. Similarly, Pardiscal, another lady who has been abducted through the use of magic, is able to send a letter to her beloved Gloris, explaining what has happened, and assuring him that she is still chaste (J.T. 5600).

32. The second public reading of the Brackenseil is undertaken by a scribe (J.T. 1871,1) At the first public reading, the communicative situation is less clear.

While Linda B. Parshall, *The Art of Narration in Wolfram's 'Parzival' and Albrecht's 'Jüngerer Titurel'*. Anglica Germanica Series 2 (Cambridge: Cambridge University Press,1981), p. 143 believes that "Jescute reads the script aloud to the assembled court," the text merely states that she let the text be heard (J.T. 1505,3), leaving open the possibility that it was read out by somebody else.

33. At the return of Tschinotulander and his troops from the Orient, Artus gives orders that letters be sent to the wives of all the men (J.T. 4431,3). Similarly, when the Arthurian court discovers the disappearance of the three hundred ladies, Artus orders messengers to go with letters to the King of Morocco. However, upon receiving the latter's written reply (J.T. 2476,3–4), he reads it *tougen* (J.T. 2480,1) [privately] before sharing the news with the court.

34. Cf. the reception of Papyres' letter: *Den prief von im zelesene het man al die wochen* (J.T. 5309,1) [One had several weeks to read his letter]. Similar formulations are used in the case of Beakuns (J.T. 5309,3–4) and Ladamus (J.T. 5313).

35. Secundille reads the letter from Amicare of Larifoticone *in suᵉzem done* (J.T. 5338,2) [in a sweet tone]. It is unclear whether this phrase refers to the rhetorical / metrical qualities of the letter itself, or whether it should be taken to mean that Secundille reads the letter aloud in a sweet voice. The latter reading would conform to the pattern whereby the entire court has access to the contents of the love-letters.

36. See chapter 3, section I.

37. For a detailed discussion of the *golt der selden*, see Hans Hennig Rausch, *Methoden und Bedeutung naturkundlischer Rezeption und Kompilation im 'Jüngeren Titurel'*. Mikrokosmos 2 (Frankfurt am Main: Peter Lang, 1977), pp. 35–141.

38. For the symbolic importance of the salamander shield, and for the extent to which Tschinotulander's inability to achieve harmony amongst the elements might be indicative of a spiritual imbalance on his part, see Finckh, *Minor Mundus*, pp. 334–344.

39. J.T. 4970,3–4: ". . . *ich weiz niht hoᵉher fursten in dem riche,* " / *der weideman so jehende was,* "*nu hat iz nieman so billiche.*" ["I do not know any greater prince in the empire," the huntsman said. "Now nobody has so great a right to it."]

40. Ackerin is said to read through the battle plans that he had previously asked to have drawn up (J.T. 3119). The Babylonian brothers arrange for a written statement of their chosen vassals' contractual obligations to be drawn up: *Daz wart nu ordenliche mit schrift gemachet stete* (J.T. 911,1) [This was now set down in writing, as is proper]. When Artus promises reward to anybody who defeats Ithers, he adds: *daz wirt mit schrift versigelt und bewæret.* (J.T. 1379,4) [this is signed, sealed, and delivered.] The formulation in J.T. 2580,1 (*Do gar mit schrift vol endet wart al ir schifladunge* [their loading of the ship was recorded in full]) emphasizes the importance of paper-work in the ordinary conduct of war. Similarly, the hyperbolic statements in J.T. 854,4 (*mit schrifte ist unverendet ir gelt* [the full extent of their wealth has never been set down in writing]) and in J.T. 6255,2–3 (*nie wart geschriben uf zedele diu lenge siner lande ob und under,* / *tagweide vierzic an der wit gemezzen* [The length of his lands from one end to another was never recorded on *cedulae*. In width it measured forty days' journey]) underscores the fact that it would be normal practice for details of material possessions to be recorded in writing. Similarly, Artus' founding of religious houses at the end of the work involves appropriate documentation and inscriptions (J.T. 5954–5956).

41. See for example J.T. 2881 for the statement that written records give a full account of the feudal powers of Ackerin's ancestor Asswerus.

42. The phrase *gehugde buᵒch* essentially means "chronicle." It is used in J.T. 4078,1, when the narrator insists that the best information about Artus is to be found in Latin

chronicles as opposed to German texts. The phrase should therefore not be understood as a pure metaphor—unlike, for example, the phrase *libro de la mia memoria* [book of my memory] used in the opening sentence of Dante's *Vita Nuova*, ed. Michele Barbi, in *Le Opere di Dante. Testo Critico della Società Dantesca Italiana* (Florence: Società Dantesca Italiana, 1960), p. 1 [pp. 1–49])—although it clearly underscores the function of books in supplementing human memory.

43. Hartmann von Aue, *Iwein* 230–802.

44. *Die Klage* 4295–4319, ed., German trans., and commentary by Elisabeth Lienert, based on the text by Karl Bartsch, Schöninghs mediävistische Editionen 5 (Paderborn: Ferdinand Schnöningh, 2000). Cf. Michael Curschmann, "Hören—Lesen—Sehen. Buch und Schriftlichkeit im Selbstverständnis der volkssprachlichen literarischen Kultur Deutschlands um 1200," *Beiträge zur Geschichte der deutschen Sprache und Literatur* 106 (1984): 227–228 [218–257].

45. Pleinfeld (*Blienvelde*) is a Franconian town close to Eschenbach (or Wolframs Eschenbach, as it has been known since 1917); Albrecht appears to invoke this place as a variation on Eschenbach.

46. For further discussion of this dialogue and its bearing on the relationship between 'Wolfram' and vrou Aventiure, see chapter 4.

47. Isidore of Seville, *Etymologiarum Libri XX*, 1.3.1–2 and 1.41.1–2, ed. Wallace Martin Lindsay, 2 vols., Scriptorum classicorum bibliotheca Oxoniensis, (Oxford: Oxford University Press 1911). Cf. Titurel's injunction to the Grail community: *di lere heiz dir schriben, so kan si niht vervallen von unwitzen* (J.T. 648,4) [have this teaching written down, so that it cannot fall into oblivion through your folly.]

48. Cf. Wenzel, "Boten und Briefe," in *Gespräche–Boten–Briefe*, p. 89: "In den Archiven von Schriftgesellschaften wird eine Akkumulation von unterschiedlichen Wissensbeständen möglich, die zur Erweiterung und Korrektur persönlicher Gedächtnisleistungen herangezogen werden kann. Die tendenziell unbegrenzte Ansammlung von Informationen sprengt den Horizont verkörperter, lebendiger Erinnerung (*brain memory*) und schafft die Bedingung für abstraktes Wissen und unverkörperte Erinnerung (*script memory*)." [In the archives of textual societies it becomes possible to accumulate a variety of factual contents that can be drawn on to supplement and to correct personal acts of personal recollection. The potentially unlimited collection of points of information bursts the confines of embodied, living recollection ("brain memory"), providing the necessary condition for abstract knowledge and unembodied recollection ("script memory").]

49. Irvine, *Textual Culture*, p. 101.

50. Curtius, *European Literature*, pp. 304–305.

51. The point about literal magnification is made by Ekunat in a speech to Tschinotulander: *Sam der berillus groͤzet di schrift in im ze lesene, / din herze dem genoͤzet, dar inne alle tugende mit wesene / wahsent hoch, breit, wit und ouch di lenge.* (J.T. 1433,1–3) [Just as the beryl magnifies script to be read through it, so your heart, in which all the existing virtues grow in height, width, breadth, and length, is the equivalent of the beryl.] The beryl's power to magnify virtues has previously been set out by the narrator, in the context of explaining the meaning of the name "Parille": *Ein sin sun Parille hiez er nach dem steine, / durch daz der ougen wille da mit erget. er machet groz uz kleine, / uz cleinen tugenden machte er di grozen.* (J.T. 99,1–3) [He named one of his sons Parille/Beryl after the stone, which benefits the eyes. It makes small things great: out of small virtues it makes great ones.] For the use of the beryl for purposes of magnification (and for the link with the modern German term "Brille" [glasses]), see Thomas Bein, "Maria als Vergrößerungsglas—außerliterarische Realien und

poetische Bildlichkeit," in *Die Funktion außer—und Innerliterarischer Faktoren für die Entstehung deutscher Literatur des Mittelalters und der frühen Neuzeit*, ed. Christa Baufeld, Göppinger Arbeiten zur Germanistik 603 (Göppingen: Kümmerle, 1994), pp. 117–139.

52. For Albrecht's idiosyncratic approach to the nature of the Gamaniol (based loosely on the chameleon), see Rausch, *Methoden*, pp. 168–200.

53. The narrator's underscoring of the fact that the chronicles relating to the Grail community still survive in many place *der schrift vil unberoubet* (J.T. 5869,2) [entirely undeprived of the text] implies that this could not necessarily be expected as a matter of course. Similarly, when he discusses the virtue of the early Grail community on the basis of written records (J.T. 166,2: *als uns di schrift noch kundet* [as the text still informs us]), the *noch* serves to highlight the convenient, but nonetheless exceptional, survival of the *schrift*.

54. It is a literary commonplace that jewels should be scattered in jousts or battles. See for example *Nibelungenlied* 34,2–4 and 2209,2–3, ed. Hermann Reichert (Berlin: de Gruyter, 2005). Here, unlike in the J.T., the jewels are not bearers of any kind of meaning beyond serving as a mark of the wealth of the combatants.

55. Titurel finds the outline of the temple represented diagrammatically on the ground (J.T. 340.1), so he knows exactly how and where to set about building it. The Grail also provides further guidance with respect to building materials (J.T. 370,2–3).

56. For this idea, see for example sermon no. 58 (*Von ma^enger hande schrift der mentschait*) in *Der sogenannte St. Georgener Prediger. Eine Überlieferung von deutschen Klosterpredigten Bertholds von Regensburg aus der Freiburger und der Karlsruher Handschrift*, ed. Karl Rieder, Deutsche Texte des Mittelalters 10 (Berlin: Weidmann, 1908), p. 248 [pp. 283–287]: *Ain ander schrift hat úns ôch ûnser herre gegeben, haz ist der laýgen schrift; won der lúte ist vil die der schrift nit kunnent die an den bu°chen ist geschriben, und dar umb hât in Got ain ander schrift geben, da si an lernent wie si nach dem hymelriche sont werben. dú schrift ist daz gema^elde in der kirchen von den hailgen, wie sú lebtent und waz si durch Got tatent und waz si durch in arbait littent.* [Our Lord has also given us another form of writing that is the script of the laity; for there are many people who cannot read the writing with which books are written and therefore God has given them another form of writing, from which they may learn how to strive for heaven. This writing is the paintings in the churches of the saints, of how they lived and what they did for the sake of God and what they suffered on his account.]

57. This banner, featuring heathen script of pure gold (J.T. 3048,3) becomes part of Tschinotulander's normal equipment.

58. *Graswalt* is the land belonging to Tschinotulander (cf. *Titurel* 88,2 and 97,2); for the identification of this with Graisivaudan in the Val d'Isère (north of Grenoble), see Wolfram von Eschenbach, *Titurel*, ed. Brackert and Fuchs-Jolie, p. 208. This place-name is also discussed in chapter 2, section I of this monograph.

59. J.T. 2171, describing Tschinotulander's attacks on his enemies, makes it clear that it is normal practice for knights to wear inscripted helmets.

60. See also J.T. 1396,34 which notes that Tschinotulander wore the crown-like garland, with letters saying that Sigune was still pure and chaste.

61. In J.T. 2638,4, the narrator refers to the promise of reward that was written onto Tschinotulander's crown. This is contrasted with the grim reward (i.e., death) which others receive in the battle all around him.

62. This metaphor is consistent with the narrator's own image in J.T. 1765,4 and J.T. 1766,1 of Amor as a scribe recording developments within love-stories.

63. Harpham, *Ascetic Imperative*, p. 14.

64. For parallels between writing and corporeality, see Curtius, *European Literature*, p. 312; and especially Warren Ginsberg, "*Ovidius ethicus?* Ovid and the Medieval Commentary Tradition," in *Desiring Discourse: The Literature of Love, Ovid through Chaucer*, ed. James J. Paxson and Cynthia A. Gravlee (London: Associated University Press, 1998), pp. 62–71. Basing his ideas on Harpham, *Ascetic Imperative*, Ginsberg argues that "the scriptural qualities of a text thus enacted a kind of ascesis . . . that provided a paradigm for the ascetic's desire to mortify his flesh." (p. 68). For the biblical and patristic associations of text, scroll, and skin, see also Burt Kimmelman, "The Trope of Reading in the Fourteenth Century," in *Reading and Literacy in the Middle Ages and the Renaissance*, ed. Frederick Moulton, Arizona Studies in the Middle Ages and the Renaissance 8 (Turnhout: Brepols, 2004), p. 27 and p. 30 [pp. 25–44]. He also discusses the textualization of the body in the mystical tradition (pp. 41–44).

65. For a general discussion of intertextuality in the J.T., see chapter 5, section I. See in particular chapter 5, n25, for discussion of whether it is Ypomidon or the narrator who makes reference to Siegfried in J.T. 3364,1.

66. The literature on the reception of Ovid in the Middle Age is extensive. See in particular Karl Bartsch, *Albrecht von Halberstadt und Ovid im Mittelalter*, Bibliothek der gesammten deutschen National-Literatur 38 (Quedlinburg: G. Basse, 1861); Franco Munari, *Ovid im Mittelalter* (Zürich: Artemis, 1960); Karl Stackmann, "Ovid im deutschen Mittelalter," *Arcadia* I (1966): 231–254; Ralph Hexter, *Ovid and Medieval Schooling: Studies in Medieval School Commentaries on Ovid's 'Ars Amatoria', 'Epistulae ex Ponto', and 'Epistulae Heroidum'*, Münchener Beiträge zur Mediävistik und Renaissance-Forschung 38 (Munich: Arbeo Gesellschaft, 1986); Peter L. Allen, *The Art of Love. Amatory Fiction from Ovid to the Romance of the Rose* (Philadelphia: University of Philadelphia Press, 1992); Renate Kistler, *Heinrich von Veldeke und Ovid*, Hermaea 71 (Tübingen: Niemeyer, 1993), especially pp. 24–25; Tracy Adams, *Violent Passions. Managing Love in Old French Verse Romance*. Studies in Arthurian and Courtly Cultures (New York: Palgrave Macmillan, 2005), pp. 37–73. For mediaeval biographies of Ovid, see Fausto Ghisalberti, "Medieval Biographies of Ovid," *Journal of the Warburg and Courtauld Institute* 9 (1946): 10–59.

67. Pseudo-Ovid, *De nvncio sagaci. De mercatore. Extrait de La Comédie latine en France au XIIe siècle*, ed. Alphonse Dain (Paris: Les belles lettres, 1932). Cf. Peter Dronke, "Pseudo-Ovid, *Facetus* and the Arts of Love," *Mittellateinisches Jahrbuch* 11 (1976): 130 [126–131]. The fact that the second line of *De nvncio* (*Sperabam curis finem fecisse futuris*) is quoted in one of the celebrated love-letters in Tegernsee MS Clm 19411 (202a; IV.3.3 in Jürgen Kühnel Kühnel, *Dû bist mîn, ih bin dîn. Die lateinischen Liebes- und Freundschafts- Briefe des clm 19411. Abbildungen, Text und Übersetzung*, Literae 52 (Göppingen: Kümmerle, 1977), p. 88) suggests that the work was known in German-speaking areas. However, note also the existence of a different pseudo-Ovidian text with a similar name: *Liber trium puellarum* (cf. Bartsch, *Albrecht von Halberstadt*, p. xxxviii).

68. The story focuses on a messenger assisting his friend in the seduction of a young girl; the seduction is successful, and it appears likely that by the end, the messenger will also have enjoyed the girl in some way.

69. The Christian side includes numerous nameless masters who are particularly associated with the Grail; see Lorenz, *Wolfram-Fortsetzung*, pp. 97–107. One important named figure is Trefizent, described as *der buˣche gar ein meister wise* (J.T. 5929,3) [a wise master learned in all the books]; this individual appears to be based on the hermit who advises Parzival in book 9 of Wolfram's work.

70. J.T. 3125,1–3 point out that according to the old books, it is often the case that a smaller force has been victorious over the larger one, because those who thought themselves doomed had not feared any losses. The particular exempla adduced are

those of Judas Maccabeus (J.T. 3126) and Alexander the Great (J.T. 3127). For Albrecht's knowledge of the Alexander-material, see R. William Leckie Jr., "Albrecht von Scharfenberg and the 'Historia de preliis Alexandri Magni'," *Zeitschrift für deutsches Altertum und deutsche Literatur* 99 (1970): 120–139.

71. Secureiz is making the point that proper, courtly, fighting require periods of formal cessation to allow the virtuously energetic knight to recuperate—otherwise he will wear himself out and eventually be defeated by a more cowardly type who will have been husbanding his resources in an ungallant manner. This is illustrated by the siege of Troy, which eventually leads to the defeat of the noble Trojans, who slip up after defending themselves for ten years. On the basis of this, Secureiz resolves to be *ein vrid geb* (J.T. 3549,3) [a guarantor of peace (i.e., of appropriate breaks)] in the coming battle.

72. The term *praeceptor amoris* derives from Ovid, *Ars armatoria* 17, ed. Henri Bornecque (Paris; Les belles lettres, 1960). For discussion of the context, see Hexter, *Ovid,* pp. 21–22.

73. Gregorius (Hartmann von Aue, *Gregorius* 1565–1624, ed. Burghart Wachinger based on the text by Paul Hermann, 13th edn., Altdeutsche Textbibliothek 2 (Tübingen: Niemeyer, 1984)), Parzival (*Parzival* 126,9–14) and Gawan (*Parzival* 66,15–22) all experience an urgent desire to embark upon knighthood.

74. Cf. Gottfried von Straßburg, *Tristan* 2085–2086: *der buoche lêre und ir getwanc / was sîner sorgen anevanc* [Book-learning and the associated discipline formed the start of his sorrows.]

75. Guggenberger, *Minnethematik,* p. 73 believes the texts in question to have been medieval courtly romances, and goes as far as to suggest that Titurel's reference to Ovid is to be taken as a circumlocution for the Ovidian content to be found in courtly romances. However, while there is some merit to the suggestion that Titurel might first have come across love in courtly romances, Guggenberg's reading does not do justice to the numerous references made in the text to Ovid as an author (rather than just as a ciphre for "courtly love").

76. For the use of Ovid in the schoolroom, see Hexter, *Ovid.*

77. Allen, *Art of Love,* pp. 53–54. Adams, *Violent Passions,* p. 37 argues that the Ovid received by medieval composers of romance was a composite figure, both a practical expert on the conduct of love affairs and "a philosopher who theorized upon love from a Neoplatonic perspective." Accordingly, Ovid's advice on love was taken "in a positive light, as offering models for mitigating amour, the imperious urge to consummate unleashed by elemental forces."

78. The nature of *minne* and *unminne* [love and its opposite] is later discussed by 'Wolfram' and vrou Aventiure, the latter claiming that the true *minne* has nothing to do with the Ovidian arrows (J.T. 4023). Guggenberger, *Minnethematik,* p. 153 notes that the Ovidian arrows of gold and lead, which have become familiar in Middle High German literature via Veldeke, are in the J.T. associated purely with heathen idolatry of Amor: a Babylonion knight has them depicted on his banner (J.T. 4036–4037). For further discussion of this, see chapter 4.

79. In terms of *leckerie* [lechery], even the adult Titurel is said to be like a child of seven (J.T. 463,4).

80. Alan of Lille, *De arte praedicatoria,* PL 210:179; quoted by Hexter, *Ovid,* p. 17.

81. Ginsberg, "Ovidius," in *Desiring Discourse* discusses the curious transformation of Ovid into an "ethical pedagogue" (p. 62) and a "voice of moral integrity" (p. 63), arguing that "the commentators . . . couldn't maintain that the amatory poems were themselves inducements to . . . ascetic conduct; when they classified works as ethical, they were not offering Ovid's poems for the reader's emulation as much as their

own textual performance. Certainly the utility of the commentaries derived in part from their ability to serve Ovid's works by making them accessible. Their ultimate value, though, had to reside in the facticity of the commentary itself, since Ovid's poems entered the ambit of ethical discourse only when they were submitted to moral or grammatical explication. In promoting their ethical Ovid, medieval scholiasts therefore were actually presenting an image of themselves as writers." (p. 67).

82. When telling the Arthurian court about Secundille's love for Anfortas, Ekuba also invokes Ovid as a measure of literary competence: *swer sin liehten luter claren varwe / zerehte pru͡efen solte, ich wǣne, Ovidio zerunne garwe.* (J.T. 5304,3–4) [If anybody were to do justice to his bright, radiant appearance—I believe this would defeat even Ovid.] Note a similar statement from an equally worldly character (Gawan), in Wirnt von Grafenberg, *Wigalois* 990–992: *. . . wan hêt sich ie gevlizzen / Ôvîdîus mit lobe dar / ern möhte si niht volloben gar.* [even if Ovid had devoted himself to formulating praise, he would not have been able to praise her exhaustively.]

83. Sigune also praises Tschinotulander's eloquence in J.T. 5226,1 and 5452,1.

84. Cf. the narrator's criticism of Lunete and Laudine in *Parzival* 436,4–10.

85. So, for example, in the dialogue about *minne / unminne* (J.T. 4016–4026) [love and its opposite], vrou Aventiure finds it necessary to take the narrator to task for ostensibly favoring an 'Ovidian' approach to love. Cf. Guggenberger, *Minnethematik*, pp. 149–155; and chapter 4 of this monograph.

86. The pairing of Ovid with a master of the natural world, the Byzantine Emperor Heraclius, who was regarded as an expert on precious stones, means that he is not only seen as a skilled wordsmith, but also as a man of learning. Heraclius is also mentioned in *Parzival* 773,22 and in *Willehalm* 331. Cf. Ulrich Engelen, *Die Edelsteine in der deutschen Dichtung des 12. und 13. Jahrhunderts*, Münstersche Mittelalterschriften 27 (Munich: Fink, 1978), p. 44; Wolfram von Eschenbach, *Parzival*, ed. Nellmann, 2:765; Lorenz, *Wolfram-Fortsetzung*, p. 98. For the wider importance of Heraclius for the J.T., see also chapter 5, sections II and III.

87. Kiening, *Körper und Schrift*, pp. 179–198. Guibert de Nogent, *Autobiographie*, ed. and trans. Edmond-René Labande, Les classiques de l'histoire de France au moyen âge 34 (Paris: Les belles lettres, 1981).

88. Kiening, *Körter und Schrift*, p. 189.

89. Ginsberg, "Ovidius," in *Desiring Discourse*, p. 67.

90. Ginsberg, "Ovidius," in *Desiring Discourse*, p. 66. See also p. 69; "Because love in Ovid is always a textual affair, all his amatory poems, but especially the *Ars*, which openly appropriates the forms of didacticism, make us see that ethical abstinence is itself a species of desire."

91. Ginsberg, "Ovidius," in *Desiring Discourse*, p. 68.

92. The work of Ovid thus forms a counterpart to the so-called bridge of virtue that later constitutes a test for the Arthurian court and which affirms the knightly excellence of Tschinotulander (J.T. 2382–2429). However, whereas Tschinotulander is tested within a secular, courtly framework, the function of the Ovid-episode is to set Titurel apart from this world and to demonstrate his suitability for Grail kingship.

2 First and Second Language: Names, Etymologies, and Natural Phenomena

1. Cf. Eckhard Hegener, *Studien zur "zweiten Sprache" in der religiösen Lyrik des zwölften Jahrhunderst. Adam von St. Victor. Walter von Châtillon*, Beiheft 6 zum Mittellateinischen Jahrbuch (Wuppertal: Kastellaun, 1971), p. 11: "Die erste Sprache ist die Sprache in

der zwischenmenschlichen Begegnung, die 'zweite Sprache' ist die Sprache dessen, der nicht nur durch Worte, sondern auch durch Taten und Dinge als Folgen seiner Taten spricht." [The first language is that used in human interaction, the "second language" is the language of him who speaks not only through words, but also through actions and through the things which result from his actions.] However, for the present discussion, divine communication through actions (beyond the act of creation itself) is of subordinate importance.

2. See also the following studies by Hennig Brinkmann: "Die 'Zweite Sprache' und die Dichtung des Mittelalters," in *Methoden in Wissenschaft und Kunst des Mittelalters*, ed. Albert Zimmermann, Miscellanea Mediaevalia 7, (Berlin: de Gruyter, 1970), pp. 155–171; "Die Zeichenhaftigkeit der Sprache, des Schrifttums und der Welt im Mittelalter," *Zeitschrift für deutsche Philologie* 93 (1974): 1–11; "Die Sprache als Zeichen im Mittelalter," in *Gedenkschrift für Jost Trier*, ed. Hartmut Beckers and Hans Schwarz (Cologne: Böhlau, 1975), pp. 23–44; *Mittelalterliche Hermeneutik* (Darmstadt: Wissenschaftliche Buchgesellschaft, 1980).

3. While the traditions of "Vierfacher Schriftsinn" [four levels of allegorical interpretation] encouraged medieval writers to take a particular interest in determining the *significationes* of the natural objects mentioned in the Bible, the scope of second language was not limited to these objects, but potentially extended to everything created by God. For example, Alan of Lille, *Elucidatio in Cantica Canticorum*, PL 210:53 characterizes *omnis creatura* [every creature] as *significans* [carrying signification].

4. On the exegesis of the pelican, see Christoph Gerhardt, *Die Metamorphosen des Pelikans: Exempel und Auslegung in mittelalterlicher Literatur. Mit Beispielen aus der bildenden Kunst und einem Bildanhang*, Trierer Studien zur Literatur 1 (Frankfurt am Main: Peter Lang, 1979).

5. Hegener, *Studien*, p. 10.

6. Augustine, *De doctrina christiana*, ed. Joseph Martin, Corpus Christianorum. Series Latina 32 (Turnhout: Brepols, 1962), II, i (2), pp. 32–33 distinguishes between *signa data* [given signs] and *signa naturalia* [natural signs]: the former are used intentionally by rational beings in order to communicate (e.g., words; or in the case of God, created objects), whereas the latter merely occur in nature (e.g., smoke denotes a sign of a fire). In *De doctrina christiana* II, x (15), p. 41, Augustine also distinguishes *signa translata* [transferred signs] from *signa propria* [proper signs] for example, the term *pecus* [head of cattle] is the *signum proprium* for the animal, and the *signum translatum* for the Evangelist Matthew, to whom the animal refers. Cf. Hegener, *Studien*, pp. 7–8; Traude-Marie Nischik, *Das volkssprachliche Naturbuch im späten Mittelalter. Sachkunde und Dinginterpretation bei Jacob von Maerlant und Konrad von Megenberg*, Hermaea 48 (Tübingen: Niemeyer, 1986), p. 52.

7. There are numerous examples of this commonplace. The following statement, taken from Alexander Neckham's prologue to the second book of natural history, is particularly apposite given its scientific context (quoted by Roswitha Klinck, *Die lateinische Etymologie des Mittelalters*, Medium Aevum 17 (Munich: Fink, 1970), p. 166): *Mundus ergo ipse, calamo Dei inscriptus, littera quaedam est intelligenti, repraesentans artificis potentiam, cum sapientia eiusdem et benignitate. Sicut autem totus mundus inscriptus est, ita totus littera est, sed intelligenti et naturas rerum investiganti, ad cognitionem et laudem Creatoris.* [The world itself, inscripted with the pen of God, is to the intelligent mind, like a piece of lettering that represents the power of the creator, together with his wisdom and benevolence. Since the whole world is inscripted, it all constitutes lettering that furthers the understanding and praise of the creator, but only for the man who is intelligent and bent on investigating the natures of things.] For other examples of this

topos, see chapter 1, nn21–23; Rausch, *Methoden*, pp. 13–14; Michael Stolz, *"Tum"-Studien. Zur dichterischen Gestaltung im Marienpreis Heinrichs von Mügeln*, Bibliotheca Germanica 36 (Tübingen: Francke, 1996), pp. 236–237.

8. Cf. Hegener, *Studien*, p. 5: "Worte sind Zeichen. Zeichen aber ersetzen Dinge. Die Sprache ist also nur Ersatz. Deshalb ist sie für Augustinus von geringerer Bedeutung als die Dinge." [Words are signs. But signs substitute for things. So language is only substitution. Therefore Augustine ascribes less importance to it than to things.]

9. Augustine, *De doctrina christiana* II, xxiv (37), p. 59. On the linguistic pessimism of Augustine, see Arno Borst, *Der Turmbau von Babel. Geschichte der Meinungen über Ursprung und Vielfalt der Sprachen und Völker*, 4 vols. (Stuttgart: Hiersemann, 1957–1963), pp. 393–399. Later prominent authorities who argue the case against the God-given status of language (and against a neat correlation of *verbum* and *res*) include Anselm of Canterbury, Abelard, Richard of St. Hugo, Albert the Great, and Thomas Aquinas (Borst, *Turmbau*, pp. 605–606, 631–637, 722, and 807–811). Whilst there are very few attempts to make a philosophical case for the God-given status of language, certain popular writers favored the "traditional" view that God invented language: these include the poet Prudentius, who conveniently regards Latin as the only true language and Christ as the *verborum dator* [giver of language] (Borst, *Turmbau*, p. 410), and Honorius of Autun who maintained, against Abelard, that Adam did not gradually work out a linguistic system for himself while in Paradise, but was in full command of a God-given language from the moment of his creation (Borst, *Turmbau*, p. 654).

10. Borst, *Turmbau*, p. 397 (with reference to Augustinian thinking). For references to other writers' treatment of this important motif, see Borst, *Turmbau*, p. 1948, n209.

11. Borst, *Turmbau*, p. 632.

12. Isidore, *Etymologiarum Libri XX*, 1.7.1.

13. For example, although Rupert of Deutz, *Commentarium In Genesim* II.33, PL 167:281 notes that Adam spoke Hebrew, he still uses Latin words to illustrate the point that Adam named things on the basis of their properties (e.g., *porcus* [pig] from *spurcus* [filth]). Cf. Borst, *Turmbau*, p. 648. By contrast, Aquinas, in *Summa Theologiae* 2a, 2ae, 45.2.2 and ad 2, 35:164–166 robustly attacks the validity of Latin etymologies (e.g., *sapientia* [wisdom] from *sapida scientia* [relished knowledge]), on the ground that they do not work in Greek and therefore do not have any universal application.

14. That Latin writers generally offer limited discussion of the status of vernacular etymologies is unsurprising, given the low esteem in which vernacular languages were generally held. For example, Borst, *Turmbau*, p. 728 points out that the Latin grammarian Alexander of Villa-Dei characterizes vernacular languages as corrupted forms of Latin.

15. For the account of etymology offered by Peter Helias, see Klinck, *Etymologie*, pp. 13–14, 35–36, and 67; Klaus Grubmüller, "Etymologie als Schlüssel zur Welt? Bemerkungen zur Sprachtheorie des Mittelalters," in *Verbum et Signum. Beiträge zur mediävistischen Bedeutungsforschung. Festschrift für Friedrich Ohly*, ed. Hans Fromm, 2 vols. (Munich: Fink, 1975), 1:220–221 [1:209–230]; Uwe Ruberg, "Verfahren und Funktionen des Etymologisierens in der mittelhochdeutschen Literatur," in *Verbum et Signum. Beiträge zur mediävistischen Bedeutungsforschung. Festschrift für Friedrich Ohly*, ed. Hans Fromm, 2 vols. (Munich: Fink, 1975), 1:299–300 [1:295–330]; Suzanne Reynolds, *Medieval Reading: Grammar, Rhetoric and the Classical Text* (Cambridge: Cambridge University Press, 1996), pp. 83–84.

16. For examples of expository etymologies, see n56 below. For etymological statements in Middle High German, see Willy Sanders, "Grundzüge und Wandlungen

der Etymologie," *Wirkendes Wort* 17 (1967): 361–384; and Willy Sanders, "Die Anfänge wortkundlichen Denkens im deutschen Mittelalter," *Zeitschrift für deutsche Philologie* 88 (1969): 57–78.

17. Friedrich Ohly, "Vom geistigen Sinn des Wortes im Mittelalter," in Friedrich Ohly, *Schriften zur mittelalterlichen Bedeutungsforschung* (Darmstadt: Wissenschaftliche Buchgesellschaft, 1983), p. 29 [pp. 1–31]; originally published in *Zeitschrift für deutsches Altertum und deutsche Literatur* 89 (1958): 1–23.

18. Augustine, *De doctrina christiana* II, xvi (24), pp. 49–50; Hegener, *Studien*, p. 8.

19. For Augustine, the aural component (*sonus, vox*) is central to the *verbum*. The word on the page is therefore incomplete: a sign of a sign. Christoph Huber, *Wort sint der dinge zeichen. Untersuchungen zum Sprachdenken der mittelhochdeutschen Spruchdichtung bis Frauenlob*, Münchener Texte und Untersuchungen 89 (Munich: Artemis, 1977), p. 9 quotes *Principia dialecticae* V, PL 32:1410: *Cum enim est in scripto, non verbum, sed verbi signum est.* [When it is written down, it is not a word, but a sign of a word.]. See also the discussion in chapter 1 of the ascetic subordination of the written to the spoken word. On the necessity of the first language for the interpretation of natural phenomena, see Hegener, *Studien*, p. 27; Nischik, *Naturbuch*, p. 53.

20. Hegener, *Studien*, pp. 38–40.

21. Finckh, *Minor Mundus*, p. 378.

22. Most of Albrecht's personal names are unique identifiers; although he takes over certain doublings from Wolfram (e.g., the two Kundries and the two Claudittes), he does not develop this trend of letting the same name refer to quite unconnected people. Unless it serves to highlight a genealogical connection, the recycling of a name is rare (although the J.T. does feature two minor characters called Darius, and two called Florie). Instead, as is argued in this chapter, Albrecht uses more complicated devices (e.g., the temporary transfer of a name from one character to another) in order to bring about a dissociation of linguistic marker from personal identity.

23. To a very limited extent, Albrecht also engages with the etymologization of common nouns. For example, the narrator notes the commonplace link between *adel* [nobility] and *adelar* [eagle] (J.T. 1145,1 and 1862); comments on the link between the Latin terms *mal* [evil] and *malum* [apple] (J.T. 6036–6038), and claims that the term *karfunkel* [carbuncle or garnet] is a shortened form of *klarifunkel*, since this stone shines (i.e., remains *klar* or bright) in the dark (J.T. 3014). In the case of place-names, he also provides a few derivations *ex origo* (cf. Klinck, *Etymologie*, pp. 10–11; Huber, *Wort*, p. 165): for example, he explains that *Salvaterre*, the name of the Grail territory, comes from *Salvator* [savior] (J.T. 323), and *Luoteringen* [Lorraine] from *Lohrangrine* (J.T. 6041); and that the noun *tiger* [tiger] is derived from the river *Tigris* (J.T. 1676–1677).

24. Similarly, the Christian view is that the planets actually serve human beings (J.T. 1654), whereas the heathen Babylonians make the mistake of worshipping the sun (J.T. 2971), thereby reversing the natural order of things.

25. For a detailed discussion of Tschinotulander's salamander shield, see Finckh, *Minor Mundus*, pp. 334–344.

26. Klaus Zatloukal, "Erzählwelt in der Nußschale. Die Bildungsweise der Eigennamen Albrechts und die Großform 'Jüngerer Titurel,'" in *Namen in deutschen literarischen Texten des Mittelalters. Symposion Kiel 9–12.9.1987*, ed. Friedhelm Debus and Horst Pütz, Kieler Beiträge zur deutschen Sprachgeschichte 12 (Neumünster: Karl Wachholtz, 1989), pp. 173 [pp. 173–187]. See also Klaus Zatloukal, "Eigennamen und Erzählwelten im 'Jüngeren Titurel,'" *Wolfram-Studien* 8 (1984), 96 [94–106].

27. Zatloukal, "Nußschale," in *Namen in deutschen literarischen Texten*, pp. 173–175.

28. While the narrative reports that the children are named after their parents, Albrecht is in fact naming the parents after the children (whose names are pre-formed in the works of Wolfram). Similarly, in J.T. 444, the narrator claims that Richaude passes on to her son the name of her father Frimutel, although in fact it is Albrecht who names Richaude's father after the character created by Wolfram.

29. Wolfgang Haubrichs, "Namendeutung in Hagiographie, Panegyrik—und im 'Tristan.' Eine gattungs-und funktionsgeschichtliche Analyse," in *Namen in deutschen literarischen Texten des Mittelalters. Symposion Kiel 9–12.9.1987*, ed. Friedhelm Debus and Horst Pütz, Kieler Beiträge zur deutschen Sprachgeschichte 12 (Neumünster: Karl Wachholtz, 1989), pp. 205–224. Medieval texts often make no distinction between common nouns and proper nouns (names); for example, in Heinrich von Mügeln's *Der meide kranz* 168a–218, ed. Karl Stackmann, *Die kleineren Dichtungen Heinrichs von Mügeln. Zweite Abteilung*, Deutsche Texte des Mittelalters 84 (Berlin: Akademie Verlag, 2003), pp. 47–203, Gramatica exemplifies the noun with solely personal names. On the use of the term *nam* [noun, name] more generally in Middle High German, see Huber, *Wort*, pp. 22–45 and Rudolf Voß, "Die Idee des Namen in der höfischen Dichtung um 1200," in *Vox Sermo Res. Beiträge zur Sprachreflexion, Literatur—und Sprachgeschichte vom Mittelalter bis zur neuzeit. Festschrift Uwe Ruberg*, ed. Wolfgang Haubrichs (Stuttgart: Hirzel, 2001). pp. 21–34.

30. The beryl has the property of magnifying things, be it literally, in the case of script (J.T. 1433,1), or metaphorically, in the case of virtues (J.T. 99,2–3). Cf. chapter 1, n51. In the prologue (J.T. 39), the narrator also plays on the similarity between the name of another stone, namely the crystal, and the name of Christ. On this point, see Ruberg, "Verfahren," in *Verbum et Signum*, p. 310 and also chapter 5, section III of this monograph.

31. J.T. 1059,3–4: *ich furhte, daz ich mere nu verliese / Herzelouden, mines bruᵒder kint, daz die den tot vor herzeleide kiese.* [I fear that I might also lose Herzeloude, the child of my brother, as a result of her dying of heartache.] However, the narrator also introduces a number of apparently meaningful names into the text, with no glossing and no clear connection between meaning and identity: for example the names *Penitenz* (J.T. 439,1) and *Terribilis* (J.T. 2071,4). Cf. Zatloukal, "Nußschale," in *Namen in deutschen literarischen Texten*, p. 177. On the "mathematical" names *Abacus* and *Algorismus* (J.T. 2051,2–3), see Wolfgang Wegner, *Albrecht, ein poeta doctus rerum naturae? Zu Umfang und Funktionalisierung naturkundlicher Realien im 'Jüngeren Titurel,'* Europäische Hochschulschriften 1.1562 (Frankfurt am Main: Peter Lang, 1995), pp. 70–73.

32. Similarly J.T. 5169,3: *und hiez von Graswaldan nach gruᶜner varwe* [and was called "of Graswald / grass-forest" on account of the green color].

33. Translation (originally *interpretatio ex Graeco*) is one of three standard forms of etymology listed by Isidore, the other two being derivations and compositions; see Herbert Backes, *Die Hochzeit Merkurs und der Philologie: Studien zu Notkers Martian-Übersetzung* (Sigmaringen: Jan Thorbecke, 1982), p. 80. For etymological translation involving languages other than Greek and Latin, see also Wolfgang Haubrichs, "*Veriloquium nominis.* Zur Namensexegese im frühen Mittelalter. Nebst einer Hypothese über die Identität des 'Heliand'-Autors," in *Verbum et Signum. Beiträge zur mediävistischen Bedeutungsforschung. Friedrich Ohly Festschrift*, ed. Hans Fromm, 2 vols. (Munich: Fink, 1975), 1:241–242 [1:231–266].

34. Cf. Wolfram von Eschenbach, *Parzival*, ed. Nellmann, 2:531.

35. For a general discussion of the link between allegory and etymology, see Klinck, *Etymologie*, pp. 62–63.

36. J.T. 1199,3–4: *welt ir du^etsch ir vriundes namen erchennen? / 'den wilden von den blu°men, Ekunat,' sol man den fursten nennen.* [Do you want to hear the name of her beloved in German? One should call the prince 'Ekunat, the wild one of the flowers']; *Titurel* 157,3–4: *welt ir tutsch ir friundes namen erchennen? / der herzoge Ehcunaver von Blo^vme div wilde, alsus horte ich in nennen* [Do you want to hear the name of her beloved in German? The Duke Ekcunaver of the Wild Flower, that is what I have heard him called.] Cf. *Joachim Heinzle, Stellenkommentar zu Wolframs Titurel. Beiträge zum Verständnis des überlieferten Textes*, Hermaea 30 (Tübingen: Niemeyer, 1972), p. 202; Wolfram von Eschenbach, *Titurel*, ed. Brackert and Fuchs-Jolie, p. 257.

37. Strictly speaking, the etymological interpretations of the names of the three mistresses is provided, not by the narrator himself, but by Ekuba, as part of her long speech to the Arthurian court about the love-life of Secundille. However, the narrator clearly intrudes into Ekuba's speech with his reference to Kyot in 5354,3–4. J.T. 5355,3–4 contains a further reference to Kyot.

38. According to Borchling, *Der jüngere Titurel*, p. 90, *Barbidele* is originally the name of a herb. Cf. *Titurel* 514: *Aloe pardisee barbudele* [barbudele, the balm of Paradise].

39. Presumably the same etymological description would apply to this woman's namesake (the beloved of Ekunat and the author of the Brackenseil).

40. Zatloukal, "Nußschale," p. 177 claims that in the whole of the J.T. only one figure (Parille) has a name that relates semantically to his character. In any case, Parille is also a very minor character.

41. Nyholm, *Studien zum sogenannten geblümten Stil*, p. 119.

42. Untranslated personal names with this root include *Floragune, Florant Turkoyte, Floreis, Florie* (used for two figures), *Florjone, Florose*; untranslated place names include *Flordibale, Floristelle, Floritane, Florischanze*. The battle-cry of Anfortas is *Floriamur* (J.T. 2012,4, 2138,1). *Ekunat de Silvat* is translated as *der wilde von den blu°men* (J.T. 1199,4) [the wild one of the flowers]; see n36 above and also chapter 3, section I.

43. Haubrichs, "*Veriloquium*," in *Verbum et Signum*, p. 234.

44. Within the genre of heroic epic, the names *Hildebrand/Hadubrand* and *Hugdietrich/Wolfdietrich* constitute striking father-son pairings. For further discussion of names within this genre, see George T. Gillespie, *A Catalogue of Persons Named in German Heroic Literature* (Oxford: Oxford University Press, 1973); and Haubrichs, "*Veriloquium*," in *Verbum et Signum*, p. 234. Within courtly romance, Tristan may be deemed to bear a French translation of his father's name, on the grounds that the form *Riwalin* may be understood as *Riuwalin* (i.e., "small sorrow"), an equivalent to the element *triste* in the son's name. See Ruberg, "Verfahren," in *Verbum et Signum*, p. 311 and Lambertus Okken, *Kommentar zum Tristan-Roman Gottfrieds von Straßburg*. Amsterdamer Publikationen zum sprache und Literatur 57–58, 2nd edn., 2 vols. (Amsterdam: Rodopi, 1996), p. 56.

45. In Heinrich von Freiberg's *Tristan* continuation, *Tantrisel* (the name of Tristan's young relative) constitutes a diminutive form of *Tantris*, the pseudonym constructed by Tristan by reversing the order of the two syllables in his name.

46. In Gottfried von Straßburg's *Tristan*, the blonde Isolde bears the same name as her mother, Queen Isolde. In *Kudrun*, Hagen's wife and daughter are both called Hilde. In J.T. 3204,4, Ekuba (whose name is glossed as *tugent*) is said to have been named after her mother.

47. In the *Nibelungenlied, Sieg*mund and *Sieg*lind share a stem with their son *Sieg*fried. In Konrad von Würzburg's *Engelhard*, the princess *Engel*trut chooses to marry *Engel*hard (rather than the equally attractive Dietrich) simply because of the common element

in their two names. In the J.T., there are similar onomastic connections between *Flor*diprintze (the ruler of *Flor*dibale), his wife Alba*flore*, and their child *Flor*amie.

48. In inventing new names from his characters, Albrecht himself sometimes avails himself of the technique of fusing two halves of existing names: so the names *Cast*able and Halz*ibier* produce the form *Kastibier*, and similarly Elisi*bant* and Secun*dille* produce *Dillibande* (Zatloukal, "Nußschale," p. 175). However, the narrator does not draw attention to the way in which these names have been constructed and no genealogical links are expressed in these cases.

49. Haubrichs, "*Veriloquium*, " in *Verbum et Signum*, p. 234, n17. A further early historical parallel (*Hiltrudis* from *Hildegaudus* and *Agentrudis*) is adduced by Zatloukal, *Salvaterre*, pp. 81–82, n157.

50. For a German (theological) variant on the principle that the union of *nomen* and *verbum* results in *oratio*, see Frauenlob's *Marienleich* 16.14–17 (*Leichs, Sangsprüche, Lieder* 1,16.14–17, ed. Karl Stackmann and Karl Bertau, 2 vols., Abhandlungen der Akademie der Wissenschaften in Göttingen, philologisch-historische Klasse, 3. Folge 119–120 (Göttingen: Vandenhoeck and Ruprecht, 1981): *Daz wort mir von der höhe quam / und ward in mir ein so gebenditer nam: / der name hie wart, daz wort was ane werden ie. / von disen zwein ein rede wart gevlochten.* [The Word/verb came to me from on high and turned into such a blessed name/noun within me: the name/noun came into existence here, the Word/verb has always been, without ever coming into existence. A sentence/utterance was woven from these two.] For a similar formulation, see Alan of Lille, *Anticlaudianus* 460–466, ed. Robert Bossuat, Textes philosophiques du moyen âge 1 (Paris: Vrin, 1955).

51. On the participle, see Alan of Lille, *Anticlaudianus* 467–469: *Cur partem capiens ab utroque, rependat utrinque / Dictio quod debetur ei, sic reddit utrumque / Quod neutrum, mediumque tenens mediatur utrinque* [why a word, formed partly from a noun and another from a verb, repays to each what is owed it and noun and verb together give a meaning that neither could separately, when the word, holding a middle position, effects a union between them [trans. James J. Sheridan, *Anticlaudianus or The Good and Perfect Man* (Toronto: Pontifical Institute of Medieval Studies, 1973), pp. 88–89]]; and Heinrich von Mügeln's *Der meide kranz* 197–199, in which Gramatica sets out *und wie das participium / uß zweierlei nature kum, / uß namen und uß wortes art.* [and how the participle comes together from two natures, from the classes of the noun and of the verb].

52. Note the equivalent formulation in J.T. 276,3: *diu* [= *di frucht*] *nach ir beider namen wart genammet.* [The offspring was named after both their names.]

53. Wegner, *Albrecht*, pp. 262–269 makes an unconvincing attempt to link the seven letters of the name to the seven chambers of the womb.

54. Zatloukal, *Salvaterre*, p. 83 states that even today this kind of feeble explanation would be capable of assuaging a woman's sense of indignation.[!]

55. For critical literature discussing this particular approach to letters of the alphabet, see Johannes de Tepla, *Epistola cum Libello ackerman und Das büchlein ackerman. Nach der Freiburger Hs. 163 und nach der Stuttgarter Hs. HB X 23*, ed. and German trans. Karl Bertau, 2 vols. (Berlin: de Gruyter, 1994), 2:97. For the notion that certain letters might really "belong" to individual persons (including members of the Trinity), see the formulation (quoted by Ruberg "Verfahren," in *Verbum et Signum*, p. 304) which is used by Heinrich von Kröllwitz in his *Vater-Unser* commentary 856–859, ed. Gottfried Christian Friedrich Lisch, Bibliothek der gesammten deutschen National-Literatur 19 (Quedlinburg: G. Basse, 1839) to argue that the term *sunne* [sun] is sanctified because it contains letters properly belonging to the Son: *Sô ist der*

name ouch ûzgenumen / unde an deme beginne irgraben / mit des suns bu°chstaben; / nâch dem hât er ouch heilicheit. [So the name has been set apart and inscribed at the beginning with the letters of the Son. As a result, it too possesses sanctity.]

56. In addition to the traditional etymologies focusing on the origins of a word (in terms of derivation, composition, and translation, as set out in n33 above), the twelfth and thirteenth centuries saw the development of the notion of etymology as a technique for the *expositio* of the qualities inherent in the object or person in question. For an assessment of this new trend, see particularly Grubmüller, "Etymologie," in *Verbum et Signum*. One popular technique of etymological *expositio* involved treating words like acronyms: i.e., letting each letter of a word or name stand for a term that helps explain the meaning of the word in question. For example, *flos* [flower] can be presented as a contracted form of any of these four lines: *feni labens [h]onor seorsum; funduns late odorem suum; fructus libans opem sequentis; faciens laetum odorem suavitatis* [the honor of hay sliding separately; pouring widely its odor; then pouring a wealth of fruit; making a happy odor of sweetness]. See Klinck, *Etymologie*, p. 69: "Die Bezeichnung *flos* erweist sich somit gleichsam als eine Art Chiffre, in der die Eigenschaften des Dinges in gedrängster Form erfaßt sind. Der Etymologie wird die Funktion des Dechiffrierens zugewiesen." [The term *flos* therefore reveals itself as a kind of cipher, in which the properties of the object are set out in abbreviated form. Etymology takes on the function of deciphering.] See also Ruberg, "Verfahren," in *Verbum et Signum*, p. 325, who quotes the German-language discussion of the Latin term **mulieres** [women] provided in the *St. Georgener Prediger* pp. 283–287. Here, the meaning of each letter is given in Latin (*munda, verecundia, leta, iusta, erecta, robusta, electa, sociata*) [clean, truthful, joyful, just, upright, firm, chosen, sharing her life] and then translated into German; this example implies that letter-by-letter *expositio* only really "works" in Latin. Conversely, Frauenlob readily transfers this technique entirely to the vernacular, when he analyses **wîp** [woman] as **Wunne Irdisch Paradis** (V,102.11) [bliss—earthly—paradise]. On this line, see also Huber, *Wort*, p. 166, note 173. This form of *expositio* complements the analysis *ex origo* of the same term also offered by Frauenlob (V, 104.14: *sus wib von Wippeone quam* [thus the term "wip" came from Wippeon"].

57. Karl Bertau, *Wolfram von Eschenbach. Neun Versuche über Subjektivität und Ursprünglichkeit in der Geschichte* (Munich: C. H. Beck: 1983), pp. 166–189 discusses the extent to which Wolfram may be said to deconstruct or otherwise pun on his own name and lists the possible meanings of the two component elements; however, it should be noted that none of Wolfram's own works contain an example as direct as the one in the J.T. quoted above. For the *ram* element, Bertau lists raven, dirt, goal, frame, branch, and ram [=*aries*] as possible meanings. This proliferation of possible meanings makes the translation of J.T. 3598,1 particularly difficult. For examples of the etymological interpretations of other names involving the element *ram*, see Haubrichs, "*Veriloquium*," in *Verbum et Signum*, p. 247 (*Ram*wold) and p. 253 (Adal*ram*); in both of these cases, *ram* taken to mean *aries*.

58. See Huber, *Wort*, p. 13.

59. See Klinck, *Etymologie*, p. 13; Huber, *Wort*, p. 141.

60. Surprisingly, perhaps, nothing is made of the argument that the syllable *el* might be imbued with particular sanctity. An example of such an argument is quoted by Haubrichs, "*Veriloquium*," in *Verbum et Signum*, p. 249: "Den Abt Samuel von Lorsch erinnert der Fuldaer Abt an die letzte Silbe seines Namens, die hebräisch (*el*) den Names Gottes bedeute, was bedeute, daß der Name Gottes sinem Wesen gleichsam eingeprägt sei." [The Abbot of Fulda reminds Samuel, the Abbot of Lorsch

that the last syllable of his first name signifies the name of God in Hebrew (*el*) and that the name of God should similarly be impressed upon his nature.]

61. Similarly, Laudine is sometimes designated by the alternative form *Laudalie* (J.T. 1344,1 and 1782,1). As in the case of *Secundare*, this unfamiliar variant appears to have been introduced for the convenience of rhyme.

62. Wuth, "*was, strâle* und *permint*, " in *Gespräche—Boten—Briefe*, p. 75. Technically, Wuth is wrong to assert that the syllable (as opposed to the letter) constitutes the smallest unit of speech, since medieval writings on grammar tended to stress the point that there is a sound to match each letter (cf. for example Reynolds, *Medieval Reading*, p. 8). Nonetheless, he makes a valid point about the opposition between the oral mode of expression chosen by Dido and the written mode chosen by Lavine.

63. Although the narrator in J.T. 2603–2604 states that the heathens, for all their learning and polish, are essentially no more than talking birds (i.e., with no real understanding of the discourse they are ostensibly engaged in), this passage relates specifically to the religious blindness of the heathens and should not be read as a claim that heathen speech or writing is generally devoid of meaning.

64. For the opposition between 'Schriftlichkeit' and 'Mündlichkeit,' and for the difficulties in translating these terms, see the introduction to chapter 4.

65. Zatloukal, "Eigennamen und Erzählwelten," 99 notes that whereas Tschinotulander is referred to by name 87 times, there are approximately 490 occasions on which other formulations replace the name.

66. Cf. J.T. 3701,1: *Den Gamureten beiden, dem lebenden und dem toten* [to the two 'Gamurets,' the living one and the dead one]. For Tschinotulander's gradual assumption of the Gamuret role, see Lorenz, *Wolfram-Fortsetzung*, pp. 260–268. The fusion of identities between Parzifal and Prester John is superficially similar, but actually less compelling, given that the latter is a hereditary title rather than a unique personal identifier. After the translation of the Grail to the East, into the kingdom of the Prester John (the first of whom was baptized by the apostle Thomas), Parzifal rules as Grail King for ten years under the name of Prester John, after which the son of Feirefiz takes over.

67. Finckh, *Minor Mundus*, pp. 326–378 also examines the way in which Albrecht's scientific references relate to the notion of man as a microcosm mirroring the macrocosmic universe.

68. Cf. Wolfram von Eschenbach, *Willehalm* 2,19. For the extent to which the personality of 'Wolfram' is modeled on that of the narrators of *Parzival* and *Willehalm*, see chapter 4.

69. Wegner, *Albrecht*, p. 35.

70. The fundamentally homiletic nature of its assertion is underscored by the similarity of the strophe to a formulation used in a Berthold von Regensburg sermon. See Röll, "Berthold," 75–76; also n71 below and the Introduction, n16.

71. Kundrie has been sent from the land of Secundille to Munsalvæsche. For the way in which the encounter between these two worlds in signaled in *Parzival* 782, see Almut Suerbaum, "*Siben sterne si dô nante heidensch.* Language as a Marker of Difference in Wolfram's *Parzival* and Adolf Muschg's *Der Rote Ritter*," *Oxford German Studies* 33 (2004): 37–50. In the J.T., the three masters addressing Tschinotulander *waren geleret in Arabie* (J.T. 2683,2) [were trained in Arabia] but seem to have a Christian perspective on interpreting the planets; indeed, the contents of their discourse coincides with that of the Berthold von Regensburg sermon '*Von den siben planêten.*' See Röll, "Berthold," 73–74; Wegner, *Albrecht*, pp. 60–62;

and the Introduction, n16. By contrast with these hermeneutically sophisticated masters, purely heathen astrologers who seek to predict specific outcomes are often presented rather negatively in the J.T., as Wegner, *Albrecht*, pp. 63–64 points out. Christian astronomers/astrologers do not fare very much better when faced with practical problems: although the physicians and astronomers who are summoned to assess the plight of Pelaie in J.T. 6013–6014 give a correct diagnosis (i.e., Pelaie's indisposition is not caused by magic, but is related to the imbalance of her humors), they are unable to provide a solution and thus to prevent the death of Loherangrin.

72. J.T. 2804,2: *ze mu°te Luna keret*. This phrase is difficult to translate as it stands, although comparison with the Berthold sermon suggest that *mu°te* should be taken to mean *demu°te* (in the equivalent phrase, Bethold uses the term *demüetekeit*). This yields the meaning that "Luna teaches humility." Cf. Wegner, *Albrecht*, p. 61.

73. On the other hand, the magical impact of certain *realia* are to be taken seriously. For example, the narrator notes that all beasts, herbs, and stones possess additional powers within a 100-mile radius of Paradise (J.T. 1679).

74. For the range and nature of the Artus-criticism articulated by Wolfram (and by Hartmann von Aue), see Schirok, "*Artûs der meienbære man*," in *Gotes und der werlde hulde*.

75. *Parzival* 281.14–22.

76. On the technical details of this object, see Wegner, *Albrecht*, pp. 69–70. A heathen counterpart to this object is mentioned in J.T. 2851–2853: the canopy covering the ladies of Ackerin's household is made of blue cloth and adorned with images of the sun, moon, and stars. As well as obviously referring to the real heavens, this object, like the ceiling in the Grail temple, is also deemed to possess a further level of meaning; however, given the heathen context, the presumed *significatio* turns out to be a spurious one. The heathens have chosen the blue color in memory of Gamuret, who loved *got in himele* (J.T. 2851,4) [God in heaven]. While this is itself is a promising starting point, the heathens do not go on to make the "correct" extrapolation from creation to creator (cf. Titurel's formulation in J.T. 6302). Instead, for the heathens, the meaning of the canopy is inextricably tied up with Gamuret himself, who is elevated into the ranks of their gods. On the heathen predilection for objects with a cosmological significance, see Finckh, *Minor Mundus*, pp. 363–364.

77. See Engelen, *Edelsteine*, pp. 198–201 for the literary traditions regarding the ornamentations of domes and ceilings.

78. When this spiritual truth is articulated by Titurel in J.T. 574, it forms the start of another chain of substitutions: the written words on the page are *signa* referring to the spoken words of the narrator, which in turn replace the supposedly "historical" words of Titurel spoken on that particular occasion.

79. For example, the temperament of the crocodile (J.T. 3886: *wan niht so zornic lebt sam kokodrille* [for no creature is as fierce as the crocodile]) makes it an appropriate emblem for the aggressive heathen Ypomidon.

80. On "living" heraldic beasts, see Rausch, *Methoden*, pp. 98, 208–209, and 276–277.

81. In the narrative context, the salamander may also be taken to signify the erotic passion of Tschinotulander for Sigune. Note also the range of heraldic beasts (including salamanders), which the heathens believe they are using to signify their love interests, but which, according to vrou Aventiure in J.T. 4027–4029, really signify *unminne* [the opposite of love]. For further discussion of the heraldic emblems of the heathens, see Rausch, *Methoden*, p. 108. This erotic dimension to the salamander is consistent with Finckh's interpretation of the shield as a didactic key object that provides the audience with a visual reminder of the importance of balance (*maze*)

between the elements, on a micro- as well as on a macrocosmic level (Finckh, *Minor Mundus*, pp. 334–344).

82. J.T. 5879,1: *Und was der bracke lebende? niht, iz was sin bilde.* [And was the hound alive? No, it was an image of it.] Similarly, the ecidemon borne by Secureiz is *nicht lebende* (J.T. 3011,1) [not alive], but so skillfully constructed that it *wirt gesehn in lebelichem wane.* (J.T. 3011,3) [gives the impression of being alive].

83. See for example J.T 3662,4: *des ro^ete gap da ro^ete, daz vor im fluzzen vil der bluotes lacken.* [The redness of the dragon produced more redness, so that lakes of blood flowed before it.]

84. For discussion of this episode, see Leckie, "Historia de preliis," p.136. As Leckie correctly points out, Albrecht's narrator is less interested in the correct technique of using mirrors for dealing with a basilisk, and more in the moral exegesis of the basilisk and the mirrors to signify the victory of virtue over evil (J.T. 3989–3994).

85. Rausch, *Methoden*, pp. 201–298.

3 The Brackenseil and the Grail: Chasing the Texts

1. Haug, *Literaturtheorie*, p. 371. Parshall, *Narration*, p. 147 also highlights parallels between the Grail and the Brackenseil. With reference to J.T. 1517 (describing the effect of the first public reading), she notes that "The Gral relieves the body of suffering, and the leash likewise lessens pain by bringing joy to the heart. Yet the inscription's influence is of shorter duration. More importantly, its effect is on one's perceptions whereas the Gral actually affects the material world. The leash remains a covetable object, bound to the courtly mundane world."

2. Haug, *Literaturtheorie*, p. 372.

3. Even Sigune appears, at least initially, to value the Backenseil more than the Grail. In J.T.1504, the narrator states that if Munt Salvasch had been Sigune's to dispose of, she would willingly have sacrificed it in order to obtain the leash.

4. For the notion that literature constitutes a particularly female preoccupation, see Jürgen Wolf, *"vrowen phlegene ze lesene. Beobachtungen zur Typik einiger für den Gebrauch von Frauen bestimmten Textsorten," Wolfram-Studien* 19 (2006): 169–190. Wolf surveys the tangible, material manifestations of female engagement with textuality in the German Middle Ages.

5. See Parshall, *Narration*, pp. 85–86.

6. The splendors of Tasme, which belonged to Secureiz, the noble heathen inadvertently killed by Tschinotulander, are described in J.T. 3386–3403. Tschinotulander brings the city back as a gift for Artus (J.T. 4463). In *Parzival*, by contrast, *Thasmê* is said to be a city still located in the land of Secundille (629, 20–21).

7. For the range of meanings of *borte*, see Elke Brüggen, *Kleidung und Mode in der höfischen Epik des 12. und 13. Jahrhunderts*, Beihefte zum Euphorion 23 (Heidelberg: Winter, 1989), pp. 207–209.

8. In this chapter, my translations of passages from *Titurel* itself or of Albrecht's reworking of the *Titurel* passages draw freely on Wolfram von Eschenbach, *Parzival, with Titurel and the love-lyrics*, trans. Cyril Edwards with an essay on the Munich *Parzival* illustrations by Julia Walworth, Arthurian Studies 56 (Cambridge: D.S. Brewer, 2004).

9. Finckh, *Minor Mundus*, p. 374. Uta Drecoll, *Tod in der Liebe—Liebe im Tod: Untersuchungen zu Wolframs "Titurel" und Gottfrieds "Tristan" in Wort und Bild* (Frankfurt am Main: Peter Lang, 2000), p. 22 comments on references to clothing of Arabic provenance in *Parzival* and other courtly texts.

10. Drecoll, *Tod*, p. 48. On the styling and costliness of medieval girdles, see Brüggen, *Kleidung*, pp. 92–94; and more generally Ilse Fingerlin, *Gürtel des hohen und späten Mittelalter*, Kunstwissenschaftliche Studien 46 (Munich: Deutscher Kunstverlag, 1971).

11. See Elke Krotz, "Der Leser an der Leine. Zu Wolframs 'Titurel,'" in *helle döne schöne. Versammelte Arbeiten zur älteren und neueren deutschen Literatur. Festschrift für Wolfgang Walliczek*, ed. Horst Brunner, Göppinger Arbeiten zur Germanistik 668 (Göppingen: Kümmerle, 1999), p. 190 [pp. 167–200].

12. For the translation of Ekunat's name, see chapter 2, n36.

13. For Albrecht's general association of flowers with virtue and sanctity, see chapter 2, section I. Clauditte's letter suggests that virtues grow from Ekunat's person, just as flowers grow from roots (J.T. 1879); and that in particular the flower of his constancy will yield fruits from which the whole world will derive moral benefits (J.T. 1880–1881). The notion that Ekunat will serve as a lesson to a wider audience already points ahead to the transition from the private to the public domain.

14. Albrecht is one of the earliest exponents of the "geblümten Stil," a supposedly florid mode of literary expression characterized by syntactic and metaphorical complexity that was popular in the thirteenth and fourteenth centuries; prominent *blümer* include Frauenlob and Heinrich von Mügeln. For a general discussion of the practice of literary *blümen* (of which Albrecht was an important exponent) see Nyholm, *Studien zum sogenannten geblümten Stil*. On the question of whether Clauditte is a *blümer*, Elisabeth Schmid, "'Dâ stuont âventiur geschriben an der strangen': Zum Verhältnis von Erzählung und Allegorie in der Brackenseilepisode von Wolframs und Albrechts 'Titurel,'" *Zeitschrift für deutsches Altertum und deutsche Literatur* 117 (1988): 90–91, n18 [79–97] argues somewhat unconvincingly against interpreting the terms *wilde* and *blu^eme* as stylistic categories in the Brackenseil (J.T. 1879–1882). Schmid does, however, concede the terms do operate in this way in other parts of the J.T.

15. Schmid, "âventiur," 89–92.

16. For the semantic link between *wilt* and *walt*, see Christian Schmid-Cadalbert, "Der wilde Wald. Zur Darstellung und Funktion eines Raumes in der mittelhochdeutschen Literatur," in *Gotes und der werlde hulde. Literatur in Mittelalter und Neuzeit. Festschrift für Heinz Rupp zum 70. Geburtstag*, ed. Rüdiger Schnell (Bern: Francke, 1989), pp. 25–27 [pp. 24–47].

17. Note the earlier formulation in J.T. 1493: *Wan er nu der wilde hiez und wilt do jagete, / di schrift gelichez bilde an diesem wilden brieve hie nu sagete. / ouch hiez der bracke hu^eten wol der verte / walt und daz gevilde, und im daz mit gewalte nieman werte.* [Since he was called the wild one and hunted game, the writing on this "wild" letter provided an appropriate image. The hound also meant "stay on the track" through woods and fields, and nobody was able to prevent him from this.]

18. Schmid, "âventiur," 92.

19. Note the similar formulations in Wolfram's *Titurel* 158 and in J.T. 1200. In the J.T., the narrator makes frequent passing references to the established translation of Ekunat's name, e.g., J.T. 1415,1: *Der von den blu^omen wilde chom herlich geblu^emet* [the wild one of the flowers came splendidly adorned with flowers] and J.T. 1432,1: *Sust jach der wilde florie, Ekunat, der furste* [thus spoke the wild flower, the Duke Ekunat].

20. J.T. 1880,1: *Der wilde vor untæte wer du ie zu vluhte* [You were always fleeing from wrong-doing]: J.T. 1881,3–4: *daz si bi dir hie nemen gelichez bilde / und sich den tugenden nahen und aller missewende werden wilde.* [That they might learn from your example so as to draw near to virtue and flee from all misdeeds.]

21. Finckh, *Minor Mundus*, p. 377 states that a leash by its very nature signifies the imposition of restraint, and links the image of the leashed hound with that of the salamander trapped within Tschinotulander's shield. Note also the opposition between the terms *wild* and *zam* in the narrator's formulation in J.T. 59,4 of his own corrective literary programme: *durch sinneriche lere muoz ich di wilden mær hie zam gestellen.* [Through wise teaching I must tame the wild tales.] The term *wilde mære* is associated with Wolfram's opus, on the basis of *Parzival* 503,1 (*Ez naehet nu wilden maeren* [Wild tales are drawing near]) and also of Gottfried von Straßburg's polemic against an unnamed literary rival (generally assumed to be Wolfram) in *Tristan* 4665–6 (*vindaere wilder maere / der maere wildenære* [Finder of wild tales, hunter of stories]).

22. Haug, *Literaturtheorie*, p. 374 comments on the way in which wisdom is combined with magic; however, he goes too far with the suggestion (p. 375) that the Brackenseil might be read as emblematic of Albrecht's own rhetorical and stylistic aims.

23. On the sirens in classical and medieval literature, see Okken, *Tristan-Roman*, pp. 277–287.

24. For the ambivalent attitude adopted toward the figure of Solomon, see chapter 5, section II.

25. In *Titurel*, considerable emphasis is placed on the narrative contents of the inscription, the story of the ill-fated relationship between Florie (Clauditte's sister) and Ilinot (the son of Artus) being intertwined with the description of Clauditte's own situation (151–158). Furthermore, Sigune's assertion to Schionatulander that *aventiure* were written on the leash (170,1) highlights the narrative mode. Although Albrecht incorporates these strophes into the J.T. with minimal change, none of this material features in the text which is quoted verbatim in J.T. 1874–1927, at the time of the second public reading. The fact that Artus weeps for Florine and Ylinot at the time of the first public reading (J.T. 1509–1512) suggests that this narrative material may have been read out on that occasion; but it is clearly not deemed part of the "proper" inscription recorded by the narrator. Cf. Parshall, *Narration*, pp. 149 and 255, n48.

26. Note also the use of the second person plural in the closing injunction (J.T. 1927,3): *des bracken names sol iu niht versmahen* [You (pl.) should not despise the hound's name].

27. This portion of the treatise is modeled on the exposition of the ideal man by Reinmar von Zweter (*Die Gedichte Reinmars von Zweter*, ed. Gustav Roethe (Leipzig: Hirzel, 1887), 'Sprüche' 99–100). Cf. Christoph Gerhardt, "Reinmar von Zweters 'Idealer Mann' (Roethe Nr. 99/100)," *Beiträge zur Geschichte der deutschen Sprache und Literatur* 109 (1987): 51–84 and 222–251; and Michael Curschmann, "Facies peccatorum-Vir bonus: Bild-Text-Formel zwischen Hochmittelalter und früher Neuzeit," in *Poesis et Pictura. Festschrift Dieter Wuttke*, ed. Stephan Füssel and Joachim Knape, Saecula Spiritalia, Sonderband (Baden-Baden: Valentin-Koerner, 1989), pp. 160 and 173–175 [pp. 157–189].

28. Both *Titurel* 149–150 and J.T. 1191–1192 make the point that although *Gardivias* is the name of a dog, the glossing of this name as *hu^ete der verte* [stay on the track] constitutes good advice to noble people. In the J.T. 1884–1927, this gloss is cited like a refrain in every strophe of the Brackenseil treatise. Ekunat later bears an emblematic representation of the hound and leash, with a much-expanded version of the refrain inscribed on the latter: *Des bracken namen groze mit schrift zelesene verre: / "vil tief in selden schoze habent ist der kneht und ouch der herre / der wol verte hu^ot an allen orten."* (J.T. 4543,1–3) [The name of the hound could be read in large script, far and wide: "Whatever lord or page stays on the track at all times is placed deep in the lap

of good fortune."] This secondary artifact with its variant reading is to be distinguished from the real Brackenseil that Ekunat wears in the final battle with Orilus. Cf. chapter 2, section II and n58 below.

29. Although this formulation is not included in the full text quoted at the second public reading, both *Titurel* 149 and the J.T. appear to suggest that it forms part of what Sigune reads. See Drecoll, *Tod*, p. 46; also note 25 above. A much-expanded version of the refrain *hu͡te der verte* is provided in J.T. 4543.

30. The first of the 'Sprüche' in the *Reichston* of Walther von der Vogelweide (*Leich, Lieder, Sangsprüche*, 14th edn. by Christoph Cormeau based on the text by Karl Lachmann (Berlin: de Gruyter, 1996), Lachmann no. 8,4–8,27, Cormeau no. 2,I,1–24) addresses the impossibility of fitting *êre* [honor] and *varnde guot* [wealth] (which constitute different aspects of worldly favor) together with *gotes hulde* [the favor of God] into one single *schrîn* [box]. 'Wolfram' alludes to Walther's *Reichston* in J.T. 607,2–4 when he asks vrou Aventiure how it is possible for the Grail community to achieve worldly honor and wealth without forfeiting the favor of God. For a general survey of the topos of pleasing God and the world, see Klaus Hofbauer, *Gott und der Welt gefallen. Geschichte eines gnomischen Motivs im hohen Mittelalter*, Europäische Hochschulschriften 1630 (Frankfurt am Main: Peter Lang, 1997). Note also the reference in Gottfried von Straßburg's *Tristan* 8004–8019 to *moraliteit*, defined as the art of pleasing both God and the world. On biblical and classical models for Gottfried's presentation of *moraliteit*, see also Okken, *Tristan-Roman*, pp. 371–372.

31. For the distinction between *auctor* and *compilator*, see Alastair Minnis, *Medieval Theory of Authorship: Scholastic Literary Attitudes in the Later Middle Ages*, 2nd edn. (Aldershot: Wildwood House, 1988), pp. 94–95.

32. Cf. J.T. 1190,3: *die schrift ein vrowe lerte* [a lady gave instructions regarding this text].

33. Horst Wenzel, "Vom Körper zur Schrift. Boten, Briefe, Bücher," in *Performativität und Medialität*, ed. Sybille Krämer (Munich: Fink, 2004), p. 275 [pp. 269–291].

34. The rabbit was renowned in the Middle Ages for its sexual promiscuity and speed of reproduction. See W. Kemp, "Hase," in *Lexikon der christlichen Ikonographie*, ed. Engelbert Kirschbaum, 8 vols. (Rome: Herder 1968–1976), 2:221 [221–225]. The short comic tale *Das Häslein* (*Die deutsche Literatur: Texte und Zeugnisse: Mittelalter*, 2 vols., ed. Helmut de Boor (Munich: Beck, 1963–1965), 2:1456–1463), in which a naive young girl gives away her virginity in exchange for a rabbit, provides a clear illustration of this association.

35. *Titurel* 145,4: *gevâhe ich imer hunt an solhez seil, ez belîbet bî mir, swenne ih in lâze.* [If I were ever to catch a dog wearing such a leash, I would keep the leash, even if I let the dog go.]

36. Ursula Liebertz-Grün, "Erkenntnistheorie im Literalisierungsprozeß. Allegorien des *lesens* in Wolframs Metaerzählung Gardeviaz," *Germanisch-Romanische Monatsschrift* 51 (2001): 388–389 [385–395]. For an alternative interpretation of the dog, which still emphasizes the inherent open-endedness confronting the reader of *Titurel*, see Krotz, "Der Leser und der Leine," in *helle döne schöne*, especially p. 167, where she suggests that Gardivias represents Wolfram himself, who is chased by an audience misguidedly determined to find out every last detail relating to the narrative world of *Parzival*: "Wolfram aber signalisiert seinem Publikum: Ihr seid genauso neugierig wie Sigune. Ich bin wie der Hund, den alle wegen des Brackenseiles jagen. Ich will aber nicht der Hund sein, der Geschichten apportiert." [Wolfram is telling his audience: You are just as curious as Sigune. I am like the dog which everybody hunts for the Brackenseil. But I do not want to be the dog that fetches stories.] Seminal studies engaging with the challenges of interpreting the fragmentary *Titurel* include

Helmut Brackert, "Sinnspuren. Die Brackenseilinschrift in Wolframs von Eschenbach 'Titurel,'" in *Erzählungen in Erzählungen. Für Dieter Kartschoke*, ed. Harald Haferland and Norbert Mecklenburg (Munich: Fink, 1996), pp. 155–175; Christian Kiening and Susanne Köbele, "Wilde Minne. Metapher und Erzählwelt in Wolframs Titurel," *Beiträge zur Geschichte der deutschen Sprache und Literatur* 120 (1998): 234–265. Further bibliography is provided in Wolfram von Eschenbach, *Titurel*, ed. Brackert and Fuchs-Jolie, pp. 287–294.

37. Liebertz-Grün, "Erkenntnistheorie," p. 387.

38. Admittedly, Albrecht has also composed an additional strophe (J.T. 1184) in which he provides a more detailed description of the dog than is found in Wolfram's *Titurel*. However, this description is not immediately associated with the hypothetical choice between dog and leash.

39. Haug, *Literaturtheorie*, p. 370.

40. By chasing after game, it stays on the symbolic track appropriate to its nature, even if this does not coincide with any literal track discernible in the woods.

41. As noted by Schmid, "âventiur," 84–85, this change also heightens the role played by chance and misfortune in the J.T.

42. Finckh, *Minor Mundus*, p. 376: "Wie im Fall des Salamanderschildes und des Graltempels vermitteln die gottgewollten Kräfte, die den Naturdingen innewohnen, zwischen der bloßen Materialität des 'Schlüsselobjektes' und seiner ethischen Botschaft." [As in the case of the salamander shield and the Grail temple, the divinely appointed powers inherent in *naturalia* mediate between the pure materiality of the "key object" and its ethical message.]

43. Peter Strohschneider, "Unlesbarkeit von Schrift. Literaturhistorische Anmerkungen zu Schriftpraxen in der religiösen Literatur des 12. und 13. Jahrhunderts," in *Regeln der Bedeutung. Zur Theorie der Bedeutung literarischer Texte*, ed. Fotis Jannidis (Berlin: de Gruyter, 2003), pp. 591–627.

44. Peter Strohschneider, "Text-Reliquie. Über Schriftgebrauch und Textpraxis im Hochmittelalter," in *Performativität und Medialität*, ed. Sybille Krämer (Munich: Fink, 2004), p. 252 [pp. 249–267]. These ideas are also discussed in Peter Strohschneider, "Textheiligung. Geltungsstrategien legendarischen Erzählens im Mittelalter am Beispiel von Konrads von Würzburg 'Alexius,'" in *Geltungsgeschichten. Über die Stabilisierung und Legitimierung institutioneller Ordnungen. Im Auftrag des Sonderforschungsbereichs 537*, ed. Gert Melville and Hans Vorländer (Cologne: Böhlau, 2002), pp. 109–147; and in Strohschneider, "Unlesbarkeit von Schrift," in *Regeln der Bedeutung*.

45. Strohschneider, "Text-Reliquie," in *Performativität und Medialität*, p. 250.

46. *Priester Wernhers Maria. Bruchstücke und Umarbeitungen*, ed. Hans Fromm based on the text by Carl Wesle, 2nd edn., Altdeutsche Textbibliothek 26 (Tübingen: Niemeyer, 1969); Strohschneider, "Text-Reliquie," in *Performativität und Medialität*, p. 261.

47. Strohschneider, "Textheiligung," in *Geltungsgeschichten*, p. 111 notes that the opposition between hermeneutic and nonhermeneutic approaches to hagiographical texts mirrors the opposition between two distinctive attitudes to the saints themselves, who may be seen either as "imitable Vorbilder" [imitable role-models] and "ethische Virtuosen" [ethical virtuosi] or as "magische Helfer" [magical helpers]. Clearly only the former approach encourages introspective reflection and ethical self-discipline.

48. On this aspect of Arthurian culture, see Guggenberger, *Minnethematik*, pp. 113–115.

49. Finckh, *Minor Mundus*, p. 377.

50. At the time of the first reading, the narrator seemed less critical of the courtiers' susceptibility to the overwhelming impact of the stones. See J.T. 1507: *Von edelkeit der steine was disiu kraft der worte. / als man der schrift ein cleine / vernam, ie gerner man si*

furbaz horte. / da mite was di schrift also geheret / durch Ekunat, den fursten. [The words' power derived from the nobility of the stones. When one heard a bit of the text, one wanted to hear more. Therefore the text was very much praised, for the sake of Ekunat, the Duke.]

51. At this stage, Sigune has only read the personal, erotically-oriented introduction, but has not yet reached the body of the discourse. Cf. Finckh, *Minor Mundus*, p. 374.

52. In J.T. 5233,2, Sigune laments: *was mohte brack und seil nu des engelten* [What good might hound and leash now do?] The *seil* [leash] has thus become as disposable to her as the *bracke* [hound].

53. Cf. J.T. 5057,4–5058,1: *mit suͤzen worten vreudenrich gesprochen / Ab dem bracken seile.* [With sweet words from the Brackenseil, spoken joyfully].

54. Ong, *Orality and Literacy*, p. 73 "When a speaker is addressing an audience, the members of the audience normally become a unity, with themselves and with the speaker . . . Writing and print isolate . . ."

55. Artus is again involved in negotiations in J.T. 4479–4491.

56. Note Ekunat's predilection for quoting Ovid, as discussed in chapter 1, section III.

57. During the great battle with the heathens, Ekunat does draw strength from his memory of the *edeln, hohen, minniclichen gruͤze* (J.T. 3591,3) [noble, lofty, loving greeting] which Clauditte sent him on the Brackenseil. This enables him to kill Sermiduns von Irdibol with a blow so powerful that not only the skull, but also the tongue of the latter is cut in two (J.T. 3592,4).

58. In this battle, Ekunat wears an effigy of the dog (made of combustible *swamben* (J.T. 5889,2) [sponge] and *harm velle* (J.T. 5889,1) [ermine]), but with the real leash wrapped around it. In the earlier battle between the forces of Artus and those of Lucius, Ekunat is also said to wear on his helmet *den bracken mit dem seile* (J.T. 4542,4) [the hound with the leash], complete with the motto of "Stay on the track" (J.T. 4543,2–4). Clearly, the dog is only a representation of the real thing; and it would seem that here the leash too has merely been replicated, and its message simplified, since at this stage of the narrative, the real leash is still in the possession of Jescute. See also the discussion of heraldic emblems in chapter 2, section II, and n28 above.

59. Parshall, *Narration*, p. 141.

60. Cf. J.T. 1296,3–4: *di schrift zulesene was er kunste sunder, / er daht in: dirre vremde brief ist uz gesant durch aventiure wunder.* [He did not possess the ability to read the text. He thought to himself: This strange letter has been sent to us as part of a marvelous *aventiure.*]

61. With this separation, the real Gardivias fades out of the story; while the conflict concentrates on the leash, the image of the dog becomes part of Ekunat's heraldic identity (see nn28 and 58 above).

62. Tschinotulander hears the text twice (at the second public reading and when Sigune reads it to him), with no consequential modification in his attitude.

63. For that reason, the Brackenseil is not mentioned by either party when the kinsmen meet each other at the Arthurian court (J.T. 1417–1445). Cf. Parshall, *Narration*, p. 142.

64. On one level, Tschinotulander is not to blame for this mistake, since he can only see the dog from a distance. However, the fact that he is too far away to see whether this dog is wearing a leash underscores the fact that he is focused on the wrong thing, namely on the dog rather than on the leash.

65. Tschinotulander's unwillingness to accept the boundaries of *rechter maze* [proper moderation] is explicitly discussed in J.T. 3568–3569; soon afterward, this shortcoming is linked to the fact that he *uber sach* (J.T. 3573,2) [ignored] the central Brackenseil message to *huͤte der verte* (J.T. 3573,1) [stay on the track].

66. Cf. the narrator's exclamation: *we, daz ie man die strangen sach geschribene!* (J.T. 1940,3)
    [Alas, that one ever saw the inscription on the leash!] Even Orilus appears to take this
    view in J.T. 4476–4478. Note especially the formulation *Daz seil Unselde heizet min
    halben immer mere.* (J.T. 4477,1) [On my account, the leash will always be called
    Misfortune.]

67. Whilst the notion of *translatio imperii* plays little or no role in Wolfram's two Grail
    texts, the related notion of *translatio studii* is arguably implicit in Wolfram's myth of an
    exotic two-tiered source for *Parzival* (consisting of the astrological findings of the
    Jewish/heathen Flegetanis as mediated and expanded into French by Kyot the
    Provençal; and then translated by Wolfram's narrator). More remote, but still seman-
    tically related to *translatio imperii* and *translatio studii*, is the rhetorical notion of *transla-
    tio* as metaphor: a term or image is "translated" into a new and nonliteral context, in
    which, as with allegory, the words appear to say one thing, but actually signify some-
    thing else. On the semantic field of *translatio*, see Annette Volfing, "Albrecht's *Jüngerer
    Titurel*: Translating the Grail," *Arthurian Literature* 22 (2005): 49–63.

68. Although the relationship between Sigune and Tschinotulander is never consum-
    mated, the erotic attraction between the two is evaluated negatively by the narrator:
    see Guggenberger, *Minnethematik*, pp. 183–187. It is also noteworthy that Ekunat
    and Clauditte, the other high-profile courtly couple, ultimately decide to withdraw
    from the world and its pleasures (J.T. 5923–5926).

69. For further discussion of the ways in which the J.T. thematizes the failure of overt
    didacticism, see chapter 5, section II.

70. For a summary of the arguments on each side, see Zatloukal, *Salvaterre*, pp. 231–236.

71. On one level, the eucharistic association of the Grail goes back to Wolfram and even
    to Chrétien (although this association is with the eucharistic bread, rather than with
    the wine). In *Parzival*, the Grail gains much of its power from the fact that on every
    Good Friday, a dove brings a communion wafer down from heaven and places it on
    the Grail; whereas in *Perceval*, the Grail contains the communion wafer that keeps
    the father of the Fisher King alive.

72. Dietrich Huschenbett, "Über Wort, Sakrament und Gral in Spruchdichtung, *Jüngerem
    Titurel*—und bei Wolfram?," in *bickelwort und wildiu mære. Festschrift für Eberhard
    Nellmann zum 65. Geburtstag*, ed. Dorothee Lindemann, Göppinger Arbeiten zur
    Germanistik 618 (Göppingen: Kümmerle, 1995), pp. 184–198; also Huschenbett, *Stil
    und Komposition*, pp. 135–148.

73. Huschenbett, "Über Wort, Sakrament und Gral," in *bickelwort und wildiu mære*, p. 197:
    "Für Albrecht ist der Gral ein Transporteur von Gottes Wort, das durch . . . Schrift
    ausgedrückt wird . . ." [For Albrecht, the Grail is a vessel for the word of God,
    which . . . is expressed in writing . . .].

74. According to Huschenbett, "Über Wort, Sakrament und Gral," in *bickelwort und
    wildiu mære*, pp. 197–198, the Grail is shown ". . . als Gegenstand . . . , der für die
    Macht des (geschriebenen) Wortes steht" [. . . as an object, which represents the
    power of the (written) word].

75. The practice of the Grail to communicate through writing continues even after the
    translatio to India, when its other miraculous properties (e.g., that of feeding its
    followers) have become redundant.

76. For the interpretation of J.T. 516.1, see also Zatloukal, *Salvaterre*, p. 231.

77. See also Finckh, *Minor Mundus*, p. 369 for parallels between the construction of the
    Grail temple and the construction of Albrecht's text.

78. Given that it is a fundamental principle of metaphysics that a physical object cannot
    exist is more than one place, Aquinas argues that the body of Christ is not present in

the eucharist *localiter* [in a localized way], but rather spiritually, as is appropriate to the sacrament. (*Summa Theologiae* 3a, 75.1.3 and ad 3, 58:52–55 and 58–59). He then raises the question of whether the principle of natural concomitance (according to which accidents cannot be separated from their substance) means that the dimensions of Christ,s body must be present *localiter* [spatially, locally] within the transubstantiated bread (*Summa Theologiae* 3a, 76.5.3, 58:108–109). However, after due consideration, he concludes that this is not the case: whilst it follows from the principle of natural concomitance that the accidents must be present with the substance in the sacrament, this can apply only to intrinsic accidents, and the quality of being in a particular place is an extrinsic rather than an intrinsic accident. (*Summa Theologiae* 3a, 76.5.ad 3, 58:110–111). It is consistent with this exposition to pursue an analogy whereby the Grail is present *localiter* in the kingdom of Prester John, and also spiritually within the members of Albrecht's audience. Cf. Volfing, "Translating the Grail," 60–61.

79. For an overview of critical opinion on Gottfried's "noble hearts" and on the religious imagery in the prologue to *Tristan*, see Christoph Huber, *Gottfried von Straßburg: Tristan*, Klassiker Lektüren 3 (Berlin: Erich Schmidt, 2000), pp. 41–46.

80. Guggenberger, *Minnethematik*, p. 242.

4 'Albrecht,' 'Wolfram,' and vrou Aventiure: Arguing with the Text

1. Haug, *Literaturtheorie*, p. 194. See also Walter Haug, "Mündlichkeit, Schriftlichkeit und Fiktionalität," in *Modernes Mittelalter: Neue Bilder einer populären Epoche*, ed. Joachim Heinzle (Frankfurt am Main: Insel, 1994), pp. 356–397. Ursula Schaefer, "Die Funktion des Erzählers zwischen Mündlichkeit und Schriftlichkeit," *Wolfram-Studien* 18 (2004): 87–91 [83–97] provides a short, but very helpful, overview of the Mündlichkeit / Schriftlichkeit dichotomy (and of the limited extent to which these terms map onto the English terms orality and literacy). See also the following other studies by Ursula Schaefer: *Vokalität. Altenglische Dichtung zwischen Mündlichkeit und Schriftlichkeit*, ScriptOralia 39 (Tübingen: Narr, 1992); "Zum Problem der Mündlichkeit," in *Modernes Mittelalter: Neue Bilder einer populären Epoche*, ed. Joachim Heinzle (Frankfurt am Main: Insel, 1994), pp. 357–375; "Individualität und Fiktionalität. Zu einer mediengeschichtlichen und mentalitätsgeschichtlichen Wandel im 12. Jahrhundert," in *Mündlichkeit—Schriftlichkeit—Weltbildwandel. Literarische Kommunikation und Deutungsschemata von Wirklichkeit in der Literatur des Mittelalters und der frühen Neuzeit*, ed. Werner Röcke and Ursula Schaefer (Tübingen: Narr, 1996), pp. 50–70. For the differences between literacy, textualization, and textual culture (all of which may serve as translations of Schriftlichkeit, depending on context and nuance), see chaper 1 of this monograph. Given the absence of any set English equivalents for Mündlichkeit and Schriftlichkeit, the terms are most conveniently left untranslated when used in contrast to each other.

2. Schaefer, "Die Funktion des Erzählers," 93–94.

3. See chapter 1, n5.

4. Green, *Medieval Listening*, p. 171 describes this mode of reception as "indeterminate"; Schaefer, *Vokalität* deploys the key term in her title to describe essentially the same cultural practice.

5. For the view that all writing fictionalizes its audience, see Walter J. Ong, "The Writer's Audience Is Always a Fiction," *PMLA* 90 (1975): 9–22. See also Manfred Günter Scholz, *Hören und Lesen. Studien zur primären Rezeption der Literatur im 12.*

und 13. Jahrhundert (Wiesbaden: Steiner, 1980), particularly pp. 11–12, for the distinction between the potential and the fictional audiences of Middle High German texts.

 6. See Monika Unzeitig, "Von der Schwierigkeit zwischen Autor und Erzähler zu unterscheiden. Eine historisch vergleichende Analyse zu Chrétien und Hartmann," *Wolfram-Studien* 18 (2004): 76 [59–81]: "Indem fiktive Rezipienten in der Situation des Erzählens Einwände an Hartman adressiert formulieren, entsteht die Illusion, als könne die Geschichte noch verändert werden, als sei das Werk ein 'opus in fieri,' dessen Produktion in der Rezeptionssituation erfolge." [When fictional recipients within the narrative situation formulate objections that are addressed to Hartman, this gives rise to the illusion that the story can still be changed, as though the work constitutes an *opus in fieri*, produced as it is being received.]

 7. Unzeitig, "Autor und Erzähler," 60.

 8. Unzeitig, "Autor und Erzähler," 60. For the metaphor of authorial signatures within the text, see also Thomas Bein, "Zum Autor im mittelalterlichen Literaturbetrieb und im Diskurs der germanischen Mediävistik," in *Rückkehr des Autors: Zur Erneuerung eines umstrittenen Begriffs*, ed. Fotis Jannidis (Tübingen: Niemeyer, 1999), pp. 303–320.

 9. Lorenz, *Wolfram-Fortsetzung*, p. 112 follows Joachim Bumke, *Mäzene im Mittelalter. Die Gönner und Auftraggeber der höfischen Literatur in Deutschland 1150–1300* (Munich: Beck, 1979), pp. 15–16 in identifying this patron as the Wittelsbacher Ludwig II (1253–1294). For a full discussion of Albrecht's patrons, see Lorenz, *Wolfram-Fortsetzung*, pp. 112–129 and pp. 129–148. See also Peter Kern, "Albrechts Gönner und die Wolfram-Rolle im 'Jüngeren Titurel'," *Wolfram-Studien* 8 (1984):138–152.

10. Vrou Aventiure variously calls him *Wolfram* (J.T. 244,4), *friunt von Blienvelde* (J.T. 608,4; J.T. 5236,1), *friunt von Eschenbach* (J.T. 4017,4), *vil edel ritter von eschenbach* (J.T. 5092,1), and *ram der wolfe* (J.T. 3598,1). For a discussion of the last of these modes of address, see chapter 2, section I. See also Mertens, "Wolfram als Rolle," pp. 209–214.

11. See chapter 1, n45.

12. See nn69 and 74 below.

13. Lorenz, *Wolfram-Fortsetzung*, p. 112.

14. The Vf is quoted from the transcription by Lorenz, *Wolfram-Fortsetzung*, pp. 68–72.

15. Strohschneider, "Gotfrid-Fortsetzungen," 97, quoted by Lorenz, *Wolfram-Fortsetzung*, p. 81. Lorenz does regard Strohschneider's principle as applying to the J.T.

16. Vf 4.

17. Vf 15 also affirms Albrecht's admiration for Wolfram. This strophe is still couched in hyperbolic terms, but without the exaggerated irony of the angel image.

18. Vf 14,1: *Er was in menschen modele vnd niht ein engel hilich* [He was cast is the mould of a man and was not a holy angel].

19. Vf 14,3: *alle edliv chvnst sich bezzert, vnd niht bosert, vnd wehet* [All noble art improves and becomes more splendid, rather than declining]. For the notion of *aemulatio* as an aggressive and competitive way of positioning oneself in relation to a literary precursor (as opposed to the more humble attitude implicit in *sequela* or *imitatio*), see G. W. Pigman, "Versions of Imitation in the Renaissance," *Renaissance Quarterly* 33 (1980): 1–32; and Annette Volfing, *John the Evangelist and Medieval German Writing: Imitating the Inimitable* (Oxford: Oxford University Press, 2001), pp. 1–7.

20. See Annette Volfing, "*Parzival* and *Willehalm*—Narrative Continuity?," in *Wolfram's 'Willehalm': 15 Essays*, ed. Martin H. Jones and Timothy McFarland (Rochester, NY and Woodbridge, Suffolk: Camden House, 2002), pp. 45–59. The J.T. certainly

presents both of these texts as the works of that 'Wolfram' who is also its narrator (cf. J.T. 5989 which criticizes the beginning of *Willehalm* and end of *Parzival*).

21. Schröder, *Wolfram-Nachfolge*, pp. 34–74 assembles numerous examples of stylistic parallelisms, with which he seeks to underpin his rejection of the J.T. as an act of untalented plagiarism. Whilst this unsophisticated assessment of the work has been superseded by the methodologies adopted in more recent scholarship, Schröder's lists still provide a useful basis for further consideration of the nature of Albrecht's engagement with Wolfram's texts. For a historical overview of critical responses to the J.T., see the introduction to this monograph.

22. J.T. 4890,4: *der kunst han ich deheine; und han ich kunst, die muoz mir sin gemeren.* [I have no artistic skill, and if I have any, it needs to be increased through inspiration.] Cf. *Willehalm* 2,22: *wan hân ich kunst, die gît mir sin.* [If I have any artistic skill, it comes through inspiration.] On the meaning of *sin* in this context, see Friedrich Ohly, "Wolframs Gebet an den heiligen Geist im Eingang des 'Willehalm,'" *Zeitschrift für deutsches Altertum und deutsche Literatur* 91 (1961–62): 19–37 [1–37]; for further bibliography on the prologue to *Willehalm*, see Bumke, *Wolfram*, p. 239 and p. 242.

23. J.T. 68,2: *kunstlos, an meisterschefte bin ich der schrifte* [I am unskilled, without mastery of the written word.] Cf. *Parzival* 115,27: *ine kan decheinen buochstap* [I do not know a single letter] and *Willehalm* 2,19–20: *swaz an den buochen stât geschriben, / des bin ich künstelôs beliben.* [I have acquired no knowledge of that which is written in the books.] For a survey of interpretations of these apparent claims to illiteracy, see Bumke, *Wolfram*, pp. 5–8.

24. J.T. 3596,1: *Min kone, min kint, min bruoder stet nicht wan zeinem libe.* [My wife, my child, my brother are all as one body.] Cf. *Parzival* 752,8–10: *beidiu mîn vater und ouch duo / und ich, wir wâren gar al ein, / doch ez an drîen stücken schein.* [Both my father, and you, and I too, were but one, though seen as three distinct entities.]

25. While Curschmann, "Das Abenteuer des Erzählens" identifies a number of distinctive roles or stances that are assumed successively by the *Parzival*-narrator (e.g., the poet, the destitute knight, the country bumpkin, the frustrated 'Minnediener'), Albrecht seems particularly interested in foregrounding the lecherous tendencies of this figure. On the cruder aspects of the *Parzival*-narrator (as manifested most strikingly in *Parzival* 424,3–6), see also Eberhard Nellmann, *Wolframs Erzähltechnik. Untersuchungen zur Funktion des Erzählers* (Wiesbaden: Steiner, 1973), p. 14 and Wolfram von Eschenbach, *Parzival*, ed. Nellmann, 2:655.

26. The *Parzival*-narrator also fantasizes about kissing his own female characters: *Parzival* 130,14–16 (Jeschute) and 450,1–8 (the daughters of Kahenis).

27. On the *Parzival*-narrator's dialogic interaction with his audience, see especially Joachim Bumke, *Die Blutstropfen im Schnee: Über Wahrnehmung und Erkenntnis im "Parzival" Wolframs von Eschenbach*, Hermaea 94 (Tübingen: Niemeyer, 2001), pp. 111–121.

28. Parshall, *Narration*, p. 217 notes that whereas the *Parzival*-narrator tends to address characters present in the scene being described, the narrator of the J.T. often addresses absent characters: "This change is consistent with the narrator's role as moralizer and explicator in the JT. His interventions do not serve to enhance his own dramatic presence or the immediacy of the action taking place. Rather they serve to point out relationships, to foreshadow or otherwise tie events together in a significant and cogent fashion, and to emphasise his omniscient grasp of the material."

29. This is inevitably an oversimplification. For a detailed discussion of the semantic field of *aventiure* just within Wolfram's *Parzival* (and of *avanture* in Chrétien's

Perceval), see Dennis Howard Green, "The concept *âventiure* in *Parzival*," in *Approaches to Wolfram von Eschenbach. Five Essays*, ed. Dennis Howard Green and Leslie Peter Johnson, Mikrokosmos 5 (Bern: Peter Lang, 1978), pp. 83–161. Green identifies seven separate meanings for *aventiure* (knightly exploit; risk, danger; miracle, wonder; the supernatural; chance, hazard, fortune; divine providence; news) even before addressing the narrative aspects to the term (story, account; the poet's source; the poet's own story.)

30. For similar uses of the term, see Hartmann von Aue, *Erec*, ed. Manfred Günter Scholz, German trans. Susanne Held, Bibliothek des Mittelalters 5 (Frankfurt am Main: Deutscher Klassiker Verlag, 2004), lines 221, 492, 4340, 5292, 7399, 7962, 7975, 8384, 8481; *Iwein* 261, 372, 377, 527, 549, 631, 3918, 6331.

31. For similar formulations, see *Erec* 185, 281, 743, 2239, 2897, 7835. These formulations coexist with the idea of a written source. See for example *Erec* 8698: *ob uns daz buoch niht liuget* [if the book is not lying to us.]

32. For discussion of this key passage, see in particular Fritz Peter Knapp, "Subjektivität des Erzählers und Fiktionalität der Erzählung bei Wolfram von Eschenbach und anderen Autoren des 12. und 13. Jahrhunderts," *Wolfram-Studien* 17 (2002): 10–29; also Friedrich Ohly, "Cor amantis non angustum. Vom Wohnen im Herzen," in Friedrich Ohly, *Schriften zur mittelalterlichen Bedeutungsforschung* (Darmstadt: Wissenschaftliche Buchgesellschaft, 1983), pp. 128–155 [pp. 148–154] (originally published in *Gedenkschrift für William Foerste*, ed. Dietrich Hoffmann and Willy Sanders, Niederdeutsche Studien 18 (Cologne: Böhlau 1970). pp. 454–476); Nellmann, *Wolframs Erzähltechnik*, p. 54; Hans-Jörg Spitz, "Wolframs Bogengleichnis: ein typologisches Signal," in *Verbum et Signum. Beiträge zur mediävistischen Bedeutungsforschung. Friedrich Ohly Festschrift*, ed. Hans Fromm, 2 vols. (Munich: Fink, 1975), 2:263–264 [247–276]; Green, "*âventiure*," in *Approaches to Wolfram von Eschenbach*, pp. 124–125.

33. *Iwein* 2971–3024. Note also the intervention from vrou Minne in *Iwein* 7027–7031.

34. On this passage, and on the truth-value of the *Iwein* narrative generally, see Wolfgang Dittmann, "*Dune hâst nicht wâr, Hartmann!* Zum Begriff der *wârheit* in Harmanns 'Iwein,'" in *Festgabe für Ulrich Pretzel zum 65. Geburtstag*, ed. Werner Simon (Berlin: Erich Schmidt, 1963), pp. 150–161.

35. The narrator in *Parzival* apostrophizes vrou Minne in 291,1–293,16, 294,21–30 and 586,26–587,6. For further detailed discussion of the first two passages, see Bumke, *Blutstropfen*, pp. 122–128. Note also the narrator's reference to vrou Liebe in 291,17 and his address to a unique male variation (*her minnen druc*) [Lord Pressure of Love] in 533.

36. In *Parzival* 532,1–18, the narrator mentions the arrows of Cupido, the darts of Amor, and the torch of their mother Venus. Veldeke's *Eneasroman* is largely responsible for starting reception of this mythological material into the Middle High German courtly tradition. See Kistler, *Heinrich von Veldeke*, pp. 124–129.

37. This is made clear not only by the narrator's evocation of erotic scenarios such as incest (*Parzival* 291,22: *sippiu âmîs*) which are not enacted within the narrative, but also by his articulation of his own love-problems. On the implications of the narrator's erotic relationship(s) for the interpretation of *Parzival*, see Annette Volfing, "*Welt ir nu hœren fürbaz?* On the Function of the Loherangrin-episode in Wolfram von Eschenbach's *Parzival*," *Beiträge zur Geschichte der deutschen Sprache und Literatur* 126 (2004): 65–84.

38. For example *Parzival* 291,19–20: *Vrou Minne, ir pflegt untriuwen / mit alten siten niuwen.* [vrou Minne, you are following your old, treacherous habits in a new way.]

39. For the difficulties associated with assessing the level of animation of a personified figure, see Annette Volfing, "*offenlich beslafen het der Grahardois sin eigen swester. Allegorie und Personifikation in der 'Crone' und im 'Jüngeren Titurel*,'" *Wolfram-Studien* 18 (2004): 305–321. Other personifications referred to in the J.T. include *Fortune/Fortuna* (J.T. 131,4; 1637,2; 2628,2; 2648,4; 3252,2; 4233,4; 4280,3; 4475,2); *geluck* [fortune] complete with wheel (J.T. 5277,2; 5334,2); *Selde* (J.T. 4280,3; 5277,3); and *Selikeit* (J.T. 4353,4). None of these is endowed with a high level of animation, although conceptually, the whole cluster of abstractions associated with good and bad luck is extremely important for the work (not least in relation to the fatal *golt der selden*); cf. Guggenberger, *Minnethematik*, pp. 155–159. In J.T. 4209,2, *Fortune* is also presented as a heathen deity.

40. See especially Guggenberger, *Minnethematik*, p. 150.

41. Immediately after this dialogue, we learn that the heathen Sabelles does indeed have Amor and his two arrows as decoration on his helmet (J.T. 4035–4037).

42. J.T. 608,4–609,1: *ey, friunt von Blienvelde, du sprichst mir zallen ziten væreliche! / Du wenst mich han gekrenket und dine witz gemeret.* [Stop, my friend from Pleinfeld, you always address me with malicious intent! You think you have put me in my place and increased your reputation as a wit.].

43. Ohly, "*Cor amantis*," in *Bedeutungsforschung*, pp. 148–154 places the opening of Book 9 of *Parzival* within the broad tradition underlying the 'Minnesang' commonplace of the beloved dwelling in the heart. This tradition in turn is shown to be associated structurally and thematically with the spatial and dialogic paradigms of the Song of Songs, and hence, given the widespread mariological interpretation of this text, with the Incarnation.

44. See Dagmar Hirschberg, "Zum Aventiure-Gespräch von der Bedeutung *warer minne* im 'Jüngeren Titurel*,'" *Wolfram-Studien* 8 (1984): 108 [107–119]; Ragotzky, *Wolfram-Rezeption*, pp. 137–138. For these occasions when the narrator addresses vrou Aventiure without receiving a reply, it is useful to invoke the notion of the "half-dialogue," as described by Peter Wiehl, *Die Redeszene als episches Strukturelement in den Erec- und Iwein-Dichtungen Hartmanns von Aue und Chrestiens de Troyes*, Bochumer Arbeiten zur Sprach—und Literaturwissenschaft 10 (Munich: Fink, 1974), pp. 54–55.

45. See Guggenberger, *Minnethematik*, pp. 81–88. For Albrecht's engagement with other Middle High German literary figures and with classical authorities, see chapter 5.

46. See Guggenberger, *Minnethematik*, pp. 206–207. For the reference to Walther von der Vogelweide, see chapter 3, n30.

47. See Guggenberger, *Minnethematik*, pp. 156–159.

48. See Hirschberg, "Aventiure-Gespräch"; Guggenberger, *Minnethematik*, pp. 149–155.

49. See Guggenberger, *Minnethematik*, pp. 162–164.

50. The facts of the narrative approximate to the narratological concept of *histoire*, as opposed to *discours* (the presentation of the *histoire*). Cf. Gérard Genette, *Narrative Discourse Revisited*, trans. Jane E. Lewin (Ithaca: Cornell University Press), pp. 13–14.

51. For the interpretation of J.T. 4022,1 (*sin werde aventiure* [his worthy aventiure]) as referring to *Willehalm*, see Guggenberger, *Minnethematik*, pp. 150–151. For the general importance of *Willehalm* as a thematic backdrop to the J.T., see also Lorenz, *Wolfram-Fortsetzung*, pp. 303–316.

52. Designating vrou Aventiure as a "muse" (as does Parshall, *Narration*, p. 217) is therefore unhelpful.

53. The narrator acknowledges in J.T. 5850,2–4 that the narrative overlap between the J.T. and *Parzival* is only partial: *wie er bi ir und Trefizent nu were / und ander sin geverte,*

daz seit ein ander bu°ch mit gantzem mere . . . [Another book gives a full account of how he visited Sigune and Trevrizent, and of his other doings . . .] The term *mere* here appears to suggest something analogous to a given *kere* of the *aventiure*: *Parzival* and the J.T. cover different aspects of the same fundamental facts (*histoire*) and therefore end up offering different accounts, with different moral and aesthetic consequences. For the narrator's reluctance to repeat material from *Parzival*, see also J.T. 5263,4: *macht ich zwo rede uz einer, so jehe mir kunst niht ordenlicher stiure* [if I were to make two stories out of one, art would not credit me with appropriate assistance.]

54. On the theme of *selde* in the J.T., see n39 above.

55. As has been shown by Green, "*âventiure*," in *Approaches to Wolfram von Eschenbach* (n29 above), there is nothing to prevent the abstract noun *aventiure* from referring to a written source; however, once the concept is explicitly personified as a speaking woman, it is less easily dissociated from the notion of an oral transmission of the narrative.

56. Similarly, in J.T. 2993,3–4, Kyot is given the credit for the transmission of the aventiure from the heathen to the Christian world.

57. On the invocation of Kyot in this and other trivial contexts in *Parzival*, see Knapp, "Subjektivität des Erzähler," 15. In the J.T., it is *aventiure*, albeit unpersonified, who holds the potential answers to trivial questions (e.g., J.T. 1819,4: *wer di andern wæren? des sult ir di aventiure pfenden.* [As to who the others were, you should try to prise that out of *aventiure*]). Admittedly, toward the end of the J.T., the narrator does refer to the existence of written chronicles that supposedly back up his (nontrivial) claim that Sigune and Tschinotulander are buried together and that two vines grow out of their mouths (J.T. 5869).

58. For further discussion of these names, see chapter 2, section I.

59. Cf. *Parzival* 452,29–453,10: *an den ervert nu Parzivâl / diu verholnen mære umbe den grâl. / Swer mich dervon ê frâgte / unt drumbe mit mir bâgte, / ob ichs im niht sagte, / unprîs der dran bejagte. / mich batez helen Kyôt / wand im diu âventiure gebôt / daz es immer man gedæhte, / ê ez diu âventiure bræhte / mit worten an der mære gruoz / daz man dervon doch sprechen muoz.* [From him [i.e., Trevrizent], Parzival will now learn the hidden account of the Grail. Anybody who asked me about this earlier and hassled me for not telling him earned nothing but shame. Kyot asked me to conceal it because *aventiure* forbade him to mention it until *aventiure* itself had come to that point precisely where one should speak of it.] There is some ambiguity as to the meaning of the term *aventiure* in this passage. Whilst Edwards (Wolfram, *Parzival, with Titurel and the love-lyrics*, p. 145) simply translates the term as "the adventure" on both occasions, Hatto (Wolfram von Eschenbach, *Parzival*, trans. A. T. Hatto (London: Penguin, 1980), p. 232) translates the first occurrence of the term as "his source" and the second occurrence as "the story." This is consistent with the notion that Kyot engages with written sources (*Parzival* 455,4: *in latînschen buochen* [in Latin books]). By contrast, it would be possible to read *aventiure* as a continuation of the female personification featured at the start of Book 9, in which case Kyot would occupy an intermediate position between the narrator and vrou Aventiure: she gives him oral instructions, which he then passes on (presumably in written form) to the narrator. On this point, see Spitz, "Wolframs Bogengleichnis," in *Verbum et Signum*, p. 264. Note also J.T. 2935, where the narrator makes the presumptuous move of lecturing vrou Aventiure on the inappropriateness of premature revelations: *ob man zu vru° daz sagete, vrowe Aventiur, daz stu°nd unhoveliche.* [It would be uncourtly, vrou Aventiure, to reveal this too early.]

60. See chapter 5, section I.

61. The characterization of a narrative as either *krump* or *sliht* derives from Wolfram's famous bow-metaphor (*Parzival* 241,9–30) which suggests that a certain distortion of the sinew is necessary to make the arrow travel in a straight line; a mode of narration may therefore be simultaneously crooked and straight. Note, however, the claim for ultimate "straightness" of the narrative made in *Parzival* 805,14–15: *ez ist niht crump alsô der boge, / diz maere ist wâr unde sleht.* [This story goes straight and truthfully, not curved like a bow.] On this metaphor, see Bernd Schirok, "Die senewe ist ein bîspel. Zu Wolframs Bogengleichnis," *Zeitschrift für deutsches Altertum und deutsche Literatur* 115 (1986): 21–36; and Peter Kern, "*ich sage die senewen âne bogen.* Zur Reflexion über die Erzählweise in *Parzival*," *Wolfram-Studien* 17 (2002): 46–62. On the use of the terms *krump* and *sliht* in the J.T., (where the former is interpreted negatively and the latter positively), see Lorenz, *Wolfram-Fortsetzung*, pp. 83–86, and particularly Thomas Neukirchen, "Dirre aventiure kere. Die Erzählperspektive Wolframs im Prolog des 'Jüngeren Titurel' und die Erzählstrategie Albrechts," *Wolfram-Studien* 18 (2004): 283–303.

62. For a discussion of German attempts to translate J.T. 65, see Neukirchen, "Dirre aventiure kere," 288–292.

63. As a parallel, note the curious passage in J.T. 2527, when Tschinotulander is said to have slept with his own sister, who is subsequently revealed to be nothing other than virtue personified. For a detailed discussion of this passage, see Volfing, "offenlich beslafen," 314–321. For the way in which this strategy of eroticizing virtue differs from Clauditte's flawed attempt to seduce her reader(s) toward virtue (discussed in chapter 3), see chapter 5.

64. Neukirchen, "*krumb* und *sliht.*"

65. Guggenberger, *Minnethematik*, p. 78.

66. J.T. 22–65. See Peter Kern, "Der Kommentar zu 'Parzival' 1,13f. im Prolog des 'Jüngeren Titurel,'" in *Studien zur deutschen Literatur und Sprache des Mittelalters. Festschrift für H. Moser zum 65. Geburtstag*, ed. Werner Besch (Berlin: Erich Schmidt, 1974), pp. 185–199. There are also striking echoes of the prologue to *Willehalm*; cf. Lorenz, *Wolfram-Fortsetzung*, p. 303, n569.

67. E.g. J.T. 20,3: *ich wil di krumb an allen orten slichten* [I intend to straighten out all crookedness]; J.T. 59,4: *durch sinneriche lere muᵒz ich di wilden mær hie zam gestellen* [through wise teaching I must tame the wild tale here]; 65,2: *darumb sol ich si wisen uf di rihte* [for that reason I should point her to the straight path].

68. J.T. 64 (forming part of the prologue) also mentions the demanding nature of patrons, without making it entirely clear whether it is 'Albrecht' or 'Wolfram' who is complaining. See also n73 below.

69. On the status of the Kunststrophen, see the introduction, nn14 and 30.

70. As an illustration of this model of authorship, see Mechthild von Magdeburg, *Das fließende Licht der Gottheit* 2,26, ed. Hans Neumann, Münchener Texte und Untersuchungen 100 (Munich: Artemis, 1990), p. 68: *Dú wort bezeichent mine wunderlich gotheit; dú vliessent von stunde zu stunde in dine sele us von minem goᵉtlichen munde.* [The words signify my marvelous divinity; they flow from hour to hour into your soul from my divine mouth.]. See also the prologue to Mechthild's work, in which God appears to be speaking (p. 4): *Dis buᵒch . . . bezeichent alleine mich* [This book . . . signifies nothing other than myself]. For this model of authorship generally, see Alastair J. Minnis, "Discussions of 'Authorial Role' and 'Literary Form' in Late-Medieval Scriptural Exegesis," *Beiträge zur Geschichte der deutschen Sprache und Literatur* 99 (1977): 37–65; for the Mechthild passages, see Eberhard Nellmann, "*Dis buoch bezeichent allein mich.* Zum Prolog von Mechthilds 'Fließendem Licht der

Gottheit,'" in *Gotes und der werlde hulde. Literatur in Mittelalter und Neuzeit. Festschrift für Heinz Rupp zum 70. Geburtstag*, ed. Rüdiger Schnell (Bern and Stuttgart: Francke, 1989), pp. 200–205.

71. This is primarily the case with *Willehalm*. For discussion of the nature of this inspiration, see Ohly, "Wolframs Gebet"; Hans Eggers, "Non cognovi litteraturam (zu >Pz.<115,27)," in *Festgabe für Ulrich Pretzel zum 65. Geburtstag*, ed. Werner Simon (Berlin: Erich Schmidt, 1963), pp. 162–172. Reprinted in *Wolfram von Eschenbach*, ed. Heinz Rupp, Wege der Forschung 57 (Darmstadt: Wissenschaftliche Buchgesellschaft, 1966.), pp. 533–548; Ingrid Ochs, *Wolframs Willehalm-Eingang im Lichte der frühmittelhochdeutschen geistlichen Dichtung*, Medium Aevum: Philologische Studien 14 (Munich: Fink, 1968).

72. A very similar example of him pausing belatedly to query something which (s)he has just said occurs in dialogue 2: although the narrator himself has just described Titurel as *der junge* in J.T. 265,1, he challenges vrou Aventiure in the next strophe to justify the designation of a fifty-year-old as *ein kint* [a child].

73. For the topos that story-telling is hard work, see Gottfried von Straßburg, *Tristan* 45–46: *Ich hân mir eine unmüezekeit / der werlt ze liebe vür geleit . . .* [I have taken on a burdensome task for the benefit of the world . . .] As an example of the anguish of having to narrate sad events, note the distress expressed by the narrator of *Parzival* when the hero fails to ask the question at Munsalvæsche (*Parzival* 240,4: *des pin ich für in noch unvrô.* [Because of that, I am still sorry for him.]) Both these aspects of story telling are expressed in J.T. 3731: *Ob ich den strit nu sunder seit al der tage viere / wie mangerleie kunder da was von manger richeit der zimiere, / so muᵉst ich vil unmuᵉz dar an uz borgen. / wie noch der strit ein ende genimt, daz bringet mich zegrozen sorgen!* [If I am to describe all four days of the battle, saying how many beasts of precious materials adorned the helmets—that would involve me in a lot of effort. As for saying how the battle ends—that would upset me too much.] There is a curious parallelism between the way in which 'Wolfram' is driven by vrou Aventiure and the way in which 'Albrecht' presents himself as being at the beck and call of his patrons (e.g., in J.T. 5960, immediately before he names himself to the audience). See also n68 above.

74. For the distinction between "open" and "closed" dialogues, see Gerhard Bauer, *Zur Poetik des Dialogs. Leistung und Formen der Gesprächsführung in der neueren Literatur* (Darmstadt: Wissenschaftliche Buchgesellschaft, 1969), pp. 12–16; Walter Haug, "Das Gespräch mit dem unvergleichbaren Partner. Der mystische Dialog bei Mechthild von Magdeburg als Paradigma für eine personale Gesprächsstrucktur," in *Das Gespräch*, ed. Karlheinz Stierle and Rainer Warning, Poetik und Hermeneutik 11, (Munich: Fink, 1984), pp. 253–255 [pp. 251–279]; Almut Suerbaum, "Structures of Dialogue in Willehalm," in *Wolfram's 'Willehalm': 15 Essays*, ed. Martin H. Jones and Timothy McFarland (Rochester, NY and Woodbridge, Suffolk: Camden House, 2002), pp. 231–234 [pp. 231–247].

75. For a theoretical analysis of the Lehrgespräch, see Günther Buck, "Das Lehrgespräch," in *Das Gespräch*. Poetik und Hermeneutik 11, ed. Karlheinz Stierle and Rainer Warning. (Munich: Fink, 1984), pp. 191–210; for a specifically medieval context, see also Hannes Kästner, *Mittelalterliche Lehrgespräche. Textlinguistische Analysen, Studien zur poetischen Funktion und pädagogischen Intention*, Philologische Studien und Quellen 94 (Berlin: Erich Schmidt, 1978); and Karl-Heinz Witte, *Der Meister des Lehrgesprächs und sein "In-Principio-Dialog": ein deutschsprachiger Theologe der Augustinerschule des 14. Jahrhunderts aus dem Kreise deutscher Mystik und Scholastik*, Münchener Texte und Untersuchungen 95 (Munich: Artemis, 1989), pp. 162–177. For the genre of the

medieval Streitgedicht, see Hans Walther, *Das Streitgedicht in der lateinischen Literatur des Mittlelalters*, Quellen und Untersuchungen zur lateinischen Philologie des Mittelalters 5.2 (Munich: Beck, 1920).

76. See for example Walter Haug, "Der Ackermann und der Tod," in *Das Gespräch*. Poetik und Hermeneutik 11, eds. Karlheinz Stierle and Rainer Warning (Munich: Fink 1984), pp. 281–286.

77. Ragotzky, *Wolfram-Rezeption*, p. 138 associates these dialogues specifically with the disputational schemata used in the genre of the 'Minnerede' [discourse about love], presumably with reference to texts such as Hartmann von Aue's *Die Klage*, also known as *Das (zweite) Büchlein*, ed. Herta Zutt (Berlin: de Gruyter, 1968), in which the body and the heart are in conflict. However, the religious didacticism of the J.T. makes it reasonable to look more widely at body-soul dialogues in the tradition of the *Visio Philiberti*—some of which specifically highlight the companionship between body and soul. For a general discussion of such dialogues, see Walther, *Das Streitgespräch*, pp. 63–80; for examples, see pp. 211–221. For the foregrounding of companionship, see in particular, example IX quoted by Walther on pp. 218–221, in which terms such as *conpar mea nobilis* (1.1 [my noble equal]) and *mihi socia* (31.1 [my companion]) are deployed. Note also the final affirmation of the otherwise problematic conjunction between body and soul in Mechthild von Magdeburg's *Das fließende Licht der Gottheit* 7.65, p. 310: *Die sele: "Eya min allerliebste gevengnisse, da ich inne gebunden bin, ich danken dir alles, des du hast gevolget mir."* [The soul: "Ah, my dearest prison-cell, in which I am bound, I thank you for all the time that you have followed me."] On the friend and foe relationship between body and soul in mystical literature, see also Caroline Walker Bynum, *The Resurrection of the Body in Western Christianity 200–1336* (New York: Columbia University Press, 1995), pp. 329–341.

78. Note also vrou Aventiure's formulation in dialogue 7, as she encourages him to abandon an Ovidian conception of love: *Waz wiltu dirre sunde? du bist doch min geleite* (J.T. 4018,1 [Why do you want anything to do with this sinfulness? You are, after all, my companion)]. In the prologue (J.T. 66), the narrator had envisaged a more harmonious form of traveling companionship, in which he also has the upper hand, serving as the guide and protector of *aventiure*. As the text progresses, it becomes clear that the narrator has little impact on the direction taken by vrou Aventiure. The narrator's jostling for control even involves the protagonists of the work: in J.T. 3205,2–4, after Ackerin has been speaking at some length, the narrator insists that the *stab der aventiure* [the staff of *aventiure*], itself an image associated with an itinerant existence, be returned to him.

79. J.T. 667,1: *Ich var di rechten strazen* [I take the appropriate roads].

80. For the topos of the text as a building, see David Cowling, *Building the Text. Architecture as Metaphor in Late Medieval and Early Modern France* (Oxford: Oxford University Press, 1998), especially pp. 140–144 which provide a useful overview of the rhetorical and exegetical traditions. For the deployment of this topos by the fourteenth-century *blümer* Heinrich von Mügeln in *Der Tum* (a verbal "cathedral" dedicated to Mary) see Stolz, *'Tum'-Studien*.

81. Hirschberg, "Aventiure-Gespräch," 111–112, with reference to J.T. 4017,2: *di wile ich bin spehende min hus in dinem herzen solcher nehe* [while I look at my house which is so near to your heart].

82. Hirschberg, "Aventiure-Gespräch," 112.

83. *In-principio-Dialog* 0.1–0.2 (pp. 16–18).

84. Barbara Newman, *God and the Goddesses: Vision, Poetry, and Belief in the Middle Ages* (Philadelphia: University of Pennsylvania Press, 2003), pp. 190–191.

85. Newman, *God and the Goddesses*, p. 193.

86. For Wisdom's life on the streets, see for example Prov 8.2–3. The travels of vrou Aventiure have already been discussed above.

87. Newman, *God and the Goddesses*, p. 191.

88. Ingrid Hahn, "Kosmologie und Zahl. Zum Prolog des 'Jüngeren Titurel,'" in *Geistliche Denkformen des Mittelalters*, ed. Klaus Grubmüller, Münstersche Mittelalter-Schriften 51(Munich: Fink, 1984), pp. 230–231 [pp. 226–244]; Finckh, *Minor Mundus*, pp. 367–369. For a critical assessment of this approach, see Neukirchen, "Dirre aventiure kere," 292–293, n38.

89. Guggenberger, *Minnethematik*, pp. 212–221 provides an idiosyncratic and unconvincing reading of these strophes. On his account, this passage is to be understood as an intertextual reference to the *Roman de Troie* by Benoît de Sainte-Maure and to the reception of this work in Herbort von Fritzlar's *Liet von Troye*. Guggenberger regards J.T. 2949–2950 as representing the (flawed) view of Benoît, the *meister være*, which is then repudiated by Herbort, the *meister wider strite*, in J.T. 2951 and the following strophes. Whilst Guggenberger rightly draws attention to the fact that Benoît's prologue does contain some similar topoi regarding the salvatory potential of literature (and that Herbort's text contains some images similar to those found in J.T. 2951–2952), it seems unlikely that these are distinctive enough to function as references to a supposed literary feud: whilst Albrecht's paraphrases of *Parzival* and *Willehalm* are undoubtedly deliberate and intended to be recognized as such, it seems more likely that we are here dealing with tacit borrowings of commonplaces from earlier texts. In any case, it is difficult to read J.T. 2951,1 in such a way as to suggest that the *meister være* and of the *meister wider strite* are two specific individuals with opposing views: while Guggenberger sees the *meister wider strite* as representing an improvement on the *meister være*, the final line of the strophe implies that both are equally reprehensible.

90. Thomasin von Zirclaria, *Der Wälsche Gast* 1121–1126; cf. the introduction, n2.

91. The most direct point of reference for J.T. 2951 is the cosmological passage in Sir. 24, opening with the words: *Sapientia laudabit animam suam* [Sir. 24.1: Wisdom praises herself]. Note also the image of *Sapientia artifex* [Wisdom the creator] in Wis. 7.21, 7.24–26, and 14.2.

92. J.T. 528. See the discussion of this strophe in chapter 3, section II.

93. Vf 2–3. See Lorenz, *Wolfram-Fortsetzung*, pp. 86–97.

94. See for example Mechthild von Magdeburg's presentation of the cosmos as a house built through words in *Das fließende Licht der Gotheit* 3.1, p. 74: *Da sach ich die scho^epnisse und die ordenunge des gottes huses das er selber mit sinem munde hat gebuwen . . . Dú schoepfnisse des huses heisset der himmel . . .* [There I say the creation and the ordering of the house of God that he has built with his own mouth . . . The creation of the house is called the heavens . . .] The image of the house of Wisdom is also taken up by Heinrich von Mügeln, *Der meide kranz* 1495–1496; cf. Annette Volfing, *Heinrich von Mügeln. 'Der meide kranz.' A Commentary*, Münchener Texte und Untersuchungen 111, (Tübingen: Niemeyer, 1997), p. 259.

95. Cf. Mary Alberi, "The 'Mystery of the Incarnation' and Wisdom's House (Prov. 9,1) in Alcuin's *Disputatio de vera philosophia*," *Journal of Theological Studies* 48.2 (1997): 505–516. On the other hand, there are precedents for a textual interpretation of the house of Wisdom. Honorius of Autun, for example, identifies the seven pillars with the seven most important books of the Bible (*Speculum ecclesiae*, PL 172:1101).

96. It is noteworthy that both Tschinotulander (J.T. 1355,3) and Teanglis (J.T. 1296,3–4) associate the Brackenseil with *aventiure* in the sense of 'a knightly challenge,' rather than in the literary sense.

97. See n29 above for the semantic field of *aventiure*. It is possible, albeit probably undesirable, to translate the term *aventiure* in both *Titurel* 170,1 and J.T. 1215,1 along the lines of "something remarkable" (i.e., without prejudice to the issue of whether or not the discourse is narrative.)

98. See the discussion of this strophe in chapters 3 and 5.

5 Justifying the Text: The Poetological Program

A monograph by Thomas Neukirchen on Albrecht's *Jüngerer Titurel* was published in 2006 when this book was already in press. It was therefore not possible for me to incorporate it into my discussion.

1. For an overview of the German literary sources for the J.T., see Huschenbett, "Albrecht, Dichter des 'Jüngeren Titurel,'" in *Verfasserlexikon*, 1:166–167. In addition to the explicit intertextual references discussed in this chapter, Huschenbett's list includes the Alexander narratives, *Herzog Ernst*, Heinrich von Türlin's *Die Krone*, and Reinbot von Durne's *Heiliger Georg*. Walter Röll, "Quellen des Wortschatzes im 'Jüngeren Titurel,'" *Wolfram-Studien* 8 (1984): 49–66 adduces linguistic similarities with a large number of other texts, including Gottfried's *Tristan*, Ulrich von Türheim's *Rennewart*, and the works of Rudolf von Ems, Konrad von Würzburg, Neidhart, Tannhäuser, and Reinmar von Zweter. For the verbal parallels between the J.T. and German sermon material ascribed to Berthold von Regensburg, see the introduction to this monograph, n16. Specific use of French sources is more difficult to demonstrate, although Albrecht is likely to have known some French Grail texts. Guggenberger, *Minnethematik*, pp. 212–221 also argues, not altogether convincingly, that Albrecht draws on the *Roman de Troie* of Benoît de Sainte-Maure and on Herbort von Fritzlar's *Liet von Troye*. For the problems with this argument, see chapter 4, n90. For a survey of Albrecht's Latin sources, see Lorenz, *Wolfram-Fortsetzung*, pp. 135–138.

2. For the extent to which the religious concerns of *Parzival* are compatible with the symbolic structure associated with the works of Chrétien and Hartmann, see Walter Haug, "Die Symbolstruktur des höfischen Epos und ihre Auflösung bei Wolfram von Eschenbach," *Deutsche Vierteljahrsschrift für Literaturwissenschaft und Geistesgeschichte* 45 (1971): 668–705.

3. Ulrich von Zatzikhoven's *Lanzelet* charts the Arthurian hero's string of sexual conquests without showing any hint of moral disapproval. Cf. Nicola McLelland, *Ulrich von Zatzikhoven's Lanzelet: Narrative Style and Entertainment*, Arthurian Studies 46 (Cambridge UK: D.S. Brewer, 2000).

4. Walter Haug, "Paradigmatische Poesie. Der spätere deutsche Artusroman auf dem Weg zu einer 'nachklassischen' Ästhetik," *Deutsche Vierteljahrsschrift für Literaturwissenschaft und Geistesgeschichte* 54 (1980): 212 [204–231].

5. Haug, "Paradigmatische Poesie," 227–229.

6. For an overview of the exemplum as a rhetorical category, see Nigel F. Palmer, "Exempla," in *Medieval Latin. An Introduction and Bibliographical Guide*, ed. F. A.C. Mantello and A.G. Rigg (Washington DC: Catholic University of America Press, 1996), pp. 582–588.

7. The historical Khusro (or Chosroes) II Parvez was the last significant Sassanide king (590–627). Medieval narratives tend to refer to this figure as *Cosdras*.

8. In J.T. 5036–5038, Sigune summarizes Enite's hardships and wishes that she too could set out with Tschinotulander. In J.T. 6005–6010, Enite, Sigune, and Kiburc are presented as exemplary wives, in contrast to Loherangrin's second wife Pelaie.

9. On this point, see Green, *Medieval Listening*, pp. 34–35; also Draesner, *Wege durch erzählte Welten*, pp. 204–206; and Wand, *Wolfram und Hartmann*, pp. 15–19.

10. Erek's failure on the bridge is recounted in J.T. 2398. There follows an apostrophe to Hartmann (J.T. 2402) in which the narrator's competitive aggression is cloaked with politeness: he insists that Hartmann is too well bred to object to having his supremacy challenged. For Erek's support for Orilus, see J.T. 4531. Note the spelling of the name in the J.T. Cf. the introduction, n26.

11. Witege is mentioned in *Willehalm* 384,23–385,12. For the range of stories associated with Witege within the genre of 'Dietrichepik,' see George T. Gillespie, *A Catalogue of Persons Named in German Heroic Literature* (Oxford: Oxford University Press, 1973), pp. 145–147. References to the heroic epic or to the Dietrichepik in *Parzival* are as follows: Wolfhart (420,22); Gunther and Rumold (420,26–28); Sibche, Ermrîche (421,24–28).

12. For references to Veldeke, see *Parzival* 292,18–19 and 482,2 (Eneas); J.T. 4889. For Walther, see *Parzival* 297,24–25; J.T. 607,2.

13. For this aspect of *Der saelden hort*, see Annette Volfing, *John the Evangelist and Medieval German Writing: Imitating the Inimitable* (Oxford: Oxford University Press, 2001), pp. 169–183.

14. Cf. Ridder, *Minne—und Aventiureromane*, p. 37.

15. For an overview of the idiosyncrasies of this text, see Hans Hugo Steinhoff, "Göttweiger Trojanerkrieg," in *Die deutsche Literatur des Mittelalters. Verfasserlexikon*, ed. Kurt Ruh, 2nd edn., 10 vols. (Berlin: de Gruyter: 1978–1999), 3:199–201. Whilst ostensibly an 'Antikenroman' [romance set in antiquity] recounting the fall of Troy, the *Göttweiger Trojanerkrieg* draws extensively on the narrative models associated with Arthurian romance and even endows certain protagonists with distinctively Arthurian names (e.g., Gahmuret from *Parzival*, Larie from Wirnt von Grafenberg's *Wigalois*). Like the J.T., this text is also narratologically complex, with a narrator who is sometimes identified as Wolfram von Eschenbach, but who sometimes refers to Wolfram as a separate individual. There are also numerous dialogues between 'Wolfram' and an allegorical figure (in this case, vrou Minne) controlling the events of the narrative.

16. The chronological aspects of the J.T. (both in relation to other Arthurian romances and to history more generally) are also discussed by Alfred Ebenbauer, "Tschionatulander und Artus. Zur Gattungsstruktur und zur Interpretation des Tschionatulanderlebens im 'Jüngeren Titurel,'" *Zeitschrift für deutsches Altertum und deutsche Literatur* 108 (1979): 397–403 [374–407].

17. Dennis Howard Green, "Fiktionalität und weiße Flecken in Wolframs 'Parzival,'" *Wolfram-Studien* 17 (2002): 30–45.

18. For the historical anchoring of *Parzival*, see Horst Brunner, "*Artus der wise höfsche man*. Zur immanenten Historizität der Ritterwelt im 'Parzival' Wolframs von Eschenbach," in *Germanistik in Erlangen. Hundert Jahre nach der Gründung des Deutschen Seminars*, ed. Dietmar Peil, Erlanger Forschungen, Reihe A, Geisteswissenschaften 31 (Erlangen: Universitätsbund Erlangen-Nürnberg, 1983), pp. 61–73; and Joachim Bumke, "Parzival und Feirefiz—Priester Johannes—Loherangrin: Der offene Schluß des *Parzival* von Wolfram von Eschenbach," *Deutsche Vierteljahrsschrift für Literaturwissenschaft und Geistesgeschichte* 65 (1991), 236–264. For the very different ways in which historicity is also foregrounded in the courtly romances of the thirteenth and fourteenth centuries, see Ridder, *Minne—und Aventiureromane*, pp. 147–154.

19. Albrecht also follows the examples of earlier writers (notably Veldeke and Wolfram) in that he uses familiar events from recent history as comparators for intradiegetic

developments. See for example J.T. 4060, which claims that Ypomidon had even more followers than Otto of Saxony.

20. *Parzival* 455,9–12 describes how Kyot read the chronicles of Britain, France, and Ireland in order to find information about the Grail. Eventually he found what he needed in Anjou. Whilst only one chronicle provides the information that Kyot wants, Albrecht suggests that information about Sigune and Tschinotulander (specifically about their burial) may be found in many places: *Ob ir des niht geloubet, so vragt in Salvaterre. / der schrift vil unberoubet sint der lande kronik nah und verre: / Frankrich, Anschowe und in Katelangen, / dar zuo in Graswaldane, in Britanje, man vindetz ouch in Spangen.* (J.T. 5869) [If you do not believe this, then ask in Salvaterre. The chronicles of the lands both close by and far away are not without a written account of this: in France, Anjou, in Catalonia, as well as in Graswalt and Britain. You will also find it in Spain.] For intradiegetic reliance on chronicles, see also the discussion in chapter 1. For the location of Graswalt, see chapter 1, n58.
21. The historical Emperor Heraclius lived 575–641.
22. Wegner, *Albrecht*, p. 41 reads J.T. 4078 as an explicit reference to the work of Geoffrey of Monmouth.
23. See chapter 1, n42.
24. See chapter 2, section II.
25. The identity of this speaker is not without ambiguity. The strophe, together with the subsequent story about Radoltz of Kanias is embedded into a long speech addressed by Ypomidon to Secureiz. Strictly speaking, one should therefore ascribe knowledge of the heroic epic to the two heathens in question, and discount the authority of the strophe to allow for the fact that it is spoken by a heathen, and a villainous one at that. A more satisfying solution would be to argue that this strophe constitutes an intrusion by the narrator into the discourse of Ypomidon. An equivalent example occurs in J.T. 5354 when Ekuba apparently makes an unmotivated and anachronistic reference to Kyot and this strophe is best regarded as an intrusion on the part of the narrator. Cf. chapter 2, n37.
26. *Tristan* 8601–8623.
27. J.T. 3369,4; *an snelheit und an varwe und an der stimme diu menscheit sich verkerte* [their human form was distorted with respect to speed, color, and voice].
28. For the origins of the story of Adam's daughters and for its presentation in Middle High German literature (notably in the *Wiener Genesis*, the *Lucidarius*, Wolfram's *Parzival*, and *Reinfried von Braunschweig*), see Roy Wisbey, "Wunder des Ostens in der 'Wiener Genesis' und in Wolframs 'Parzival,'" in *Studien zur frühmittelhochdeutschen Literatur. Cambridger Colloquium 1971*, ed. Leslie Peter Johnson, Publications of the Institute of Germanic Studies of the University of London 19 (Berlin: Erich Schmidt, 1974), pp. 190–198 [pp. 180–214]. In *Reinfried von Braunschweig* 19,628–19,932 ed. Carl von Kraus, Bibliothek des Litterarischen Vereins in Stuttgart 109 (Stuttgart: Litterarischer Verein, 1871). This story is invoked specifically in order to explain the existence of a fierce population (possibly modeled on the descendants of Radoltz in the J.T.) who are made entirely of *horn* and who fight on the side of the Amazons. In the *Reinfried* version, the guilty women are not Adam's immediate daughters, but later female descendants living after the flood: Adam's insights having survived the flood by being inscribed onto a pillar, the women read the information about the properties of the different herbs and resolve to put this to the test, with the result that a range of monstrous populations are brought into the world. Nonetheless, far from insisting on the truthfulness of this account, the narrator of *Reinfried* admits that he has never seen monstrous people himself.

29. Wegner, *Albrecht*, p. 201.

30. *Parzival* 518,1–519,9.

31. *Willehalm* 35,12–17 and 395,22–24.

32. *Parzival* 518,29: *sus wart verkêrt diu mennischeit* [humanity was thus distorted].

33. Note also the inclusion of *wurtz* in earlier catalogues of created objects, e.g., J.T. 284,1–2 and 1662,1–2.

34. See J.T. 4209,1: *Hie mit sint underscheiden di heiden und di cristen.* [Heathens and Christians differ in this respect.]

35. For further discussion of Albrecht's approach to the cultural attainments of the heathens, see chapter 1, n14.

36. Elke Brüggen, "Fiktionalität und Didaxe. Annäherungen an die Dignität lehrhafter Rede im Mittelalter," in *Text und Kultur. Mittelalterliche Literatur 1150–1450*, ed. Ursula Peters (Stuttgart: Metzler: 2001), p. 574 [pp. 546–574].

37. For an older overview of Albrecht's didactic method, see Zatloukal, *Salvaterre*, pp. 25–46.

38. Neukirchen, "Dirre aventiure kere," 287.

39. See Huschenbett, "Albrecht, Dichter des 'Jüngeren Titurel,'" in *Verfasserlexikon*, 1:170; and Finckh, *Minor Mundus*, p. 327. Rausch, *Methoden*, p. 11 compares the didactic programme of Albrecht to that of Vincent of Beauvais, emphasizing the connection between "Wissensvermittlung" [transmission of knowledge] und *tugende ler* [the instruction of virtue].

40. Wegner, *Albrecht*, p. 39 characterizes the J.T. as being "der *lere* verpflichtet" [committed to *lere*] and as forming "ein Geflecht aus fiktionalen Elementen einerseits und Versatzstücken einer erfahrbaren Wirklichkeit, den Realien, andererseits" [a tangle consisting of fictional elements on the one hand, and of *realia* on the other, set pieces taken from an experiential reality].

41. Finckh, *Minor Mundus*, p. 339.

42. See the introduction, and J.T. 646–647.

43. In Gottfried's *Tristan*, the relationship between narrative and excurses is famously problematic (cf. Huber, *Tristan*, pp. 118–119). However, even in Hartmann's *Iwein*, there are occasional tensions between the murky events of the narrative and the narrator's ostensible insistence that all is well. For this narrator's (possibly ironic) endorsement of Laudine's marriage to Iwein, see Thomas Cramer, "Sælde und êre in Hartmanns 'Iwein,'" in *Hartmann von Aue: Wege der Forschung*, ed. Hugo Kuhn and Christoph Cormeau (Darmstadt: Wissenschaftliche Buchgesellschaft, 1973), p. 435 [pp. 426–449]; originally published in *Euphorion* 60 (1966): 30–47. On moral ambiguity more generally in *Iwein*, see Alan Roberstshaw, "Ambiguity and Morality in *Iwein*," in *Hartmann von Aue: Changing Perspectives. London Hartmann Symposium 1985*, ed. Timothy McFarland and Silvia Ranawake, Göppinger Arbeiten zur Germanistik 486 (Göppingen: Kümmerle, 1988), pp. 117–128.

44. J.T. 1283 and 2521. Cf. Guggenberger, *Minnethematik*, pp. 102–103 and 141.

45. Views are similarly polarized with respect to the Brackenseil text, as has been discussed in chapter 3, section I.

46. Finckh, *Minor Mundus*, p. 333.

47. In particular, Tschinotulander's military exploits in the Orient are endowed with some of the moral glamor attaching to crusades, notwithstanding the facts that the conflict itself is an internal one between two heathen parties, and that Tschinotulander is fighting to win the love of a lady. Cf. Guggenberger, *Minnethematik*, p. 155; Finckh, *Minor Mundus*, p. 343; Lorenz, *Wolfram–Fortsetzung*, pp. 282–292.

48. On this excursus, see Guggenberger, *Minnethematik*, pp. 212–221. However, note the caveats expressed in chapter 4, n90 about some of Guggenberger's assertions.

49. This argument opens with the analogy discussed in detail in chapter 4 between the author creating the text and the figure of Wisdom creating the world. In the following strophes, the narrator compares life on earth to a journey undertaken by the blind, who therefore need the guidance of fully-sighted masters (J.T. 2952–2956).

50. See chapter 1, section III.

51. On this excursus, see Guggenberger, *Minnethematik*, pp. 221–223.

52. *Kunst* [art, knowledge, skill] and *meisterschaft* [mastery, acknowledged expertise] are both loaded terms within Middle High German literature. In the prologue to Wolfram's *Willehalm* (2,19–22), *kunst* is linked to *sin* to form a specifically poet-ological unit (see chapter 4, n22). By contrast, the J.T. links *kunst* with *witze*, using both terms more widely to refer to the intelligent handling of learned material by poets and nonpoets alike (cf. Wegner, *Albrecht*, pp. 33–34). For the range of meanings associated with the term *meisterschaft* within the didactic tradi-tion of the genre of 'Spruchdichtung,' see Karl Stackmann, *Der Spruchdichter Heinrich von Mügeln: Vorstudien zur Erkenntnis seiner Individualität*, Probleme der Dichtung: Studien zur deutschen Literaturgeschichte 3 (Heidelberg: C. Winter, 1958), pp. 94–98.

53. Note also J.T. 5281, which links book knowledge to virtue in general and to chaste, spiritual love in particular.

54. The rhetorical strategy of endowing terms with new meanings is familiar from the genre of 'Minnesang.' Most famously, in Walther von der Vogelweide's song *Saget mir ieman waz ist minne* (*Leich, Lieder, Sangsprüche* ed. Lachmann no. 69,1; Cormeau no. 44), the lyrical persona breaks with common usage by stipulating that the term 'Minne' should be used only to refer to happy, reciprocal love.

55. The mixture of illustrative comparators may be illustrated by reference to J.T. 2483, in which Arthur's aunt Accedille is said to be wiser than *Thetis* or *Sibille*.

56. For further discussion of these figures, see section III below.

57. See Mishtoomi Bose, "From Exegesis to Appropriation: The Medieval Solomon," *Medium Ævum* 64 (1996): 187–210.

58. Cf. chapter 1, n30.

59. This is essentially the view of Brode, *Sprach- und Werkstil*, pp. 198–199. Cf. Zatloukal, *Salvaterre*, pp. 145–157 for a critique of this.

60. Cf. the discussion of J.T. 2949–2951 in chapter 4.

61. Zatloukal, *Salvaterre*, p. 146.

62. The inscriptions inside and outside the Temple are discussed in chapter 1. For the textual nature of both Temple and cosmos, see Finckh, *Minor Mundus*, p. 361: "Für ihn [Albrecht] ist die Welt von Gott als lesbare und interpretierbare Lehrschrift angelegt. Der Tempel stellt demnach eine Art Codeschlüssel für dieses 'Buch der Welt' dar, eine Hilfe zum Dechiffrieren der göttlichen Botschaft in der Natur." [For Albrecht, the world is set out as a legible and interpretable didactic text by God. Accordingly, the temple constitutes a kind of code to this "Book of the World," an aid to deciphering the divine message in nature.]

63. Mathias Herweg, "Der Kosmos als Innenraum. Ein persischer Thronsaal und seine Rezeption im Mittelalter," *Deutsche Vierteljahrsschrift für Literaturwissenschaft und Geistesgeschichte* 80 (2006):3–54.

64. Herweg, "Der Kosmos als Innenraum" provides a survey of this motif in Latin and Middle High German literature, with particular reference to the *Kaiserchronik* and to Otte's *Eraclius*.

65. See also Finckh, *Minor Mundus*, p. 346: "Ohne das harmonische Zusammenspiel von menschlicher und göttlicher Kraft wäre Titurels Werk gar nicht denkbar gewesen." [Titurel's achievement would have been unthinkable without the harmonious interaction of human and divine power.]

66. Finckh, *Minor Mundus*, pp. 368–369. For a criticism of this position, see Neukirchen, "Dirre aventiure kere," 292–293, n38.

67. Christian Thelen, *Das Dichtergebet in der deutschen Literatur des Mittelalters*, Arbeiten zur Frühmittelalterforschung 18 (Berlin: de Gruyter, 1989), p. 458 notes that Albrecht replaces Wolfram's idea of a universal "Gotteskindschaft" (i.e., the idea that all people are the children of God) with a more special relationship between God and poet.

68. C. Stephen Jaeger, "Der Schöpfer der Welt und das Schöpfungswerk als Prologmotiv in der mittelhochdeutschen Dichtung," *Zeitschrift für deutsches Altertum und deutsche Literatur* 107 (1978), 1–18.

69. In one version (the so-called 'Reisefassung') of *Brandans Meerfahrt*, the protagonist destroys the book because he regards the marvels as unbelievable. As punishment, he is the ordered by God to set out to see the wonders for himself, so that he will be able to re–create the book. Cf. Walter Haug, "Brandans Meerfahrt," in *Die deutsche Literatur des Mittelalters. Verfasserlexikon*, ed. Kurt Ruh, 2nd edn., 10 vols. (Berlin: de Gruyter: 1978–1999), 1:985–991. Note also the related motif in the *Wartburgkrieg* of Zabulon's magical book that is hidden on the magnetic mountain, only to be retrieved by Virgil and taken to Brandan. Cf. Wachinger, "Wartburgkrieg," 10:753–756. *Reinfried von Braunschweig* 20,989–21,722 features an episode about this magical book on the magnetic mountain. Cf. Alfred Ebenbauer, "Reinfried von Braunschweig," in *Die deutsche Literatur des Mittelalters. Verfasserlexikon*, ed. Kurt Ruh, 2nd edn., 10 vols. (Berlin: de Gruyter: 1978–1999), 7:1171–1176.

70. Minnis, "Discussions of 'Authorial Role,'" 39–42.

71. The historical Phocas was a Byzantine Emperor who reigned 602–610.

72. For Wolfram's conflation of Heraclius with Hercules, see Wolfram von Eschenbach, *Parzival*, ed. Nellmann, 2:765. Albrecht follows Wolfram in this respect. His association in J.T. 108 of *Ercules* with learned, intellectual figures such as Aristotle, Solomon, and Ovid strongly suggests that he is invoking the learning of Heraclius rather than the legendary strength of Hercules.

73. For the various ways in which medieval thinkers engaged with the issues of Aristotle's moral and intellectual excellence and of his chances of salvation, see Steven Williams, *The Secret of Secrets: The Scholarly Career of a Pseudo-Aristotelian Text in the Latin Middle Ages* (Ann Arbor: University of Michigan Press, 2003), pp. 272–289.

74. For the story of Aristotle being ridden by Phyllis, see Hellmut Rosenfeld, "Aristotles und Phyllis," in *Die deutsche Literatur des Mittelalters. Verfasserlexikon*, ed. Kurt Ruh, 2nd edn., 10 vols. (Berlin: de Gruyter: 1978–1999), 1:434–436.

75. See chapter 3, section II.

76. Cf. Hahn, "Kosmologie und Zahl," in *Geistliche Denkformen*, pp. 232–236; Finckh, *Minor Mundus*, pp. 370–372.

77. Aquinas, *Summa theologiae* 3a, 60.2, 56:8 defines the sacrament as *signum rei sacræ inquantum est sanctificans homines* [a sign of a sacred reality inasmuch as it has the property of sanctifying men.]

78. J.T. 76–82 explain that all four elements are equally subordinate to the will of God. However, in situations of conflict, water is able to overpower each of the other three elements (J.T. 42,1: *sint got daz wazzer eine fur allen elementen hat gesterket* [since God

has made water more powerful than any other element]). In discussing the matter of baptism, Aquinas, *Summa theologiae* 3a, 66.3, 57:14 highlights the many uses of water, noting that *quidam philosophi posuerunt aquam omnium rerum principium*. [Some philosophers postulated water as the principle of everything.] Whilst water plays an obvious part in baptism, it also holds a symbolic significance for all the sacraments, given that they all derive their power from the passion of Christ, when water (together with blood) flowed from his side wound. Cf. Aquinas, *Summa theologiae* 3a, 62.5, 56:68; for Christ's association with water and blood, see also 1 John 5,6. This may explain the readiness of the J.T. to associate water not only with baptism, but also with the other sacraments (J.T. 43,1 and 48,4), even though they do not use water as part of their ritual.

79. In J.T. 31,4, water is presented as washing away the stains on the spiritual robes of the baptized (J.T. 31,4). Cf. Aquinas, *Summa theologiae* 3a, 66.3.ad 3, 57:14: *ex latere Christi fluxit aqua ad abluendum* [Water flowed from the side of Christ for the purpose of washing]. For the tears of the penitent, see J.T. 46.

80. For the tradition of seeking trinitarian analogies in natural phenomena, see Peter Kern, *Trinität, Maria, Inkarnation. Studien zur Thematik der deutschen Dichtung des späteren Mittelalters*, Philologische Studien und Quellen 55 (Berlin: Erich Schmidt, 1971), pp. 150–163.

81. Hahn, "Kosmologie und Zahl," in *Geistliche Denkformen*, pp. 235–244 discusses the numerological implications of this juxtaposition of "Gott und Natur, *creator* und geschaffene Welt, die Drei und die Vier." [God and nature, creator and created world, the Three and the Four].

82. In J.T. 85, the closing strophe of the prologue, the narrator implicitly juxtaposes God's redemptive opus with his own literary undertaking in J.T.: *Iedoch swie wir ersterben doch muoz wir leben immer, / da nach als wir hie werben. solche mære kund ich vol enden nimmer. / ein ander werk han ich hie under handen . . .* [Although we die, we will live for ever, according to how we act here. I could never provide a complete account of this. I have another project to embark upon . . .] The phrase *ein ander werk* contrasts not only with the (hypothetical) literary narration of salvation history, but also with God's actual *werk* of directing salvation history.

83. For the importance of sacramental language generally, see Aquinas, *Summa theologiae* 3a, 60.6, 56:20–25. For a reminder that in baptism, the source of the sanctification does not derive from the water itself, but from the application of the water to man *sub forma præscripta verborum* [with the prescribed form of words], see *Summa theologiae* 3a, 66.1 (57:6).

84. The scientific and exegetical traditions relating to the crystal are extensive, whilst the enidorium (otherwise known as *enhydros* or *enydros*) is more obscure. See Kern, "Der Kommentar zu 'Parzival,'" in *Festschrift für H. Moser*, pp. 192–195; Engelen, *Edelsteine*, pp. 25 and 91–92 (for the enidorium) and pp. 334–343 (for the crystal). Other stones with quasi-miraculous properties feature as building materials for the temple: notably asbestos (J.T. 333), which burns forever without being consumed), and the heliotrope (J.T. 334), which can regulate temperatures according to the season. For the ways in which the crystal, the *enidorium*, asbestos and the heliotrope are all presented in the J.T. as demonstrations of the power of God, see Engelen, *Edelsteine*, p. 338. Nonetheless, the last two stone are not mentioned in the prologue and have no poetological significance.

85. For details, see Christel Meier, *Gemma spiritalis. Methode und Gebrauch der Edelsteinallegorese von frühen Christentum bis ins 18. Jahrhundert.* Münstersche Mittelalter-Schriften 34,1. Munich: Fink, 1977, p. 264; Wegner, *Albrecht*, pp. 86–87.

86. J.T. 354–355 mention the crystal, whilst J.T. 370 makes it clear that all the building materials are provided by the Grail. Cf. Finckh, *Minor Mundus*, pp. 346 and 372.
87. Gottfried von Straßburg, *Tristan* 4629.
88. For discussion of the full extent to which the prologue to the J.T. paraphrases *Parzival*, see Kern, "Der Kommentar zu 'Parzival,'" in *Festschrift für H. Moser*.

BIBLIOGRAPHY

Texts and Translations

Alan of Lille. *Anticlaudianus: Texte critique avec une introduction et des tables*. Ed. Robert Bossuat. Textes philosophiques du moyen âge 1. Paris: Vrin, 1955.

———. *Anticlaudianus or The Good and Perfect Man*. Trans. James J. Sheridan. Toronto: Pontifical Institute of Medieval Studies, 1973.

———. *Elucidatio in Cantica canticorum*. PL 210:51–110.

———. *De incarnatione Christi rhytmus perelegans* (second version). PL 210:579–580.

———. *Summa de arte prædicatoria*. PL 210:109–198.

Albrecht. *Albrechts von Scharfenberg Jüngerer Titurel (J.T.)*. Ed. Werner Wolf (I–II,2) and Kurt Nyholm (II,2–III,2). 5 vols. (I; II,1; II,2; III,1; III,2). Deutsche Texte des Mittelalters 45, 55, 61, 73, 77. Berlin: Akademie-Verlag, 1955–1992.

———. *Das Verfasserfragment (Vf)*. Andrea Lorenz, *Der Jüngere Titurel als Wolfram-Fortsetzung. Eine Reise zum Mittelpunkt des Werks*. Deutsche Literatur von den Anfängen bis 1700 36. Bern: Peter Lang, 2002. pp. 68–72.

Aquinas, Thomas. *Summa Theologiae: Latin Text and English Translation, Introduction, Notes, Appendices and Glossaries*. Ed. Thomas Gilby. 61 vols. London: Blackfriars, 1963–1980.

Augustine. *Confessiones*. Ed. Lucas Verheijen. Corpus Christianorum. Series Latina 27. Turnhout: Brepols, 1981.

———. *De doctrina Christiana*. Ed. Joseph Martin. Corpus Christianorum. Series Latina 32. Turnhout: Brepols, 1962.

———. *Principia dialecticae*. PL 32:1409–1420.

Benoît de Sainte-Maure. *Roman de Troie*. Ed. Léopold Constans. 6 vols. Paris: Firmin-Didot, 1904–1912.

Berthold von Regensburg. *Vollständige Ausgabe seiner deutschen Predigten*. Ed. Franz Pfeiffer and Joseph Strobl. 2 vols. Vienna: Braumüller, 1862–1880.

[The Bible] *Biblia sacra iuxta vulgatam clementinam*. Ed. Alberto Colunga and Lorenzo Turrado. Biblioteca de autores cristianos. Madrid: La Editorial Catolica S.A., 1982.

Brun von Schönebeck. *Das Hohe Lied*. Ed. Arwed Fischer. Bibliothek des Litterarischen Vereins in Stuttgart 198. Tübingen: Litterarischer Verein, 1893.

Chrétien de Troyes. *Le Roman de Perceval ou Le Conte du Graal. Édition critique d'après tous les manuscripts*. Ed. Keith Busby. Tübingen: Niemeyer, 1993.

Dante Aligheri. *Vita Nuova*. Ed. Michele Barbi. *Le Opere di Dante. Testo Critico della Società Dantesca Italiana*. Florence: Società Dantesca Italiana, 1960. pp. 1–49.

Frauenlob (Heinrich von Meißen). *Leichs, Sangsprüche, Lieder*. Ed. Karl Stackmann and Karl Bertau. 2 vols. Abhandlungen der Akademie der Wissenschaften in Göttingen, philologisch-historische Klasse, 3. Folge 119–120. Göttingen: Vandenhoeck and Ruprecht, 1981.

Geoffrey of Monmouth. *Histoira regum Britanniae*. Ed. Jacob Hammer. Cambridge, Mass.: Medieval Academy of America, 1951.

Der sogenannte St. Georgener Prediger. Eine Überlieferung von deutschen Klosterpredigten Bertholds von Regensburg aus der Freiburger und der Karlsruher Handschrift. Ed. Karl Rieder. Deutsche Texte des Mittelalters 10. Berlin: Weidmann, 1908.

Gottfried von Straßburg. *Tristan*. Ed. and German trans. Rüdiger Krohn based on the text by Friedrich Ranke. 3rd edn. 2 vols. Universal-Bibliothek 4471–4472. Stuttgart: Reclam, 1984.

Göttweiger Trojanerkrieg. Ed. Alfred Koppitz. Deutsche Texte des Mittelalters 29. Berlin: Weidmann, 1926.

Guibert de Nogent. *Autobiographie*. Ed. and French trans. Edmond-René Labande. Les classiques de l'histoire de France au moyen âge 34. Paris: Les belles lettres, 1981.

Hartmann von Aue. *Erec*. Ed. Manfred Günter Scholz. German trans. Susanne Held. Bibliothek des Mittelalters 5. Frankfurt am Main: Deutscher Klassiker Verlag, 2004.

————. *Gregorius*. Ed. Burghart Wachinger based on the text by Paul Hermann. 13th edn. Altdeutsche Textbibliothek 2. Tübingen: Niemeyer, 1984.

————. *Iwein*. Ed. Ludwig Wolf based on the text by Georg Friedrich Benecke and Karl Lachmann. 7th edn. 2 vols. Berlin: de Gruyter, 1968.

————. *Die Klage. Das (zweite) Büchlein aus dem Ambraser Heldenbuch*. Ed. Herta Zutt. Berlin: de Gruyter, 1968.

Das Häslein. Die deutsche Literatur: Texte und Zeugnisse: Mittelalter. Ed. Helmut de Boor. 2 vols. Munich: Beck, 1963–1965. 2:1456–1463.

Heinrich von Freiberg. *Tristan*. Ed. Alois Bernt. Halle: Niemeyer, 1906. Reprinted Tübingen: Niemeyer, 1978.

Heinrich von Kröllwitz. *Vaterunser*. Ed. Gottfried Christian Friedrich Lisch. Bibliothek der gesammten deutschen National-Literatur 19. Quedlinburg: G. Basse, 1839.

Heinrich von Mügeln, *Der meide kranz. Die Kleineren Dichtungen Heinrichs von Mügeln. Zweite Abteilung*. Ed. Karl Stackmann with Michael Stolz. Deutsche Texte des Mittelalters 84. Berlin: Akademie Verlag, 2003. pp. 47–203.

Heinrich von dem Türlin. *Die Krone (Verse 1–12281). Nach der Handschrift 2779 der Österre-ichischen Nationalbibliothek*. Ed. Fritz Peter Knapp and Manuela Nieser, on the basis of preliminary work by Alfred Ebenbauer. Altdeutsche Textbibliothek 112. Tübingen: Niemeyer, 2000. *Die Krone (Verse 12282–30042). Nach der Handschrift Cod. Pal. germ. 374 der Universitätsbibliothek Heidelberg*. Ed. Alfred Ebenbauer and Florian Kragl, on the basis of preliminary work by Fritz Peter Knapp and Klaus Zatloukal. Altdeutsche Textbibliothek 118. Tübingen: Niemeyer, 2005.

Heinrich von Veldeke. *Eneasroman: Mittelhochdeutsch—Neuhochdeutsch*. Ed. and trans. Dieter Kartschoke based on the text by Ludwig Ettmüller. Universal-Bibliothek 8303. Stuttgart: Reclam, 1989.

Herbort von Fritslar. *Liet von Troye*. Ed. Georg Karl Fromman. Bibliothek der gesammten deutschen National-Literatur 5. Quedlingburg and Leipzig: H. Rückert, 1837. Reprinted Amsterdam: Rodopi, 1966.

Herzog Ernst. Ed. Karl Bartsch. Vienna: Braumüller, 1869.

Honorius of Autun. *Elucidarium*. PL 172:1109–1176.

————. *Speculum ecclesiae*. PL 172:807–1108.

Hugo von Montfort. *Das poetische Werk. Texte—Melodien—Einführung*. Ed. Wernfried Hofmeister with an appendix by Agnes Grond. Berlin:de Gruyter, 2005.

In-principio-Dialog. Ed. Karl-Heinz Witte. *Der Meister des Lehrgesprächs und sein "In-Principio-Dialog": ein deutschsprachiger Theologe der Augustinerschule des 14. Jahrhunderts aus dem Kreise deutscher Mystik und Scholastik*. Münchener Texte und Untersuchungen 95. Munich: Artemis, 1989.

Isidore of Seville. *Isidori Etymologiarum Libri XX*. Ed. Wallace Martin Lindsay. 2 vols. Scriptorum classicorum bibliotheca Oxoniensis. Oxford: Oxford University Press, 1911. Reprinted 1985.

Johann von Würzburg. *Johanns von Würzburg Wilhelm von Österreich aus der Gothaer Handschrift*. Ed. Ernst Regel. Deutsche Texte des Mittelalters 3. Berlin: Weidmann, 1906.

Johannes von Tepl. *Der Ackermann: Frühneuhochdeutsch / Neuhochdeutsch*. Universal-Bibliothek 18075. Ed. and German trans. Christian Kiening. Stuttgart: Reclam, 2000.

————. *Epistola cum Libello ackerman und Das büchlein ackerman. Nach der Freiburger Hs. 163 und nach der Stuttgarter Hs. HB X 23*. Ed. and German trans. Karl Bertau, 2 vols. Berlin: de Gruyter, 1994.

John of Salisbury. *Metalogicon*. Ed. J. B. Hall and K. S. B. Keats-Rohan. Corpus Christianorum, Continuatio Mediaevalis 98. Turnhout: Brepols, 1991.

Die Kaiserchronik eines Regensburger Geistlichen. Ed. Edward Schroeder. Monumenta Germaniae Historica. Deutsche Chroniken 1. Hannover: Hahn, 1892.

Die Klage. Ed., German trans. and commentary by Elisabeth Lienert, based on the text by Karl Bartsch. Schöninghs Mediävistisches Editionen 5. Paderborn: Ferdinand Schnöningh, 2000.

Konrad, Pfaffe. *Das Rolandslied des Pfaffen Konrad*. Ed. Dieter Kartschoke. Universal-Bibliothek 2745. Stuttgart: Reclam, 1993.

Konrad von Würzburg. *Engelhard*. Ed. Ingo Reiffenstein. 3rd edn., based on the text of Paul Gereke. Altdeutsche Textbibliothek 17. Tübingen: Niemeyer, 1982.

Kudrun. Ed. Karl Stackmann based on the text by Karl Bartsch. Altdeutsche Textbibliothek 115. Tübingen: Niemeyer, 2000.

Lucidarius aus der Berliner Handschrift. Ed. Felix Heidlauf. Deutsche Texte des Mittelalters 28. Berlin: Weidmann, 1915.

Mechthild von Magdeburg. *Das fliessende Licht der Gottheit*. Münchener Texte und Untersuchungen 100. Ed. Hans Neumann. Munich: Artemis, 1990.

Muschg, Adolf. *Der Rote Ritter. Eine Geschichte von Parzivâl*. Frankfurt am Main: Suhrkamp, 1993.

Das Nibelungenlied. Text und Einführung. Ed. Hermann Reichert. Berlin: de Gruyter, 2005.

Otte. *Eraclius*. Ed. Winfried Frey. Göppinger Arbeiten zur Germanistik 348. Göppingen: Kümmerle, 1983.

Ovid, *Ars amatoria*. Ed. Henri Bornecque. Paris; Les belles lettres, 1960.

Pseudo-Ovid. *De nvncio sagaci. De mercatore. Extrait de La Comédie latine en France au XIIe siècle*. Ed. Alphonse Dain. Paris: Les belles lettres, 1932.

Püterich von Reichertshausen, Jakob. *Ehrenbrief*. Ed. Fritz Behrend and Rudolf Wolkan. Weimar: Gesellschaft der Bibliophilen, 1920.

Reinbot von Durne. *Der Heilige Georg*. Ed. Carl von Kraus. Germanistische Bibliothek 3,1. Heidelberg: C. Winter, 1907.

Reinfried von Braunschweig. Ed. Carl von Kraus. Bibliothek des Litterarischen Vereins in Stuttgart 109. Stuttgart: Litterarischer Verein, 1871.

Reinmar von Zweter. *Die Gedichte Reinmars von Zweter*. Ed. Gustav Roethe. Leipzig: Hirzel, 1887.

Rupert of Deutz. *Commentarium In Genesim* II.33, PL 167:199–566.

Der saelden hort. Alemannisches Gedicht vom Leben Jesu, Johannes des Täufers und der Magdalena. Ed. Heinrich Adrian. Deutsche Texte des Mittelalters 26. Berlin: Weidmann, 1927.

Thomasin von Zirclaria. *Der Wälsche Gast*. Bibliothek der gesamten deutschen National-Literatur 30. Ed. Heinrich Rückert. Quedlinburg: G. Basse,1852. Reprinted with a foreword and index by Friedrich Neumann. Deutsche Neudrucke: Texte des Mittelalters. Berlin: de Gruyter, 1965.

Tristan als Mönch. Ed. Betty C. Bushey. Göppinger Arbeiten zur Germanistik 119. Göppingen: Kümmerle, 1974.

Ulrich von Türheim. *Rennewart. Aus der Berliner und Heidelberger Handschrift.* Ed. Alfred Hübner. Deutsche Texte des Mittelalters 39. Berlin and Zurich: Akademie-Verlag, 1964.

———. *Tristan.* Ed. Thomas Kerth. Altdeutsche Textbibliothek 89. Tübingen: Niemeyer, 1979.

Ulrich von dem Türlin. *'Arabel'-Studien. Prolegomena zu einer neuen Ausgabe Ulrichs von dem Türlin.* Ed. Werner Schröder. 6 vols. Mainz: Akademie der Wissenschaften und Literatur, Geistes- und Sozialwissenschaftlichen Klasse, 1982–1993.

———. *Willehalm.* Ed. Samuel Singer. Bibliothek der Mittelhochdeutschen Literatur in Böhmen IV. Prague: Verlag des Vereins für Geschichte der Deutschen in Böhmen, 1893. Reprinted Hildesheim: G. Olms, 1968.

Ulrich von Zatzikhoven. *Lanzelet.* Ed. K. A. Hahn. Frankfurt am Main: Brönner. Reprinted Deutsche Neudrucke. Texte des Mittelalters. Berlin: de Gruyter, 1965.

Virginal. Ed. J. Zupitza. *Dietrichs Abenteuer von Albrecht von Kemenaten nebst den Bruchstücken von Dietrich und Wenezlar.* Deutsches Heldenbuch 5. Berlin: Weidmann, 1870. pp. 1–200.

Walther von der Volgelweide. *Leich, Lieder, Sangsprüche.* 14th edn. by Christoph Cormeau based on the text by Karl Lachmann. Berlin: de Gruyter, 1996.

Der Wartburgkrieg. Ed. Karl Simrock. Stuttgart and Augsburg: Cotta, 1858.

Der Wartburgkrieg. Ed. Tom Albert Rompelmann. Amsterdam: H.J. Paris. 1939.

Priester Wernhers Maria. Bruchstücke und Umarbeitungen. Ed. Hans Fromm based on the text by Carl Wesle. 2nd edn. Altdeutsche Textbibliothek 26. Tübingen: Niemeyer, 1969.

Wiener Genesis. Ed. Kathryn Smits. Philologische Studien und Quellen 59. Berlin: Erich Schmidt, 1972.

Wirnt von Gravenberg. *Wigalois. Text—Übersetzung—Stellenkommentar.* Ed., German trans. and notes by Sabine Seelbach and Ulrich Seelbach based on the text by J.M.N. Kapteyn. Berlin: de Gruyter, 2005.

Wolfram von Eschenbach. Werke. Ed. Karl Lachmann. Berlin: Georg Reimer, 1833. 6th edn. Berlin: de Gruyter, 1926.

Wolfram von Eschenbach. *Parzival.* Ed. and commentary by Eberhard Nellmann based on the text of Karl Lachmann. German trans. by Dieter Kühn. 2 vols. Bibliothek des Mittelalters 8.1–2. Frankfurt am Main: Deutscher Klassiker Verlag, 1994.

———. *Parzival.* Trans. A. T. Hatto. London: Penguin, 1980.

———. *Parzival, with Titurel and the Love-lyrics.* Trans. Cyril Edwards with an essay on the Munich *Parzival* illustrations by Julia Walworth. Arthurian Studies 56. Cambridge: D.S. Brewer, 2004.

———. *Titurel. Text—Übersetzung—Stellenkommentar.* Ed. Helmut Brackert and Stephan Fuchs-Jolie. Berlin: de Gruyter, 2003.

———. *Willehalm. Nach der Handschrift 857 der Stiftsbibliothek St. Gallen.* Ed. Joachin Heinzle. Altdeutsche Textbibliothek 108. Tübingen: Niemeyer, 1994.

Critical Studies

Adams, Tracy. *Violent Passions. Managing Love in the Old French Verse Romance.* Studies in Arthurian and Courtly Cultures. New York: Palgrave Macmillan, 2005.

Alberi, Mary. "The 'Mystery of the Incarnation' and Wisdom's House (Prov. 9,1) in Alcuin's *Disputatio de vera philosophia.*" *Journal of Theological Studies* 48.2 (1997): 505–516.

Allen, Peter L. *The Art of Love. Amatory Fiction from Ovid to the Romance of the Rose.* Philadelphia: University of Philadelphia Press, 1992.

Ashcroft, Jeffrey. "*dicke Karel wart genant*: Konrad's *Rolandslied* and the Transmission of Authority and Legitimacy in Wolfram's *Willehalm*." *Wolfram's "Willehalm": Fifteen Essays*. Ed. Martin H. Jones and Timothy McFarland. Rochester, NY and Woodbridge, Suffolk: Camden House, 2002. pp. 21–43.

Backes, Herbert. *Die Hochzeit Merkurs und der Philologie: Studien zu Notkers Martian-Übersetzung*. Sigmaringen: Jan Thorbecke, 1982.

Barber, Richard. *The Holy Grail. Imagination and Belief*. London: Allen Lane, 2004.

Barber, Richard and Cyril Edwards. "The Grail Temple in *Der Jüngere Titurel*." *Arthurian Literature* 20 (2003): 85–102.

Bartsch, Karl. *Albrecht von Halberstadt und Ovid im Mittelalter*. Bibliothek der gesammten deutschen National-Literatur 38. Quedlinburg: G. Basse, 1861.

Bauer, Gerhard, *Zur Poetik des Dialogs. Leistung und Formen der Gesprächsführung in der neueren Literatur*. Darmstadt: Wissenschaftliche Buchgesellschaft, 1969.

Bein, Thomas. "Zum Autor im mittelalterlichen Literaturbetrieb und im Diskurs der germanischen Mediävistik." *Rückkehr des Autors: Zur Erneuerung eines umstrittenen Begriffs*. Ed. Fotis Jannidis. Tübingen: Niemeyer, 1999. pp. 303–320.

———. "Maria als Vergrößerungsglas—außerliterarische Realien und poetische Bildlichkeit." *Die Funktion außer- und Innerliterarischer Faktoren für die Entstehung deutscher Literatur des Mittelalters und der frühen Neuzeit*. Ed. Christa Baufeld. Göppinger Arbeiten zur Germanistik 603. Göppingen: Kümmerle, 1994. pp. 117–139.

Bertau, Karl. *Wolfram von Eschenbach. Neun Versuche über Subjektivität und Ursprünglichkeit in der Geschichte*. Munich: C. H. Beck: 1983.

Böer, L. "Briefe," *Marienlexikon*. Ed. Remigius Bäumer and Leo Scheffczuk. 6 vols. St Ottilien: Eos, 1988–1994. 1:584–589.

Borchling, Conrad. *Der jüngere Titurel und sein Verhältnis zu Wolfram von Eschenbach*. Göttingen: Dieterich'sche Universitäts-Buchdruckerei, 1897.

Borst, Arno. *Der Turmbau von Babel. Geschichte der Meinungen über Ursprung und Vielfalt der Sprachen und Völker*. 4 vols. Stuttgart: Hiersemann, 1957–1963.

Bose, Mishtoomi. "From Exegesis to Appropriation: The Medieval Solomon." *Medium Ævum* 64 (1996): 187–210.

Brackert, Helmut. "*Da stuont daz minne wol gezam*. Minnebriefe im späthöfischen Roman." *Zeitschrift für deutsche Philologie* 93 (1974): 1–18.

———. "Sinnspuren. Die Brackenseilinschrift in Wolframs von Eschenbach 'Titurel.'" *Erzählungen in Erzählungen. Für Dieter Kartschoke*. Ed. Harald Haferland and Norbert Mecklenburg. Munich: Fink, 1996. pp. 155–175.

Brinkmann, Hennig. "Die 'Zweite Sprache' und die Dichtung des Mittelalters." *Methoden in Wissenschaft und Kunst des Mittelalters*. Ed. Albert Zimmermann. Miscellanea Mediaevalia 7. Berlin: de Gruyter, 1970. pp. 155–171.

———. "Die Zeichenhaftigkeit der Sprache, des Schrifttums und der Welt im Mittelalter." *Zeitschrift für deutsche Philologie* 93 (1974): 1–11.

———. "Die Sprache als Zeichen im Mittelalter." *Gedenkschrift für Jost Trier*. Ed. Hartmut Beckers and Hans Schwarz. Cologne: Böhlau, 1975. pp. 23–44.

———. *Mittelalterliche Hermeneutik*. Darmstadt: Wissenschaftliche Buchgesellschaft, 1980.

Brode, Hanspeter. *Untersuchungen zum Sprach- und Werkstil des 'Jüngeren Titurel' von Albrecht von Scharfenberg*. Dissertation. Freiburg in Breigau, 1966.

Brüggen, Elke. *Kleidung und Mode in der höfischen Epik des 12. und 13. Jahrhunderts*. Beihefte zum Euphorion 23. Heidelberg: Winter, 1989.

———. "Fiktionalität und Didaxe. Annäherungen an die Dignität lehrhafter Rede im Mittelalter." *Text und Kultur. Mittelalterliche Literatur 1150–1450*. Ed. Ursula Peters. Stuttgart: Metzler, 2001. pp. 546–574.

Brunner, Horst. "*Artus der wise höfsche man*. Zur immanenten Historizität der Ritterwelt im 'Parzival' Wolframs von Eschenbach." *Germanistik in Erlangen. Hundert Jahre nach der Gründung des Deutschen Seminars*. Ed. Dietmar Peil. Erlanger Forschungen, Reihe A, Geisteswissenschaften 31. Erlangen: Universitätsbund Erlangen-Nürnberg, 1983. pp. 61–73.

Buck, Günther. "Das Lehrgespräch." *Das Gespräch*. Ed. Karlheinz Stierle and Rainer Warning. Poetik und Hermeneutik 11. Munich: Fink, 1984. pp. 191–210.

Bumke, Joachim. *Mäzene im Mittelalter. Die Gönner und Auftraggeber der höfischen Literatur in Deutschland 1150–1300*. Munich: Beck, 1979.

———. "Parzival und Feirefiz—Priester Johannes—Loherangrin: Der offene Schluß des *Parzival* von Wolfram von Eschenbach." *Deutsche Vierteljahrsschrift für Literaturwissenschaft und Geistesgeschichte* 65 (1991). 236–264.

———. *Wolfram von Eschenbach*. Sammlung Metzler 36. 7th edn. Stuttgart: Metzler, 1997.

———. *Die Blutstropfen im Schnee: Über Wahrnehmung und Erkenntnis im "Parzival" Wolframs von Eschenbach*, Hermaea 94. Tübingen: Niemeyer, 2001.

Bussmann, Britta. "Mit tugent und kunst. Wiedererzählen, Weitererzählen und Beschreiben in Albrechts Jüngerem Titurel" *Übertragungen. Formen und Konzepte von Reproduktion in Mittelalter und Früher Neuzeit*. Ed. Britta Bussmann and others. Trends in Medieval Philology 5. Berlin and New York: de Gruyter, 2005. pp. 437–461.

Bynum, Caroline Walker. *The Resurrection of the Body in Western Christianity 200–1336*. New York: Columbia University Press, 1995.

Carruthers, Mary. *The Book of Memory. A Study of Memory in Medieval Culture*. Cambridge: Cambridge University Press, 1990.

Clanchy, Michael T. *From Memory to Written Record. England 1066–1307*. 2nd edn. Oxford: Basil Blackwell, 1993.

Cowling, David. *Building the Text. Architecture as Metaphor in Late Medieval and Early Modern France*. Oxford: Oxford University Press, 1998.

Coxon, Sebastian. *The Presentation of Authorship in Medieval German Narrative Literature 1220–1290*. Oxford: Oxford University Press, 2001.

Cramer, Thomas. "*Sælde und êre* in Hartmanns 'Iwein.'" *Euphorion* 60 (1966): 30–47. Reprinted *Hartmann von Aue: Wege der Forschung*. Ed Hugo Kuhn and Christoph Cormeau. Darmstadt: Wissenschaftliche Buchgesellschaft, 1973. pp. 426–449.

Curschmann, Michael. "Das Abenteuer des Erzählens. Über den Erzähler in Wolframs 'Parzival.'" *Deutsche Vierteljahrsschrift für Literaturwissenschaft und Geistesgeschichte* 45 (1971): 627–667.

———. "Hören—Lesen—Sehen. Buch und Schriftlichkeit im Selbstverständnis der volkssprachlichen literarischen Kultur Deutschlands um 1200." *Beiträge zur Geschichte der deutschen Sprache und Literatur* 106 (1984): 218–257.

———. "Facies peccatorum—Vir bonus: Bild-Text-Formel zwischen Hochmittelalter und früher Neuzeit." *Poesis et Pictura. Festschrift Dieter Wuttke*. Ed. Stephan Füssel and Joachim Knape. Saecula Spiritalia, Sonderband. Baden-Baden: Valentin-Koerner, 1989. pp. 157–189.

Curtius, Ernst Robert. *European Literature and the Latin Middle Ages*. Trans. Willard R. Trask. London: Routledge and Kegan, 1953.

Deinert, Wilhelm. *Ritter und Kosmos im Parzival. Eine Untersuchung der Sternkunde Wolframs von Eschenbach*. Münchener Texte und Untersuchungen 2. Munich: Beck, 1960.

Dietl, Cora. *Minnerede, Roman und historia. Der 'Wilhelm von Österreich' Johanns von Würzburg*. Germanistische Forschungen, N.F. 87. Tübingen: Niemeyer, 1990.

Dittmann, Wolfgang. "*Dune hâst nicht wâr*, Hartmann! Zum Begriff der *wârheit* in Harmanns 'Iwein.'" *Festgabe für Ulrich Pretzel zum 65. Geburtstag*. Ed. Werner Simon. Berlin: Erich Schmidt, 1963. pp. 150–161.

Draesner, Ulrike. *Wege durch erzählte Welten. Intertextuelle Verweise als Mittel der Bedeutungskonstitution in Wolframs 'Parzival.'* Mikrokosmos 36. Frankfurt am Main: Peter Lang, 1993.

Drecoll, Uta. *Tod in der Liebe—Liebe im Tod: Untersuchungen zu Wolframs 'Titurel' und Gottfrieds 'Tristan' in Wort un Bild.* Frankfurt am Main: Peter Lang, 2000.

Dronke, Peter: "Pseudo-Ovid, *Facetus* and the Arts of Love." *Mittellateinisches Jahrbuch* 11 (1976): 126–131.

Ebenbauer, Alfred. "Tschionatulander und Artus. Zur Gattungsstruktur und zur Interpretation des Tschionatulanderlebens im 'Jüngeren Titurel.'" *Zeitschrift für deutsches Altertum und deutsche Literatur* 108 (1979): 374–407.

———. "Reinfried von Braunschweig." *Die deutsche Literatur des Mittelalters. Verfasserlexikon.* Ed. Kurt Ruh. 2nd edn. 10 vols. Berlin: de Gruyter: 1978–1999. 7:1171–1176.

Edwards, Cyril. "The Grail Temple in *Der Jüngere Titurel.*" *Arthurian Literature* 20 (2003): 85–102.

Eggers, Hans. "Non cognovi litteraturam (zu >Pz.< 115,27)." *Festgabe für Ulrich Pretzel zum 65. Geburtstag.* Ed. Werner Simon. Berlin: Erich Schmidt, 1963. pp. 162–172. Reprinted in *Wolfram von Eschenbach.* Ed. Heinz Rupp. Wege der Forschung 57. Darmstadt: Wissenschaftliche Buchgesellschaft, 1966. pp. 533–548.

Engelen, Ulrich. *Die Edelsteine in der deutschen Dichtung des 12. und 13. Jahrhunderts.* Münstersche Mittelalterschriften 27. Munich: Fink, 1978.

Finckh, Ruth. *Minor Mundus Homo. Studien zu Mikrokosmos-Idee in der mittelalterlichen Literatur.* Palaestra 306. Göttingen: Vandenhoeck and Ruprecht, 1999.

Fingerlin, Ilse. *Gürtel des hohen und späten Mittelalter.* Kunstwissenschaftliche Studien 46. Munich: Deutscher Kunstverlag, 1971.

Gellrich, Jesse M. *The Idea of the Book in the Middle Ages. Language Theory, Mythology, and Fiction.* Ithaca: Cornell University Press, 1985.

Genette, Gérard. *Narrative Discourse. Translation of "Discours du récit," a portion of Figures III.* Trans. Jane E. Lewin. Ithaca: Cornell University Press, 1980.

———. *Narrative Discourse Revisited.* Trans. Jane E. Lewin. Ithaca: Cornell University Press.

Gerhardt, Christoph. *Die Metamorphosen des Pelikans: Exempel und Auslegung in mittelalterlicher Literatur. Mit Beispielen aus der bildenden Kunst und einem Bildanhang.* Trierer Studien zur Literatur 1. Frankfurt am Main: Peter Lang, 1979.

———. "Reinmar von Zweters 'Idealer Mann' (Roethe Nr. 99/100)." *Beiträge zur Geschichte der deutschen Sprache und Literatur* 109 (1987): 51–84 and 222–251.

Gervinus, Georg Gottfried. *Geschichte der deutschen Dichtung.* 5th edn. 5 vols. Leipzig: W. Engelmann, 1871–1874.

Ghisalberti, Fausto. "Medieval Biographies of Ovid." *Journal of the Warburg and Courtauld Institute* 9 (1946): 10–59.

Gillespie, George T. *A Catalogue of Persons Named in German Heroic Literature.* Oxford: Oxford University Press, 1973.

Ginsberg, Warren. "*Ovidius ethicus?* Ovid and the Medieval Commentary Tradition." *Desiring Discourse: The Literature of Love, Ovid through Chaucer.* Ed. James J. Paxson and Cynthia A. Gravlee. London: Associated University Press, 1998. pp. 62–71.

Green, Dennis Howard. "The concept *âventiure* in *Parzival.*" *Approaches to Wolfram von Eschenbach. Five Essays.* Mikrokosmos 5. Ed. Dennis Howard Green and Leslie Peter Johnson. Bern: Peter Lang, 1978. pp. 83–161.

———. *Medieval Listening and Reading: The Primary Reception of German Literature 800–1300.* Cambridge: Cambridge University Press, 1994.

———. "Fiktionalität und weiße Flecken in Wolframs 'Parzival.'" *Wolfram-Studien* 17 (2002): 30–45.

Green, Dennis Howard. "Terminologische Überlegungen zum Hören und Lesen im Mittelalter." *Eine Epoche im Umbruch. Volkssprachliche Literalität 1200–1300*. Ed. Christa Bertelsmeier-Kierst and Christopher Young. Tübingen, Niemeyer, 2003. pp. 1–22.

Grubmüller, Klaus. "Etymologie als Schlüssel zur Welt? Bemerkungen zur Sprachtheorie des Mittelalters." *Verbum et Signum. Beiträge zur mediävistischen Bedeutungsforschung. Festschrift für Friedrich Ohly*. Ed. Hans Fromm. 2 vols. Munich: Fink, 1975. 1:209–230.

———. "Die Konzeption der Artusfigur bei Chrestien und in Ulrichs *Lanzelet*: Mißverständnis, Kritik oder Selbständigkeit? Ein Diskussionsbeitrag." *Chrétien de Troyes and the German Middle Ages*. Ed. Martin H. Jones and Roy Wisbey. Arthurian Studies 26. Cambridge: D.S. Brewer, 1993. pp. 137–149.

Grünkorn, Gertrud. *Die Fiktionalität des höfischen Roman um 1200*. Philologische Studien und Quellen 129. Berlin: Erich Schmidt, 1994.

Guggenberger, Herbert. *Albrechts Jüngerer Titurel: Studien zur Minnethematik und zur Werkkonzeption*. Göppinger Arbeiten zur Germanistik 566. Göppingen: Kümmerle, 1992.

Haferland, Harald. *Höfische Interaktion. Interpretationen zur höfischen Epik und Didaktik um 1200*. Forschungen zur Geschichte der älteren deutschen Literatur 10. Munich: Fink, 1989.

Hagenlocher, Albrecht. "Littera Meretrix. Brun von Schönebeck und die Autorität der Schrift im Mittelalter." *Zeitschrift für deutsches Altertum und deutsche Literatur* 118 (1989): 131–163.

Hahn, Ingrid. "Kosmologie und Zahl. Zum Prolog des 'Jüngeren Titurel.'" *Geistliche Denkformen des Mittelalters*. Münstersche Mittelalter-Schriften 51. Ed. Klaus Grubmüller. Munich: Fink, 1984. pp. 226–244.

Harpham, Geoffrey Galt. *The Ascetic Imperative in Culture and Criticism*. Chicago: University of Chicago Press, 1987.

Haubrichs, Wolfgang. "*Veriloquium nominis*. Zur Namensexegese im frühen Mittelalter. Nebst einer Hypothese über die Identität des 'Heliand'-Autors." *Verbum et Signum. Beiträge zur mediävistischen Bedeutungsforschung. Friedrich Ohly Festschrift*. Ed. Hans Fromm. 2 vols. Munich: Fink, 1975. 1:231–266.

———. "Namendeutung in Hagiographie, Panegyrik—und im 'Tristan.' Eine gattungs-und funktionsgeschichtliche Analyse." *Namen in deutschen literarischen Texten des Mittelalters. Symposion Kiel 9–12.9.1987*. Ed. Friedhelm Debus and Horst Pütz. Kieler Beiträge zur deutschen Sprachgeschichte 12. Neumünster: Karl Wachholtz, 1989. pp. 205–224.

Haug, Walter. "Die Symbolstruktur des höfischen Epos und ihre Auflösung bei Wolfram von Eschenbach." *Deutsche Vierteljahrsschrift für Literaturwissenschaft und Geistesgeschichte* 45 (1971): 668–705.

———. "Paradigmatische Poesie. Der spätere deutsche Artusroman auf dem Weg zu einer 'nachklassischen' Ästhetik." *Deutsche Vierteljahrsschrift für Literaturwissenschaft und Geistesgeschichte* 54 (1980): 204–231.

———. "Brandans Meerfahrt." *Die deutsche Literatur des Mittelalters. Verfasserlexikon*. Eds. Kurt Ruh and others. 2nd edn. 10 vols. Berlin: de Gruyter: 1978–1999. 1:985–991.

———. "Das Gespräch mit dem unvergleichbaren Partner. Der mystische Dialog bei Mechthild von Magdeburg als Paradigma für eine personale Gesprächsstrucktur." *Das Gespräch*. Ed. Karlheinz Stierle and Rainer Warning. Poetik und Hermeneutik 11. Munich: Fink, 1984. pp. 251–279.

———. "Der Ackermann und der Tod." *Das Gespräch*. Ed. Karlheinz Stierle and Rainer Warning. Poetik und Hermeneutik 11. Munich: Fink 1984, pp. 281–286.

———. *Literaturtheorie im deutschen Mittelalter. Von den Anfängen bis zum Ende des 13. Jahrhunderts*. 2nd edn. Darmstadt: Wissenschaftliche Buchgesellschaft, 1992.

Hegener, Eckhard. *Studien zur "zweiten Sprache" in der religiösen Lyrik des zwölften Jahrhunderst. Adam von St. Victor. Walter von Châtillon*. Beiheft 6 zum Mittellateinischen Jahrbuch. Wuppertal: Kastellaun, 1971.

Heinzle, Joachim. *Stellenkommentar zu Wolframs Titurel. Beiträge zum Verständnis des überlieferten Textes.* Hermaea 30. Tübingen: Niemeyer, 1972.

Herweg, Mathias. "Der Kosmos als Innenraum. Ein persischer Thronsaal und seine Rezeption im Mittelalter." *Deutsche Vierteljahrsschrift für Literaturwissenschaft und Geistesgeschichte* 80 (2006): 3–54.

Hexter, Ralph. *Ovid and Medieval Schooling: Studies in Medieval School Commentaries on Ovid's "Ars Amatoria," "Epistulae ex Ponto," and "Epistulae Heroidum."* Münchener Beiträge zur Mediävistik und Renaissance-Forschung 38. Munich: Arbeo Gesellschaft, 1986.

Hirschberg, Dagmar. "Zum Aventiure-Gespräch von der Bedeutung *warer minne* im 'Jüngeren Titurel.'" *Wolfram-Studien* 8 (1984): 107–119.

Hofbauer, Klaus. *Gott und der Welt gefallen. Geschichte eines gnomischen Motivs im hohen Mittelalter.* Europäische Hochschulschriften 1630. Frankfurt am Main: Peter Lang, 1997.

Huber, Christoph. *Wort sint der dinge zeichen. Untersuchungen zum Sprachdenken der mittelhochdeutschen Spruchdichtung bis Frauenlob.* Münchener Texte und Untersuchungen 89. Munich: Artemis, 1977.

———. "Zur mittelalterlichen Roman-Hermeneutik: Noch einmal Thomasin von Zerklaere und das Integumentum." *German Narrative Literature of the Twelfth and Thirteenth Centuries. Studies Presented to Roy Wisbey on his Sixty-fifth Birthday.* Ed. Volker Honemann. Tübingen: Niemeyer, 1994. pp. 27–38.

———. *Gottfried von Straßburg: Tristan.* Klassiker Lektüren 3. Berlin: Erich Schmidt, 2000.

Huschenbett, Dietrich. "Albrecht, Dichter des 'Jüngeren Titurel.'" *Die deutsche Literatur des Mittelalters. Verfasserlexikon.* Ed. Kurt Ruh. 2nd edn. 10 vols. Berlin: de Gruyter: 1978–1999. 1:158–173.

———. "Albrecht von Scharfenberg." *Die deutsche Literatur des Mittelalters. Verfasserlexikon.* Ed. Kurt Ruh. 2nd edn. 10 vols. Berlin: de Gruyter: 1978–1999. 1:200–206.

———. *Albrechts 'Jüngerer Titurel'. Zu Stil und Komposition.* Medium Aevum. Philologische Studien 35. Munich: Fink, 1979.

———. "Bibliographie zum 'Jüngeren Titurel.'" *Wolfram-Studien* 8 (1984): 169–176.

———. "Über Wort, Sakrament und Gral in Spruchdichtung, *Jüngerem Titurel*—und bei Wolfram?" *bickelwort und wildiu mære. Festschrift für Eberhard Nellmann zum 65. Geburtstag.* Ed. Dorothee Lindemann. Göppinger Arbeiten zur Germanistik 618. Göppingen: Kümmerle, 1995. pp. 184–198.

Irvine, Martin. *The Making of Textual Culture. "Grammatica" and Literary Theory 350–1100.* Cambridge: Cambridge University Press, 1994.

Jackson, William Henry and Silvia Ranawake (eds.) *The Arthur of the Germans: The Arthurian Legend in Medieval German and Dutch Literature.* Cardiff: University of Wales Press, 2002.

Jaeger, C. Stephen. "Der Schöpfer der Welt und das Schöpfungswerk als Prologmotiv in der mittelhochdeutschen Dichtung." *Zeitschrift für deutsches Altertum und deutsche Literatur* 107 (1978): 1–18.

Martin H. Jones and Roy Wisbey (eds.) *Chrétien de Troyes and the German Middle Ages.* Arthurian Studies 26. Cambridge: D.S. Brewer, 1993.

Kästner, Hannes. *Mittelalterliche Lehrgespräche. Textlinguistische Analysen, Studien zur poetischen Funktion und pädagogischen Intention.* Philologische Studien und Quellen 94. Berlin: Erich Schmidt, 1978.

Kellermann, Karina and Christopher Young. "You've got mail! Briefe, Büchlein, Boten im 'Frauendienst' Ulrichs von Liechtenstein." *Eine Epoche im Umbruch. Volkssprachliche Literalität 1200–1300.* Ed. Christa Bertelsmeier-Kierst and Christopher Young. Tübingen, Niemeyer, 2003. pp. 317–344.

Kemp, W. "Hase." *Lexikon der christlichen Ikonographie.* Ed. Engelbert Kirschbaum. 8 vols. Rome: Herder 1968–1976. 2:221–225.

Kern, Peter. *Trinität, Maria, Inkarnation. Studien zur Thematik der deutschen Dichtung des späteren Mittelalters*. Philologische Studien und Quellen 55. Berlin: Erich Schmidt, 1971.

———. "Der Kommentar zu 'Parzival' 1,13f. im Prolog des 'Jüngeren Titurel.'" *Studien zur deutschen Literatur und Sprache des Mittelalters. Festschrift für H. Moser zum 65. Geburtstag*. Ed. Werner Besch. Berlin: Erich Schmidt, 1974. pp. 185–199.

———. "Albrechts Gönner und die Wolfram-Rolle im 'Jüngeren Titurel.'" *Wolfram-Studien* 8 (1984): 138–152.

———. "*ich sage die senewen âne bogen*. Zur Reflexion über die Erzählweise in *Parzival*." *Wolfram-Studien* 17 (2002): 46–62.

Kiening, Christian. *Zwischen Körper und Schrift. Texte vor dem Zeitalter der Literatur*. Frankfurt am Main: Fischer, 2003.

Kiening, Christian and Susanne Köbele. "Wilde Minne. Metapher und Erzählwelt in Wolframs Titurel." *Beiträge zur Geschichte der deutschen Sprache und Literatur* 120 (1998): 234–265.

Kimmelman, Burt. "The Trope of Reading in the Fourteenth Century." *Reading and Literacy in the Middle Ages and the Renaissance*. Arizona Studies in the Middle Ages and the Renaissance 8. Ed. Frederick Moulton. Turnhout: Brepols, 2004. pp. 25–44.

Kistler, Renate. *Heinrich von Veldeke und Ovid*. Hermaea 71. Tübingen: Niemeyer, 1993.

Klinck, Roswitha. *Die lateinische Etymologie des Mittelalters*. Medium Aevum 17. Munich: Fink, 1970.

Knapp, Fritz Peter. "Subjektivität des Erzählers und Fiktionalität der Erzählung bei Wolfram von Eschenbach und anderen Autoren des 12. und 13. Jahrhunderts." *Wolfram-Studien* 17 (2002): 10–29.

Köhn, Rolf. "Latein und Volkssprache, Schriftlichkeit und Mündlichkeit in der Korrespondenz des lateinischen Mittelalters." *Zusammenhänge, Einflüsse, Wirkungen. Kongressakten zum ersten Symposium des Mediävistenverbandes in Tübingen 1984*. Ed. Joerg Fichte. Berlin: de Gruyter, 1986. pp. 340–356.

Krotz, Elke. "Der Leser an der Leine. Zu Wolframs 'Titurel.'" *helle döne schöne. Versammelte Arbeiten zur älteren und neueren deutschen Literatur. Festschrift für Wolfgang Walliczek*. Ed. Horst Brunner. Göppinger Arbeiten zur Germanistik 668. Göppingen: Kümmerle, 1999. pp. 167–200.

Kühnel, Jürgen. *Dû bist mîn, ih bin dîn. Die lateinischen Liebes- und Freundschafts- Briefe des clm 19411. Abbildungen, Text und Übersetzung*. Literae 52. Göppingen: Kümmerle, 1977.

Kunitzsch, Paul. "Caldeis und Côati." *Deutsche Vierteljahrsschrift für Literaturwissenschaft und Geistesgeschichte* 49 (1975): 372–377.

Lachmann, Karl. "Titurel und Dante." (Review of Rosenkranz, *Über den Titurel*), *Hallische Allgemeine Literatur-Zeitung* 238 (1829): 351–357.

Leckie Jr., R. William. "Bestia de funde. Natural Science and the 'Jüngerer Titurel.'" *Zeitschrift für deutsches Altertum und deutsche Literatur* 96 (1967): 263–277.

———. "Gamaniol, der vogel. Natural Science and the 'Jüngerer Titurel.'" *Zeitschrift für deutsches Altertum und deutsche Literatur* 98 (1969): 133–144.

———. "Albrecht von Scharfenberg and the 'Historia de preliis Alexandri Magni.'" *Zeitschrift für deutsches Altertum und deutsche Literatur* 99 (1970): 120–139.

Lieb, Ludger and Stephan Müller (eds.). *Situationen des Erzählens. Aspekte narrativer Praxis im Mittelalter*. Quellen und Forschungen 20. Berlin: de Gruyter, 2002.

Liebertz-Grün, Ursula. "Erkenntnistheorie im Literalisierungsprozeß. Allegorien des *lesens* in Wolframs Metaerzählung Gardeviaz." *Germanisch-Romanische Monatsschrift* 51 (2001): 385–395.

Lofmark, Carl. *The Authority of the Source in Middle High German Narrative Poetry*. Bithell Series of Dissertations 5. London: Institute of Germanic Studies, 1981.

Lorenz, Andrea. *Der Jüngere Titurel als Wolfram-Fortsetzung. Eine Reise zum Mittelpunkt des Werks.* Deutsche Literatur von den Anfängen bis 1700 36. Bern: Peter Lang, 2002.

McLelland, Nicola. *Ulrich von Zatzikhoven's Lanzelet: Narrative Style and Entertainment.* Arthurian Studies 46. Cambridge: D.S. Brewer, 2000.

Meier, Christel. *Gemma spiritalis. Methode und Gebrauch der Edelsteinallegorese von frühen Christentum bis ins 18. Jahrhundert.* Münstersche Mittelalter-Schriften 34,1. Munich: Fink, 1977.

Mertens, Volker. *Der deutsche Artusroman.* Universal-Bibliothek 17609. Stuttgart: Reclam, 1998.

———. *Der Gral: Mythos und Literatur.* Universal-Bibliothek 18261. Stuttgart: Reclam, 2003.

———. "Wolfram als Rolle und Vorstellung. Zur Potologie der Authentizität im 'Jüngeren Titurel." *Geltung der Literatur. Formen ihrer Autorisierung und Legitimierung im Mittelalter.* Ed. Beate Kellner and others. Philologische Studien und Quellen 190. Berlin: Erich Schmidt, 2005. pp. 203–226.

Minnis, Alastair J. "Discussions of 'Authorial Role' and 'Literary Form' in Late-Medieval Scriptural Exegesis." *Beiträge zur Geschichte der deutschen Sprache und Literatur* 99 (1977): 37–65.

———. *Medieval Theory of Authorship: Scholastic Literary Attitudes in the Later Middle Ages.* 2nd edn. Aldershot: Wildwood House, 1988.

Munari, Franco. *Ovid im Mittelalter.* Zürich: Artemis, 1960.

Nellmann, Eberhard. *Wolframs Erzähltechnik. Untersuchungen zur Funktion des Erzählers.* Wiesbaden: Steiner, 1973.

———. "*Dis buoch bezeichent allein mich.* Zum Prolog von Mechthilds 'Fließendem Licht der Gottheit.'" *Gotes und der werlde hulde. Literatur in Mittelalter und Neuzeit. Festschrift für Heinz Rupp zum 70. Geburtstag.* Ed. Rüdiger Schnell. Bern and Stuttgart: Francke, 1989. pp. 200–205.

Neukirchen, Thomas. "*krumb* und *sliht.* Über die sogenannten Hinweis- und Kunststrophen im Überlieferungszweig I des 'Jüngeren Titurel.'" *Zeitschrift für deutsches Altertum und deutsche Literatur* 132 (2003): 62–76.

———. "*Dirre aventiure kere.* Die Erzählperspektive Wolframs im Prolog des 'Jüngeren Titurel' und die Erzählstrategie Albrechts." *Wolfram-Studien* 18 (2004): 283–303.

———. "Bibliographie zum 'Jüngeren Titurel' 1984–2002." *Wolfram-Studien* 18 (2004): 405–424.

Newman, Barbara. *God and the Goddesses: Vision, Poetry, and Belief in the Middle Ages.* Philadelphia: University of Pennsylvania Press, 2003.

Nischik, Traude-Marie. *Das volkssprachliche Naturbuch im späten Mittelalter. Sachkunde und Dinginterpretation bei Jacob von Maerlant und Konrad von Megenberg.* Hermaea 48. Tübingen: Niemeyer, 1986.

Nyholm, Kurt. *Studien zum sogenannten geblümten Stil.* Acta Academiae Aboensis, ser. A, Humaniora 33.2. Åbo: Åbo akademi, 1971.

———. "Pragmatische Isotypien im 'Jüngeren Titurel.' Überlegungen zur Autor-Hörer/Leser-Situation." *Wolfram-Studien* 8 (1984): 120–137.

Ochs, Ingrid. *Wolframs Willehalm-Eingang im Lichte der frühmittelhochdeutschen geistlichen Dichtung.* Medium Aevum. Philologische Studien, 14. Munich: Fink, 1968.

Ohly, Friedrich. "Vom geistigen Sinn des Wortes im Mittelalter." *Zeitschrift für deutsches Altertum und deutsche Literatur* 89 (1958): 1–23. Reprint. Friedrich Ohly. *Schriften zur mittelalterlichen Bedeutungsforschung.* Darmstadt: Wissenschaftliche Buchgesellschaft, 1983. pp. 1–31.

———. "Cor amantis non angustum. Vom Wohnen im Herzen." *Gedenkschrift für William Foerste.* Niederdeutsche Studien 18. Ed. Dietrich Hoffmann and Willy Sanders.

Cologne: Böhlau, 1970. pp. 454–476. Reprint. Friedrich Ohly, *Schriften zur mittelalterlichen Bedeutungsforschung.* Darmstadt: Wissenschaftliche Buchgesellschaft, 1983. pp. 128–155.

Ohly, Friedrich. "Wolframs Gebet an den heiligen Geist im Eingang des 'Willehalm.'" *Zeitschrift für deutsches Altertum und deutsche Literatur* 91 (1961–1962):1–37.

Okken, Lambertus. *Kommentar zum Tristan-Roman Gottfrieds von Straßburg.* Amsterdamer Publikationen zum sprache und Literatur 57–58. 2 vols. 2nd edn. Amsterdam: Rodopi, 1996.

Ong, Walter J. "The Writer's Audience Is Always a Fiction." *PMLA* 90 (1975): 9–22.

———. *Orality and Literacy. The Technologizing of the Word.* New York: Routledge, 1982. Reprint. 2002.

Palmer, Nigel, F. "Exempla." *Medieval Latin. An Introduction and Bibliographical Guide.* Ed. F. A. C. Mantello and A. G. Rigg. Washington DC: Catholic University of America Press, 1996. pp. 582–588.

Parshall, Linda B. *The Art of Narration in Wolfram's "Parzival" and Albrecht's "Jüngerer Titurel."* Anglica Germanica Series 2. Cambridge: Cambridge University Press, 1981.

Peschel-Rentsch, Dietmar. *Pferdemänner. Sieben Essays über Sozialisation und ihre Wirkungen in mittelalterlicher Literatur.* Erlangen Studien 117. Erlangen: Universitätsbund Erlangen-Nürnberg, 1998.

Petersen, Karen-Maria. "Zum Grundriß des Graltempels." *Festschrift für Kurt Herbert Halbach zum 70. Geburtstag.* Ed. Rose Beate Schäfer-Maulbetsch. Göppinger Arbeiten zur Germanistik 70. Göppingen: Kümmerle, 1972. pp. 271–306.

Pigman, G. W. "Versions of Imitation in the Renaissance." *Renaissance Quarterly* 33 (1980): 1–32.

Ragotzky, Hedda. *Studien zur Wolfram-Rezeption. Die Entstehung und Verwandlung der Wolfram-Rolle in der deutschen Literatur des 13. Jahrhunderts.* Studien zur Poetik und geschichte der Literatur 20. Stuttgart: Kohlhammer, 1971.

Rausch, Hans-Henning. *Methoden und Bedeutung naturkundlischer Rezeption und Kompilation im "Jüngeren Titurel."* Mikrokosmos 2. Frankfurt am Main: Peter Lang, 1977.

Reuvekamp-Felber, Timo. "Briefe als Kommunikations- und Strukturelemente in der 'Virginal.'" *Beiträge zur Geschichte der deutschen Sprache und Literatur* 125 (2003): 56–81.

Reynolds, Suzanne. *Medieval Reading: Grammar, Rhetoric and the Classical Text.* Cambridge: Cambridge University Press, 1996.

Ridder, Klaus. *Mittelhochdeutsche Minne- und Aventiureromane: Fiktion, Geschichte und literarische Tradition im späthöfischen Roman: 'Reinfried von Braunschweig,' 'Wilhelm von Österreich,' 'Friedrich von Schwaben.'* Quellen und Forschungen 12. Berlin: de Gruyter, 1998.

Robertshaw, Alan. "Ambiguity and Morality in *Iwein.*" *Hartmann von Aue: Changing Perspectives. London Hartmann Symposium 1985.* Ed. Timothy McFarland and Silvia Ranawake. Göppinger Arbeiten zur Germanistik 486. Göppingen: Kümmerle, 1988. pp. 117–128.

Röll, Walter. *Studien zu Text und Überlieferung des sogenannten Jüngeren Titurel.* Germanische Bibliothek, reihe 3, Untersuchungen und Einzeldarstelllungen. Heidelberg: C. Winter, 1964.

———. "Quellen des Wortschatzes im 'Jüngeren Titurel.'" *Wolfram-Studien* 8 (1984): 49–66.

———. "Berthold von Regensburg und der 'Jüngere Titurel'." *Wolfram-Studien* 8 (1984): 67–93.

Rosenfeld, Hellmut. "Aristotles und Phyllis.." *Die deutsche Literatur des Mittelalters. Verfasserlexikon.* Ed. Kurt Ruh. 2nd edn. 10 vols. Berlin: de Gruyter: 1978–1999. 1:434–436.

Rosenkranz, Karl. *Über den Titurel und Dantes Komödie.* Halle: Reinicke, 1829.

Ruberg, Uwe. "Verfahren und Funktionen des Etymologisierens in der mittelhochdeutschen Literatur." *Verbum et Signum. Beiträge zur mediävistischen Bedeutungsforschung. Festschrift für Friedrich Ohly.* Ed. Hans Fromm. 2 vols.. Munich: Fink, 1975. 1:295–330.

———. "Zur Poetik der Eigennamen in Gottfrieds 'Tristan.'" *Sprache—Literatur—Kultur. Studien zu ihrer Geschichte im deutschen Süden und Westen. Festschrift für Wolfgang Kleiber.* Ed. Albrecht Greule and Uwe Ruberg. Stuttgart: Steiner, 1989. pp. 301–320.

Sanders, Willy. "Grundzüge und Wandlungen der Etymologie." *Wirkendes Wort* 17 (1967): 361–384.

———. "Die Anfänge wortkundlichen Denkens im deutschen Mittelalter." *Zeitschrift für deutsche Philologie* 88 (1969): 57–78.

Schaefer, Ursula. *Vokalität: Altenglische Dichtung zwischen Mündlichkeit und Schriftlichkeit.* ScriptOralia 39. Tübingen: Narr, 1992.

———. "Zum Problem der Mündlichkeit." *Modernes Mittelalter: Neue Bilder einer populären Epoche.* Ed. Joachim Heinzle. Frankfurt am Main: Insel, 1994. pp. 357–375.

———. "Individualität und Fiktionalität. Zu einer mediengeschichtlichen und mentalitätsgeschichtlichen Wandel im 12. Jahrhundert." *Mündlichkeit—Schriftlichkeit—Weltbildwandel. Literarische Kommunikation und Deutungsschemata von Wirklichkeit in der Literatur des Mittelalters und der frühen Neuzeit.* Ed. Werner Röcke and Ursula Schaefer. Tübingen: Narr, 1996. pp. 50–70.

———. "Die Funktion des Erzählers zwischen Mündlichkeit und Schriftlichkeit." *Wolfram-Studien* 18 (2004): 83–97.

Schirok, Bernd. "Die senewe ist ein bîspel. Zu Wolframs Bogengleichnis." *Zeitschrift für deutsches Altertum und deutsche Literatur* 115 (1986): 21–36.

———. "*Artûs der meienbære man*—Zum Stellenwert der 'Artuskritik' im klassischen deutschen Artusroman." *Gotes und der werlde hulde. Literatur in Mittelalter und Neuzeit. Festschrift für Heinz Rupp zum 70. Geburtstag.* Ed. Rüdiger Schnell. Bern: Francke, 1989. pp. 58–81.

Schlegel, August Wilhelm. *Geschichte der deutschen Sprache und Poesie. Vorlesungen an der Universität Bonn seit dem Wintersemester 1818–1819.* Deutsche Literaturdenkmale des 18. und 19. Jahrhunderts, 3. Folge, Nr. 27. Ed. Joself Körner. Berlin: B. Behr, 1913.

Schmid, Elisabeth. "Priester Johann oder die Aneignung des Fremden." *Germanistik in Erlangen. Hundert Jahre nach der Gründung des Deutschen Seminars.* Erlanger Forschungen, Reihe A, Geisteswissenschaften 31. Ed. Dietmar Peil. Erlangen: Universitätsbund Erlangen-Nürnberg, 1983. pp. 75–93.

———. "'Dâ stuont âventiur geschriben an der strangen': Zum Verhältnis von Erzählung und Allegorie in der Brackenseilepisode von Wolframs und Albrechts 'Titurel.'" *Zeitschrift für deutsches Altertum und deutsche Literatur* 117 (1988): 79–97.

Schmid-Cadalbert, Christian. "Der wilde Wald. Zur Darstellung und Funktion eines Raumes in der mittelhochdeutschen Literatur." *Gotes und der werlde hulde. Literatur in Mittelalter und Neuzeit. Festschrift für Heinz Rupp zum 70. Geburtstag.* Ed Rüdiger Schnell. Bern: Francke, 1989. pp. 24–47.

Scholz, Manfred Günter. *Hören und Lesen. Studien zur primären Rezeption der Literatur im 12. und 13. Jahrhundert.* Wiesbaden: Steiner, 1980.

Schröder, Werner. *Wolfram-Nachfolge im "Jüngeren Titurel": Devotion oder Arroganz.* Frankfurter wissenschftliche Beiträge 150. Frankfurt am Main: Klostermann, 1982.

Singleton, Charles S. *An Essay on the Vita Nuova.* Baltimore and London: John Hopkins University Press, 1949. Reprint. 1977.

Spitz, Hans-Jörg. "Wolframs Bogengleichnis: ein typologisches Signal." *Verbum et Signum. Beiträge zur mediävistischen Bedeutungsforschung. Friedrich Ohly Festschrift.* Ed. Hans Fromm. 2 vols. Munich: Fink, 1975. 2:247–276.

Stackmann, Karl. *Der Spruchdichter Heinrich von Mügeln: Vorstudien zur Erkenntnis seiner Individualität*. Probleme der Dichtung: Studien zur deutschen Literaturgeschichte 3. Heidelberg: C. Winter, 1958.

———. "Ovid im deutschen Mittelalter." *Arcadia* I (1966): 231–254.

Starkey, Kathryn. *Reading the Medieval Book. Word, Image, and Performance in Wolfram von Eschenbach's Willehalm*. Poetics of Orality and Literacy. Notre Dame: University of Notre Dame Press, 2004.

Steinhoff, Hans Hugo. "Göttweiger Trojanerkrieg." *Die deutsche Literatur des Mittelalters. Verfasserlexikon*. Ed. Kurt Ruh. 2nd edn. 10 vols. Berlin: de Gruyter, 1978–1999. 3:199–201.

Stock, Brian. *The Implications of Literacy. Written Language and Models of Interpretation in the Eleventh and Twelfth Centuries*. Princeton: Princeton University Press, 1983.

Stolz, Michael. *'Tum'-Studien. Zur dichterischen Gestaltung im Marienpreis Heinrichs von Mügeln*. Bibliotheca Germanica 36, Tübingen: Francke, 1996.

Störmer-Caysa, Uta. "Die Architektur eines Vorlesebuches. Über Boten, Briefe und Zusammenfassungen in der Heidelberger 'Virginal.'" *Zeitschrift für Germanistik* N.F. 7 (2002): 12–24.

Strohschneider, Peter. "Gotfrid-Fortsetzungen. Tristans Ende im 13. Jahrhundert und die Möglichkeiten nachklassischer Epik." *Deutsche Vierteljahrsschrift für Literaturwissenschaft und Geistesgeschichte* 65 (1991): 70–98.

———. "Textheiligung. Geltungsstrategien legendarischen Erzählens im Mittelalter am Beispiel von Konrads von Würzburg 'Alexius.'" *Geltungsgeschichten. Über die Stabilisierung und Legitimierung institutioneller Ordnungen. Im Auftrag des Sonderforschungsbereichs 537*. Ed. Gert Melville and Hans Vorländer. Cologne: Böhlau, 2002. pp. 109–147.

———. "Unlesbarkeit von Schrift. Literaturhistorische Anmerkungen zu Schriftpraxen in der religiösen Literatur des 12. und 13. Jahrhunderts." *Regeln der Bedeutung. Zur Theorie der Bedeutung literarischer Texte*. Ed. Fotis Jannidis. Berlin: de Gruyter, 2003. pp. 591–627.

———. "Text-Reliquie. Über Schriftgebrauch und Textpraxis im Hochmittelalter." *Performativität und Medialität*. Ed. Sybille Krämer. Munich: Fink, 2004. pp. 249–267.

Suerbaum, Almut. "Structures of Dialogue in *Willehalm*." *Wolfram's "Willehalm": 15 Essays*. Ed. Martin H. Jones and Timothy McFarland. Rochester, NY and Woodbridge, Suffolk: Camden House, 2002. pp. 231–247.

———. "*Siben sterne si dô nante heidensch*. Language as a Marker of Difference in Wolfram's *Parzival* and Adolf Muschg's *Der Rote Ritter*." *Oxford German Studies* 33 (2004): 37–50.

Thelen, Christian. *Das Dichtergebet in der deutschen Literatur des Mittelalters*. Arbeiten zur Frühmittelalterforschung 18. Berlin: de Gruyter, 1989.

Thornton, Alison G. *Weltgeschichte und Heilsgeschichte in Albrechts von Scharfenberg Jüngerem Titurel*. Göppinger Arbeiten zur Germanistik 211. Göppingen: Kümmerle, 1977.

Trendelenburg, Gundula. *Studien zum Gralraum im Jüngeren Titurel*. Göppinger Arbeiten zur Germanistik 78. Göppingen: Kümmerle, 1972.

Unzeitig, Monika. "Von der Schwierigkeit zwischen Autor und Erzähler zu unterscheiden. Eine historisch vergleichende Analyse zu Chrétien und Hartmann." *Wolfram-Studien* 18 (2004): 59–81.

Volfing, Annette. *Heinrich von Mügeln. "Der meide kranz"*. *A Commentary*. Münchener Texte und Untersuchungen 111. Tübingen: Niemeyer, 1997.

———. *John the Evangelist and Medieval German Writing: Imitating the Inimitable*. Oxford: Oxford University Press, 2001.

———. "Parzival and Willehalm—Narrative Continuity?" *Wolfram's "Willehalm": 15 Essays*. Ed. Martin H. Jones and Timothy McFarland. Rochester, NY and Woodbridge, Suffolk: Camden House, 2002. pp. 45–59.

————. "*offenlich beslafen het der Grahardois sin eigen swester.* Allegorie und Personifikation in der 'Crone' und im 'Jüngeren Titurel.'" *Wolfram-Studien* 18 (2004): 305–321.

————. "The Song of Songs as Fiction: Brun von Schönebeck's *Das Hohe Lied.*" *Vir ingenio mirandus. Studies Presented to John L. Flood.* Ed. William Jones. Göppinger Arbeiten zur Germanistik 710. Göppingen: Kümmerle, 2003. pp. 137–154.

————. "*Welt ir nu hæren fürbaz?* On the Function of the Loherangrin-episode in Wolfram von Eschenbach's *Parzival.*" *Beiträge zur Geschichte der deutschen Sprache und Literatur* 126 (2004): 65–84.

————. "Albrecht's *Jüngerer Titurel*: Translating the Grail." *Arthurian Literature* 22 (2005): 49–63.

Voß, Rudolf. "Die Idee des Namens in der höfischen Dichtung um 1200." *Vox Sermo Res. Beiträge zur Sprachreflexion, Literatur- und Sprachgeschichte vom Mittelalter bis zur neuzeit. Festschrift Uwe Ruberg.* Ed. Wolfgang Haubrichs. Stuttgart: Hirzel, 2001. pp. 21–34.

Wachinger, Burghart. *Sängerkrieg. Untersuchungen zur Spruchdichtung des 13. Jahrhunderts.* Münchener Texte und Untersuchungen 42. Munich: Beck, 1973.

————. "Wartburgkrieg." *Die deutsche Literatur des Mittelalters. Verfasserlexikon.* Ed. Kurt Ruh. 2nd edn. 10 vol. Berlin: de Gruyter, 1978–1999. 10:740–766.

Walther, Hans. *Das Streitgedicht in der lateinischen Literatur des Mittlelalters.* Quellen und Untersuchungen zur lateinischen Philologie des Mittelalters 5.2. Munich: Beck, 1920.

Wand, Christine. *Wolfram von Eschenbach und Hartmann von Aue: Literarische Reaktionen auf Hartmann im "Parzival."* 2nd edn. Herne: Verlag für Wissenschaft und Kunst, 1992.

Wand-Wittkowski, Christine. *Briefe im Mittelalter. Der deutschsprachige Brief als weltliche und religiöse Literatur.* Herne: Verlag für Wissenschaft und Kunst, 2000.

Warning, Rainer. "Der inszenierte Diskurs. Bemerkungen zur pragmatischen Relation der Fiktion." *Funktionen des Fiktiven.* Poetik und Hermeneutik 10. Ed. Dieter Henrich und Wolfgang Iser. Munich: Fink, 1983. pp. 183–206.

Wegner, Wolfgang. *Albrecht, ein poeta doctus rerum naturae? Zu Umfang und Funktionalisierung naturkundlicher Realien im "Jüngeren Titurel."* Europäische Hochschulschriften 1.1562. Frankfurt am Main: Peter Lang, 1995.

Wenzel, Horst. "Boten und Briefe. Zum Verhältnis körperlicher und nicht-körperlicher Nachrichtenträger." *Gespräche—Boten—Briefe. Körpergedächtnis und Schriftgedächtnis im Mittelalter.* Ed. Horst Wenzel. Philologische Studien und Quellen 143. Berlin: Erich Schmidt, 1997. pp. 86–105.

————. "Vom Körper zur Schrift. Boten, Briefe, Bücher." *Performativität und Medialität.* Ed. Sybille Krämer. Munich: Fink, 2004. pp. 269–291.

Wiehl, Peter. *Die Redeszene als episches Strukturelement in den Erec- und Iwein-Dichtungen Hartmanns von Aue und Chrestiens de Troyes.* Bochumer Arbeiten zur Sprach- und Literaturwissenschaft 10. Munich: Fink, 1974. pp. 54–55.

Williams, Steven. *The Secret of Secrets: The Scholarly Career of a Pseudo-Aristotelian Text in the Latin Middle Ages.* Ann Arbor: University of Michigan Press, 2003.

Wisbey, Roy. "Wunder des Ostens in der 'Wiener Genesis' und in Wolframs 'Parzival.'" *Studien zur frühmittelhochdeutschen Literatur. Cambridger Colloquium 1971.* Ed Leslie Peter Johnson. Publications of the Institute of Germanic Studies of the University of London 19. Berlin: Erich Schmidt, 1974). pp. 180–214.

Wolf, Jürgen. "*vrowen phlegene zu lesene.* Beobachtungen zur Typik einiger für den Gebrauch von Frauen bestimmten Textsorten." *Wolfram-Studien* 19 (2006): 169–190.

Wuth, Henning. "*was, strâle* und *permint.* Mediengeschichtliches zum Eneasroman Heinrichs von Veldeke." *Gespräche—Boten—Briefe. Körpergedächtnis und Schriftgedächtnis im Mittelalter.* Ed. Horst Wenzel. Philologische Studien und Quellen 143. Berlin: Erich Schmidt, 1997. pp. 63–76.

Wyss, Ulrich. "Den 'Jüngeren Titurel' lesen." *Germanistik in Erlangen. Hundert Jahre nach der Gründung des Deutschen Seminars.* Ed. Dietmar Peschel. Erlanger Forschungen, Reihe A, Geisteswissenschaften 31. Erlangen: Universitätsbund Erlangen-Nürnberg 1983. pp. 95–113.

Zatloukal, Klaus. "India—ein idealer Staat im 'Jüngeren Titurel.'" *Strukturen und Interpretationen. Studien zur deutschen Philologie. Festschrift für Blanka Horacek.* Ed. Alfred Ebenbauer. Philologica Germanica. Vienna: Braumüller, 1974. pp. 401–445.

———. *Salvaterre. Studien zu Sinn und funktion des Gralsbereiches im "Jüngeren Titurel."* Wiener Arbeiten zur germanistischen Altertumskunde und Philologie 12. Vienna: Halosar, 1978.

———. "Eigennamen und Erzählwelten im 'Jüngeren Titurel.'" *Wolfram-Studien* 8 (1984): 94–106.

———. "Erzählwelt in der Nußschale. Die Bildungsweise der Eigennamen Albrechts und die Großform 'Jüngerer Titurel.'" *Namen in deutschen literarischen Texten des Mittelalters. Symposion Kiel 9–12.9.1987.* Ed. Friedhelm Debus and Horst Pütz. Kieler Beiträge zur deutschen Sprachgeschichte 12. Neumünster: Karl Wachholtz, 1989. pp. 173–187.